AN EXEGETICAL SUMMARY OF
GALATIANS

AN EXEGETICAL SUMMARY OF GALATIANS

Second Edition

Robert Stutzman

SIL International

Second Edition
© 2006, 2008 by SIL International

Library of Congress Catalog Card Number: 2008923527
ISBN: 978-155671-201-2

Printed in the United States of America

All Rights Reserved
No part of this publication may be reproduced, stored in a retrieval system, or transmitted in any form or by any means without the express permission of SIL International. However, brief excerpts, generally understood to be within the limits of fair use, may be quoted without written permission.

Copies of this and other publications
of SIL International may be obtained from

International Academic Bookstore
SIL International
7500 West Camp Wisdom Road
Dallas, TX 75236-5699, USA

Voice: 972-708-7404
Fax: 972-708-7363
academic_books@sil.org
www.ethnologue.com

PREFACE

Exegesis is concerned with the interpretation of a text. Exegesis of the New Testament involves determining the meaning of the Greek text. Translators must be especially careful and thorough in their exegesis of the New Testament in order to accurately communicate its message in the vocabulary, grammar, and literary devices of another language. Questions occurring to translators as they study the Greek text are answered by summarizing how scholars have interpreted the text. This is information that should be considered by translators as they make their own exegetical decisions regarding the message they will communicate in their translations.

The Semi-Literal Translation

As a basis for discussion, a semi-literal translation of the Greek text is given so that the reasons for different interpretations can best be seen. When one Greek word is translated into English by several words, these words are joined by hyphens. There are a few times when clarity requires that a string of words joined by hyphens have a separate word, such as "not" (μή), inserted in their midst. In this case, the separate word is surrounded by spaces between the hyphens. When alternate translations of a Greek word are given, these are separated by slashes.

The Text

Variations in the Greek text are noted under the heading TEXT. The base text for the summary is the text of the fourth revised edition of *The Greek New Testament,* published by the United Bible Societies, which has the same text as the twenty-sixth edition of the *Novum Testamentum Graece* (Nestle-Aland). Dr. J. Harold Greenlee researched the variants and has written the notes for this part of the summary. The versions that follow different variations are listed without evaluating their choices.

The Lexicon

The meaning of a key word in context is the first question to be answered. Words marked with a raised letter in the semi-literal translation are treated separately under the heading LEXICON. First, the lexicon form of the Greek word is given. Within the parentheses following the Greek word is the location number where, in the author's judgment, this word is defined in the *Greek-English Lexicon of the New Testament Based on Semantic Domains* (Louw and Nida 1988). When a semantic domain includes a translation of the particular verse being treated, **LN** in bold type indicates that specific translation. If the specific reference for the verse is listed in *A Greek-English Lexicon of the New Testament and Other Early Christian Literature* (Bauer, Arndt, Gingrich, and Danker 1979), the outline location and page number is given. Then English equivalents of the Greek word are given to show how it is translated by commentators who offer their own translations of the whole text and, after a semicolon, all the versions in the list of abbreviations for translations. When reference is made to "all versions," it refers to only the versions in the list of translations. Sometimes further comments are made about the meaning of the word or the significance of a verb's tense, voice, or mood.

The Questions

Under the heading QUESTION, a question is asked that comes from examining the Greek text under consideration. Typical questions concern the identity of an implied actor or object of an event word, the antecedent of a pronominal reference, the connection indicated by a relational word, the meaning of a genitive construction, the meaning of figurative language, the function of a rhetorical question, the identification of an ambiguity, and the presence of implied information that is needed to understand the passage correctly. Background information is also considered for a proper understanding of a passage. Although not all implied information and background information is made explicit in a translation, it is important to consider it so that the translation will not be stated in such a way that prevents a reader from arriving at the proper interpretation. The question is answered with a summary of what commentators have said. If there are contrasting differences of opinion, the different interpretations are numbered and the commentaries that support each are listed. Differences that are not treated by many of the commentaries often are not numbered, but are introduced with a contrastive 'Or' at the beginning of the sentence. No attempt has been made to select which interpretation is best.

In listing support for various statements of interpretation, the author is often faced with the difficult task of matching the different terminologies used in commentaries with the terminology he has adopted. Sometimes he can only infer the position of a commentary from incidental remarks. This book, then, includes the author's interpretation of the views taken in the various commentaries. General statements are followed by specific statements, which indicate the author's understanding of the pertinent relationships, actors, events, and objects implied by that interpretation.

The Use of This Book

This book does not replace the commentaries that it summarizes. Commentaries contain much more information about the meaning of words and passages. They often contain arguments for the interpretations that are taken and they may have important discussions about the discourse features of the text. In addition, they have information about the historical, geographical, and cultural setting. Translators will want to refer to at least four commentaries as they exegete a passage. However, since no one commentary contains all the answers translators need, this book will be a valuable supplement. It makes more sources of exegetical help available than most translators have access to. Even if they had all the books available, few would have the time to search through all of them for the answers.

When many commentaries are studied, it soon becomes apparent that they frequently disagree in their interpretations. That is the reason why so many answers in this book are divided into two or more interpretations. The reader's initial reaction may be that all of these different interpretations complicate exegesis rather than help it. However, before translating a passage, a translator needs to know exactly where there is a problem of interpretation and what the exegetical options are.

ABBREVIATIONS

COMMENTARIES AND REFERENCE BOOKS

Alf Alford, Henry. 1857. *The Greek New Testament,* Vol. 3. Reprint with revision by E. F. *Harrison*, 1968. Chicago: Moody Press.

BAGD Bauer, Walter. *A Greek-English Lexicon of the New Testament and Other Early Christian Literature.* Translated and adapted from the 5th ed., 1958 by William F. Arndt and F. Wilbur Gingrich. 2d English ed. revised and augmented by F. Wilbur Gingrich and Frederick W. Danker. Chicago: University of Chicago Press, 1979.

BNTC Dunn, James D. G. *The Epistle to the Galatians.* Black's New Testament Commentary. London: A. & C. Black: Peabody, MA: Hendrickson, 1993.

BST Stott, John R.W. *Only One Way The Message of Galatians.* The Bible Speaks Today. Downers Grove, IL: InterVarsity Press, 1968.

Herm Betz, Hans Dieter. *Galatians: A Commentary on Paul's Letter to the Churches in Galatia.* Hermeneia—A Critical and Historical Commentary on the Bible. Minneapolis, MN: Fortress Press, 1979.

ICC Burton, Ernest De Witt. *A Critical and Exegetical Commentary on the Epistle to the Galatians.* International Critical Commentary. Edinburgh: T & T Clark; distr. in USA by Books International, Inc., Herndon, VA, 1920.

LN Louw, Johannes P., and Eugene A. Nida. *Greek-English Lexicon of the New Testament Based on Semantic Domains.* New York: United Bible Societies, 1988.

Lns Lenski, R. C. H. *The Interpretation of St. Paul's Epistles to the Galatians, to the Ephesians, and to the Philippians.* 1937. Reprint. Minneapolis, MN: Augsburg Publishing House, 1961.

Lt Lightfoot, J. B. *Commentaries on Galatians, Philippians, Colossians, and Philemon.* 1890–1897 Reprint. Peabody, MA: Hendrickson, 1981.

Mor Morris, Leon. *Galatians: Paul's Charter of Christian Freedom.* Downers Grove, IL:InterVarsity Press, 1996.

NAC George, Timothy. *Galatians.* The New American Commentary. Nashville, TN: Broadman & Holman, 1994.

NCBC Guthrie, Donald. *Galatians.* New Century Bible Commentary, Rev. ed. Grand Rapids: Eerdmans; London: Marshall Pickering, 1974.

NIBC Jervis, Ann. *Galatians,* New International Biblical Commentary. Peabody, MA: Hendrickson, 1999.

NIC Fung, Ronald Y. K. *The Epistle to the Galatians.* New International Commentary on the New Testament. Grand Rapids: Eerdmans, 1988.

NIGTC	Bruce, F. F. *The Epistle to the Galatians: A Commentary on the Greek Text*. New International Greek Testament Commentary. Grand Rapids: Eerdmans; Carlisle, England: Paternoster Press, 1982.
NTC	Hendriksen, William. *Exposition of Galatians*. New Testament Commentary. Grand Rapids: Baker Book House, 1968.
SSA	Rogers, Elinor MacDonald. *A Semantic Structure Analysis of Galatians*. Ed. by John Callow. Dallas, TX: Summer Institute of Linguistics, 1989.
TH	Arichea, Daniel C., and Eugene A. Nida. *A Translator's Handbook on Paul's Letter to the Galatians*. New York: United Bible Societies, 1976.
TNTC	Cole, R. Alan. *The Letter of Paul to the Galatians: An Introduction and Commentary*. Tyndale New Testament Commentaries, 2nd ed. Grand Rapids: Eerdmans, 1989.
WBC	Longenecker, Richard N. *Galatians*. Word Biblical Commentary. Dallas, TX; Milton Keynes, England: Word Books. 1990.

GREEK TEXT AND TRANSLATIONS

GNT	The Greek New Testament. Edited by B. Aland, K. Aland, J. Karavidopoulos, C. Martini, and B. Metzger. 4th ed. London, New York: United Bible Societies, 1993.
CEV	The Holy Bible, Contemporary English Version. New York: American Bible Society, 1995.
GW	God's Word. Grand Rapids: World Publishing, 1995.
KJV	The Holy Bible. Authorized (or King James) Version. 1611.
NASB	New American Standard Bible. La Habra, Calif.: Lockman Foundation, 1995.
NCV	New Century Version. Dallas: Word Publishing, 1991.
NET	The Net Bible. New English Translation, New Testament. Version 9.206. WWW.NETBIBLE.COM: Biblical Studies Press, 1999.
NIV	The Holy Bible, New International Version. Grand Rapids: Zondervan, 1984.
NLT	The Holy Bible, New Living Translation. Wheaton, Ill.: Tyndale House Publishers, 1996.
NRSV	The Holy Bible: New Revised Standard Version. New York: Oxford University Press, 1989.
REB	The Revised English Bible. Oxford: Oxford University Press and Cambridge University Press, 1989.
TEV	Good News Bible, Today's English Version. 2nd ed. New York: American Bible Society, 1992.

GRAMMATICAL TERMS

act.	active	infin.	infinitive
excl.	exclusive	mid.	middle
fut.	future	opt.	optative
impera	imperative	pass.	passive
imperf.	imperfect	perf.	perfect
incl.	inclusive	pres.	present
indic.	indicative	subj.	subjunctive

EXEGETICAL SUMMARY OF GALATIANS

DISCOURSE UNIT: 1:1–2:21 [TNTC]. The topic is the argument from experience.

DISCOURSE UNIT: 1:1–5 [BST, GNT, Mor, NAC, NCBC, NIC, NIGTC, TNTC, WBC; GW, NASB, NCV, NET, NLT, NRSV]. The topic is the introduction [Mor, NCBC; NASB], the apostolic salutation [GNT, NAC, NIC, NIGTC, WBC; NET, NRSV], the greeting [TNTC; GW], greetings from Paul [NLT], the apostle Paul's authority and gospel [BST], Christians are saved by grace [NCV].

1:1 Paul (an) apostle[a] not from[b] men[c] nor through[d] man[e]

LEXICON—a. ἀπόστολος (LN 53.74) (BAGD 3. p. 99): 'apostle' [BAGD, BNTC, Herm, Mor, SSA, WBC; all versions], 'special messenger' [LN].

b. ἀπό with genitive object (LN 90.15) (BAGD 4. p. 88): 'from' [BAGD, BNTC, Herm, LN, Mor, WBC; NASB, NET, NIV, TEV], 'by' [LN; GW, NCV, NLT, NRSV, REB], 'of' [KJV]. The phrase οὐκ ἀπ' ἀνθρώπων 'not from men' is translated 'no mere human chose...me to this work' [CEV], 'not because a group of people appointed me' [SSA].

c. ἄνθρωπος (LN 9.1, 9.24) (BAGD 1. p. 68): 'man' [BAGD, LN (9.24)], 'human being' [BAGD, LN (9.1)]. The plural form is translated 'men' [Herm, Mor, WBC; KJV, NASB, NET, NIV], 'a group' [GW, NLT], 'a group of people' [SSA], '(no) mere human' [CEV], 'human authority' [REB], 'human beings' [BNTC; NCV, TEV], 'human commission' [NRSV].

d. διά with genitive object (LN 90.4) (BAGD 2. p. 180): 'through' [BNTC, Herm, LN, Mor, WBC; NASB], 'by' [BAGD, LN; GW, KJV, NIV, NLT, REB, TEV], 'from' [NCV, NRSV]. The phrase οὐδὲ δι' ἀνθρώπου 'nor through man' is translated 'no mere human...appointed me to this work' [CEV], 'nor by human agency' [NET], 'nor because a human being sent me to be an apostle' [SSA].

e. ἄνθρωπος (LN 9.1, 9.24) (BAGD 1. p. 68): 'man' [BAGD, Herm, LN (9.24), Mor, WBC; KJV, NIV], 'human being' [BAGD, BNTC, LN (9.1), SSA; NLT], 'human beings' [NCV], 'mere human' [CEV], 'individual' [GW], 'human act' [REB], 'human means' [TEV], 'human agency' [NET], 'agency of man' [NASB], 'human authorities' [NRSV].

QUESTION—What relationship is indicated by ἀπό 'from'?

It indicates the source of Paul's apostleship [BNTC, ICC, Mor, NAC, NCBC, SSA, TH, TNTC, WBC]. It refers to the remote originating cause [Alf, BAGD]. From 1:16, 17 it appears that Paul has in mind the apostles or the church in Jerusalem [ICC].

QUESTION—What relationship is indicated by διά 'through'?

It indicates the means by which he became an apostle, by either a sending person or agency [BNTC, ICC, Mor, NAC, NCBC, NIC, NIGTC, SSA, TH,

TNTC, WBC; NASB, NET, NIV, NRSV, TEV], the nearer instrumental cause [Alf].

QUESTION—What is the significance of the change from the plural ἀπ' ἀνθρώπων 'from *men*' to the singular δι' ἀνθρώπου 'through *man*'?

1. The change from the plural to the singular is probably not significant [TH, TNTC]. The second form is singular to better make a contrast with the next phrase 'through Jesus Christ' [Alf, Lt]. The singular form is generic in order to deny any human agency at all [Alf, ICC, Lns] and could be best translated 'through man' rather than 'through a man' [ICC].
2. The change is significant. He is an apostle 'not from men' in the sense that he was not appointed to be an apostle by any group, such as the church in Antioch. He is an apostle 'not through man' in the sense that he was not appointed to be an apostle by any individual man such as Ananias or Barnabas [BST]. Paul included the plural and the singular to emphasize that he was not appointed to be an apostle by any group or by any individual [NIBC].

but[a] through[b] Jesus Christ and God (the) Father

LEXICON—a. ἀλλά (LN 89.125): 'but' [BNTC, Herm, LN, Mor, SSA, WBC; all versions except CEV, NCV, NLT], not explicit [CEV, NCV, NLT, which begin a new sentence here].

b. διά with genitive object (LN 90.4): 'through' [BNTC, Herm, LN, Mor, WBC; NASB, NCV, NRSV], 'by' [LN; CEV, GW, KJV, NET, NIV, REB], 'from' [NLT, TEV]. The entire clause is translated 'but Jesus Christ and God the Father have appointed and sent me to be an apostle' [SSA], 'I was chosen to be an apostle by Jesus Christ and by God the Father' [CEV], 'my call is from Jesus Christ and from God the Father' [NLT], 'whose call to be an apostle (came) from Jesus Christ and God the Father' [TEV].

QUESTION—What relationship is indicated by ἀλλά 'but'?

It indicates a strong positive contrast with the previous negative phrases [Herm, Mor, NAC, WBC]. The phrase 'but *through* Jesus Christ and God the Father' is in contrast with both preceding negative phrases 'not *from* men nor *through* man' and it is the positive correlative of 'not *through* man' [ICC].

QUESTION—What relationship is indicated by διά 'through'?

Although διά in the preceding phrase 'nor through (διά) 'man' refers to mediation, here it cannot mean through the mediation of both Jesus and God the Father. When referring to God, this conjunction is used in the more general sense of agency [NIGTC]. By adding 'and God the Father', Paul is not thinking of the agency through which he became an apostle, but that Jesus and the Father are jointly the immediate and direct source of his office [ICC]. The channel of Paul's authority (διά 'through') coincides with its source (ἀπό 'from') [Lt]. Paul is thinking of his original commission described in Acts 26:16–18 and here he indicates that Christ was not just an intermediate used by another. God the Father's name is joined with his so that both are placed on the absolute and supreme level; there was no higher one who could commission him and at the same time no lower one did so [Lns]. Διά makes it clear that the gift was direct from God and Christ and that there was no human involved [Mor]. It should be understood in terms of ultimate source rather than agency [WBC].

QUESTION—Whose Father is God?
1. The designation 'God Father' is used to refer to God the Father [Alf, Lns; all versions]. It is a unit name used to distinguish the first person of the Trinity [Lns]. It is to be taken generally [Alf].
2. This refers to God's relationship to all Christians [NIBC, TH]. In 1:4 Paul uses the phrase 'according to the will of the God and Father of us'. Paul was writing to believers in Galatia and so here and in 1:4 the inclusive sense of 'our' Father is intended [TH].

the (one) having-raised him from[a] (the) dead,[b]
LEXICON—a. ἐκ with genitive object (LN 84.4): 'from' [BNTC, Herm, LN, Mor, WBC; all versions except GW], 'out from, out of' [LN]. See b. [SSA; GW].
   b. νεκρός (LN 23.121) (BAGD 2. p. 535): 'dead' [BAGD, BNTC, Herm, LN, Mor, WBC; all versions except CEV, GW, TEV], 'death' [CEV, TEV]. This phrase is translated 'who brought him back to life' [GW], 'the Father had resurrected Jesus' [SSA].

QUESTION—What is the function of this description of God the Father?
This is not to be taken as though specifying which God the Father is referred to [TH]. This reminds the readers that it was the risen Christ who had commissioned Paul to be an apostle [ICC, NIGTC].

1:2 and all the brothers[a] with[b] me,
LEXICON—a. ἀδελφός (LN 11.23): 'Christian brother, fellow believer' [LN]. The plural form is translated 'Lord's followers' [CEV], 'brothers' [BNTC, Herm, Mor, SSA, WBC; NET, NIV], 'brothers and sisters' [NLT], 'members of God's family' [NRSV], 'friends' [REB], 'believers' [GW, TEV], 'brethren' [KJV, NASB], 'those of God's family' [NCV]. 'Brothers' is a common New Testament designation of believers in Christ [NIC].
   b. σύν with dative object (LN 89.107) (BAGD 1. p. 781): 'with' [BAGD, BNTC, Herm, LN, Mor, SSA, WBC; all versions except NLT, TEV], 'together with' [LN]. This preposition is also translated as a verb: 'join' [NLT, TEV].

QUESTION—How were the brothers connected with the writing of this letter?
They joined in the greeting, but were not joint writers of the letter [ICC, Lns, Mor, NIC, TNTC; NLT, REB, TEV]. Paul uses first person singular in 1:6 [ICC]. These brothers knew what Paul was writing and agreed with him [Alf, BNTC, Lns].

QUESTION—What is meant by ἀδελφοί 'brothers'?
1. The term 'brothers' refers to all the fellow Christians living in the place where Paul was staying [ICC, Lns, NTC, TNTC]: and all the fellow believers here with me.
2. This refers to the men who were Paul's fellow missionaries traveling with him [Alf, Herm, ICC, Lt, Mor, NCBC, NIC]: and the brothers here with me.

to-the churches[a] of Galatia,
LEXICON—a. ἐκκλησία (LN 11.32) (BAGD 4. p. 241): 'church' [BAGD, BNTC, Herm, LN, Mor, SSA, WBC; all versions], 'congregation' [LN].
QUESTION—How are the two nouns related in the genitive construction ταῖς ἐκκλησίαις τῆς Γαλατίας 'the churches of Galatia'?
The churches are the various local Christian congregations located in Galatia [NAC, NCBC, NIBC, NIC, TH, TNTC, WBC].

1:3 grace[a] to-you and peace[b] from[c] God our Father and Lord Jesus Christ
TEXT—Instead of πατρός ἡμῶν καὶ κυριου 'our Father and Lord', some manuscripts read πατρός καὶ κυριου ἡμῶν 'Father and our Lord' and other manuscripts read πατρός καὶ κυριου 'Father and Lord'. GNT reads πατρός ἡμῶν καὶ κυριου 'our Father and Lord' with a B decision, indicating that the text is almost certain.
LEXICON—a. χάρις (LN 25.89, 88.66) (BAGD 2. p. 877): 'grace' [BAGD, BNTC, Herm, Mor, WBC; all versions except CEV, GW], 'favor' [BAGD, LN (25.89)], 'kindness' [LN (88.66)], 'good will' [LN (25.89); GW]. This noun is also translated as a verb phrase: 'to be kind to' [CEV], 'to graciously help' [SSA]. Grace is God's undeserved love [TH], his free favor [BNTC, BST, ICC, Lns, NCBC, NIC, NTC, TH], his unmerited goodwill [NAC, NIGTC].
b. εἰρήνη (LN 22.42) (BAGD 2. p. 227): 'peace' [BAGD, BNTC, Herm, LN, Mor, WBC; all versions]. This noun is also translated as a verb phrase: 'to cause to be peaceful' [SSA].
c. ἀπό with genitive object (LN 90.15) (BAGD 4. p. 88): 'from' [BAGD, BNTC, Herm, LN, Mor, WBC; all versions except CEV, TEV]. The entire clause is translated 'I pray that God the Father and our Lord Jesus Christ will be kind to you and will bless you with peace' [CEV], 'May God our Father and the Lord Jesus Christ give you grace and peace' [TEV], 'I pray that God, our Father, and the Lord Jesus Christ will graciously help you and cause that you be peaceful' [SSA].
QUESTION—What is the function of this clause?
1. It is a greeting [BNTC, Lns, Mor, NCBC, NIC, TH, TNTC].
2. It is in the form of a prayer or wish [Herm, SSA; CEV, KJV, NLT, TEV]: may grace and peace be to you from God and the Lord Jesus Christ.
3. It is a statement [GW]: grace and peace are yours from God and the Lord Jesus Christ.

QUESTION—What is meant by εἰρήνη 'peace'?
Peace refers to their total well being [Lns, NTC, TH], their spiritual well being [TNTC]. It is a state of wholeness and freedom that the grace of God brings [BNTC, ICC, NAC, NIC]. Peace includes the state of being reconciled with God and the resultant condition of satisfaction and happiness [Lns] and an inner conviction that all is well [NTC]. It is one of the major fruits of the Spirit [NCBC].

1:4 the (one) having-given[a] himself for[b] our sins[c],
LEXICON—a. aorist act. participle of δίδωμι (LN 57.71) (BAGD 6. p. 193): 'to give' [BNTC, Herm, LN, Mor, WBC; all versions except GW, NLT], 'to give up, to sacrifice' [BAGD]. The phrase τοῦ δόντος ἑαυτὸν 'the one having given himself' is translated 'he died' [NLT], 'the Lord Jesus Christ died voluntarily' [SSA], 'Christ took the punishment' [GW].
  b. ὑπέρ with genitive object (LN **90.36**) (BAGD 1.ε. p. 838): 'for' [BNTC, Herm, LN, Mor, WBC; all versions], 'on behalf of' [**LN**], 'for the sake of' [LN]. The phrase ὑπὲρ τῶν ἁμαρτιῶν ἡμῶν 'for our sins' is translated 'in order to atone for the sins, or to remove them' [BAGD], 'in order that he might benefit us (incl.) who have sinned' [SSA].
  c. ἁμαρτία (LN 88.289): 'sin' [BNTC, Herm, LN, Mor, WBC; all versions]. It is an act contrary to both God's will and law [LN]. This noun is also translated as a verb with 'us' as the subject: 'to sin' [SSA].
QUESTION—What is meant by τοῦ δόντος ἑαυτ'ον 'the one having given himself'?
To give himself means that Christ gave his life or voluntarily died [ICC, Lns, NAC, NCBC, NTC, SSA, TH]. It means that Christ died as an offering [Alf].
QUESTION—What relationship is indicated by ὑπέρ 'for'?
It indicates that Christ's death was for the benefit of us who have sinned [SSA]. Christ's death brought about the removal of our sins [Lns, Mor, NIC, TH], the forgiveness of our sins [NIGTC].

in-order-that[a] he-might-deliver[b] us out-of[c] the present[d] evil[e] age[f]
LEXICON—a. ὅπως (LN 89.59) (BAGD 2. p. 577): 'in order to' [LN; GW, NLT, TEV], 'for the purpose of' [LN], 'in order that' [BAGD, BNTC, Herm, Mor, SSA, WBC], 'so that' [LN; NASB], 'that' [KJV], 'to' [CEV, NCV, NET, NIV, NRSV, REB].
  b. aorist mid. subj. of ἐξαιρέω (LN 85.43) (BAGD 2. p. 272): 'to deliver' [BAGD, Mor; KJV], 'to set free' [BAGD; NRSV, TEV], 'to rescue' [BAGD, BNTC, Herm, WBC; CEV, NASB, NET, NIV, NLT, REB], 'to take out, to remove' [LN], 'to release' [SSA], 'to free' [GW, NCV].
  c. ἐκ with genitive object (LN 84.4, 90.16): 'out of' [LN (84.4); REB], 'out from' [LN (84.4)], 'from' [BNTC, Herm, LN (84.4, 90.16), Mor, SSA, WBC; all versions except REB].
  d. perf. act. participle of ἐνίστημι (LN **67.41**) (BAGD 1. p. 266): 'present' [BAGD, BNTC, Herm, LN, Mor, WBC; all versions except CEV, NCV, NLT]. The phrase τοῦ αἰῶνος τοῦ ἐνεστῶτος πονηροῦ 'the present evil

age' is translated 'this evil world' [CEV], 'this evil world we live in' [NCV], 'this evil world in which we live' [NLT], 'the evil ways in which human beings who do not know him think and act' [SSA].
- e. πονηρός (LN 88.110) (BAGD 1. p. 691): 'evil' [BAGD, BNTC, Herm, LN, Mor, SSA, WBC; all versions except REB], 'wicked' [BAGD, LN; REB].
- f. αἰών (LN 41.38, 67.143) (BAGD 2. p. 27): 'age' [BAGD, BNTC, Herm, LN (67.143), Mor, WBC; NASB, NET, NIV, NRSV, REB, TEV], 'world' [LN (41.38); CEV, GW, KJV, NCV, NLT], 'world system' [LN (41.38)], 'ways in which human beings who do not know him think and act' [SSA].

QUESTION—What relationship is indicated by ὅπως 'in order to'?

It indicates purpose [Lns, Mor, NIC, SSA, TH, WBC]: Christ died in order to set us free from the power of sin in the world.

QUESTION—What is the present evil age?

The present evil age refers to the evil attitudes and activities of this present time [Alf, BNTC, ICC, Lns, Mor, NIC]. It refers to the present world system that is apart from God [Lt, NIGTC, NTC, SSA]. It includes both the present age of world history and the way of life that characterizes it [NIGTC, WBC]. It is the present age that began with Christ's death and it is an evil age because Satan rules in it [Lns]. It is the present age in contrast to the age to come [Mor].

QUESTION—In what way are we delivered?

It does not refer to being taken out of this present world at the coming of the Lord [ICC]. He delivered us by dying for our sins which have tied us to this age and although still living in the world, we are no longer part of it [Lns]. Deliverance from the present world system is by empowering us to overcome the evil around us [ICC, NIC, SSA]. Deliverance includes both justification in the present time and deliverance from God's wrath at the coming of Christ [ICC, TH]. Deliverance here is not a removal from the world but a rescue from the evil that dominates it [NIGTC, WBC].

in-accordance-with[a] the will[b] of-the God and Father of-us,

LEXICON—a. κατά with accusative object (LN 89.8): 'in accordance with' [BNTC, LN], 'according to' [Herm, Mor, WBC; KJV, NASB, NET, NIV, NRSV], 'in obedience to' [TEV]. The phrase κατὰ τὸ θέλημα τοῦ θεοῦ 'in accordance with the will of God' is translated 'as our God willed' [REB], 'as God planned' [NCV], 'just as God planned' [NLT], 'because that was what our God wanted' [GW], 'this occurred because God willed it' [SSA], 'Christ obeyed God' [CEV].
- b. θέλημα (LN 30.59) (BAGD 2. p. 354): 'will' [BAGD, BNTC, Herm, LN, Mor, WBC; KJV, NASB, NET, NIV, NRSV, TEV], 'plan, purpose, intent' [LN], not explicit [CEV]. This noun is also translated as a verb: 'to will' [SSA; REB], 'to want' [GW], 'to plan' [NCV, NLT].

QUESTION—What is this phrase connected with?
1. It is connected with τοῦ δόντος ἑαυτὸν 'who gave himself' [GW, NLT, TEV]: Christ gave up his life according to the will of our God and Father.
2. It is connected with ἐξέληται ἡμᾶς 'to deliver us' [NASB, NCV, NIV, NRSV, REB]: Christ's purpose was to deliver us from this present evil world, for this was the will of our God and Father.
3. It is connected with the whole clause τοῦ δόντος ἑαυτ'ον ἐξέληται ἡμᾶς 'who gave himself to deliver us' [BST, ICC, Lns, Mor, NTC, SSA, TH, TNTC, WBC]: Christ gave up his life to deliver us according to the will of our God and Father.

QUESTION—What is ἡμῶν 'of us' connected with?
1. It is connected with both 'God and Father' [Lns, Lt, NTC, TH; GW, NASB, NET, NIV, NRSV, REB, TEV]: our God and Father. Since only one person is involved, it means 'our God, who is our Father' [TH].
2. It is connected with only 'Father' [Alf, SSA; KJV, NLT]: God and our Father. This occurred because God, who is our Father, willed it [SSA].

1:5 to-whom (be/is) the glory[a] into[b] the ages[c] of-the ages. Amen.[d]

LEXICON—a. δόξα (LN 33.357, 87.4) (BAGD 3. p. 204): 'glory' [BNTC, Herm, LN (33.357), Mor, WBC; all versions], 'praise' [LN (33.357)], 'honor' [BAGD, LN (87.4)]. This noun is also translated as an adjective: '(God is) glorious' [SSA]. It refers to the majesty or the splendor of God [BNTC, Mor]. It refers to the praise and worship of God by his people [ICC, NAC, NIGTC, TH, WBC].
b. εἰς with accusative object (LN 84.22): 'into' [LN], 'through' [NLT], not explicit [BNTC, Herm, Mor, SSA, WBC; all versions except NLT].
c. αἰών (LN 67.95, 67.143) (BAGD 1. p. 27): 'age, era' [LN (67.143)]. The phrase εἰς τοὺς αἰῶνας τῶν αἰωνων 'into the ages of the ages' is translated 'for ever and ever' [BNTC, Herm, LN (67.95), Mor, WBC; all versions except GW, NASB, NLT], 'for evermore' [BAGD, SSA; NASB], 'ages of eternity' [NLT], 'forever' [GW].
d. ἀμήν (LN 72.6) (BAGD 1. p. 45): 'amen' [BAGD, BNTC, Herm, Mor, SSA, WBC; all versions], 'truly' [BAGD, LN], 'indeed' [LN].

QUESTION—What is the antecedent to which ᾧ 'to whom' refers?
It refers to God [Alf, ICC, Lns, Lt, Mor, NAC, NCBC, NIC, NIGTC, NTC, SSA, TH, WBC; CEV, GW, NCV, NLT, TEV].

QUESTION—What is the function of this clause?
1. This is a wish or an exhortation [ICC, NTC, TH; KJV, NASB, NET, NIV, NRSV, REB, TEV]: to whom *be* the glory forever. When the verb 'be' is supplied in a translation, it is not clear if this expresses the wish 'may God be glorified or praised forever' or if it is an exhortation 'let us glorify or praise him forever'. The alternative is specified by only a few commentaries. TH is explicit in suggesting it means 'let us praise God' or 'God deserves praise', or 'people should praise God'. If the alternative verb were to be supplied, 'to him *is* the glory', then glory should be

ascribed to him, so there is little difference in the resultant meaning [NTC].
2. This is an affirmation [Lns, Lt, NCBC, NIC, SSA; CEV, GW, NCV, NLT]: to whom *is* the glory forever.

QUESTION—What is the significance of the ἀμήν 'amen'?

It confirms Paul's declaration [BNTC, Lns, Mor, NIC]. This was the usual ending to a prayer and means 'May it be so' [TH]. For those who take this to end an affirmation rather than a prayer it means 'this is true' [SSA].

DISCOURSE UNIT: 1:6–2:21 [Mor; REB]. The topic is the gospel [Mor], one gospel for all [REB].

DISCOURSE UNIT: 1:6–10 [BST, GNT, Mor, NAC, NCBC, NIC, NIGTC, WBC; CEV, GW, NASB, NCV, NET, NIV, NLT, NRSV, TEV]. The topic is false teachers and faithless Galatians [BST], the different gospel the Galatians preached [Mor], the apostolic curse [NAC], the apostasy of the Galatians [NCBC], condemnation of the counterfeit gospel [NIC], no other gospel [GNT, NIGTC; NIV, NRSV, TEV], the occasion for writing/issues at stake [WBC; NET], the only true message [CEV], there is only one good news [NLT], follow the good news we gave you [GW], perversion of the gospel [NASB], the only good news [NCV].

DISCOURSE UNIT: 1:6–9 [TNTC]. The topic is the introduction to the subject of the letter.

1:6 I-marvel[a] that so[b] quickly[c] you-are-turning-away[d]

LEXICON—a. pres. act. indic. of θαυμάζω (LN 25.213) (BAGD 1. p. 352): 'to marvel' [LN, Mor; KJV], 'to be amazed' [LN; NASB, NCV], 'to be surprised' [BAGD; GW, TEV], 'to wonder' [BAGD, LN], 'to be astonished' [BNTC, Herm, WBC; NET, NIV, NRSV, REB], 'to be shocked' [CEV, NLT], 'to be severely disappointed' [SSA].
  b. οὕτως (LN 78.4) (BAGD 3. p. 598): 'so' [BAGD, BNTC, Herm, LN, Mor, SSA, WBC; all versions except TEV], not explicit [TEV].
  c. ταχέως (LN 67.56, **67.110**) (BAGD 1. p. 806): 'quickly' [BNTC, Herm, **LN** (67.110), Mor, WBC; all versions except KJV, NLT, TEV], 'too quickly, too easily, hastily' [BAGD], 'soon' [LN (67.56), SSA; KJV, NLT], 'very soon' [LN (67.56)], 'in no time at all' [TEV].
  d. pres. mid. indic. of μετατίθημι (LN **34.27**) (BAGD 2.b. p. 513): 'to turn away' [BAGD, BNTC, **LN**, Mor; NCV, NLT, REB], 'to turn away from' [**LN**], 'to turn from' [CEV], 'to desert' [BAGD, Herm, WBC; GW, NASB, NET, NIV, NRSV, TEV], 'to no longer devote (yourselves to God)' [SSA], 'to be removed' [KJV]. The present tense indicates that they were in the process of turning away [ICC, Mor, SSA, WBC] and the change had not yet been completed [BNTC, Lns]. Their desertion may still be stopped [Herm, NTC, SSA, TH, TNTC].

QUESTION—What is meant by οὕτως ταχέως 'so quickly'?
1. This is a temporal reference [Alf, BNTC, Herm, ICC, NAC, NIC, SSA, TH]: so soon you are turning away. This refers to so soon after they had accepted the true gospel [ICC, NIC, TH], or it refers to so soon after Paul had left them [BNTC, SSA], or it refers to so soon after the false teachers introduced a false gospel [BNTC].
2. This is a temporal-manner reference [Lns, NCBC, NTC]: so quickly you are turning away. It did not take much time for the false teachers to turn them away from the true gospel [NCBC].

from[a] the (one) having-called[b] you in[c] (the) grace[d] of-Christ into[e] (a) different[f] gospel,[g]

TEXT—Some manuscripts omit Χριστοῦ 'of Christ'. GNT includes this word in brackets with a C decision, indicating that the Committee had difficulty in making the decision. Χριστοῦ 'Christ' is omitted by CEV, REB.

LEXICON—a. ἀπό with genitive object (LN 89.122): 'from' [BNTC, LN, Mor; CEV, KJV, NLT, REB], not explicit [Herm, SSA, WBC; GW, NASB, NCV, NET, NIV, NRSV, TEV].

b. aorist act. participle of καλέω (LN 33.307) (BAGD 2. p. 399): 'to call' [BAGD, BNTC, Herm, LN, Mor, SSA, WBC; all versions except CEV], 'to choose' [CEV].

c. ἐν with dative object (LN 13.8, 83.13, 84.22, 89.76, 90.10) (BAGD 2. p. 261): 'in' [BNTC, Herm, LN (13.8, 83.13), Mor; GW, NLT, NRSV], 'with' [LN (13.8, 90.10)], 'within, inside' [LN (83.13)], 'into' [LN (84.22); KJV], 'by' [LN (89.76, 90.10), WBC; NASB, NCV, NET, NIV, REB, TEV], 'by means of, through' [LN (89.76)], 'because of' [CEV]. The phrase ἐν χάριτι 'in the grace' is translated 'graciously' [BAGD]. Not explicit [SSA].

d. χάρις (LN 25.89, 88.66) (BAGD 3. p. 878): 'grace' [BAGD, BNTC, Herm, LN (88.66), Mor, WBC; all versions except CEV, GW, NLT], 'kindness' [LN (88.66); GW], 'wonderful kindness' [CEV], 'favor, good will' [LN (25.89)], 'love and mercy' [NLT]. The phrase χάριτι Χριστοῦ 'the grace of Christ' is translated 'what Christ freely provides/gives' [SSA].

e. εἰς with accusative object (LN 84.22) (BAGD 4. p. 229): 'into' [LN; KJV], 'to' [BAGD, BNTC, Herm, WBC; GW], 'for' [Mor; NASB], 'devoting yourselves to' [SSA], 'and following' [NET, REB], 'and are turning to' [NIV, NRSV], 'and are accepting' [TEV], 'and believing' [NCV]. Some begin a new sentence here: 'You have believed' [CEV], 'You are already following' [NLT].

f. ἕτερος (LN 58.36, 58.37) (BAGD 2. p. 315): 'different' [BAGD, Herm, LN (58.36), Mor, SSA, WBC; all versions except CEV, KJV, TEV], 'another' [BAGD, BNTC, LN (58.37); CEV, KJV, TEV].

g. εὐαγγέλιον (LN 33.217) (BAGD 2. p. 318): 'gospel' [BAGD, BNTC, Herm, LN, Mor, WBC; KJV, NASB, NET, NIV, NRSV, REB, TEV], 'good news' [BAGD, LN; GW, NCV], 'message' [SSA; CEV], 'way' [NLT].

QUESTION—To whom does τοῦ καλέσαντος 'the one having called' refer to?
1. God, the Father, is the one who called them [Alf, BNTC, BST, Herm, ICC, Lt, Mor, NAC, NCBC, NIBC, NIC, NIGTC, NTC, SSA, TH, TNTC, WBC; CEV, NCV, NLT]. This refers to God's call which was brought to them through Paul's preaching [ICC, NIC]. Another view is that this refers to an internal call by which the Holy Spirit applied the gospel invitation to their hearts [NTC].
2. Christ is the one who called them [Lns; GW]. In Romans 1:6 Paul speaks of the Christians as being called by Jesus Christ [Lns].

QUESTION—What relationship is indicated by ἐν 'in'?
1. It indicates the means or instrument by which they were called [BNTC, Lt, NIC, WBC; NASB, NCV, NET, NIV, REB, TEV]: the one who called you by means of the message about the grace of Christ.
2. It indicates the purpose for which they were called [ICC, SSA; KJV]: the one who called you in order that you receive Christ's grace. This refers to a change of state in which their relation towards God made them the objects of the grace of Christ so that they participated in its benefits [ICC]. God's purpose was that they might have the life Christ freely provides [SSA].
3. It indicates the manner of the call [Lns]: the one who graciously called you.
4. It indicates the reason God called them [CEV]: the one who called you because of his grace.

1:7 which is not another,[a]

LEXICON—a. ἄλλος (LN 58.37) (BAGD 1. p. 40): 'another' [BAGD, Herm, LN, Mor; KJV, NASB, NET, NRSV, REB], 'other' [BNTC, LN; NCV, TEV], 'different in kind' [BAGD], 'altered' [SSA], not explicit [GW, NIV, NLT]. The phrase οὐκ ἔστιν ἄλλο 'is not another' is translated 'when there is really only one true message' [CEV], 'is not the same' [WBC].

QUESTION—In what way is ἕτερος 'different' in 1:6 different in meaning to ἄλλος 'another' in 1:7?
1. There is a significant difference between the words [Alf, ICC, Lns, Lt, Mor, NIBC, NTC, SSA, WBC]. The word ἕτερος means another of a different kind and ἄλλος means another of the same kind [Mor, NIBC, WBC]. 'Different' distinguishes between the two while 'other' adds to one [Lt]. The gospel is different because there is not another gospel [Lns].
2. There is no significant difference between the two words [BNTC, Herm, NIC, TH]. Paul had called the false teaching another version of the gospel in the previous verse, but here Paul denies that it can even be called that since there is no other substitute for the gospel that Paul had preached [TH].

if[a] not some (persons) there-are the-(ones) troubling[b] you
LEXICON—a. εἰ (LN 89.65, **89.131**) (BAGD 8. p. 220): 'if' [LN (89.65)]. The phrase εἰ μή 'if not' is translated 'except that' [BNTC, **LN** (89.131), WBC], 'except' [SSA], 'but' [BAGD, Herm, LN (89.131); CEV, GW, KJV, NCV, NET, NRSV, TEV], 'only' [Mor; NASB, REB], 'evidently' [NIV], not explicit [NLT].
    b. pres. act. participle of ταράσσω (LN 25.244) (BAGD 2. p. 805): 'to trouble' [Mor; KJV], 'to stir up' [BAGD], 'to disturb' [BAGD, BNTC, Herm; NASB, NET], 'to unsettle' [BAGD, SSA; REB], 'to throw into confusion' [BAGD; NIV], 'to distress' [LN], 'to distress greatly' [LN], 'to cause great mental distress' [LN], 'to cause trouble' [CEV], 'to confuse' [WBC; GW, NCV, NRSV], 'to upset' [TEV], 'you are being fooled' [NLT].
QUESTION—What is meant by εἰ μή 'except that'?
The previous statement is now qualified to explain that the different gospel is not another gospel except that some pretend that another gospel is the true gospel [Lns]. It is another gospel only so far that certain ones want to pervert the true gospel [Alf]. It suggests that no one would think of calling this substitute message a 'gospel' except with the intention of confusing the Christians [NIGTC, WBC].

and wishing[a] to-pervert[b] the gospel[c] of-Christ.
LEXICON—a. pres. act. participle of θέλω (LN 25.1): 'to wish' [LN], 'to want' [BNTC, Herm, LN; CEV, GW, KJV, NASB, NCV, NET, NRSV], 'to desire' [LN, SSA, WBC], 'to try' [NIV, REB, TEV], 'to will' [Mor], not explicit [NLT].
    b. aorist act. infin. of μεταστρέφω (LN 13.64) (BAGD p. 513): 'to pervert' [BAGD, Herm, Mor, WBC; KJV, NIV, NRSV], 'to change' [LN; NCV, TEV], 'to distort' [GW, NASB, NET, REB], 'to twist and change' [NLT], 'to alter' [SSA], 'to turn' [BNTC], not explicit [CEV].
    c. εὐαγγέλιον (LN 33.217) (BAGD 2. p. 318): 'gospel' [BAGD, BNTC, Herm, LN, Mor, WBC; KJV, NASB, NET, NIV, NRSV, REB, TEV], 'good news' [BAGD, LN, SSA; CEV, GW, NCV], 'truth' [NLT].
QUESTION—How are the two nouns related in the genitive construction τὸ εὐαγγέλιον τοῦ χριστοῦ 'the gospel of Christ'?
    1. The gospel is about Christ [Alf, Herm, NIC, NTC, TH; CEV, GW].
    2. The gospel is what Christ preached [Lns, SSA]. This is the good news that Christ revealed [SSA].
    3. The gospel that belongs to Christ [NCBC].
    4. The gospel is both about Christ and from him [WBC].

1:8 But even[a] if we or (an) angel from[b] heaven should-be-preaching[c] to-you contrary-to[d] that-which we-preached to-you,
TEXT—Instead of the present subjunctive εὐαγγελίζηται 'should be preaching' some manuscripts read the aorist subjunctive εὐαγγελίσηται 'should preach' and other manuscripts read the present indicative εὐαγγελίζεται 'is

preaching'. Some of these manuscripts omit ὑμῖν 'to you'. GNT reads the present subjunctive εὐαγγελίζηται ὑμῖν 'should be preaching to you' with a C decision, indicating that the Committee had difficulty making the decision.

LEXICON—a. καί (LN 89.93): 'even' [BNTC, Herm, LN, Mor, SSA, WBC; all versions except CEV, KJV, NCV], 'though' [KJV], 'so' [NCV]. This conjunction is also translated as a verb phrase: 'it doesn't matter' [CEV].
  b. ἐκ with genitive object (LN 84.4): 'from' [BNTC, Herm, LN, Mor, SSA, WBC; all versions], 'out from, out of' [LN].
  c. pres. mid. (deponent = act.) subj. of εὐαγγελίζω (LN 33.215) (BAGD 2. p. 317): 'to preach' [BAGD, BNTC, Mor, WBC; all versions except GW, NRSV], 'to proclaim' [BAGD, Herm; NRSV], 'to announce the gospel' [LN], 'to tell the good news' [LN, SSA; GW].
  d. παρά with accusative object (LN 89.137) (BAGD 6. p. 611): 'contrary to' [BAGD, BNTC, Herm, LN, Mor; NASB, NET, NRSV], 'other than' [SSA, WBC; NIV, REB], 'any other' [KJV, NLT], 'different from' [CEV, GW, TEV], 'something different' [NCV]. Rather than direct contradictions, it refers to subversive additions 'not in accordance with' or 'at variance with' his own teaching [ICC].

QUESTION—What relationship is indicated by ἀλλά 'but'?
Ἀλλά 'but' is the strong adversative. Paul used it to show how serious he considered the differences between his gospel and that which the Jewish-Christian preachers were preaching in Galatia [ICC, Lns, Mor, WBC]. There are some people of the kind described in 1:7, but whoever they may be, they are accursed [Alf, Lns].

QUESTION—What relationship is indicated by καί 'even'?
It indicates the extreme nature of the supposition to follow [WBC].

QUESTION—What relationship is indicated by ἐάν 'if'?
It indicates the conditions under which the curse was to become effective [Herm]. This supposes a case that is not a reality [ICC, Lns].

QUESTION—To whom does ἡμεῖς 'we' refer to?
1. This refers to several people [BNTC, Herm, Lns, Lt, NTC]. In the next verse Paul refers to himself as 'I', so here he includes his assistants [Lns, NTC].
2. This refers only to Paul [TH]: which I preached to you.

may-he-be accursed.[a]

LEXICON—a. ἀνάθεμα (LN 33.474) (BAGD 2. p. 54): 'to be accursed' [BNTC, Herm, LN, Mor, WBC; KJV, NASB, NRSV], 'to be cursed' [BAGD, LN], 'to be forever cursed' [NLT], 'to be eternally condemned' [NIV], 'to be condemned to hell' [GW, NET, TEV], 'to be judged guilty' [NCV], 'to be banned' [REB]. This phrase is translated 'I pray that God will punish anyone' [CEV], 'I appeal to God that he destroy us or such a one' [SSA].

QUESTION—Who is the implied actor of ἀνάθεμα 'accursed' and what is the intent of this clause?

The implied actor is God [Alf, BST, NAC, NCBC, NIC, SSA, TH, TNTC; CEV]. Some regard this as a petition to God [BST, TH; CEV, TEV]: may he be accursed. Others regard this as a judgment of what should take place [KJV, NASB, NET, NIV, NLT, NRSV, REB]: let him be accursed. Others regard this as a moral evaluation of what should happen [GW, NCV]: he should be accursed. Others take this to be an affirmation that it shall happen [Lns; NASB]: he shall be accursed.

1:9 As we-have-said-before[a] and now[b] again I-say,[c]

LEXICON—a. perf. act. indic. of προλέγω (LN 33.86) (BAGD 2. p. 704): 'to say before' [BAGD, BNTC, Herm, Mor, WBC; CEV, KJV, NASB, NCV, NET, NRSV, TEV], 'to say already' [LN; NIV], 'to say previously' [BAGD], 'to warn in the past' [REB], 'to tell in the past' [SSA; GW], not explicit [NLT].
- b. ἄρτι (LN 67.38) (BAGD 3. p. 110): 'now' [BAGD, BNTC, Herm, LN, Mor, SSA, WBC; all versions except CEV, NLT], 'at the present time' [BAGD], not explicit [CEV, NLT].
- c. pres. act. indic. of λέγω (LN 33.69): 'to say' [BNTC, Herm, LN, Mor, WBC; all versions except GW, NRSV, REB], 'to tell' [LN, SSA; GW], 'to warn' [REB]. The phrase πάλιν λέγω 'again I say' is translated 'I repeat' [NRSV].

QUESTION—Who does 'we' refer to in the verb προειρήκαμεν 'we have said it before'?
1. This refers to several people [Alf, BNTC, Lns, Lt, NIC, NTC, SSA]. The change from 'we' to 'I say' in this same sentence is significant. Paul does not spare himself or his friends and assistants if they should preach a false message [Lns].
2. This refers only to Paul [TNTC; CEV, REB]. There is no significance in the change from the plural προειρήκαμεν 'we have said it before' to the singular λέγω 'I say' [TNTC].

QUESTION—What occasion does προειρήκαμεν 'we have said it before' refer to?
1. It refers to an earlier visit [Alf, Herm, ICC, Lns, Lt, Mor, NTC].
2. It refers to what he wrote in 1:8 [NIGTC, TNTC]. It means 'let me repeat what I have just said' [TNTC].

if anyone is-preaching[a] to-you different-from[b] that-which you-received,[c] may-he-be accursed.[d]

LEXICON—a. pres. mid. (deponent = act.) indic. of εὐαγγελίζω (LN 33.215) (BAGD 2. p. 317): 'to preach' [BAGD, BNTC, Mor, WBC; all versions except GW, NRSV], 'to proclaim' [BAGD, Herm; NRSV], 'to announce the gospel' [LN], 'to tell the good news' [LN, SSA], 'to tell' [GW].
- b. παρά with accusative object (LN 89.137) (BAGD 6. p. 611): 'different from' [CEV, GW, TEV], 'other than' [Mor, SSA, WBC; NIV, REB], 'any

other' [KJV, NLT], 'something different' [NCV], 'contrary to' [BAGD, BNTC, Herm, LN; NASB, NET, NRSV].
   c. aorist act. indic. of παραλαμβάνω (LN 33.238) (BAGD 2. p. 619): 'to receive' [BAGD, BNTC, Herm, LN, Mor, SSA; GW, KJV, NASB, NET, NRSV, REB], 'to believe' [CEV], 'to accept' [WBC; NCV, NIV, TEV], 'to welcome' [NLT].
   d. ἀνάθεμα (LN 33.474) (BAGD 2. p. 54): 'accursed' [LN], 'cursed' [BAGD, LN]. See this word at 1:8. The phrase ἀνάθεμα ἔστω 'may he be accursed' is translated 'I appeal to God that he destroy that one' [SSA], 'let God's curse fall upon that person' [NLT].
QUESTION—What relationship is indicated by εἰ 'if'?
   It indicates that Paul is no longer dealing with a supposition or a hypothetical situation and is now referring to the actual situation [Alf, Herm, NIC, TH, WBC]. He uses a general reference, but is actually referring to the people mentioned in 1:7 [TH].

DISCOURSE UNIT: 1:10–24 [TNTC]. The topic is Paul's conversion.

1:10 For now[a] am-I-trying-to-persuade/seek-approval-of[b] men[c] or God?
LEXICON—a. ἄρτι (LN 67.38) (BAGD 3. p. 110): 'now' [BAGD, BNTC, Herm, LN, Mor, WBC; GW, KJV, NASB, NET, NIV, NRSV, REB], 'at the present time' [BAGD], not explicit [SSA; CEV, NCV, NLT, TEV].
   b. pres. act. indic. of πείθω (LN 33.301) (BAGD 1.b. or 1.c. p. 639): 'to seek approval' [WBC; NRSV], 'to gain the approval of' [NET], 'to win the approval of' [GW, NIV], 'to ask for (human) approval' [REB], 'to win (human) approval' [TEV], 'to seek the favor' [NASB], 'to try to make (people) accept...to try to please (God)' [NCV], 'to try to please' [CEV], 'to strive to please' [BAGD (1.c)], 'to try to be (a people) pleaser...to please (God)' [NLT], 'to persuade' [BAGD (1.b.), BNTC, Herm, LN; KJV], 'to appeal to' [BAGD (1.b.), Mor], 'to win over' [BAGD (1.c.)], 'to convince' [LN], 'to desire the approval of' [SSA]. The present tense is conative, 'to try to please' [CEV, NCV, NLT].
   c. ἄνθρωπος (LN 9.1, 9.24) (BAGD 1. p. 68): 'man' [BAGD, LN (9.24)], 'person' [LN (9.1)], 'human being' [BAGD], 'men' [BNTC, Herm, Mor, WBC; KJV, NASB, NIV], 'people' [SSA; CEV, GW, NCV, NET, NLT]. This noun is also translated as an adjective: 'human (approval)' [NRSV, REB, TEV].
QUESTION—What relationship is indicated by γάρ 'for'?
   1. It indicates the reason why Paul pronounced such a severe judgment in the preceding verse [Alf, ICC, Lt]. This accounts for his severe judgment in the preceding verse and at the same time softens the harshness of it [Alf].
   2. It is used assertively [Lns, NTC]. It is used as an exclamation such as 'Yes, indeed' or 'Certainly' [NTC]. It is used to make the question more urgent and the implied answer more inevitable [Lns].

GALATIANS 1:10

QUESTION—To what does ἄρτι 'now' refer?
1. It refers to the severe language that he used in the previous verse [Alf, ICC, Lns, TH, WBC]: now that I have used such severe language.
2. It indicates a contrast between his present and his former purpose of life [TNTC].
3. It indicates a place of emphasis [BNTC].

QUESTION—What is meant by the verb πείθω 'to persuade/to seek approval of' and how does it differ from ἀρέσκω 'to please' in the next clause?
1. The verb πείθω in this clause means to persuade someone, not to please them [BNTC, Herm, LN (33.301), NIGTC; KJV].
   1.1 It implies that he does try to persuade men, but not God [NIGTC]: He says, 'Is it human beings or God that I am trying to persuade now?'. Paul never thought of trying to persuade God about anything, such as endorsing the anathema he had pronounced, but persuading people to be reconciled to God was his constant aim [NIGTC].
   1.2 It implies that he does not try to persuade either men or God [Herm]. This is asked in irony and denies both alternatives [Herm].
2. The verb πείθω means 'to gain the approval of someone' or 'to please someone' and is close in meaning to ἀρέσκω 'to please' in the next clause [Alf, BST, ICC, Lns, Lt, Mor, NCBC, NIBC, NTC, SSA, TH; all versions except KJV]. The verb πείθω 'to seek favor or approval' is continued by ζητῆ ἀρέσκειν 'seeking to please' to doubly enforce the meaning of πείθω [SSA]. The verb πείθω 'to seek the favor of' is repeated a little more distinctly by ἀρέσκω 'to try to please' [ICC]. It implies that Paul does try to seek God's approval, not man's [TH; TEV] and the following question has the same thought with the implied answer being that he was not trying to please men [TH].
   2.1 Both verbs are translated the same: 'to please' [CEV, NLT].
   2.2 The verbs are translated differently: 'to win/gain the approval of...to please' [GW, NET, NIV], 'to seek the favor of...to please' [NASB], 'to make (people) accept me...to please' [NCV], 'to seek approval...to please' [WBC; NRSV], 'to seek (human) approval...to seek (human) favor' [REB], 'to win human approval...to be popular with' [TEV].

Or am-I-seeking[a] to-please[b] men?[c]

LEXICON—a. pres. act. indic. of ζητέω (LN 25.9, 68.60) (BAGD 2. p. 339): 'to seek' [BNTC, Herm, LN (68.60), Mor; KJV], 'to try' [LN (68.60), WBC; all versions except KJV, NASB, REB], 'to attempt' [LN (68.60)], 'to strive' [BAGD; NASB], 'to aim at' [BAGD], 'to desire' [BAGD, LN (25.9)], 'to want' [LN (25.9)], 'to wish' [BAGD], 'to curry' [REB].
b. pres. act. infin. of ἀρέσκω (LN 25.90) (BAGD 1. p. 105): 'to please' [BNTC, Herm, LN, Mor, WBC; all versions except REB, TEV], 'to strive to please' [BAGD], 'favor with' [REB], 'to be popular with' [TEV], 'do what people prefer' [SSA]. This imperfect tense is the conative imperfect (*i.e.,* it means to attempt) [BAGD].

c. ἄνθρωπος (LN 9.1, 9.24) (BAGD 1. p. 68): 'man' [BAGD, LN (9.24)], 'person' [LN (9.1)], 'human being' [BAGD]. The plural form is translated 'people' [SSA; CEV, GW, NCV, NET, NLT, NRSV, TEV], 'men' [BNTC, Herm, Mor, WBC; KJV, NASB, NIV, REB].

QUESTION—What relationship is indicated by ἤ 'or'?

This conjunction is not contrastive but conjunctive and makes the first question clearer [Lns]. It introduces a more general and comprehensive restatement of the preceding question [ICC].

QUESTION—What is the purpose of this rhetorical question?

It repeats the preceding question for added emphasis. Also the verb in the first rhetorical question πείθω 'to please' refers to making it easy for men to accept the gospel. The verb in this question ἀρέσκω 'to please' refers to getting favor so as to become popular [NCBC]. 'Or' does not indicate an alternative, rather it is a conjunction that clarifies the preceding question [Lns]. It repeats a little more distinctly the thought of the preceding clause [ICC].

If still[a] I-were-pleasing men, I-would- not -be (a) slave[b] of-Christ.

LEXICON—a. ἔτι (LN 67.128) (BAGD 1. p. 315): 'still' [BAGD, BNTC, Herm, LN, SSA, WBC; all versions except CEV, KJV], 'yet' [LN; KJV], not explicit [Mor; CEV].

b. δοῦλος (LN **87.76**) (BAGD 4. p. 206): 'slave' [BAGD, BNTC, Herm, LN, Mor; NET], 'bondservant' [LN; NASB], 'servant' [WBC; all versions except NASB, NET]. The phrase Χριστοῦ δοῦλος οὐκ ἂν ἤμην 'I would not be a slave of Christ' is translated 'then I would not be one who willingly and completely serves Christ' [SSA]. This noun focuses on Paul's belonging to Christ [**LN**], his relationship to Christ [BAGD].

QUESTION—To what does ἔτι 'still' refer?

It refers to the time before Paul became a Christian [Herm]. It implies that he is no longer pleasing men. However, this is not to be taken absolutely, but comparatively and means that he does not please men in preference to God and he does not please men for his own advantage [ICC].

QUESTION—How are the nouns related in the genitive construction δοῦλος χριστοῦ 'slave of Christ'?

Christ is the one he obeys [ICC, Lns, Mor].

DISCOURSE UNIT: 1:11–2:21 [NCBC]. The topic is Paul's apologia.

DISCOURSE UNIT: 1:11–2:14 [NIC, NIGTC, WBC]. The topic is Paul's independent gospel and apostleship [NIC, NIGTC], autobiographical statements in Paul's defense [WBC].

DISCOURSE UNIT: 1:11–2:10 [CEV]. The topic is how Paul became an apostle.

DISCOURSE UNIT: 1:11–24 [BST, GNT, Mor, NAC; GW, NASB, NCV, NET, NIV, NLT, NRSV, TEV]. The topic is Paul called by God [NIV], Paul's message comes from Christ [NLT], Paul's vindication of his apostleship [NET, NRSV], the origins of Paul's gospel [BST], Paul's experience of the gospel [Mor], apostolic vocation [NAC], how Paul became an apostle [GNT; TEV], Jesus alone gave Paul the good news he spreads [GW], Paul defends his ministry [NASB], Paul's authority is from God [NCV].

DISCOURSE UNIT: 1:11–12 [NIC, NIGTC]. The topic is the divine origin of Paul's gospel [NIC], Paul's gospel received by revelation [NIGTC].

1:11 **For I-make-known[a] to-you, brothers,[b]**

TEXT—Instead of γάρ 'for' some manuscripts read δέ 'but'. GNT reads γάρ 'for' with a C decision, indicating that the Committee had difficulty making the decision. 'But' is read by KJV.

LEXICON—a. pres. act. indic. of γνωρίζω (LN 28.26) (BAGD 1. p. 163): 'to make known' [BAGD, LN, Mor], 'to make it quite clear' [REB], 'to solemnly assure' [NLT], 'to tell' [TEV], 'to certify' [KJV], 'to declare' [SSA]. The phrase Γνωρίζω γάρ ὑμῖν 'I make known to you' is translated 'I want you to know' [BNTC, WBC; CEV, GW, NCV, NET, NIV, NRSV], 'I would have you know' [Herm; NASB].

b. ἀδελφός (LN 11.23): 'brother, Christian brother, fellow believer' [LN]. The plural form is translated 'brothers' [BNTC, Herm, Mor, SSA, WBC; NIV], 'brethren' [KJV, NASB], 'brothers and sisters' [GW, NCV, NET, NLT, NRSV], 'my friends' [CEV, REB, TEV].

QUESTION—What relationship is indicated by γάρ 'for'?
1. It is explanatory in a broad way: so that you may understand this whole matter [Lns].
2. It indicates the grounds for his preceding statements [NTC, SSA]. It must mean something like 'In justification of the facts which I have stated, namely, that my gospel is of divine origin and is the only true gospel, so that anyone who distorts it is accursed, note the following corroborative facts selected from the story of my life' [NTC]. 'I am disappointed in you, and I appeal to God, since I declare to you...' [SSA].

that the gospel[a] preached[b] by[c] me

LEXICON—a. εὐαγγέλιον (LN 33.217) (BAGD 1. p. 318): 'gospel' [BAGD, BNTC, Herm, LN, Mor, WBC; KJV, NASB, NET, NIV, NRSV, REB, TEV], 'good news' [BAGD, LN, SSA; GW, NCV, NLT], 'message' [CEV].

b. aorist pass. participle of εὐαγγαλίζω (LN 33.215) (BAGD 2. p. 317): 'to be preached' [BAGD, BNTC, Herm, Mor, WBC; KJV, NASB, REB], 'to be proclaimed' [NRSV]. This passive voice with the gospel as the subject of the verb is also translated actively so as to make Paul the subject: 'to preach' [CEV, NCV, NET, NIV, NLT, TEV], 'to spread' [GW], 'to tell' [SSA]. The verb itself includes the idea of the contents: 'to tell the good news, to announce the gospel' [LN].

28   GALATIANS 1:11

   c. ὑπό with genitive object (LN 90.1) (BAGD 1. p. 843): 'by' [BAGD, BNTC, Herm, LN, Mor; NASB, NRSV], 'of' [KJV], not explicit [SSA, WBC; all versions except KJV, NASB, NRSV].

is not according-to^a man;^b

LEXICON—a. κατά with accusative object (LN 89.8): 'according to' [LN, Mor; NASB], 'in accordance with' [LN], 'in relation to' [LN], 'of' [BNTC; NET, NRSV, REB, TEV], 'based on' [NLT], 'after' [KJV], 'made up by' [NCV], not explicit [Herm, SSA, WBC; CEV, GW, NIV].
   b. ἄνθρωπος (LN 9.1, 9.24) (BAGD 1. p. 68): 'man' [BAGD, LN (9.24), Mor], 'person' [LN (9.1)], 'human being' [BAGD, LN (9.1)]. The phrase κατὰ ἄνθρωπον 'according to man' [KJV, NASB] is also translated 'from a human standpoint' [BAGD], 'no one made up (the message)' [CEV], 'of human origin' [BNTC; NET, NRSV, REB, TEV], 'something that man made up' [NIV], 'a human message' [SSA; GW], 'human in nature' [Herm], 'human' [WBC], 'based on mere human reasoning or logic' [NLT], 'made up by human beings' [NCV].

1:12 for I neither received^a it from^b man/a-man^c

LEXICON—a. aorist act. indic. of παραλαμβάνω (LN 27.13, 33.238) (BAGD 2. p. 619): 'to receive' [BAGD, BNTC, Herm, LN (33.238), Mor, SSA, WBC; GW, KJV, NASB, NET, NIV, NRSV, TEV], 'to receive instruction' [LN (33.238)], 'to learn' [LN (27.13)], 'to take (it) over' [REB], 'to get' [NASB], 'to be given' [CEV], not explicit [NLT].
   b. παρά with genitive object (LN 90.14): 'from' [BNTC, Herm, LN, Mor, SSA, WBC; all versions except CEV, KJV, NLT], 'by' [CEV], 'of' [KJV], not explicit [NLT]. It is a general word to indicate the idea of transmission and in this case it is the notion of passing the gospel on from hand to hand [NCBC].
   c. ἄνθρωπος (LN 9.1, 9.24) (BAGD 1. p. 68): 'man' [BAGD, Herm, LN (9.24), Mor, WBC; KJV, NASB, NIV], 'person' [LN (9.1); GW], 'human being' [BAGD, BNTC; TEV], 'some mere human' [CEV], 'anyone' [REB], 'no one' [NLT], 'humans' [NCV]. This noun is also translated as an adjective: 'human (source, origin)' [SSA; NET, NRSV].

QUESTION—What relationship is indicated by γάρ 'for'?
   1. It indicates the grounds for the previous statement [Alf, ICC, Mor, NCBC].
   2. It signals that this sentence with its two negatives is meant to be an elaboration and clarification of the preceding phrase 'that it is not from man' [TH, WBC].

QUESTION—What is meant in saying that he did not receive it from man?
   1. 'Man' refers to a human being in contrast with God [CEV, GW, NCV, NET, NRSV, TEV]: I did not receive it from a human source.
   2. 'Man' refers to any particular man who might have taught him [NIV]: I did not receive it from a man.

nor was-I-taught[a] (it) but through[b] a-revelation[c] of-Jesus Christ.
LEXICON—a. aorist pass. indic. of διδάσκω (LN 33.224) (BAGD 2. p. 192): 'to be taught' [BAGD, BNTC, Herm, LN, Mor, SSA, WBC; all versions except NCV, NET, TEV], 'to learn' [NET]. This passive form is also translated actively with 'anyone' as the subject: 'to teach' [NCV, TEV].
   b. διά with genitive object (LN 89.76, 90.8): 'through' [BNTC, Herm, LN (89.76, 90.8), Mor; NASB, NRSV, REB], 'by means of' [LN (89.76, 90.8)], 'from' [CEV], 'by' [WBC; KJV, NET, NIV, NLT], not explicit [SSA; GW, NCV, TEV].
   c. ἀποκάλυψις (LN 28.38) (BAGD 2. p. 92): 'revelation' [BAGD, BNTC, Herm, LN, Mor, WBC; KJV, NASB, NET, NIV, NLT, NRSV, REB], 'disclosure' [LN]. This noun is also translated as a verb with 'Jesus Christ' as the subject: 'to reveal' [SSA; GW, TEV], 'to show' [NCV]. Although most take it to mean that the gospel was revealed by Jesus Christ, one takes it to mean that Jesus Christ was revealed: 'my message came directly from Jesus Christ when he appeared to me' [CEV].
QUESTION—What relationship is indicated by ἀλλά 'but'?
It introduces the contrary thought [Lns, Mor]: on the contrary, it came through revelation.
QUESTION—What relationship is indicated by διά 'through'?
It indicates the means by which Paul received the gospel [WBC].
QUESTION—How are the nouns related in the genitive construction ἀποκαλύψεως Ἰησοῦ Χριστοῦ 'revelation of Jesus Christ'?
   1. It means a revelation made by God about Jesus Christ [BNTC, ICC, NCBC, NIC, NIGTC, SSA, TH, TNTC]: through what God revealed to me about Jesus Christ.
   2. It means a revelation made by Jesus Christ [BST, Lns, Lt, Mor, NTC, WBC; NCV, NIV, NLT, TEV]: through what Jesus Christ revealed to me.
   3. It means Jesus Christ was revealed [CEV]: through what Jesus told me when he appeared to me.

DISCOURSE UNIT: 1:13-17 [WBC]. The topic is Paul's early life, conversion, and commission.

DISCOURSE UNIT: 1:13-14 [NIC, NIGTC]. The topic is Paul's former life [NIC], Paul's earlier career [NIGTC].

1:13 For you heard (of) my manner-of-life[a] formerly[b] in[c] Judaism,[d]
LEXICON—a. ἀναστροφή (LN **41.3**) (BAGD p. 61): 'manner of life' [NASB, REB], 'conduct' [BAGD, LN], 'behavior' [LN], 'life' [**LN**; NCV, NRSV], 'lifestyle' [NET], 'way of life' [BNTC, Herm, Mor, WBC; NIV], 'conversation' [KJV]. This noun is also translated as a verb phrase: 'how I used to live' [CEV, TEV], 'what I was like' [NLT], 'how I had behaved' [SSA], 'the way I lived' [GW].
   b. ποτέ (LN 67.9) (BAGD 1. p. 695): 'formerly' [BAGD, Mor, SSA], 'once' [BAGD; GW], 'former' [Herm; NASB, NET], 'previous' [WBC; NIV],

'earlier' [NRSV], 'in time past' [KJV], 'when' [NLT, REB, TEV], 'previously' [BNTC], 'past' [NCV], not explicit [CEV].
   c. ἐν with dative object (LN 83.13): 'in' [BNTC, Herm, LN, Mor, WBC; KJV, NASB, NCV, NET, NIV, NRSV]. This preposition is also translated as a verb phrase: 'when I followed' [GW, NLT], 'I was devoted to' [TEV], 'when I practiced' [SSA], 'when I was still' [REB]. The phrase ἐν τῷ Ἰουδαϊσμῷ 'in Judaism' is translated 'as a Jew' [CEV].
   d. Ἰουδαϊσμός (LN 41.33) (BAGD p. 379): 'Judaism' [BAGD, BNTC, Herm, LN, Mor, WBC; NASB, NET, NIV, NRSV], 'the practice of Judaism' [LN], 'the Jewish religion' [LN, SSA; GW, NCV, NLT, TEV], 'as a Jew' [CEV], 'a practicing Jew' [REB], 'the Jews' religion' [KJV].
QUESTION—What relationship is indicated by γάρ 'for'?
   It indicates the grounds for his preceding statement [ICC, NCBC]. Paul is referring to his pre-Christian days as proof that he was not influenced by Christianity until he became a believer [NCBC]. This is evidence that he had not received the gospel from a human source [ICC].

that in-accordance-with excess^a I-was-persecuting^b the church^c of-God and pillaging^d it,

LEXICON—a. ὑπερβολή (LN **78.33**) (BAGD p. 840): 'excess' [BAGD, LN]. The phrase καθ' ὑπερβολήν 'in accordance with excess' is translated 'to an extreme degree' [**LN**; NET], 'to an extraordinary degree' [BAGD], 'beyond measure' [BAGD; KJV, NASB], 'utterly' [BAGD], 'intensely' [WBC; NIV], 'violently' [GW, NLT, NRSV], 'savagely' [REB], 'vigorously' [Herm], 'without mercy' [TEV], 'intensely and continually' [SSA], 'exceedingly' [Mor], 'excessive' [BNTC], not explicit [CEV, NCV].
   b. imperf. act. indic. of διώκω (LN 39.45) (BAGD 2. p. 201): 'to persecute' [BAGD, BNTC, Herm, LN, Mor, SSA, WBC; all versions except CEV, NCV], 'to harass' [LN], 'to be cruel to' [CEV], 'to attack' [NCV]. The imperfect tense indicates that Paul kept on persecuting the church for some time [ICC, Lns, NCBC, TH].
   c. ἐκκλησία (LN 11.32) (BAGD 4. p. 241): 'church' [BAGD, BNTC, Herm, LN, Mor, SSA, WBC; all versions except NLT], 'the Christians' [NLT]. The church is composed of those who believe in God wherever they might be [ICC, Mor, NAC, NIBC, NIC, NTC, TH, WBC].
   d. imperf. act. indic. of πορθέω (LN **20.37**) (BAGD p. 693): 'to pillage, to attack' [LN], 'to destroy' [BAGD, BNTC, Herm, LN, SSA, WBC; all versions except KJV, NLT], 'to waste' [KJV], 'to lay to waste' [Mor]. The phrase τὴν ἐκκλησίαν τοῦ θεοῦ καὶ ἐπόρθουν αὐτήν 'the church of God and pillaging it' is translated 'I tried to destroy the church of God' [BAGD], 'I attacked with the purpose of destroying the church of God' [**LN**], 'I did my best to get rid of them' [NLT]. The imperfect tense indicates an attempt made over a period of time [TH; NLT].

GALATIANS 1:13 31

QUESTION—How are the nouns related in the genitive construction τὴν ἐκκλησίαν τοῦ θεοῦ 'the church of God'?

Those who believe in God wherever they might be [ICC, Mor, NAC, NIBC, NIC, NTC, TH, WBC].

1:14 and I-was-advancing[a] in[b] Judaism[c] above[d] many contemporaries[e] in my nation,[f]

LEXICON—a. imperf. act. indic. of προκόπτω (LN **13.57**) (BAGD 2. p. 708): 'to advance' [BAGD, Herm, LN, Mor, WBC; NASB, NET, NIV, NRSV], 'to progress' [BAGD, BNTC, LN], 'to profit' [KJV], 'to become a leader' [NCV]. The phrase καὶ προέκοπτον ἐν τῷ Ἰουδαϊσμῷ ὑπέρ 'to advance above' is translated 'to practice more thoroughly' [SSA], 'to be much better than' [CEV], 'to be far ahead of' [GW], 'to be one of the most (religious)' [NLT], 'to outstrip most of' [REB], 'to be ahead of' [TEV].

b. ἐν with dative object (LN 83.13): 'in' [BNTC, Herm, LN, Mor, WBC; all versions except CEV, GW, NLT], 'when' [SSA], 'in following' [GW], not explicit [CEV, NLT].

c. Ἰουδαϊσμός (LN **41.33**) (BAGD p. 379): 'Judaism' [BAGD, BNTC, Herm, LN, Mor, WBC; NASB, NET, NIV, NRSV], 'the Jewish religion' [LN; GW, NCV], 'the practice of Judaism' [**LN**], 'the/my practice of the Jewish religion' [SSA; TEV], 'religious (Jews)' [NLT], 'the practice of our religion' [REB], 'the Jews' religion' [KJV], 'to be a Jew' [CEV].

d. ὑπέρ with accusative object (LN 87.30) (BAGD 2. p. 839): 'above' [LN, Mor; KJV], 'superior to' [LN], 'more than' [BAGD], 'much better than' [CEV], 'beyond' [BNTC, Herm, WBC; NASB, NET, NIV, NRSV], 'ahead of' [GW, TEV], 'more thoroughly' [SSA], 'better than' [NCV], not explicit [NLT]. This preposition is also translated as a verb: 'I outstripped' [REB].

e. συνηλικιώτης (LN **67.159**) (BAGD p. 789): 'contemporary' [BAGD, BNTC, LN; NASB, NET], 'Jewish contemporaries' [REB], '(anyone else) my own age' [CEV], '(Jews) of my own age' [WBC; NIV, NLT], '(my people) of the same age' [NRSV], '(Jews) of my age' [NCV, TEV], 'equals' [KJV], 'my own age' [Mor], 'Jews who were my age' [SSA], 'other (Jews) in my age group' [GW], '(my people) who were of the same age' [Herm]. This probably refers to his fellow students in Jerusalem [TNTC].

f. γένος (LN 10.1) (BAGD 3. p. 156): 'nation' [BAGD, LN; KJV, NET], 'people' [BAGD, BNTC; NRSV], 'race' [LN, Mor]. The phrase ἐν τῷ γένει μου 'in my nation' is translated 'among my countrymen' [NASB], 'among my people' [Herm], 'anyone else' [CEV], 'Jews' [SSA, WBC; GW, NCV, NIV, NLT], 'national (religion)' [REB], 'Jewish' [TEV].

QUESTION—What is meant by προκόπτω 'to advance'?

The root meaning is literally a cutting of one's way in a forward direction. If this meaning is present, then Paul meant that he had raced ahead of his

Jewish contemporaries in religious achievement [NCBC]. This can include increasing his knowledge of the Jewish teachings, attaining the Pharisaic ideal of conduct, gaining a higher standing in the Pharisaic order, and especially progressing in achieving the Pharisaic standards of righteousness [ICC]. The imperfect form indicates a continuing progress. Paul continued to advance in Jewish teachings [Mor]. It is the process of moral and spiritual development in an individual. For Paul there was a continuing process of moral and spiritual development throughout his life in Judaism [WBC].

being to-a-much-greater-degree[a] **(a) zealot**[b] **of-my paternal**[c] **traditions.**[d]

LEXICON—a. περισσοτέρως (LN 78.31) (BAGD 1. p. 651): 'to a much greater degree' [BAGD], 'far more' [BAGD, Herm, SSA, WBC; NRSV], 'far greater' [BAGD], 'more greatly' [LN], 'much more' [TEV], 'more exceedingly' [KJV], 'extremely' [NET, NIV], 'exceedingly' [BNTC, Mor], 'tried harder' [NCV], 'more extremely' [NASB], 'as hard as possible' [NLT], not explicit [CEV, GW, REB].

b. ζηλωτής (LN 11.88, 25.77) (BAGD 1. p. 338): 'zealot' [BAGD, LN (11.88)], 'zealous person' [LN (25.77)], 'enthusiast' [BAGD, LN (25.77)] 'boundless devotion' [REB]. This noun is also translated as an adjective: 'zealous' [BNTC, Herm, Mor, WBC; KJV, NASB, NET, NIV, NRSV], 'devoted' [TEV], 'fanatical' [GW]; as a verb phrase: 'to be deeply committed' [LN (25.77)], 'to enthusiastically promote' [SSA], 'to obey every (law)' [CEV], 'to try hard to follow' [NCV], 'to try as hard as possible' [NLT].

c. πατρικός (LN **10.21**) (BAGD p. 636): 'paternal' [BAGD], 'of the forefathers' [**LN**], 'of the ancestors' [LN], 'derived from (one's) father' [BAGD], 'handed down by (one's) father' [BAGD]. It probably refers to the traditions of the author's father's house, adhering strictly to the law [BAGD], 'our ancestors' [CEV], 'of my ancestors' [GW, NET, NRSV, REB], 'of my fathers' [Mor, WBC; KJV, NIV], 'of my forefathers' [Herm], 'of my religion' [NLT], 'of our ancestors' [NCV, TEV], 'my ancestors' [SSA], 'ancestral' [BNTC; NASB].

d. παράδοσις (LN 33.239) (BAGD 2. p. 616): 'tradition' [BAGD, LN], 'teaching' [LN], 'traditions' [BNTC, Herm, Mor, WBC; all versions except CEV, NCV], 'ideas taught' [SSA], 'teachings handed down' [NCV], 'law given us' [CEV].

QUESTION—What is referred to in πατρικῶν μου παραδόσεων 'of my paternal traditions'?

It refers to the teachings and practices developed in the Pharisaic schools of Second Temple Judaism. It also refers to the interpretations of a more popular nature that arose within the synagogues of Paul's day [WBC]. It refers to the well-known orally transmitted traditions which were observed by the Pharisees [ICC, NIC]. It refers to the traditions of the Jewish nation as a whole [TH]. It refers to the entire *halakah* or body of Jewish oral law which supplemented the written law [NTC]. It refers to those traditions that were handed down in the sect of the Pharisees [Alf, Lt, Mor]. It refers to the Jewish tradition of the Torah as a whole, not to Paul's specific family traditions [Herm].

DISCOURSE UNIT: 1:15–17 [NIC, NIGTC]. The topic is Paul's call to apostleship [NIC], Paul becomes an apostle [NIGTC].

1:15 **But when God was-pleased,**[a]
TEXT—Some manuscripts omit ὁ θεός 'God'. GNT includes this phrase in the text in brackets with a C decision, indicating that the Committee had difficulty making the decision.
LEXICON—a. aorist act. indic. of εὐδοκέω (LN 25.87) (BAGD 1. p. 319): 'to be pleased' [BNTC, Herm, LN, Mor, WBC; GW, KJV, NASB, NET, NIV, NLT, NRSV], 'to consider good' [BAGD], 'to determine' [BAGD], 'to decide' [CEV, TEV], 'to desire' [SSA], 'to have special plans' [NCV]. This verb is also translated as a prepositional phrase: 'in his good pleasure' [REB].
QUESTION—What relationship is indicated by δέ 'but'?
1. It indicates contrast [NIC, TH; all versions]. It indicates that a complete break occurred in Paul's life when God called him to be an apostle [NIC]. In spite of what Paul had done, God did the following [TH].
2. This section is not antithetical to what precedes but continues his argument, so δέ should be translated 'and' instead of 'but' [ICC].
QUESTION—What is meant by εὐδοκέω 'was pleased'?
It refers to God's purpose, resolve, and choice [NIC]. God was moved only by what is in himself and not by any worthiness in Paul. It also carries the thought of grace and kindness [Lns].

the (one) having-set-apart[a] **me from**[b] **(the) womb**[c] **of-my mother**
LEXICON—a. aorist act. participle of ἀφορίζω (LN 37.97) (BAGD 2. p. 127): 'to set apart' [BAGD, BNTC, LN, WBC; NASB, NCV, NET, NIV, NRSV, REB], 'to set aside' [Herm], 'to appoint' [BAGD, LN; GW], 'to select' [SSA], 'to separate' [Mor; KJV], 'to choose' [CEV, NLT, TEV].
b. ἐκ with genitive object (LN 67.131, 84.4, 90.16): 'from' [BNTC, Herm, LN (67.131, 84.4, 90.16), Mor, WBC; KJV, NASB, NET, NIV, REB], 'out from, out of' [LN (84.4)], 'since' [LN (67.131)], not explicit [SSA; CEV, GW, NCV, NLT, NRSV, TEV].
c. κοιλία (LN 8.69) (BAGD 2. p. 437): 'womb' [BNTC, Herm, LN, Mor; KJV, NASB]. The phrase ἐκ κοιλίας μητρός μου 'from the womb of my mother' is translated 'from birth' [BAGD, WBC; NET, NIV], 'before I was born' [SSA; CEV, GW, NCV, NLT, NRSV, TEV], 'from my birth' [REB].
QUESTION—What relationship is indicated by ἐκ 'from'?
1. The phrase means from the time of his birth [Alf, BAGD, ICC, WBC; NET, NIV, REB].

2. It includes the time he was in the womb [BST, Lt, NIBC, NIGTC, TNTC; CEV, GW, NCV, NLT, NRSV, TEV]. It was before he was born and did not have any impulses or principles of his own [Lt].

and having-called^a (me) through/because-of^b his grace,^c

LEXICON—a. aorist act. participle of καλέω (LN 33.312) (BAGD 2. p. 399): 'to call' [BAGD, BNTC, Herm, LN, Mor, SSA, WBC; all versions except CEV], 'to choose' [CEV].
  b. διά with genitive object (LN 89.76, 90.8) (BAGD A.III.1.e. p. 180): 'through' [BNTC, Herm, LN (89.76, 90.8), Mor; NASB, NCV, NRSV, REB], 'by virtue of' [BAGD], 'by means of' [LN (89.76, 90.8)], 'by' [WBC; GW, KJV, NET, NIV], 'in' [NLT, TEV], 'because of' [SSA], not explicit [CEV].
  c. χάρις (LN 25.89, 88.66) (BAGD 2. p. 877): 'grace' [BAGD, BNTC, Herm, LN (88.66), Mor, WBC; all versions except CEV, GW, NLT], 'kindness' [LN (88.66); GW, NLT], 'favor' [BAGD, LN (25.89)], 'good will' [BAGD, LN (25.89)]. This noun is also translated as a verb phrase: 'to be gracious' [SSA], 'to be kind' [CEV]. See this word at 1:6.

QUESTION—What relationship is indicated by διά 'through'?
  1. It indicates the means by which Paul was called [NIC; GW, KJV, NET, NIV].
  2. It indicates the reason he was called [SSA]: He called me because he is gracious. It gives God's motive for calling Paul [SSA].

QUESTION—To what did God call Paul?
  1. This was a call to become a Christian [Lns, SSA]. Paul was both selected and called to eternal life [SSA].
  2. This was a call to become an apostle [Lt, NIGTC, TH]. The call was specifically to preach to the Gentiles [Lt].
  3. The call was both to be a Christian and an apostle [NIBC, NIC, NTC].

1:16 to-reveal^a his Son in/through^b me,

LEXICON—a. aorist act. infin. of ἀποκαλύπτω (LN 28.38) (BAGD 2. p. 92): 'to reveal' [BAGD, BNTC, Herm, LN, Mor, WBC; all versions except CEV, GW, NCV], 'to disclose' [LN], 'to show' [SSA; CEV, GW, NCV].
  b. ἐν with dative object (LN 83.13, **90.56**) (BAGD IV.4. p. 261): 'in' [BAGD, BNTC, Herm, LN (83.13), Mor, WBC; KJV, NASB, NET, NIV], 'to' [**LN** (90.56), SSA; NCV, NLT, NRSV, TEV], 'by' [**LN** (90.56)], 'through' [**LN** (90.56)], 'in and through' [REB], not explicit [CEV, GW].

QUESTION—What is meant by ἐν ἐμοί 'in me'?
  1. It refers to the inwardness of the experience [Alf, ICC, Lns, NCBC, NIC, NIGTC, NTC, SSA, TH, WBC; CEV, NCV, NLT, NRSV, TEV]: he called me in order to reveal his Son in me. God showed his Son to Paul. This must be an inward revelation since the purpose of the clause in regard to others follows this clause [SSA]. It refers to the inward reality of the Christian experience [WBC]. This is what happened on the Damascus

road [NIGTC]. Paul stresses the inward and intensely personal character of God's revelation to him of the risen Jesus [NIC].
2. It refers to a revelation made through Paul to others [Lt, TNTC]: he called me to reveal his Son to others through me. As Paul kept telling others the Good News, God was revealing his Son to them [Lt].

in-order-that I-might-preach[a] him among[b] the nations,[c]
LEXICON—a. pres. mid. (deponent = act.) subj. of εὐαγγελίζω (LN 33.215) (BAGD 2.a.α. p. 317): 'to preach' [BAGD, BNTC, Herm, Mor, WBC; KJV, NASB, NET, NIV], 'to preach the Good News (about)' [TEV], 'to proclaim' [BAGD; NRSV, REB], 'to proclaim the Good News (about)' [NLT], 'to announce the gospel' [LN], 'to tell the good news' [LN; GW], 'to tell the Good News (about)' [SSA; NCV], 'to announce (his) message' [CEV].
b. ἐν with dative object (LN 83.9, 83.13): 'among' [BNTC, Herm, LN (83.9), Mor, WBC; KJV, NASB, NET, NIV, NRSV, REB], 'in' [LN (83.13), SSA], 'to' [CEV, NCV, NLT, TEV], not explicit [GW].
c. ἔθνος (LN 11.37, 11.55): 'nation' [LN (11.55)]. The plural form is translated 'heathen' [LN (11.37); KJV], 'pagans' [LN (11.37)], 'Gentiles' [BNTC, Herm, Mor, WBC; all versions except GW, KJV, NCV], 'Gentile regions' [SSA], 'people who are not Jewish' [GW], 'those who are not Jewish' [NCV].
QUESTION—What relationship is indicated by ἵνα 'in order that'?
It indicates the purpose of the preceding clause [BNTC, BST, Herm, ICC, Lns, Mor, NAC, NCBC, NIC, NIGTC, NTC, TH, TNTC, WBC]: God revealed his Son in order that I might preach the Good News about him to the Gentiles.
QUESTION—What relationship is indicated by ἐν 'among'?
It indicates the sphere and scope of his mission, which was the regions of the Gentiles and all who lived in those areas [WBC].
QUESTION—What is meant by τοῖς ἔθνεσιν 'the nations'?
It refers to all who were in Gentile lands [ICC, NIC]. It refers to the nations other than Israel [BNTC].

immediately[a] I-did- not -consult[b] (with) flesh[c] and blood
LEXICON—a. εὐθέως (LN 67.53) (BAGD p. 320): 'immediately' [BAGD, BNTC, Herm, LN, Mor, SSA, WBC; KJV, NASB, REB], 'at once' [BAGD], 'rush out' [NLT]. This is also translated 'when this happened' [GW], 'when God called me' [NCV]. This is inserted in the phrase 'to Arabia' in 1:17 as 'at once' [CEV, NRSV, TEV], 'right away' [NET], 'immediately' [NIV].
b. aorist mid. indic. of προσανατίθημι (LN **33.175**) (BAGD 2. p. 711): 'to consult with' [BAGD, BNTC, LN, WBC; NASB, NLT], 'to consult' [SSA; NIV, REB], 'to confer with' [Herm, Mor; KJV, NRSV], 'to talk this over with' [CEV], 'to ask advice of' [**LN**], 'to ask advice from'

[NET], 'to go for advice from' [TEV], 'to talk it over with' [GW], 'to get advice or help from' [NCV].
  c. σάρξ (LN 8.63, 9.11, 9.14) (BAGD 3. p. 743): 'flesh' [BNTC, Herm, LN (8.63), Mor; KJV, NASB], 'human being, people' [LN (9.11)]. The phrase σαρκὶ καὶ αἵματι 'flesh and blood' [BNTC, Herm, Mor; KJV, NASB] is also translated 'person' [LN (9.14)], 'human being' [BAGD, LN (9.14)], 'anyone' [WBC; CEV, TEV], 'any human beings' [SSA], 'any human being' [NET, NRSV], 'any man' [NIV], 'anyone else' [NLT], 'a single person' [REB], 'any other person' [GW], 'any person' [NCV].

QUESTION—Does εὐθέως 'immediately' go with the negative part of the sentence or the positive part?
  1. It should be taken with the negative part of the sentence [Lns, NTC, WBC]: I did not immediately consult with flesh and blood nor did I go up to Jerusalem to see the apostles before me.
  2. It should be taken with the positive part of the sentence [Alf, ICC, Lt, NIGTC, TH; CEV, NET, NIV, NRSV, TEV]: I immediately went into Arabia. The negative clause has been interposed with to indicate his purpose in going away [Alf]. The word 'immediately' calls for an affirmation, not just a statement of what he didn't do and the idea is, 'Immediately, instead of consulting with flesh and blood, I went into Arabia' [ICC, Lt].

QUESTION—What is meant by σαρκὶ καὶ αἵματι 'flesh and blood'?
  It is an idiom and means a living person [TH]. It is a common phrase used to denote human beings [NCBC, NIC]. He did not consult any human being [BST, Lns]. It refers to human beings generally [Herm]. It is a figure of speech for human beings in contrast to God [SSA, WBC].

1:17 nor did-I-go-up[a] to[b] Jerusalem to[c] the apostles before[d] me,

LEXICON—a. aorist act. indic. of ἀνέρχομαι (LN **15.101**) (BAGD p. 65): 'to go up' [BAGD, BNTC, Herm, LN, Mor, WBC; KJV, NASB, NET, NIV, NLT, NRSV, REB], 'to go' [SSA; GW, NCV, TEV], not explicit [CEV].
  b. εἰς with accusative object (LN 84.16): 'to' [BNTC, Herm, LN (84.16), Mor, SSA, WBC; all versions except CEV], not explicit [CEV].
  c. πρός with accusative object (LN 84.16): 'to' [BNTC, Herm, LN, Mor, SSA, WBC; all versions].
  d. πρό with genitive object (LN 67.17) (BAGD 2. p. 702): 'before' [BAGD, BNTC, Herm, LN, Mor, SSA, WBC; all versions].

QUESTION—What relationship is indicated by the verb ἀνέρχομαι 'go up'?
  Since Jerusalem is located on a hill, it is necessary to go up to it [Herm]. Besides its geographical position this also referred to its religious position as the seat of the temple and the mother-city of the church [NIC].

QUESTION—To what does the phrase πρὸ ἐμοῦ 'before me' refer?
  It refers to time [ICC, Lns, NCBC, NIGTC, SSA, TH, TNTC, WBC; CEV, GW, NCV, NIV, NLT]: those who were apostles before I was.

but I-went-away[a] into[b] Arabia
LEXICON—a. aorist act. indic. of ἀπέρχομαι (LN 15.37) (BAGD 2. p. 84): 'to go away' [BNTC, Herm, LN, SSA, WBC; NASB, NCV, NLT, NRSV], 'to go' [BAGD; CEV, GW, KJV, NIV, TEV], 'to go off' [Mor; REB], 'to depart' [NET].
  b. εἰς with accusative object (LN 84.16, 84.22): 'into' [BNTC, LN (84.22), WBC; KJV, NIV, NLT, NRSV], 'to' [Herm, LN (84.16), Mor, SSA; CEV, GW, NASB, NCV, NET, REB, TEV].
QUESTION—What relationship is indicated by ἀλλά 'but'?
It is the strong adversative and means 'on the contrary' [Lns, Mor].

and again[a] I-returned[b] to[c] Damascus.
LEXICON—a. πάλιν (LN 67.55): 'again' [BNTC, Herm, LN, Mor, WBC; KJV], 'afterwards' [CEV, NRSV, REB], 'then' [GW, NET, TEV], 'once more' [SSA; NASB], 'later' [NCV, NIV, NLT].
  b. aorist act. indic. of ὑποστρέφω (LN **15.88**) (BAGD p. 847): 'to return' [BAGD, BNTC, Herm, **LN**, Mor, SSA, WBC; all versions except GW, NCV], 'to go back' [LN; NCV], 'to come back' [LN; GW].
  c. εἰς with accusative object (LN 84.16): 'to' [BNTC, Herm, LN, Mor, SSA, WBC; all versions except KJV], 'unto' [KJV].
QUESTION —What is implied by καὶ πάλιν 'and again'?
Although Damascus has not been mentioned to this point, it implies that his readers would know that his conversion was associated with the city [ICC, SSA, TH], that it took place near the city [NCBC].

DISCOURSE UNIT: 1:18–24 [NAC, WBC]. The topic is the first visit to Jerusalem.

DISCOURSE UNIT: 1:18–20 [NIC, NIGTC]. The topic is Paul's first post-conversion visit to Jerusalem [NIC], Paul meets the Jerusalem church leaders [NIGTC].

1:18 Then after[a] three years I-went-up[b] to[c] Jerusalem to-visit[d] Cephas[e]
LEXICON—a. μετά with accusative object (LN 67.48) (BAGD B.II.1. p. 510): 'after' [BAGD, BNTC, Herm, LN, Mor, SSA, WBC; KJV, NCV, NET, NIV, NRSV], '(three years) later' [CEV, GW, NASB, NLT, REB, TEV].
  b. aorist act. indic. of ἀνέρχομαι (LN 15.101): 'to go up' [BNTC, Herm, LN, Mor, WBC; KJV, NASB, NET, NIV, NRSV, REB], 'to go' [SSA; CEV, GW, NCV, NLT, TEV].
  c. εἰς with accusative object (LN 84.16): 'to' [BNTC, Herm, LN, Mor, SSA, WBC; all versions except CEV], 'in' [CEV].
  d. aorist act. infin. of ἱστορέω (LN **34.52**) (BAGD p. 383): 'to visit' [BAGD, Herm, Mor; CEV, NRSV], 'to visit and get information from' [LN; NET], 'to get to know' [BNTC; REB], 'to get acquainted with' [WBC; NIV], 'to meet' [SSA; NCV], 'to become personally acquainted with' [GW], 'to become acquainted with' [NASB], 'for a visit with' [NLT], 'to obtain information from' [TEV], 'to see' [KJV]. It implies

visiting for the purpose of coming to know someone or something [BAGD].

e. Κηφᾶς (LN 93.211) (BAGD p. 431): 'Cephas' [BAGD, BNTC, Herm, LN, Mor, WBC; GW, NASB, NET, NRSV, REB]. This Hebrew word is also translated with its Greek form: 'Peter' [BAGD; CEV, KJV, NCV, NIV, NLT, TEV], 'Cephas/Peter' [SSA].

QUESTION—What relationship is indicated by ἔπειτα 'then'?

It draws attention to the next event in the order of sequence [BNTC, NCBC, SSA]. It shows that he considered this visit to be part of another period and not part of his reaction to the vision of Christ [Herm]. It gives the sense that Paul made his first post-conversion visit to Jerusalem only after he had gone into Arabia and later returned to Damascus [NIBC].

QUESTION—To what does μετὰ ἔτη τρία 'after three years' refer?

It refers back to the date of Paul's conversion [Alf, BST, ICC, Lns, Lt, Mor, NAC, NIC, NIGTC, NTC, SSA, TH]. This does not specify whether 'three years' means three full years, or only part of the third year [NCBC, NTC]. Perhaps it means 'in the third year' [NAC, NIGTC].

QUESTION—What relationship is indicated by ἱστορέω 'to visit'?

It indicates that Paul's purpose for visiting with Peter was to get acquainted with him [Alf, BNTC, BST, Herm, ICC, Lns, Mor, NAC, NCBC, NIBC, NIC, NTC, TNTC, WBC; GW, NASB, REB]. He also intended to get information from Peter [TEV].

and I-remained[a] with[b] him fifteen days,[c]

LEXICON—a. aorist act. indic. of ἐπιμένω (LN 85.55) (BAGD 1. p. 296 twice): 'to remain' [BAGD, LN], 'to stay' [BAGD, BNTC, Herm, LN, Mor, SSA, WBC; all versions except KJV], 'to abide' [KJV].

b. πρός with accusative object (LN 89.112) (BAGD III.7. p. 711): 'with' [BAGD, BNTC, Herm, LN, Mor, SSA, WBC; all versions].

c. ἡμέρα (LN 67.178) (BAGD 2. p. 346): 'day' [BAGD, LN], 'days' [BNTC, Herm, Mor, SSA, WBC; all versions except REB, TEV]. The phrase ἡμέρας δεκαπέντε 'fifteen days' is translated 'two weeks' [REB, TEV].

1:19 but[a] another[b] of-the apostles I-did- not-see[c] except James the brother of-the Lord.

LEXICON—a. δέ (LN 89.124): 'but' [Herm, LN, Mor, SSA; KJV, NASB, NET, NRSV], 'on the other hand' [LN], not explicit [BNTC, WBC; CEV, GW, NCV, NIV, NLT, REB, TEV].

b. ἕτερος (LN 58.37) (BAGD 1.b.α. p. 315): 'another' [BAGD, LN], 'other' [BNTC, Herm, LN, Mor, WBC; KJV, NET, NIV, NLT, REB], 'any other' [GW, NASB, NRSV, TEV], 'no other' [SSA; NCV], 'the only other (apostle I saw)' [CEV].

c. aorist act. indic. of ὁράω (LN 24.1, 34.50): 'to see' [BNTC, Herm, LN (24.1), Mor, SSA, WBC; all versions except NCV, NLT], 'to go to see, to visit' [LN (34.50)], 'to meet' [NCV, NLT].

QUESTION—What relationship is indicated by εἰ μή 'except'?
1. It indicates exception and is a retraction to the previous clause [Alf, ICC, Lt, Mor, NCBC, NIC, NIGTC, SSA, WBC; CEV, NASB, NET, NLT, NRSV, TEV]: I did not see another apostle except James. This implies that James was also an apostle. Paul surely saw other persons in Jerusalem, so this is an exception to the preceding clause and refers to the apostles he had seen [ICC].
2. It indicates exception and refers only to the verb 'I saw' [Herm, Lns, NTC; GW, NIV]: I did not see another apostle, I only saw James. This implies that James was not an apostle. Paul had seen other believers in Jerusalem, so here he is referring to the Christian leaders he had seen [NTC]. Probably the other apostles were absent from Jerusalem at the time [Lns, NTC]. James, though not regarded as an apostle, had a special position in the church [Herm].

QUESTION—How are the nouns related in the genitive construction Ἰάκωβον τὸν ἀδελφὸν τοῦ κυρίου 'James the brother of the Lord'?

It indicates that James was a biological brother of Jesus [BNTC, Mor, NAC, NCBC, NIBC, NIC, NIGTC, NTC, WBC]. This distinguishes James from other persons of the same name, such as James, the son of Zebedee and James, the son of Alphaeus [Lns, NTC, TH].

1:20 And[a] the-things-that I-am-writing[b] to-you, behold,[c] before[d] God that[e] I-am- not -lying.[f]

LEXICON—a. δέ (LN 89.94): 'and' [LN; CEV], 'now' [Herm, Mor; KJV, NASB], not explicit [BNTC, SSA, WBC; all versions except CEV, KJV, NASB].
b. pres. act. indic. of γράφω (LN 33.61) (BAGD 2.d. p. 167): 'to write' [BAGD, BNTC, Herm, LN, Mor, SSA, WBC; all versions except CEV, NLT], 'to say' [NLT], not explicit [CEV].
c. ἰδού (LN 91.10, 91.13): 'behold' [Herm, LN (91.13); KJV], 'indeed' [LN (91.10)], 'look' [LN (91.13), Mor], 'take note' [NET], 'please note' [BNTC], 'I assure you' [WBC; NASB, NIV], 'I declare' [NLT], not explicit [SSA; CEV, GW, NCV, NRSV, REB, TEV].
d. ἐνώπιον with genitive object (LN 83.33) (BAGD 2.b. p. 270): 'before' [BNTC, Herm, LN, Mor, WBC; KJV, NASB, NET, NIV, NLT, NRSV], 'in the sight of' [BAGD], 'in the presence of' [CEV]. The phrase ἐνώπιον θεοῦ 'before God' is translated 'God knows' [NCV, REB, TEV], 'God is my witness' [GW], 'I solemnly swear' [SSA].
e. ὅτι (LN 90.21) (BAGD 1.b.α. p. 588): 'that' [BAGD, LN, WBC; GW, NASB, NCV, NET, NIV, NLT, TEV], not explicit [BNTC, Herm, Mor, SSA; CEV, KJV, NRSV, REB].
f. pres. mid. (deponent = act.) indic. of ψεύδομαι (LN 33.253) (BAGD 1. p. 891): 'to lie' [BAGD, BNTC, Herm, LN, Mor, WBC; KJV, NASB, NET, NLT, NRSV, REB, TEV], 'to tell falsehoods' [BAGD, LN]. The phrase οὐ ψεύδομαι 'I am not lying' is translated 'what I'm writing is not

a lie' [GW], 'these things I write are not lies' [NCV], 'what I am writing you is no lie' [NIV], 'I am telling the truth' [CEV], 'what I am writing is true' [SSA].

QUESTION—What are the things he refers to?

He refers to all that precedes in 1:15–19 and possibly beginning at 1:13 [Herm, ICC, WBC]. This refers directly to 1:18 and 19 where he claims that he is not misrepresenting his relationship to the Twelve apostles [Alf]. Actually, he refers to what he is telling them since a scribe is writing down what he dictates until he writes in his own hand at the end (6:11) [TH]. This refers to his immediately preceding statements [BNTC]. It refers mainly to the report about his first visit to Jerusalem and especially to his last sentence in 1:19 [NIC].

DISCOURSE UNIT: 1:21–24 [NIC, NIGTC]. The topic is Paul in Syria and Cilicia.

1:21 Then[a] I-went/came[b] into[c] the districts[d] of-Syria and of-Cilicia;

LEXICON—a. ἔπειτα (LN 67.44) (BAGD 1. p. 284): 'then' [BAGD, BNTC, LN, Mor; GW, NASB, NRSV, REB], 'afterwards' [LN; KJV, NET], 'afterward' [TEV], 'after that' [Herm, WBC], 'later' [LN; CEV, NCV, NIV], 'then after this visit' [NLT], 'after I had stayed in Jerusalem with Cephas' [SSA].

b. aorist act. indic. of ἔρχομαι (LN 15.7, 15.81): 'to go' [Herm, LN (15.7), SSA, WBC; all versions except KJV, REB], 'to come' [LN (15.7, 15.81), Mor; KJV], 'to leave for' [REB], 'to go off' [BNTC].

c. εἰς with accusative object (LN 84.22): 'into' [BNTC, Herm, LN, Mor, SSA, WBC; KJV, NASB, NLT, NRSV], 'to' [CEV, GW, NCV, NET, NIV, TEV], 'for' [REB].

d. κλίμα (LN **1.79**) (BAGD p. 436): 'district' [BAGD, Mor, WBC], 'region' [Herm, LN, SSA; CEV, GW, KJV, NASB, NET, NRSV, REB], 'area' [NCV], 'province' [NLT], 'place' [TEV], 'territory' [BNTC], not explicit [NIV].

QUESTION—What relationship is indicated by ἔπειτα 'then'?

It connects this event with what immediately preceded, which was Paul's visit to Jerusalem [TH]. It introduces a new set of events after Paul's first visit as a Christian to Jerusalem [WBC]. It is used again to assure his readers that no suspicious gaps are left in the narrative [NIGTC]. It shows Paul's concern to provide an orderly record [BNTC].

1:22 and I-was being-unknown[a] by-face[b] to-the churches[c] of-Judea the (ones) in[d] Christ.

LEXICON—a. pres. pass. participle of ἀγνοέω (LN 28.13) (BAGD 2. p. 11): 'to be unknown' [BAGD], 'to not be known' [LN]. The passive periphrastic phrase ἤμην...ἀγνοούμενος 'I was being unknown' is translated 'I was unknown' [BNTC, WBC; KJV, NASB, NET, NIV, NRSV, REB], 'I was not known' [Mor], 'I remained personally unknown'

[Herm]. This is also translated actively with 'the churches' as the subject: 'did not know me' [GW, NLT, TEV], 'had never met me' [NCV], 'had not met me' [SSA], '(no one) had ever seen me' [CEV].
b. πρόσωπον (LN 8.18, 9.9) (BAGD 1.b. p. 721): '(by) face' [BAGD, LN (8.18), Mor; KJV], '(in) person' [LN (9.9); CEV, NET], '(by) sight' [BNTC; NASB, NRSV, REB], not explicit [NCV]. This noun is also translated as an adjective: 'personally' [BAGD, Herm, SSA, WBC; GW, NIV, NLT, TEV].
c. ἐκκλησία (LN 11.32) (BAGD 4.b. p. 241): 'church' [BAGD, BNTC, Herm, LN, Mor, SSA, WBC; all versions except REB], 'congregation' [BAGD, LN; REB].
d. ἐν with dative object (LN 83.13) (BAGD I.5.d. p. 260): 'in' [BNTC, Herm, LN, Mor, WBC; KJV, NASB, NCV, NET, NIV, NRSV]. The phrase ταῖς ἐκκλησίαις ταῖς ἐν Χριστῷ 'the churches the ones in Christ' is translated 'the churches of Christ' [GW], 'the Christians in the churches' [NLT], 'the Christian congregations' [REB], 'one who belonged to Christ's churches' [CEV], 'persons in the churches' [SSA], 'the members of the churches' [TEV]. The preposition indicates a close personal relation [BAGD]. It indicates the personal, local, and dynamic relation of a believer to Christ [WBC].

QUESTION—Since Jerusalem was located in Judea, how could Paul say that he was unknown to the churches of Judea?

Paul had persecuted the church in Jerusalem (Acts 9:13) and had visited Peter and James in Jerusalem (1:18–19), so the statement cannot be taken so literally that it means that no one had ever seen him in Jerusalem [ICC]. This means that he was not known to the church at large in Jerusalem [NIGTC]. In speaking of the church in Judea, Paul had in mind those churches which were chiefly outside Jerusalem [ICC]. It is clear that Paul is excluding the church in Jerusalem [Lns, Lt, NCBC, NTC]. Paul's point is that he was personally unknown to the Judean churches [BNTC, Mor]. The province of Judea is much larger than the city of Jerusalem, so it is reasonable to presume that many of the country churches in this area could not have recognized him in a crowd, even though they had heard of him [NAC]. He was privately known to individual members of the churches, but he was personally unknown to the churches as a whole since he had never preached in their assemblies [NIC].

1:23 But only[a] they-were hearing[b]

LEXICON—a. μόνον (BAGD 2.a. p. 528): 'only' [BAGD, BNTC, Herm, Mor, WBC; all versions except NLT, REB], 'just' [SSA], 'simply' [REB]. See b. [NLT].
b. pres. act. participle of ἀκούω (LN 24.52, 33.212): 'to hear' [BNTC, Herm, LN (24.52, 33.212), Mor, SSA, WBC; all versions except NLT, REB, TEV], 'to receive news' [LN (33.212)]. This phrase is translated 'all

they knew was that people were saying' [NLT], 'they had simply heard it said' [REB], 'they knew only what others were saying' [TEV].

QUESTION—What is meant by μόνον 'only'?

It is used as an adverb to limit the previous clause of 1:22 and indicates that what follows is the only exception to their ignorance about him that is referred to in verse 22 [ICC, WBC].

QUESTION—Who is the subject of ἦσαν ἀκούοντες 'they were hearing'?

The subject is the members of the churches mentioned in 1:22 [Alf, ICC, Lns, NIC, NIGTC, NTC, TH, WBC].

"The (one) persecuting[a] us at-one-time[b] now is-preaching[c] the faith[d] that at-one-time he-was-trying-to-destroy,"[e]

LEXICON—a. pres. act. participle of διώκω (LN 39.45) (BAGD 2. p. 201): 'to persecute' [BAGD, Herm, LN, Mor, SSA, WBC; all versions except CEV, NCV, REB], 'to harass' [LN], 'to attack' [NCV], 'to be cruel to' [CEV]. This verb is also translated as a noun: 'our persecutor' [BNTC; REB].

b. ποτε (LN 67.9) (BAGD 1. p. 695): 'formerly' [BAGD, Mor, SSA, WBC; NIV, NRSV], 'at some time' [LN], 'at some time or other, at one time' [BAGD], 'in times past' [KJV], 'once' [Herm; NASB, NET], 'was' [NCV], 'used to' [NLT, TEV], not explicit [CEV, GW]. This word is also translated as an adjective: 'former (persecutor)' [BNTC; REB].

c. pres. mid. (deponent = act.) indic. of εὐαγγελίζω (LN 33.215) (BAGD 2.a.β. p. 317): 'to preach' [BAGD, BNTC, Herm, Mor, WBC; all versions except GW, NET, NRSV], 'to announce the gospel' [LN], 'to tell the good news' [LN, SSA], 'to proclaim' [BAGD; NET, NRSV], 'to spread' [GW].

d. πίστις (LN 31.102, **31.104**) (BAGD 2.d.α. p. 663; 3. p. 664): 'the faith' [BNTC, Herm, LN (31.102, **31.104**), Mor, WBC; GW, KJV, NASB, NIV, NRSV, TEV], 'the Christian faith' [LN (31.102)], 'body of faith, body of belief' [BAGD], 'beliefs' [**LN** (31.104)], 'doctrine' [BAGD, **LN** (31.104)], '(the good news) which we believe' [SSA], 'the message' [CEV], 'the same faith' [NCV], 'the good news of the faith' [NET, REB], 'the very faith' [NLT].

e. imperf. act. indic. of πορθέω (LN 20.37) (BAGD p. 693): 'to try to destroy' [BAGD, BNTC, Herm, LN, SSA, WBC; all versions except KJV], 'to destroy' [Mor; KJV], 'to attack' [LN, SSA]. The imperfect tense is conative [ICC].

QUESTION—To what does τὴν πίστιν 'the faith' refer to?

1. It refers to the content of what is believed [Herm, Lns, NIGTC, NTC, TH, WBC].
2. It refers to the act of believing [ICC]. The preachers urged them to have faith in the gospel they preached [ICC].

1:24 and they-were-glorifying[a] God in[b] me.
LEXICON—a. imperf. act. indic. of δοξάζω (LN 33.357, 87.8, 87.24) (BAGD 1. p. 204): 'to glorify' [BNTC, LN (33.357, 87.24), Mor; KJV, NASB, NET, NRSV], 'to give glory to' [NLT], 'to praise' [BAGD, Herm, LN (33.357), SSA, WBC; CEV, GW, NCV, NIV, REB, TEV], 'to honor' [BAGD, LN (87.8)], 'to magnify' [BAGD].
  b. ἐν with dative object (LN 83.13, 89.26) (BAGD I.2. p. 258): 'in' [LN (83.13), Mor; KJV], 'because of, on account of' [LN (89.26)]. The phrase ἐν ἐμοί 'in me' is translated 'because of me' [BAGD, BNTC, Herm, WBC; all versions except GW, KJV, REB], 'for me' [BAGD], 'because they heard how God had changed me' [SSA], 'for what had happened to me' [GW, REB].
QUESTION—What relationship is indicated by ἐν 'in'?
  It indicates the reason they glorified God [Alf, ICC, TH, WBC]: they glorified God because of me. Paul provided the occasion and the reason for glorifying God. They praised God for what he had done in Paul [TNTC], for what he had done through Paul or caused Paul to do [TH].

DISCOURSE UNIT: 2:1–10 [BST, GNT, Mor, NAC, NIC, NIGTC, TNTC, WBC; GW, NASB, NCV, NET, NIV, NLT, NRSV, TEV]. The topic is later relations with Jerusalem church leaders [TNTC], Paul's second post-conversion visit to Jerusalem [NIC], the second visit to Jerusalem [NAC, WBC], the conference in Jerusalem [NIGTC], Paul's agreement with the Jerusalem church [Mor], Paul accepted by the other apostles [GNT; NCV, NIV, NLT], Paul was accepted as an apostle by the leaders in Jerusalem [GW], the council at Jerusalem [NASB], confirmation from the Jerusalem apostles [NET], Paul and the other apostles [NRSV, TEV], only one gospel [BST].

2:1 Then[a] after/through[b] fourteen years again[c] I-went-up[d] into[e] Jerusalem with[f] Barnabas, taking-along[g] Titus also;[h]
TEXT—Instead of πάλιν ἀνέβην 'again I went up' some manuscripts read ἀνέβην πάλιν 'I went up again' and other manuscripts read ἀνέβην 'I went up'. GNT reads πάλιν ἀνέβην 'again I went up' with an A decision, indicating that the text is certain.
LEXICON—a. ἔπειτα (LN 67.44) (BAGD 1. p. 284): 'then' [BAGD, BNTC, Herm, Mor, SSA, WBC; GW, KJV, NASB, NET, NLT, NRSV], 'later' [LN, WBC; TEV], 'afterwards' [LN], not explicit [CEV, NCV, NIV, REB].
  b. διά with genitive object (LN 67.60, 67.136) (BAGD A.II.2. p. 180): 'after' [BAGD, BNTC, Herm, Mor; KJV, NASB, NCV, NET, NRSV], 'through' [BAGD], 'during' [LN (67.136)]. The phrase δι' ἐτῶν 'through years' is translated 'some years later' [LN (67.60)]. The phrase διὰ δεκατεσσάρων ἐτῶν 'through fourteen years' is translated 'fourteen years elapsed' [SSA], 'fourteen years later' [WBC; CEV, GW, NIV, NLT, REB, TEV].

c. πάλιν (LN 67.55) (BAGD 1.a. p. 606): 'again' [Herm, LN, Mor, WBC; all versions except CEV, TEV], 'back' [BAGD], 'once again' [BNTC], not explicit [CEV]. The phrase πάλιν ἀνέβην 'again I went up' is translated 'I went back' [TEV], 'I returned' [SSA].
d. aorist act. indic. of ἀναβαίνω (LN 15.101) (BAGD 1.a.α. p. 50): 'to go up' [BAGD, LN], 'traveled up' [BNTC], 'went up' [Herm, Mor, WBC; KJV, NASB, NET, NIV, NRSV, REB], 'returned' [SSA], 'went' [CEV, GW, NCV], 'went back' [NLT, TEV].
e. εἰς with accusative object (LN 84.16, 84.22): 'into' [LN (84.22)], 'to' [BNTC, Herm, LN (84.16), Mor, SSA, WBC; all versions].
f. μετά with genitive object (LN 89.108) (BAGD A.II.1.a. p. 508): 'with' [BAGD, BNTC, LN, Mor, WBC; all versions], 'together with' [Herm, LN], 'in the company of' [LN], 'in company with' [BAGD]. The phrase μετὰ Βαρναβᾶ 'with Barnabas' is translated 'Barnabas accompanied me' [SSA].
g. aorist act. participle of συμπαραλαμβάνω (LN **15.169**) (BAGD p. 779): 'to take along' [BAGD, Herm, **LN**, WBC; CEV, GW, NASB, NET, NIV], 'to take along (with me)' [NRSV, TEV], 'to bring along (with)' [LN], 'to take' [SSA], 'to take (with me)' [BNTC, Mor; KJV, NCV, REB]. This is also translated with 'Titus' as the subject: 'to come along' [NLT].
h. καί (LN 89.93): 'also' [BNTC, Herm, LN, Mor, SSA; CEV, GW, KJV, NASB, NCV, NIV], 'as well' [WBC], 'too' [NET, NLT], not explicit [NRSV, REB, TEV].

QUESTION—What relationship is indicated by ἔπειτα 'then'?

Paul uses ἔπειτα to indicate sequence [SSA] and to assure his readers that he hasn't omitted anything [BNTC, NIC, NIGTC, WBC].

QUESTION—Does διά mean 'after' or 'through'?
1. It means *after* fourteen years had passed [Alf, BNTC, BST, ICC, Lns, Lt, Mor, NAC, NIC, NTC, TH; KJV, NASB, NCV, NET, NRSV].
2. It means *through* or *during* fourteen years [ICC, Lt, SSA]. It means that throughout the fourteen years he had not contacted those in Judea and Jerusalem [SSA].

QUESTION—What time period is being specified by 'fourteen years'?
1. It was fourteen years after his first journey to Jerusalem [ICC, Lns, Lt, NTC, TH]. The point he is making is how long after he last saw the apostle Peter that he again went to see the apostles in Jerusalem [TH].
2. It was fourteen years after his conversion [Alf, BST, NAC]. It was after three years from his conversion he first went to Jerusalem and it was fourteen years after his conversion that he again went to Jerusalem [Alf].

QUESTION—What relationship is indicated by πάλιν 'again'?

This was another trip Paul made to Jerusalem. It does not necessarily mean 'for the second time'. It can mean 'once again' without stating how many trips had been made to Jerusalem before [NTC]. Some think it indicates that this was his second visit to Jerusalem [BST, Herm, NAC, NIC, NIGTC,

WBC]. Some take it to refer to his third visit to Jerusalem for the council with the apostles and elders (Acts 15) [Alf, Lns, Lt, NTC].

QUESTION—What relationship is indicated by μετά 'with'?

It indicates that this time Paul had Barnabas as a colleague [NIC] who accompanied him [SSA]. It signals association without the idea of inferiority or subordination [WBC]. However, it was Barnabas who accompanied Paul, and not the other way around [ICC, NCBC, TH] since Paul was the leader of the party [ICC].

QUESTION—What is the function of the participle συμπαραλαβών 'taking along'?

It expresses an attendant circumstance [SSA]: and I took Titus along also. The wording places Titus in a subordinate position [Herm, ICC, SSA, WBC].

2:2 and I-went-up[a] in-accordance-with[b] revelation;[c]

LEXICON—a. aorist act. indic. of ἀναβαίνω (LN 15.101): 'to go up' [Herm, LN, Mor, SSA, WBC; KJV, NASB, NRSV], 'to travel up' [BNTC], 'to go' [all versions except KJV, NASB, NRSV].
- b. κατά with accusative object (LN 89.8) (BAGD II.5.a.δ. p. 407): 'in accordance with' [BAGD, BNTC, Herm, LN, Mor], 'in response to' [WBC; GW, NIV, NRSV, REB], 'because of' [BAGD, SSA; NASB, NET], 'because' [CEV, NCV, NLT, TEV], 'by' [KJV].
- c. ἀποκάλυψις (LN 28.38) (BAGD 2. p. 92): 'revelation' [BAGD, BNTC, Herm, LN, Mor, WBC; GW, KJV, NASB, NET, NIV, NRSV, REB]. This is translated 'what God revealed to me/someone' [SSA], 'God had told me' [CEV], 'God showed me' [NCV], 'God revealed to me' [NLT, TEV].

QUESTION—What relationship is indicated by δέ 'and'?

It carries on the narrative and it also carries on the refutation [Alf].

QUESTION—Does the preposition κατά mean 'in accordance with' or 'because of'?

1. It means 'in accordance with' [BNTC, ICC, LN, Mor, SSA, WBC; GW, NIV, NRSV, REB]: I went up in accordance with what God revealed to me. It was Paul's response to the revelation [ICC, NAC, WBC; GW, NIV, NRSV, REB]. Although SSA translates with 'because', its comments explain that the preposition is not directly causal.
2. It indicates the reason Paul went to Jerusalem [Herm, NIC, TH; CEV, NASB, NCV, NET, NLT, TEV]: I went up because this is what God revealed I should do.

QUESTION—To what does ἀποκάλυψις 'revelation' refer?

Perhaps the revelation was a direct communication that guided Paul to go there [NAC], or the revelation was a confirmation of the church's previous decision in Antioch that Paul should go, or perhaps the revelation was the one given to Agabus about a famine in Judea that required being sent with famine relief [SSA]. It refers to what God had revealed to him. God revealed to him that he should make this journey [Mor]. It refers to God making himself or his will known, probably not verbal [TH]. It refers to disclosing the divine will concerning a specific matter [ICC].

and I-set-forth[a] to-them the gospel that I-preach[b] among[c] the gentiles,[d]

LEXICON—a. aorist mid. (deponent = act.) indic. of ἀνατίθημι (LN **33.151**) (BAGD 2. p. 62): 'to set forth, to make clear' [LN], 'to set before' [Mor, WBC; NIV], 'to lay before' [BAGD, BNTC, Herm; NRSV], 'to explain' [CEV, NLT, REB, TEV], 'to show' [GW], 'to submit' [NASB], 'to tell' [NCV], 'to present' [SSA; NET], 'to communicate' [KJV].

b. pres. act. indic. of κηρύσσω (LN 33.256) (BAGD 2.b.β. p. 431): 'to preach' [BAGD, Herm, LN, Mor, WBC; all versions except GW, NRSV], 'to proclaim' [BAGD, BNTC, SSA; NRSV], 'to spread' [GW].

c. ἐν with dative object (LN 83.9, 90.56): 'among' [BNTC, Herm, LN (83.9), Mor, WBC; GW, KJV, NASB, NET, NIV, NRSV], 'to' [LN (90.56); CEV, NCV, NLT, REB, TEV], 'in (Gentile regions)' [SSA].

d. ἔθνος (LN 11.37, 11.55): 'gentile, nation' [LN (11.55)]. The plural form is translated 'Gentiles' [BNTC, Herm, Mor, WBC; all versions except GW, NCV], 'people who are not Jewish' [GW], 'non-Jewish people' [NCV], 'heathen, pagans' [LN (11.37)], 'Gentile regions' [SSA].

QUESTION—What relationship is indicated by ἐν 'among'?

This does not limit his preaching to Gentiles and it covers his practice of going to Jewish synagogues in those lands [Mor]. It refers to people living in Gentile lands [ICC, TH, WBC].

but according-to privacy[a] (to) the-(ones) seeming[b] (to be important),

LEXICON—a. ἴδιος (LN 92.21) (BAGD 4. p. 370): 'privacy' is translated as an adverb: 'individually, separately' [LN]. The phrase κατ' ἰδίαν 'according to privacy' is translated 'privately' [BAGD, BNTC, Herm, Mor, SSA, WBC; CEV, KJV, NIV, NLT], 'in private' [NASB, NCV, NRSV], 'in a private meeting' [GW, NET, TEV], 'at a private interview' [REB].

b. pres. act. participle of δοκέω (LN **87.42**) (BAGD 2.b. p. 202): 'to seem' [BAGD]. The phrase τοῖς δοκοῦσιν 'the ones seeming' is translated 'prominent persons' [**LN**], 'important persons, influential persons' [LN], 'influential men' [BAGD], 'those held in repute' [BNTC], 'those who were recognized as leaders' [Mor], 'those reputed to be important' [WBC], 'those whom your new teachers highly respect' [SSA], 'those who were of reputation' [NASB], 'those of repute' [REB], 'them which were of reputation' [KJV], 'those who seemed to be leaders' [NIV], 'the ones who seemed to be the most important leaders' [CEV], 'those recognized as important people' [GW], 'the leaders' [TEV], 'their leaders' [NCV], 'the acknowledged leaders' [NRSV], 'the leaders of the church' [NLT], 'the influential people' [NET], 'the men of eminence' [Herm]. The phrase refers to those who are generally recognized to be important [LN].

QUESTION—How many meetings did Paul have?
1. He had one meeting [Alf, BST, Mor, NAC, NIC, NIGTC, TH, TNTC, WBC; all versions except CEV, NCV]: I set forth to them the gospel that I preach, but it was a private meeting with those of repute. The conjunction 'but' limits the preceding 'them' and has the meaning "when I say 'to them', I mean to those of repute" [Alf, NIGTC].
2. He had two meetings [Herm, ICC, Lns, Lt, NCBC, NTC; CEV, NCV]: I set forth to them, the whole church, the gospel that I-preach, but I also had a private meeting with those of repute. The first meeting was with 'them', the Christian community [ICC] in a public meeting [Lns].

QUESTION—How does Paul use the phrase 'those seeming to be important'?
These words describe the church leaders as the influential men of the church in Jerusalem [ICC, NIC] and there is nothing in the passage that indicates he is speaking of those leaders in irony [Alf, ICC, NTC]. Even though this terminology seems to imply some resentment, Paul is not belittling the leaders themselves [NTC, SSA]. Rather he is mocking those who opposed him in Galatia [SSA] by quoting their own words with which they exalted James, Peter, and John at the expense of Paul [NTC].

lest-somehow[a] I-should-be-running[b] or had-run in vain.[c]

LEXICON—a. μή πως (LN 89.62) (BAGD 2. p. 519). The phrase μή πως (or μήπως) 'lest somehow' is translated 'lest, in order that not' [LN], 'so that not' [Herm, LN], 'lest somehow' [BNTC, WBC], 'lest by any chance' [Mor], 'lest by any means' [KJV], '(fearing) that perhaps' [BAGD], 'for fear that' [NASB, NIV], 'I wanted to make sure that' [CEV], 'to see whether' [GW], 'I did not want' [NCV, TEV], 'to make sure that' [NET, NLT, REB], 'in order to make sure that' [NRSV], 'in order that...not' [SSA].

b. pres. act. subj. of τρέχω (LN 15.230, 41.14) (BAGD 2.a. p. 825): 'to run' [BAGD, BNTC, Herm, LN (15.230), Mor, WBC; KJV, NASB, NET, NIV, NRSV, REB], 'to behave' [LN (41.14)]. The phrase τρέχω ἢ ἔδραμον 'I should be running or had run' is translated 'all my efforts' [GW], 'my ministry' [NLT], 'my work in the past and my future work' [CEV], 'my work in the past or in the present' [TEV], 'my past work and the work I am now doing' [NCV], 'what I was doing and what I had done' [SSA].

c. κενός (LN 89.53): 'vain' [BNTC, Herm, LN, Mor, WBC; KJV, NASB, NET, NIV, NRSV, REB], 'without result, without effect' [LN]. This word is also translated as a verb: 'to be wasted' [GW, NCV], 'to be for nothing' [CEV], 'to be useless' [NLT], 'to be a failure' [TEV], 'to be invalidated' [SSA].

QUESTION—What relationship is indicated by the clause introduced by μή πως 'lest somehow'?
1. It expresses the purpose of the private meeting [BST, Herm, Lt, NTC, SSA; CEV, NCV, NET, NLT, NRSV, REB, TEV].

2. Along with a negative purpose it includes Paul's apprehension [Alf, BNTC, ICC, Mor, NIC, TH, WBC; NASB, NIV]. Paul feared that disapproval by the apostles would interfere with his work and hinder it [ICC].
3. It expresses the thrust of the question he put before the private meeting: "with the question whether…" [Lns]. Paul was not in doubt and the implied answer was 'certainly not' [Lns].

QUESTION—What is meant by τρέχω ἢ ἔδραμον 'I should be running or had run'?

This is a figure of a foot race and refers to his ministry [BNTC, Herm, Lt, Mor, SSA, WBC].

2:3 But not-even[a] Titus the (one) with[b] me, being a-Greek/Greek,[c] was-compelled[d] to-be-circumcised;[e]

LEXICON—a. οὐδέ (LN 69.7, 69.8) (BAGD 3. p. 591): 'not even' [BAGD, BNTC, Herm, LN (69.8), Mor, SSA, WBC; NASB, NET, NIV, NLT, REB], 'and not' [LN (69.7)], 'still…not' [CEV], 'even…not' [NRSV], 'neither' [LN (69.7); KJV], not explicit [GW, NCV, TEV].
b. σύν with dative object (LN 89.107) (BAGD 1.c. p. 781): 'with' [BAGD, BNTC, Herm, LN, Mor, WBC; all versions except NLT, REB, TEV]. This preposition is also translated as a noun phrase: 'my companion' [NLT, REB, TEV], as a verb: 'accompanied' [SSA].
c. Ἕλλην (LN 11.40, 11.90) (BAGD 2.a. p. 252): 'Greek' [BNTC, Herm, LN (11.40, 11.90), Mor, SSA, WBC; all versions except NLT], 'Gentile' [BAGD, LN (11.40); NLT]. Here 'Greek' is equivalent to Gentile [ICC, Lt, TH].
d. aorist pass. indic. of ἀναγκάζω (LN 37.33) (BAGD 1. p. 52): 'to be compelled' [BAGD, BNTC, Herm, LN, Mor, WBC; KJV, NASB, NET, NIV, NRSV, REB], 'to be forced' [LN; CEV, GW, NCV, TEV], not explicit [SSA; NLT].
e. aorist pass. infin. of περιτέμνω (LN 53.51) (BAGD 1. p. 652): 'to be circumcised' [BAGD, BNTC, Herm, LN, Mor, SSA, WBC; all versions].

QUESTION—What relationship is indicated by ἀλλά 'but'?

It does not express an opposing qualification, but serves to strengthen the more general statement just made [NCBC]. It indicates that the preceding is to be considered a settled matter and forms a transition to something new [Mor]. It indicates that Paul's views prevailed [TH].

QUESTION—What relationship is indicated by οὐδέ 'not even'?

It lays stress on the evidential value of Titus' case: if it is true for Titus, the Greek, it is true in principle [Herm, WBC]. It points out the prominence of Paul's companion, Titus, and thus the weight that his non-circumcision could have in the fight against legalism [SSA].

QUESTION—Who is the implied actor of ἀναγκάζω 'was compelled'?

The actors are the false brothers [ICC, NAC, NIBC, SSA], the Judaizers [Lns].

2:4 **but because-ofᵃ the sneaked-inᵇ false-brothers,ᶜ**

LEXICON—a. διά with accusative object (LN 90.44): 'because of' [BNTC, Herm, LN; CEV, KJV, NASB, NET, NRSV], 'because' [SSA, WBC; NCV, NIV], 'on account of' [LN, Mor], 'except for' [NLT], not explicit [GW, TEV]. The phrase διὰ δὲ 'but on account of' is translated 'that course was urged only as a concession to' [REB].

  b. παρείσακτος (LN **34.29**) (BAGD p. 624): 'sneaked in' [BAGD; CEV] 'falsely pretending, joined falsely' [LN], 'secretly brought in' [BAGD, Herm; NASB, NRSV], 'smuggled in' [BAGD, BNTC], 'brought in secretly' [Mor], 'infiltrated' [WBC; NIV], 'brought in' [GW], 'had come into our group secretly' [NCV], 'with false pretenses' [NET], 'unawares brought in' [KJV], not explicit [NLT, REB, TEV]. The phrase τοὺς παρεισάκτους ψευδαδέλφους 'the sneaked in false brothers' is translated 'those who falsely pretended to be fellow believers' [**LN**], 'some persons who were encouraged by other persons' [SSA].

  c. ψευδάδελφος (LN 11.36) (BAGD p. 891): 'false brother' [BAGD, LN], 'false brothers' [BNTC, Herm, Mor, WBC; NET, NIV], 'false Christians' [GW], 'false brethren' [KJV, NASB], 'false believers' [NCV, NRSV], 'so-called Christians—false ones' [NLT], 'sham Christians' [REB]. This noun is also translated as a verb phrase: 'pretending to be believers' [TEV], 'pretended to be followers' [CEV], 'pretended that they were brothers' [SSA]. This refers to someone who pretends to be a fellow believer in Christ [BAGD, LN], but his unbrotherly conduct shows that he is not [BAGD].

QUESTION—What relationship is indicated by διά 'because of'?

  1. This is connected with verse 1 to explain why Paul set forth the gospel privately [SSA; CEV, NCV]: I set forth the gospel privately…because of the false brothers who had slipped in. 'We went there because of those who pretended to be followers' [CEV], 'we talked about this problem because some false believers had come into our group secretly' [NCV].

  2. This is connected with verse 3 to explain why there was a demand to have Titus circumcised [Alf, ICC, Lns, NCBC, NTC; NET, NIV, NLT, REB]: Titus was not compelled to be circumcised because of the false brothers who had slipped in. The suggestion that Titus had to be circumcised would not have arisen except for the false brothers [NTC]. 'This matter arose because…' [NIV], 'That course was urged only as a concession to …' [REB].

  3. This begins an unfinished sentence [BNTC, BST, Lt, WBC; NRSV]: But because of the sneaked-in false brothers…. Instead of completing the sentence with something like 'the leading Apostles urged me to yield', a long parenthesis is introduced so that the sentence remains unfinished [Lt]. The verse ends with a dash before the comment in 2:5 [NRSV].

QUESTION—Who is the implied actor of παρείσακτος 'sneaked in'?

  1. This has the passive sense and implies that someone other than the false brothers had sneaked them in [BNTC, Herm, Lns, NIBC, SSA, TNTC;

GW, KJV, REB]: the false brothers whom some person sneaked in. Some of the members of the church had invited the false brothers [BNTC, NCBC], other persons [SSA]. Perhaps it was a large group of Christians who belonged to the Pharisaic part or who were ex-priests [TNTC].
2. This refers only to the actions of the false brothers [Lt, NAC, NTC; NCV, NIV]: the false brothers who had sneaked in. These people, who were Pharisees at heart, had pretended to be brothers and had stealthily entered the church [Lt, NAC].

those-who slipped-in^a to-spy-out^b our freedom^c

LEXICON—a. aorist act. indic. of παρεισέρχομαι (LN **34.30**) (BAGD 2. p. 625): 'to slip in' [BAGD; GW, NET, NRSV], 'to slip into' [**LN**; TEV], 'to sneak in' [BAGD, BNTC, Mor; CEV, NASB, REB], 'to join unnoticed' [LN], 'to intrude' [WBC], 'to associate with/to assemble' [SSA], 'to come in' [NCV, NLT], 'to come in privily' [KJV], 'to infiltrate' [Herm; NIV].
  b. aorist act. infin. of κατασκοπέω (LN **24.50**) (BAGD p. 418): 'to spy out' [BAGD, Herm, **LN**, Mor, WBC; KJV, NASB, NET], 'to observe secretly' [LN], 'to spy on' [BNTC; NIV, NLT, NRSV, REB], 'to observe closely' [SSA]. This verb is also translated to indicate the manner they slipped in: 'as spies' [CEV, GW, TEV], 'like spies' [NCV].
  c. ἐλευθερία (LN 37.133) (BAGD p. 250): 'freedom' [BAGD, BNTC, Herm, LN, Mor, WBC; all versions except KJV, NASB, REB], 'liberty' [BAGD; KJV, NASB, REB], 'what we do because we are free' [SSA].
QUESTION—What community did the false brethren slip into?
  They got into the general Christian fellowship [Lt, WBC], the Antioch congregation [NCBC], the Jerusalem congregation [BNTC, Lns, NAC, TNTC].
QUESTION—What is meant by ἐλευθερίαν ἡμῶν 'our freedom'?
  It refers to the freedom that Christians have from bondage to the law [BNTC, BST, ICC, NCBC, NIGTC, NTC, TH, WBC] and the Mosaic ritual [Alf]. It refers to the freedom a Christian man has to remain uncircumcised [Lns, NIC].

that we-have^a in^b Christ Jesus,

LEXICON—a. pres. act. indic. of ἔχω (LN 57.1) (BAGD I.2.g. p. 333): 'to have' [BAGD, BNTC, Herm, LN, Mor, WBC; KJV, NASB, NCV, NET, NIV, NRSV, TEV], 'to possess' [BAGD, LN], 'to enjoy' [REB], 'to be given' [CEV], '(Christ Jesus) gives us' [GW], not explicit [NLT]. See b. [SSA].
  b. ἐν with dative object (LN 13.8, 83.13, 89.119) (BAGD I.5.d. p. 259): 'in' [BNTC, Herm, LN (13.8, 83.13, 89.119), Mor, WBC; KJV, NASB, NCV, NET, NIV, NLT, NRSV], 'in union with' [LN (89.119)], 'in the fellowship of' [REB]. It indicates a close personal relation [BAGD]. The phrase ἔχομεν ἐν 'we have in' is translated 'we do not trust ourselves but trust' [SSA], 'through our union with' [TEV]. The phrase ἣν ἔχομεν ἐν

Χριστῷ Ἰησοῦ 'which we have in Christ Jesus' is translated 'that Christ Jesus had given us' [CEV], 'Christ Jesus gives us' [GW].

QUESTION—What is the meaning of ἐν Χριστῷ 'in Christ'?
1. It indicates the reason that we have freedom [ICC, NIC; CEV, GW]: We have freedom because of Christ Jesus.
   1.1 It is because of what Christ Jesus has done for us [ICC; CEV, GW]. It is because of Christ's work we have freedom [ICC]. Christ gives us our freedom [CEV, GW].
   1.2 It is because we trust in Christ Jesus [SSA].
2. It refers to our association with Christ Jesus [NCBC; REB].
3. It indicates the instrument and the location of our freedom. We have freedom as the result of what Christ does in our lives (the instrument) and we have freedom through our personal relationship with Christ (the location) [WBC].

in-order-that they-will-enslave[a] us,

TEXT—Instead of the future active indicative καταδουλώσουσιν 'they will enslave', some manuscripts presumably read the aorist mid. subj. καταδουλώσωνται 'they might enslave', which is read by NRSV, although GNT does not mention this reading.

LEXICON—a. fut. act. subj. of καταδουλόω (LN **37.27**) (BAGD p. 410): 'to enslave' [BAGD, BNTC, Herm, Mor, SSA; NRSV], 'to make slaves of' [LN], 'to make someone a slave' [WBC; CEV, NCV, NET, NIV, TEV], 'to gain control over' [**LN**], 'to control' [GW], 'to bring into bondage' [KJV, NASB, REB], 'to force (us), like slaves' [NLT].

QUESTION—What relationship is indicated by ἵνα 'in order that'?
It indicates purpose [Lns, Mor, NIBC]: they slipped in to spy out our freedom in order to enslave us.

QUESTION—In what way did they want to enslave them?
Enslavement is a metaphor [TH] for making them subject to the Jewish law [ICC, Lt, NIC, NIGTC, NTC, TNTC, WBC], Jewish ritual [TH]. This was not their conscious desire, but it is Paul's evaluation of what would result in submission to such a religious system [TNTC]. They would enslave them if they convinced the Christians that instead of trusting only in Christ, they must also comply with the whole Law of Moses [SSA].

2:5 **to-whom not-even[a] for[b] (an) hour[c] did-we-yield[d] in-submission,[e]**

TEXT—Instead of οἷς οὐδέ 'to whom not even', some manuscripts read οἷς 'to whom' and other manuscripts omit both words. GNT reads οἷς οὐδέ 'to whom not even' with an A decision, indicating that the text is certain.

LEXICON—a. οὐδέ (LN 69.8): 'not even' [BNTC, LN, SSA; CEV], 'even' [BNTC, Mor, WBC; NASB, NET, NRSV], not explicit [Herm; GW, KJV, NCV, NIV, NLT, REB, TEV].
   b. πρός with accusative object (LN 78.51) (BAGD III.2.b. p. 710): 'for' [BAGD, BNTC, Herm, Mor, WBC; all versions], 'to the extent of' [LN], not explicit [SSA].

c. ὥρα (LN 67.148, 67.199) (BAGD 2.a.β. p. 896): 'hour' [BNTC, LN (67.199), Mor; KJV, NASB], '(a) while' [BAGD, LN (67.148)], '(a) moment' [BAGD, Herm, WBC; GW, NET, NIV, NRSV], 'a second' [CEV], 'a minute' [NCV, TEV], 'a single moment' [NLT], 'one moment' [REB], 'briefly' [SSA].

d. aorist act. indic. of εἴκω (LN **39.21**) (BAGD p. 222): 'to yield' [BAGD, BNTC, Herm, LN; NASB, REB], 'to give in' [LN, WBC; CEV, GW, NCV, NIV, TEV], 'to submit' [Mor; NRSV], 'to surrender' [NET], 'to give place' [KJV]. See e. [SSA; NLT].

e. ὑποταγή (LN 36.18) (BAGD p. 847): 'submission' [BAGD, BNTC, Herm, LN], 'in subjection' [NASB], 'by subjection' [KJV], not explicit [Mor, WBC; all versions except KJV, NASB, NLT]. The phrase εἴξαμεν τῇ ὑποταγῇ 'did we yield in subjection' is translated 'we resisted them' [SSA], 'we refused to listen' [NLT].

QUESTION—To whom does εἴξαμεν 'did we yield' refer?
1. It refers only to Paul [TH; REB].
2. It refers to Paul and others [Alf, BNTC, Lns, Lt, NIBC, NIGTC]. It refers to Paul and Barnabas [BNTC, Lns, Lt], and the entire delegation from Antioch (Acts 15:2) [Lns].

QUESTION—What is the meaning of ὑποταγή 'submission'?
It means that they did not yield in regards to the matter under discussion, circumcision [NCBC]. They did not do what the false brothers demanded of them [ICC]. They did not yield to the demanded submission to the Mosaic ceremonial regulations [Lns].

in-order-that the truth[a] of-the gospel[b] might-remain[c] with[d] you.

LEXICON—a. ἀλήθεια (LN 72.2) (BAGD 2.b. p. 36): 'truth' [BAGD, BNTC, Herm, LN, Mor, WBC; all versions except CEV], 'true (message)' [CEV], not explicit [SSA].

b. εὐαγγέλιον (LN 33.217) (BAGD 1.b. p. 318): 'gospel' [BAGD, BNTC, Herm, LN, Mor, WBC; KJV, NASB, NET, NIV, NRSV, REB, TEV], 'good news' [BAGD, LN; GW, NCV, NLT], 'genuine good news' [SSA], 'message' [CEV].

c. aorist act. subj. of διαμένω (LN 13.89, 68.11) (BAGD p. 186): 'to remain' [BNTC, Herm, LN (13.89, 68.11), Mor, WBC; NASB, NET, NIV, NRSV], 'to remain continually' [BAGD], 'to continue' [LN (13.89); KJV, NCV], 'to continue to exist' [LN (13.89)], 'to continue on' [SSA], 'to always be' [GW], 'to be maintained' [REB], 'to preserve' [NLT], 'to keep safe' [TEV], not explicit [CEV].

d. πρός with accusative object (LN 89.112) (BAGD III.7. p. 711): 'with' [BAGD, Herm, LN, Mor, WBC; KJV, NASB, NET, NIV, NRSV], 'for' [BNTC; NCV, NLT, REB, TEV]. The phrase διαμείνῃ πρὸς ὑμᾶς 'might remain with you' is translated 'might continue on and benefit you' [SSA], 'would always be yours' [GW], '(we wanted) you to have' [CEV].

QUESTION—How are the nouns related in the genitive construction ἀλήθεια τοῦ εὐαγγελίου 'truth of the gospel'?

It means the gospel in its integrity [Herm, Lt, NAC, WBC]. It means that the truth is contained in the gospel [ICC]. It means that truth is its substance, the divine reality it contains [Lns].

2:6 But from^a the (ones) seeming^b to-be something,^c

LEXICON—a. ἀπό with genitive object (LN 90.15): 'from' [BNTC, LN, Mor, SSA; NASB, NET, NRSV], 'for' [Herm, WBC; NIV, REB], 'of' [KJV], not explicit [CEV, GW, NCV, NLT, TEV].
b. pres. act. participle of δοκέω (LN 87.42) (BAGD 2.b. p. 202): 'to seem' [Mor; KJV, NCV, NIV, TEV], 'to be reputed' [BNTC, WBC; REB], 'to be recognized' [GW], 'to be supposed' [CEV, NRSV], not explicit [Herm; NASB, NET, NLT]. See c. [SSA]. See this verb in 2:2 where the following words εἶναί τι 'to be something' are only implied.
c. τις (LN 92.13) (BAGD 1.b.ε. p. 820): 'something' [BAGD, BNTC, LN; REB], 'somewhat' [KJV]. In the predicate position of this context, it refers to someone of prominence or distinction [LN]: 'someone important' [LN], 'important people' [GW], 'important leaders' [CEV], 'great leaders' [NLT], 'leaders' [NRSV, TEV], 'important' [Mor, WBC; NCV, NIV], 'of high reputation' [NASB], 'influential' [NET]. The phrase τῶν δοκούντων εἶναί τι 'the ones seeming to be something' is translated 'the ones whom your new teachers respect' [SSA], 'the men of eminence' [Herm].

QUESTION—What relationship is indicated by δέ 'but'?

It indicates a continuation of the narrative of 2:1–2 [ICC, WBC].

QUESTION—How is this clause connected to what follows?

Instead of ending this clause with something like 'I received nothing', Paul interrupted his thought at the end of this clause with a parenthetical comment about those leaders. In the last clause of this verse he returns to his subject but instead of completing the sentence with a verb he has another dependent clause 'for to me the ones seeming added nothing' [NTC]. Some translations make a complete sentence here by adapting the last clause: 'Those who were recognized as important people didn't add a single thing to my message' [GW], 'Those leaders who seemed to be important did not change the Good News that I preach' [NCV], 'And the leaders of the church who were there had nothing to add to what I was preaching' [NLT]. Another translation made a complete sentence by including the next clause: 'Some of them were supposed to be important leaders, but I didn't care who they were' [CEV].

—what-sort^a at-any-time^b they-were matters^c nothing to-me;

LEXICON—a. ὁποῖος (LN **58.30**) (BAGD p. 575): 'what sort, what sort of' [**LN**], 'what sort of people' [BAGD], 'what kind of' [LN]. The phrase ὁποῖοί ποτε ἦσαν 'what sort at any time' is translated 'what sort of people they were' [BAGD; GW], 'what they once were' [BNTC], 'what those ones formerly were' [SSA], 'whatever they were' [Mor, WBC;

NET, NIV], 'what they were' [Herm; NASB, TEV], 'what they actually were' [NRSV], 'whatsoever they were' [KJV]. This clause is translated 'but I didn't care who they were' [CEV], 'it doesn't matter to me if they were important or not' [NCV], 'By the way, their reputation as great leaders made no difference to me' [NLT], 'not that importance matters to me' [REB].

b. ποτέ (LN 67.9) (BAGD 3. p. 695): 'at any time, at some time, ever' [LN], 'at one time' [WBC], not explicit [Herm, Mor; all versions]. See a. [BAGD, BNTC, SSA].

c. pres. act. indic. of διφέρω (LN 58.41) (BAGD 2.c. p. 190): 'to matter' [LN]. The phrase οὐδέν μοι διαφέρει 'matters nothing to me' is translated 'it makes no difference to me' [BAGD; TEV], 'does not concern me' [SSA], 'makes no difference to me' [BNTC, Herm, WBC; GW, NASB, NET, NIV, NRSV], 'not that their importance matters to me' [REB], 'it maketh no matter to me' [KJV], 'makes no difference' [Mor]. See a. [CEV, NCV, NLT].

QUESTION—What is the meaning of ποτέ 'at any time'?
1. It has an intensive sense 'whatever' [Lns; KJV, NET, NIV].
2. It has a temporal sense 'once' [BNTC, ICC, Lt, NTC, TH]. It indicates a particular past period of time and emphasizes the idea of 'at one time' or 'formerly' [WBC].

God does- not -accept[a] (the) face[b] of-(a) man[c]—
LEXICON—a. pres. act. indic. of λαμβάνω (LN 57.125, 88.238) (BAGD 1.e.β. p. 464): 'to accept' [LN (57.125), Mor; KJV], 'to receive' [BAGD], 'to favor' [SSA]. The phrase πρόσωπον...λαμβάνει 'accepts the face' is translated 'to show partiality' [BNTC, Herm, LN (88.238); NASB, NRSV]. This entire phrase is translated 'God does not take into account human credentials' [WBC], 'God doesn't have any favorites' [CEV], 'God doesn't play favorites' [GW], 'To God everyone is the same' [NCV], 'God shows no favoritism between people' [NET], 'God does not judge by external appearance' [NIV], 'God has no favorites' [NLT], 'God does not recognize these personal distinctions' [REB], 'God does not judge by outward appearances' [TEV], 'God does not show partiality' [Herm].

b. πρόσωπον (LN 8.18) (BAGD 1.b. p. 721): 'face' [BAGD, LN]. The phrase πρόσωπον ἀνθρώπου 'face of a man' is translated 'man's person' [KJV], 'anyone's person' [Mor], 'certain/important persons' [SSA]. See a. [BNTC, Herm, WBC; all versions except KJV].

c. ἄνθρωπος (LN 9.1, 9.24): 'man' [LN (9.24)], 'person, human being' [LN (9.1)]. See b. [Mor, SSA; KJV]. See a. [BNTC, Herm, WBC; all versions except KJV].

QUESTION—What is meant by 'accepts the face of a man'?
To accept the person/face of a man is to base one's judgment and action on external and irrelevant considerations [ICC], to consider the external

circumstances of a man such as his wealth, rank, etc [Lt], to judge a person on the basis of his external circumstances such as wealth, social position, or rank [NCBC, TH], to take into account human credentials [WBC], to evaluate a person on the basis of an outward appearance or external circumstance [NAC].

for to-me the-(ones) seeming (to be something) added[a] nothing,
    LEXICON—a. aorist mid./mid. (deponent = act.) indic. of προσανατίθημι (LN **59.72**) (BAGD 1. p. 711): 'to add' [BAGD, BNTC, **LN**, Mor, SSA, WBC; CEV, GW, KJV, NET, NIV, NLT], 'to contribute' [NASB, NRSV], 'to impart' [REB], not explicit [NCV]. The phrase οὐδὲν προσανέθεντο 'added nothing' is translated 'made no new suggestions' [**LN**; TEV], 'did not make any demand upon me' [Herm].
QUESTION—What relationship is indicated by γάρ 'for'?
    1. It resumes the broken sentence [BNTC, Herm, ICC, Lt, NIGTC].
    2. It indicates the reason for saying 'what they were makes no difference to me' [Alf].

2:7 but on-the-contrary[a] seeing[b] that I-was-entrusted[c] (with) the gospel[d] of-the-uncircumcision[e] just-as[f] Peter of-the-circumcision,[g]
LEXICON—a. τοὐναντίον (LN 89.134) (BAGD 2. p. 262): 'on the contrary' [BNTC, Herm, LN, Mor, WBC; NASB, NET, NIV, NRSV, REB, TEV], 'rather, instead' [LN], 'on the other hand' [BAGD], 'in fact' [GW], 'contrariwise' [KJV], not explicit [CEV, NCV, NLT]. This is translated 'they responded very differently' [SSA].
    b. aorist act. participle of ὁράω (LN 24.1, 32.11) (BAGD 3. p. 221): 'to see' [BAGD, BNTC, Herm, LN (24.1, 32.11), Mor, WBC; all versions except CEV], 'to realize' [CEV], 'to understand' [LN (32.11), SSA].
    c. perf. pass. indic. of πιστεύω (LN 35.50) (BAGD 3. p. 662): 'to be entrusted' [BAGD, BNTC, Herm, LN, Mor, WBC; GW, NASB, NET, NIV, NRSV, REB], 'to be committed' [KJV], 'to be given' [NCV]. This passive is also translated actively with 'God' as the subject: 'to send with' [CEV], 'to commit' [SSA], 'to give the responsibility' [NLT], 'to give the task' [TEV]. The perfect tense indicates a continuous entrusting [Alf, Lns, Lt, Mor, NIGTC].
    d. εὐαγγέλιον (LN 33.217) (BAGD 2.b.α. p. 318): 'gospel' [BAGD, BNTC, Herm, LN, Mor; KJV, NASB, NET, NIV, NRSV, REB, TEV], 'good news' [LN, SSA; CEV, GW, NCV, NLT]. This is translated 'the task of preaching' [WBC].
    e. ἀκροβυστία (LN **11.53**) (BAGD 3. p. 33): 'uncircumcision' [BAGD, BNTC, Herm, Mor; KJV], 'the uncircumcised' [LN, WBC; NASB, NET, NRSV], 'Gentiles' [**LN**; CEV, NIV, NLT, REB, TEV], 'Gentile world' [BAGD, LN], 'people who are not circumcised' [GW], 'those who are not Jewish' [NCV], 'those who do not circumcise persons' [SSA].

f. καθώς (LN 64.14): 'just as' [Herm, LN, Mor, SSA, WBC; NASB, NCV, NET, NIV, NLT, NRSV, TEV], 'as' [BNTC; GW, KJV, REB], not explicit [CEV].

g. περιτομή (LN 53.51) (BAGD 4.a. p. 653): 'circumcision' [BNTC, Herm, LN, Mor; KJV], 'Jews' [BAGD; CEV, NCV, NIV, NLT, REB, TEV], 'the circumcised' [WBC; GW, NASB, NET, NRSV], 'those who circumcise persons' [SSA].

QUESTION—What relationship is indicated by ἀλλὰ τοὐναντίον 'but on the contrary'?

It signals a strong reversal from what was previously said [WBC]. They did what was completely opposite and endorsed Paul's actions [Lns, NIGTC].

QUESTION—What is the function of the participle ἰδόντες 'having seen'?

It is temporal [WBC; NET, NRSV]: when they saw.

QUESTION—Who is the implied actor of πεπίστευμαι 'I have been entrusted (with)'?

The implied actor is God [Alf, ICC, Lns, SSA, TH; CEV, NLT, TEV].

QUESTION—How are the nouns related in the genitive constructions τὸ εὐαγγέλιον τῆς ἀκροβυστίας 'the gospel of the uncircumcision' and τῆς περιτομῆς 'of the circumcision'?

They are genitives of connection and equivalent to 'in uncircumcision' and 'in circumcision' [ICC]. The genitives are objective. The gospel in both is the same good news [BNTC, Lns, Mor, NAC, NCBC, NIC, NIGTC, NTC, TH]. The same gospel is preached to the uncircumcised and to the circumcised [BNTC, Lns, Mor, NAC, NCBC, NIC, NIGTC, TH]. The gospel was preached to both [CEV, GW, NCV, NIV, NLT, REB, TEV]. The gospel was for them [NRSV].

2:8 for the (one) having-worked[a] in-Peter for[b] apostleship[c] of-the circumcision worked in-me also for the Gentiles,[d]

LEXICON—a. aorist act. participle of ἐνεργέω (LN 42.3) (BAGD 1.a. p. 265): 'to work' [BAGD, BNTC, Herm, LN, Mor, WBC; NASB, NIV, NLT, NRSV, REB], 'to empower' [SSA; NET]. The phrase ἐνεργήσας Πέτρῳ εἰς ἀποστολὴν 'having worked in Peter for apostleship' is translated 'he that wrought effectually in Peter to the apostleship' [KJV], 'who effectually worked for Peter in his apostleship' [NASB], 'who made Peter an apostle' [GW], 'who had sent Peter on a mission' [CEV], 'who empowered Peter for his apostleship' [NET], 'who was at work in the ministry of Peter as an apostle' [NIV], 'who worked through Peter making him an apostle' [NRSV], 'who worked through Peter for the benefit of' [NLT], 'who was at work in Peter's mission' [REB], 'God gave Peter the power to work as an apostle' [NCV], 'who empowered Peter in order that he might be an apostle' [SSA], 'who was at work in Peter as an apostle' [WBC], 'who was at work with Peter for the apostolate' [Mor], 'by God's power I was made an apostle' [TEV], 'he who worked through Peter for the apostolate' [Herm].

b. εἰς with accusative object (LN 89.57): 'for the purpose of, in order to' [LN]. See a. for translations in context. It indicates purpose or result [ICC].
c. ἀποστολή (LN 53.73) (BAGD p. 99): 'apostleship' [BNTC, LN; KJV, NASB, NET], 'to be an apostle' [LN], 'apostolate' [Herm, Mor], 'apostle' [SSA, WBC; GW, NCV, NIV, NRSV, TEV], 'mission' [CEV, REB]. The phrase ὁ...ἐνεργήσας...εἰς ἀποστολήν 'the one having worked for apostleship' is translated 'to make capable of being an apostle' [BAGD], 'the same God who worked through Peter for the benefit of (the Jews)' [NLT].
d. ἔθνος (LN 11.55): 'Gentile, nation' [LN], 'Gentiles' [BNTC, Herm, Mor, WBC; all versions except GW, NCV], 'people who are not Jewish' [GW], 'those who are not Jews' [NCV], 'Gentiles/in Gentile regions' [SSA].

QUESTION—What relationship is indicated by γάρ 'for'?
1. It indicates the effectiveness of their apostolic work is the positive proof of their apostolic commission [NIC].
2. It introduces an explanatory comment [Mor, SSA, TH]: that it is God having worked in Peter. This is a parenthetical comment [TH].

QUESTION—What is the meaning of ἀποστολή 'apostleship'?
1. It refers to the commission to be an apostle [ICC].
2. It refers to the activity of being an apostle [NIC, NTC, TNTC].

QUESTION—Who is the implied actor of ἐνεργέω 'having worked/worked'?
The implied actor is God [Alf, BNTC, Herm, ICC, Mor, NCBC, NTC, SSA, TH; CEV, NCV, NIV, NLT, REB, TEV].

QUESTION—In what way did God work in Peter and Paul?
1. God worked by calling them to be apostles [ICC, SSA; CEV, GW, NCV, NET, NRSV, TEV]. This interpretation refers to their inner experience by which they were commissioned for their work [TH]. Complex as it is, the point is that Paul was commissioned to be an apostle just as Peter was [SSA].
2. God worked through them in their ministry as apostles [NTC, TNTC; NASB, NIV, NLT, REB]. This interpretation refers to God working through them so that their ministry as apostles was successful [TH].

2:9 **and knowing[a] the grace[b] the (one) having-been-given[c] to-me,**

LEXICON—a. aorist act. participle of γινώσκω (LN 28.1, 32.16): 'to know' [LN (28.1), Mor, SSA, WBC], 'to understand' [LN (32.16); NCV], 'to perceive' [LN (32.16), SSA; KJV], 'to recognize' [BNTC, Herm; NASB, NET, NIV, NLT, NRSV, REB, TEV], 'to realize' [CEV], 'to acknowledge' [GW].
b. χάρις (LN 25.89, 88.66) (BAGD 4. p. 878): 'grace' [BNTC, Herm, LN (88.66), Mor, WBC; KJV, NASB, NCV, NET, NIV, NRSV], 'favor' [LN (25.89)], 'the message about his undeserved kindness' [CEV], 'special gift' [GW], 'gift' [NLT], 'privilege' [REB], 'special task' [TEV], 'what

God had freely/graciously (given)' [SSA]. It refers to the powers and capabilities requisite for the office [BAGD].
  c. aorist pass. participle of δίδωμι (LN 37.98, 57.71): 'to be given' [BNTC, Herm, LN (57.71), Mor, SSA, WBC; KJV, NASB, NET, NIV, NRSV], 'to be assigned, to be appointed' [LN (37.98)], 'to be bestowed' [REB]. The passive voice is also translated actively with 'God' as the subject: 'to give' [CEV, GW, NCV, NLT, TEV]. The implied actor is God [ICC, Lns, TH, WBC] or Christ [ICC].

QUESTION—Who is the implied actor of γνότες 'knowing'?
  The implied actors are James, Peter and John [BST, NIGTC, NTC, TH].

QUESTION—What relationship is indicated by γνότες 'knowing'?
  It means that the Jerusalem leaders recognized the hand of God in what happened when Paul preached among the Gentiles [Mor].

QUESTION—What is meant by τὴν χάριν 'the grace'?
  Paul had referred to having been called through God's grace in 1:15 and here the grace given to him is his apostleship to the Gentiles [NIGTC]. It refers to Paul's commission to preach [NCBC], the privilege of apostleship [NIC], his apostolic office [Herm]. It includes Paul's office, his ability, and his success [Lns]. By saying that his commission was given through grace, he refers to God's favor through which the commission was given [NCBC]. It is the grace of God or Christ when Paul was entrusted with the gospel to the Gentiles, and it may also include the manifested results of the ministry [ICC].

James[a] and Cephas[b] and John, the-(ones) seeming[c] to-be pillars,[d]

LEXICON—a. Ἰάκωβος (LN 93.158) (BAGD 3. p. 368): 'James' [BAGD, BNTC, Herm, LN, Mor, SSA, WBC; all versions].
  b. Κηφᾶς (LN 93.211) (BAGD p. 431): 'Cephas' [BAGD, BNTC, Herm, LN, Mor, WBC; GW, KJV, NASB, NET, NRSV, REB], 'Cephas/Peter' [SSA], 'Peter' [CEV, NCV, NIV, NLT, TEV].
  c. pres. act. participle of δοκέω (LN **36.7**) (BAGD 2.b. p. 202): 'to seem, to be recognized as being' [BAGD], 'reputed to be' [BNTC, Herm, WBC; NASB, NIV, REB], 'seemed to be' [Mor; KJV, NCV, TEV], 'supposed to be' [CEV], 'recognized' [GW], 'acknowledged' [NRSV]. The phrase οἱ δοκοῦντες στῦλοι εἶναι 'the ones seeming to be pillars' is translated 'those who seemed to be leaders' [LN], 'the ones whom your new teachers respect' [SSA], 'who had a reputation as' [NET], 'who were known as' [NLT].
  d. στῦλος (LN **7.45, 36.7**) (BAGD p. 772): 'pillar' [BAGD, **LN** (7.45)], 'leader' [**LN** (36.7)], 'pillars' [BNTC, Herm, Mor, WBC; KJV, NASB, NET, NIV, NLT, NRSV, REB], 'most important people' [GW], 'leaders' [NCV, TEV]. It is a figurative reference to the leaders of the Jerusalem church [BAGD, **LN** (7.45)]. This is translated 'they instruct/lead' [SSA], 'the backbone of the church' [CEV].

QUESTION—To whom does Ἰάκωβος 'James' refer?

It refers to James, the brother of Jesus [BNTC, Mor, NAC, NCBC, NIBC, NIGTC, NTC, TH, WBC]. James apparently was the leading figure at the church in Jerusalem [Herm].

QUESTION—To whom does Ἰωάννης 'John' refer?

John was the son of Zebedee [BNTC, Herm, NIBC, NIGTC, TH]. He is called 'the beloved disciple' in the gospel of John [NAC, WBC]. He was 'the disciple whom Jesus loved' [NTC].

QUESTION—What is meant by εἶναι στῦλοι 'to be pillars'?

It means that James, Peter and John were seen to be leaders among the Christians [Mor, WBC]. It is used in a figurative sense and implies that they provided support and defense [NIGTC]. The Jerusalem church regarded James, Peter, and John as the main support on which their local community of the church of God was built [BNTC]. It means that they gave stability to the church [NTC]. It is a designation for those who have responsibility resting upon them [ICC, TH]. This term was used by the Jews in reference to the teachers of the law [Lt].

gave[a] (the) right-hands of-fellowship[b] to-me and Barnabas, that we (go) to[c] the Gentiles, and they-themselves to the circumcision;

LEXICON—a. aorist act. indic. of δίδωμι (LN 57.71): 'to give' [BNTC, Herm, LN, Mor, WBC; CEV, KJV, NASB, NET, NIV, NRSV]. The phrase δεξιὰς ἔδωκαν κοινωνίας 'to give the right hands of fellowship' is translated 'to give a friendly handshake' [CEV], 'to shake hands, agreeing to be partners' [GW], 'to accept someone' [NCV], 'to accept as co-workers' [NLT], 'to accept as partners and to shake hands on it' [REB], 'to shake hands as a sign that all were partners' [TEV], 'to make a covenant as to how to share the work' [**LN** (34.42)]. Not explicit [SSA].

b. κοινωνία (LN 34.5) (BAGD 1. p. 439): 'fellowship' [BAGD, BNTC, LN, Mor, WBC; KJV, NASB, NET, NIV, NRSV], 'partnership' [Herm], not explicit [SSA; CEV, GW, NCV, NLT, REB, TEV].

c. εἰς with accusative object (LN 83.9, 84.16): 'to' [Herm, LN (84.16), Mor, SSA, WBC; NASB, NCV, NET, NIV, NLT, NRSV, REB], 'among' [LN (83.9); GW, TEV], 'for' [BNTC], '(work) with' [CEV], 'unto' [KJV].

QUESTION—How are the nouns related in the genitive construction δεξιὰς κοινωνίας 'the right hands of fellowship'?

Shaking hands was a symbol of fellowship with one another [NAC, NTC]. Clasped right hands were the sign of friendship and trust [TNTC]. Shaking hands indicated agreement [BNTC, NCBC, NIC, NIGTC, NTC], goodwill and approval [Mor]. The custom of giving the hand indicated a pledge of friendship or agreement [ICC]. It meant that they accepted Paul and Barnabas as partners [BST]. It pledged friendship and also acknowledged agreement [WBC]. The handshake was usually an expression of fellowship, but in this reference it was a formal conclusion to the agreement which follows [Herm, Lns]. Here it indicated that they were in agreement as to the mission of Paul and Barnabas [SSA]. It meant that they entered into a covenant, which is a binding agreement between two parties [TH].

QUESTION—What relationship is indicated by ἵνα 'that'?

It defines the content of the agreement that was mentioned in the previous clause [ICC, Lns, Mor, SSA].

QUESTION—What relationship is indicated by εἰς 'to'?

It expresses the goal of the activity of each group [BNTC, NCBC].
1. It points to two ethnic divisions, not geographic territories [Herm].
2. It points to geographical regions [SSA, TH]. It is likely that they intended that Paul go to Gentile territories to preach the gospel while Peter would remain in Jerusalem to work in the Jewish homeland [TH].

2:10 only[a] that we-should-remember[b] the poor,[c]

LEXICON—a. μόνον (LN **29.16**) (BAGD 2.b. p. 528): 'only' [BAGD, Herm, Mor; KJV]. This is translated 'all they asked was' [LN, WBC; NIV, REB, TEV], 'they requested only' [NET], 'and they merely urged' [SSA], 'they only asked' [CEV, NASB], 'the only thing they asked' [GW, NCV], 'the only thing they suggested was' [NLT], 'they asked only one thing' [NRSV], 'with the one qualification' [BNTC].

b. pres. act. subj. of μνημονεύω (LN **29.16**) (BAGD 1.a. p. 525): 'to remember' [BAGD, BNTC, Herm, LN, Mor, SSA, WBC; all versions except NLT, REB], 'to keep in mind' [BAGD; REB], 'to remember to help' [NLT]. It implies doing something about the needy [LN].

c. πτωχός (LN 57.53) (BAGD 1.a. p. 728): 'the poor' [BAGD, BNTC, Herm, LN, Mor, SSA, WBC; all versions except TEV], 'the needy in their group' [TEV].

QUESTION—What is meant by μόνον 'only'?

It expresses a concession [Herm, WBC]. It limits the whole clause and indicates that it contains the only qualification of the agreement already stated in general terms [ICC, NTC].

QUESTION—What is meant by μνημονεύωμεν 'we should remember'?
1. The present tense of this verb indicates that they already had been remembering the poor and were now told to continue doing so [BNTC, Herm, ICC, NCBC, NIBC, SSA; NIV]: continue to remember the poor. The apostles were requesting further help [SSA].
2. It means that they should make a practice of remembering the poor [TH, WBC]: always remember the poor. They were to continue to think about and constantly be concerned for the poor [TH]. It refers to a desired ongoing activity [WBC].
3. It means that they should not only continue to remember the poor, but that it should be a regular practice of the church to help the poor [NTC].

QUESTION—Who is referred to as τῶν πτωχῶν 'the poor'?

It refers to the Jewish Christians of Jerusalem [BNTC, Mor, NAC, NIBC, NIC, NIGTC, SSA, TH, WBC], the poor Christians in Judea [BST, NCBC, NTC], the poor among the Palestinian churches [Lns].

which also[a] I-was-diligent[b] to-do this same[c] (thing).
LEXICON—a. καί (LN 89.93) (BAGD II.6. p. 393): 'also' [BAGD, LN; KJV, NASB], 'likewise' [BAGD], 'even' [LN], 'too' [NET], not explicit [BNTC, Mor, SSA, WBC; all versions except KJV, NASB, NET]. This entire phrase is translated 'which request I have made my special concern to fulfill' [Herm].
   b. aorist act. indic. of σπουδάζω (LN **25.74**) (BAGD 2. p. 763): 'to be diligent' [BAGD, LN, Mor], 'to be eager' [BAGD, LN, WBC; all versions except KJV, NCV, REB], 'to be zealous, to make every effort' [BAGD], 'to really want' [NCV], 'to be forward' [KJV]. This is translated 'I have always made it my business' [REB], 'I have made my special concern' [Herm]. This verb is translated as an adverb modifying 'to do': 'eagerly' [BNTC], 'enthusiastically' [SSA].
   c. αὐτός (LN 58.31) (BAGD 1.h. p. 123): 'same' [LN; KJV], 'very same' [BAGD], 'very' [BNTC, Mor; GW, NASB, NET, NIV, REB, TEV], 'exactly' [SSA], not explicit [WBC; CEV, NCV, NLT, NRSV]. See a. [Herm].
QUESTION—What is the significance of the change from the plural μνημονεύωμεν 'we should remember' in the previous phrase to the singular ἐσπούδασα 'I was eager' in this phrase?
   Before Paul had the opportunity to fulfill this request he had separated from Barnabas [Alf, Herm, Lt]. Paul refers to the collection he took up a year after this conference [Lns].

DISCOURSE UNIT: 2:11–21 [NAC; CEV, GW, NASB, NCV, NIV, NLT]. The topic is the incident at Antioch [NAC], Paul corrects Peter at Antioch [CEV], Paul shows how Cephas was wrong [GW, NCV], Peter (Cephas) opposed by Paul [NASB, NIV], Paul confronts Peter [NLT].

DISCOURSE UNIT: 2:11–16 [BST, TNTC]. The topic is the clash with Peter [TNTC], Paul clashes with Peter in Antioch [BST].

DISCOURSE UNIT: 2:11–14 [GNT, Mor, NIC, NIGTC, WBC; NET, NRSV, TEV]. The topic is an incident at Antioch [NIC], conflict at Antioch [NIGTC], Paul's clash with Peter [Mor], the Antioch episode [WBC], Paul rebukes Peter [NET], Paul rebukes Peter at Antioch [GNT; NRSV, TEV].

2:11 **But when Cephas[a] came[b] to[c] Antioch,**
LEXICON—a. Κηφᾶς (LN 93.211) (BAGD p. 431): 'Cephas' [BAGD, BNTC, Herm, LN, Mor, WBC; GW, NASB, NET, NRSV, REB], 'Cephas/Peter' [SSA], 'Peter' [CEV, KJV, NCV, NIV, NLT, TEV].
   b. aorist act. indic. of ἔρχομαι (LN 15.81): 'to come' [BNTC, Herm, LN, Mor, SSA, WBC; all versions].
   c. εἰς with accusative object (LN 84.16): 'to' [BNTC, Herm, LN, Mor, SSA, WBC; all versions].

QUESTION—What relationship is indicated by δέ 'but'?
  It indicates a contrast between the unity of 2:7–10 and the confrontation of 2:11–14 [ICC, WBC] and it also continues the narrative of Paul's underlying agreement with the Jerusalem apostles [ICC, WBC]. It is intended to draw attention to Peter's inconsistent action in view of the agreement that was reached in 2:9 [NCBC]. It is transitional [Lns].
QUESTION—What relationship is indicated by ὅτε 'when'?
  It is indeterminate. No date is given as to when the incident took place [Herm, NAC, WBC].

I-opposed[a] him to (his) face,[b] because he-was-condemned. [c]
LEXICON—a. aorist act. indic. of ἀνθίστημι (LN **39.1**) (BAGD 1. p. 67): 'to oppose' [BAGD, BNTC, Herm, LN, SSA, WBC; all versions except CEV, KJV, NCV], 'to set (oneself) against' [BAGD], 'to withstand' [BAGD, Mor; KJV], 'to tell' [CEV], 'to challenge' [NCV].
  b. πρόσωπον (LN **83.38**) (BAGD 1.c.δ. p. 721): 'face' [BAGD, BNTC, Herm, LN, Mor, WBC; KJV, NASB, NCV, NET, NIV, NRSV, REB]. The phrase κατὰ πρόσωπον 'to his face' is translated 'face to face' [**LN**; CEV], 'in person' [**LN**], 'openly' [GW], 'publicly' [NLT], 'in public' [TEV], 'directly' [SSA].
  c. perf. pass. participle of καταγινώσκω (LN 30.118) (BAGD p. 409): 'to be condemned' [LN], 'to be blameworthy' [Mor], 'to be wrong' [SSA; all versions except KJV, NASB, NRSV], 'to be blamed' [KJV], 'to stand condemned' [BAGD, BNTC, Herm, WBC; NASB], 'to stand self-condemned' [NRSV].
QUESTION—What is meant by κατα πρόσωπον 'to his face'?
  It is an idiom that implies a direct encounter [NTC, WBC]. It means that Paul stood up to Peter face to face [ICC, TNTC]. As 2:14 indicates, this encounter was in public [Lns].
QUESTION—What relationship is indicated by ὅτι 'because'?
  This is the reason that Paul opposed Peter [Alf, Herm, ICC, Lns, NTC, TH, TNTC].
QUESTION—Who is the implied actor of κατεγνωσμένος ἦν 'he was condemned'?
  1. Peter condemned himself by his own actions [Alf, ICC, Lt, Mor, NCBC, NIGTC, NTC, TH]. It was obvious by what Peter did that he was in the wrong [TH].
  2. Peter was condemned by the previous action of the Jerusalem council [Lns]. Peter had placed himself among the Judaizers who had been condemned by the church council (Acts 15:13) [Lns].

2:12 **For before[a] certain[b] (persons) came[c] from[d] James, he-was-eating-together[e] with the Gentiles;**
TEXT—Instead of the plural τινας 'some persons' some manuscripts read the singular τινα 'some person'. GNT reads τινας 'some persons' with an A decision, indicating that the text is certain.

LEXICON—a. πρό with genitive object (LN 67.17) (BAGD 2. p. 702): 'before' [BAGD, BNTC, LN, Mor, SSA, WBC; KJV, NIV, TEV], 'prior' [NASB], 'until' [Herm; NCV, NET, NRSV, REB], 'afterward' [NLT]. The phrase πρὸ τοῦ γὰρ ἐλθεῖν τινας ἀπὸ Ἰακώβου 'for before certain persons came from James' is translated 'until James sent some Jewish followers' [CEV], 'until some men James had sent from Jerusalem arrived' [GW].
  b. τις (LN 92.12) (BAGD 1.a.α. p. 819): 'some person' [BAGD, LN], 'certain' [KJV], 'certain persons' [SSA], 'certain people' [Herm; NET, NRSV], 'certain men' [WBC; NASB, NIV], 'certain individuals' [BNTC], 'some men' [Mor; GW, TEV], 'some Jewish people' [NCV], 'some Jewish followers' [CEV], 'some Jewish friends' [NLT], 'some messengers' [REB].
  c. aorist act. infin. of ἔρχομαι (LN 15.81) (BAGD I.1.a.β. p. 310): 'to come' [BAGD, BNTC, Herm, LN, Mor, SSA, WBC; all versions except CEV, GW, TEV]. The reciprocal verb is used, making them the recipients of the action: 'to send, to be sent' [CEV, GW, TEV].
  d. ἀπό with genitive object (LN 90.15): 'from' [BNTC, Herm, LN, Mor, WBC; KJV, NASB, NCV, NET, NIV, NRSV, REB], 'sent by (James)' [TEV], not explicit [CEV, GW]. This preposition shows the connection of the people with James: '(friends) of' [NLT], 'who were associated with' [SSA].
  e. imperf. act. indic. of συνεσθίω (LN 23.12) (BAGD p. 788): 'to eat together' [LN, SSA], 'to eat with' [BAGD, BNTC, Herm, LN, Mor, WBC; all versions except REB], 'to take one's meals with' [REB].
QUESTION—What relationship is indicated by γάρ 'for'?
It indicates that what follows in the verse gives the reason that Peter stood condemned [ICC, Lns, WBC].
QUESTION—What is meant by ἀπό Ἰακώβου 'from James'?
  1. They were sent or commended by James [Alf, Herm, ICC, Lt, Mor, NCBC, NIC, NIGTC, TH; TEV]. James had probably invested them with some powers which they abused [Lt].
  2. They came from the church where James was the leader [Lns, NTC, SSA, TNTC, WBC]. They came from the Jerusalem church, but it does not imply that James had sent them [Lns, TNTC].
  3. They pretended to represent James [BST].

but when they-came, he-was-withdrawing^a and was-separating^b himself,

TEXT—Instead of the plural ἦλθον 'they came' some manuscripts read ἦλθεν 'he came' (see preceding TEXT). GNT reads ἦλθον 'they came' with an A decision, indicating that the text is certain.
LEXICON—a. imperf. act. indic. of ὑποστέλλω (LN **68.53**) (BAGD 1. p. 847): 'to withdraw' [BAGD, Mor, SSA; KJV, NASB], 'to draw back' [BAGD, BNTC, Herm, WBC; GW, NIV, NRSV, REB, TEV], 'to stop' [**LN**], 'to stop (doing this)' [NET], 'to stop (eating)' [NCV], 'to cease, to give up doing' [LN]. The two verbs 'he was withdrawing and was separating' are

translated as one verb: 'stopped eating with' [CEV], 'wouldn't eat with' [NLT].

b. imperf. act. indic. of ἀφορίζω (LN 63.28) (BAGD 1. p. 127): 'to separate oneself' [BAGD, BNTC, Herm, LN, Mor, WBC; KJV, NCV, NET, NIV], 'to hold oneself aloof' [BAGD; NASB, REB], 'to disassociate' [SSA], 'to not associate with' [GW], 'to not eat with' [TEV], 'to keep oneself separate' [NRSV], not explicit [CEV, NLT].

QUESTION—What is indicated by the imperfect tenses, ὑπέστελλεν 'he was withdrawing' and ἀφώριζεν 'he was separating'?

It suggests a process rather than a single action. Peter may have debated in his mind before he finally gave in to the circumcision party [NCBC]. It suggests that he changed from his former practice of eating with the Gentile Christians gradually [ICC, NIGTC, WBC] under pressure [ICC]. Some take the tenses to be incohative, he began to withdraw [Lns; NASB, NIV, REB].

fearing[a] the (ones) from[b] circumcision.[c]

LEXICON—a. pres. mid. (deponent = act.) participle of φοβέω (LN 25.252) (BAGD 1.b.α. p. 863): 'to fear' [BAGD, BNTC, LN, Mor, SSA; KJV, NASB], 'to be afraid' [Herm, WBC; all versions except KJV, NASB, NRSV], 'for fear of' [NRSV].

b. ἐκ with genitive object (LN 90.16) (BAGD 3.d. p. 235): 'from' [LN], 'in/from' [SSA], 'of' [BNTC, Herm, WBC; all versions except GW, TEV], not explicit [Mor]. This is translated 'the circumcision party' [BAGD]. See c. [GW, TEV].

c. περιτομή (LN 53.51) (BAGD 4.a. p. 653): 'circumcision' [LN]. The phrase τοὺς ἐκ περιτομῆς 'the ones from circumcision' is translated 'them which were of the circumcision' [KJV], 'those who belonged to the circumcision group' [NIV], 'the circumcised men' [Mor], 'the men of the circumcision' [Herm], 'the Jewish brothers' [SSA], 'the Jews' [WBC; CEV, NCV, REB], 'those of the circumcision' [BNTC], 'the circumcision faction' [NRSV], 'the party of the circumcision' [NASB], 'these legalists' [NLT], 'those who were pro-circumcision' [NET], 'those who were in favor of circumcising them' [TEV], 'those who insisted that circumcision was necessary' [GW]. The phrase means 'those of the circumcised who believe', i.e., the Jewish Christians [BAGD].

QUESTION—To whom does τοὺς ἐκ περιτομῆς 'the ones from circumcision' refer?

1. It refers to the Jews who had become Christians [Herm, ICC, Lt, SSA]. They were Jewish Christians who had come from the church in Jerusalem [ICC].
2. It refers to the circumcision party among the Jewish Christians [BST, NCBC, NTC, TNTC].
3. It refers to the Jewish militants [Mor, NAC, NIGTC, WBC]. Peter would not have feared fellow Jewish Christians, nor the men from James [NIGTC].

GALATIANS 2:13

2:13 And the rest[a] of-(the) Jews[b] also[c] joined-in-hypocrisy[d] (with) him,
TEXT—Some manuscripts omit καί 'also'. GNT does not discuss this variant but includes it in brackets in the text, indicating that the Committee was uncertain about including it.
LEXICON—a. λοιπός (LN 63.21) (BAGD 2.a. p. 479): 'rest' [BAGD, BNTC, LN, WBC; NASB, NET], 'other' [Herm, Mor, SSA; all versions except CEV, NASB, NET], 'remaining' [LN]. The phrase οἱ λοιποὶ Ἰουδαῖοι 'the rest of the Jews' is translated 'the others' [CEV].
b. Ἰουδαῖος (LN 93.172) (BAGD 2.d. p. 379): 'Jew' [BNTC, Herm, LN, Mor, SSA; KJV, NASB, NET, NIV, NRSV], 'Jewish believers' [WBC; NCV, TEV], 'Jewish Christians' [GW, NLT, REB], not explicit [CEV]. It refers to Jewish Christians [BAGD].
c. καί (LN 89.93): 'also' [BNTC, Herm, LN, SSA; GW, NET, TEV], 'in addition, even' [LN], 'likewise' [KJV], 'as were' [NCV], not explicit [Mor, WBC; CEV, NASB, NIV, NLT, NRSV, REB].
d. aorist pass. (deponent = act.) indic. of συνυποκρίνομαι (LN **88.229**) (BAGD p. 793): 'to join in hypocrisy' [LN; GW, NASB, NET, NIV, NRSV], 'to join in playing the hypocrite' [BAGD, BNTC, WBC], 'to act insincerely along with' [SSA], 'to dissemble with' [Mor; KJV], 'to show the same lack of principle' [REB], 'to hide one's true feelings' [CEV], 'to follow another's hypocrisy' [NLT], 'to start acting like cowards along with' [TEV], 'to commit the same hypocrisy' [Herm]. This entire phrase is translated 'So Peter was a hypocrite, as were the other Jewish believers who joined with him' [NCV].
QUESTION—To whom does οἱ λοιποὶ Ἰουδαῖοι 'the rest of the Jews' refer?
It refers to the other Jewish Christians at Antioch [Herm, ICC, Lns, Lt, Mor, NIBC, NIC, NIGTC, TNTC, WBC].

with-the-result-that[a] Barnabas also[b] was-led-astray-together[c] (with them) by-their hypocrisy.[d]
LEXICON—a. ὥστε (LN 89.52) (BAGD 2.a.α. p. 900): 'with the result that' [LN; NASB], 'as a result, so' [LN], 'so that' [BAGD, BNTC, Herm, LN, Mor, WBC; NET, NIV, NRSV], 'that' [CEV], 'insomuch that' [KJV], not explicit [SSA; GW, NCV, NLT, REB, TEV].
b. καί (LN 89.93): 'also' [LN; KJV], 'in addition' [LN], 'even' [BNTC, Herm, LN, Mor, SSA, WBC; all versions except KJV].
c. aorist pass. indic. of συναπάγω (LN **31.76**) (BAGD p. 784): 'to be led astray together' [LN], 'to be led astray (with)' [**LN**, WBC; NET, NIV, NRSV], 'to be led away' [BAGD], 'to be carried away' [BAGD, BNTC, Herm, Mor; KJV, NASB, REB], 'to be fooled' [CEV], 'to be swept along' [GW, TEV], 'to be influenced' [NCV], 'to be influenced to join (them)' [NLT], 'to be convinced' [SSA].
d. ὑπόκρισις (LN 88.227) (BAGD p. 845): 'hypocrisy' [BAGD, BNTC, Herm, LN, Mor, WBC; NASB, NET, NIV, NLT, NRSV], 'dissimulation' [KJV], not explicit [CEV, GW]. The phrase αὐτῶν τῇ ὑποκρίσει 'by the

hypocrisy of them' is translated 'by what these Jewish believers did' [NCV], 'by their cowardly action' [TEV], 'because they acted insincerely' [SSA], 'played false like the rest' [REB].

QUESTION—What is meant by συναπάγω 'to be led astray/to be carried away'?

In this verse it suggests that it was irrational emotion that caused Barnabas to desert the Gentile Christians [Herm, WBC]. It means that Barnabas not only felt the pressure to join the other Jewish Christians in separating themselves from the Gentile Christians, but he actually did join them [TH].

2:14 But when I-saw that not they-were-walking-straight[a] in-accordance-with[b] the truth[c] of-the gospel,[d]

LEXICON—a. pres. act. indic. of ὀρθοποδέω (LN **41.36**) (BAGD p. 580): 'to walk straight' [BAGD, BNTC], 'to walk a straight path' [TEV], 'to be straightforward' [BAGD; NASB], 'to live right' [LN], 'to walk rightly' [Mor], 'to comply' [SSA], 'to behave consistently' [NET], 'to act consistently' [Herm; NRSV], 'to walk uprightly' [KJV]. The phrase οὐκ ὀρθοποδοῦσιν πρὸς τὴν ἀλήθειαν 'they were not walking straight in accordance with the truth' is translated 'they were not really obeying the truth' [CEV], 'they were not following the truth' [NCV, NLT], 'they were not properly following the truth' [GW], 'they were not acting in line with the truth' [WBC; NIV], 'their conduct did not square with the truth' [REB].

b. πρός with accusative object (LN **89.9**) (BAGD III.5.d. p. 710): 'in accordance with' [BAGD, LN], 'according to' [LN; KJV], 'in line with' [**LN,** WBC; NIV, TEV], 'towards' [BNTC], 'with respect to' [Mor], 'about' [NASB], 'with' [Herm, SSA; NET, NRSV, REB], not explicit [CEV, GW, NCV, NLT].

c. ἀλήθεια (LN 72.2) (BAGD 2.b. p. 36): 'truth' [BAGD, BNTC, Herm, LN, Mor, WBC; all versions], 'genuine' [SSA].

d. εὐαγγέλιον (LN 33.217) (BAGD 1.b. p. 318): 'gospel' [BAGD, BNTC, Herm, LN, Mor, WBC; KJV, NASB, NET, NIV, NRSV, REB, TEV], 'good news' [LN, SSA; CEV, GW, NCV, NLT].

QUESTION—What relationship is indicated by ἀλλά 'but'?

It is a strong adversative which indicates that what is said in 2:14 is in a direct contrast to what was said in 2:12–13 [WBC]. It indicates the turning point where Paul turns to his own confrontation with Peter [Herm].

QUESTION—What is meant by ὀρθοποδοῦσιν 'they were walking straight'?

In this verse it refers to upright, unwavering, and sincere conduct [ICC, WBC]. To make a straight path refers either to a person's attitude or to a person's conduct [TH]. In this verse it is not a moral term, but describes 'orthodoxy' or the lack of it [Herm]. It means 'not to waver, not to stumble' [NIC].

QUESTION—What relationship is indicated by πρός 'in accordance with'?

It indicates the line of direction to be observed [Lt, NIC].

QUESTION—How are the nouns related in the genitive construction τὴν ἀλήθειαν τοῦ εὐαγγελίου 'the truth of the gospel'?

It is the doctrine of justification by grace through faith alone [BST]. It means that the truth is contained in the gospel [ICC; CEV]. It means the gospel in its integrity [Herm, Lt, NAC, WBC]. It means the truth is its substance, the divine reality it contains [Lns].

I-said[a] to-Cephas[b] in-front-of[c] all,[d]

LEXICON—a. aorist act. indic. of λέγω (LN 33.69): 'to say' [BNTC, Herm, LN, Mor, WBC; all versions except CEV, GW, NCV], 'to tell' [SSA; GW], 'to correct' [CEV], 'to speak' [NCV].

b. Κηφᾶς (LN 93.211) (BAGD p. 431): 'Cephas' [BAGD, BNTC, Herm, LN, Mor, WBC; GW, NASB, NET, NRSV, REB], 'Cephas/Peter' [SSA], 'Peter' [CEV, KJV, NCV, NIV, NLT, TEV].

c. ἔμπροσθεν with genitive object (LN 83.33) (BAGD 2.b. p. 257): 'in front of' [BNTC, LN; all versions except KJV, NASB, NRSV], 'in the presence of' [BAGD, WBC; NASB], 'before' [BAGD, Herm, LN, Mor; KJV, NRSV]. This is translated 'and when all the brothers there were present' [SSA].

d. πᾶς (LN 59.23): 'all' [LN; NASB], 'every' [LN], 'everyone' [BNTC; CEV, GW], 'them all' [Mor, WBC; KJV, NCV, NET, NIV, NRSV, TEV], 'all the others' [NLT], 'the whole congregation' [REB], 'all of them' [Herm]. See c. [SSA].

QUESTION—To whom does ἔμπροσθεν πάντων 'in front of all' refer?

Paul confronted Peter in front of all the members of the Antioch church [Alf, ICC, Mor, TH, WBC]. Paul confronted Peter in front of the whole assembly [NAC]. Paul confronted Peter in front of everyone not just the Jewish believers [BNTC].

"If[a] you being (a) Jew live[b] like-a-Gentile and not like-a-Jew,

LEXICON—a. εἰ (LN 89.30, 89.65): 'if' [BNTC, Herm, LN (89.65), Mor, WBC; KJV, NASB, NET, NRSV, REB], 'since' [LN (89.30); NLT], not explicit [SSA; CEV, GW, NCV, NIV, TEV].

b. pres. act. indic. of ζάω (LN 41.2) (BAGD 3.a. p. 336): 'to live' [BAGD, BNTC, Herm, LN, Mor, WBC; all versions], 'to behave' [LN], 'to conduct oneself' [LN, SSA]. It refers to conduct [BAGD].

QUESTION—What relationship is indicated by εἰ 'if'?

It marks the beginning of a conditional clause. This clause refers to something that is true, not hypothetical [ICC, TH, WBC].

QUESTION—What is the meaning of living ἐθνικῶς 'like a Gentile' and Ἰουδαϊκῶς 'like a Jew'?

These terms refer to living according to Gentile and Jewish customs. In this reference the focus is on Jewish dietary laws which the Jews observe, but the Gentiles do not [TH, WBC]. Paul did not follow the Jewish laws forbidding eating with Gentiles [ICC, TH]. By eating with the Gentiles, Peter was living like a Gentile [TH].

how[a] (can) you-compel[b] the Gentiles to-live-like-Jews?"[c]
LEXICON—a. πῶς (LN 92.16) (BAGD 1.c. p. 732): 'how' [BNTC, Herm, LN, WBC; CEV, GW, NET, NRSV, REB, TEV], 'what right, how dare you' [BAGD], 'how is it' [Mor; NASB, NIV], 'why' [KJV, NCV, NLT], not explicit [SSA].
- b. pres. act. indic. of ἀναγκάζω (LN 37.33) (BAGD 1. p. 52): 'to compel' [BAGD, BNTC, Herm, **LN**, WBC; KJV, NASB, NRSV], 'to force' [LN; CEV, NCV, NET, NIV, TEV], 'to constrain' [Mor], 'to cause' [SSA], 'to insist' [GW, REB], 'to make' [NLT].
- c. pres. act. infin. of Ἰουδαΐζω (LN **41.32**) (BAGD p. 379): 'to live like Jews' [Herm; all versions except KJV, NIV, NLT], 'to live as a Jew' [BAGD, LN], 'to live Jewish' [**LN**], 'to Judaize' [BAGD, BNTC, LN], 'to live according to Jewish customs' [BAGD], 'to conform to Jewish practices' [Mor], 'to become Jews' [WBC], 'to conduct themselves like Jews do' [SSA], 'to follow Jewish customs' [NIV], 'to obey the Jewish laws' [NLT], 'to live as do the Jews' [KJV].

QUESTION—What relationship is indicated by πῶς 'how'?
It expresses the emotions of surprise, displeasure, and agitation [ICC, WBC]. There is no possible answer, Peter cannot do that [Herm, Lns].

QUESTION—What is the meaning of Ἰουδαΐζω 'to live like Jews'?
It means to adopt a Jewish way of life [BNTC, ICC, NIC]. It means to become a Jew and not to just live like a Jew [Mor, WBC]. It means more than following Jewish dietary laws, it means forcing someone to become a Jewish convert who must follow the whole Torah [Herm].

QUESTION—How had Peter been compelling the Gentiles to live like Jews?
This verb is conative, meaning 'why are you trying to compel them?' [ICC, TNTC, WBC; NET, NLT, TEV]. It was not Peter's intention to compel them [Lt, TNTC]. By Peter's example he was exerting pressure on the Gentiles to live in a way that was acceptable to the Jews [ICC, Lt, NIGTC, TH].

DISCOURSE UNIT: 2:15–21 [BST, GNT, Mor, NIC, NIGTC, WBC; NET, NRSV, TEV]. The topic is Paul's address [NIC], the proposition of Galatians [WBC], justification by faith alone [BST, Mor], both Jews and Gentiles are justified by faith [NIGTC; NET], Jews, like Gentiles, are saved by faith [GNT], Jews and Gentiles are saved by faith [NRSV, TEV].

2:15 We by-nature[a] Jews and not sinners of[b] Gentiles,[c]
LEXICON—a. φύσις (LN 58.8) (BAGD 1. p. 869): 'nature' [LN], 'natural endowment, natural condition' [BAGD], 'by nature' [BNTC; KJV, NASB], 'by birth' [Herm, Mor, WBC; all versions except KJV, NASB, NCV], 'were born as' [SSA; NCV].
- b. ἐκ with genitive object (LN 63.20, 89.3, 90.16) (BAGD 3.b. p. 235): 'of' [LN (63.20), WBC; KJV], 'from' [Herm, LN (89.3, 90.16); GW, NASB], 'among' [LN (63.20)], 'like' [CEV, NLT], 'as' [SSA]. It denotes origin [BAGD]. Not explicit [BNTC, Mor; NCV, NET, NIV, NRSV, REB, TEV].

GALATIANS 2:15   69

c. ἔθνος (LN 11.37): 'Gentile' [LN]. The plural form is translated 'heathen, pagans' [LN], 'Gentiles' [Herm, SSA, WBC; CEV, KJV, NASB, NLT], 'other nations' [GW]. The phrase ἐξ ἐθνῶν ἁμαρτωλοί 'sinners of Gentiles' is translated 'Gentile sinners' [BNTC, Mor; NET, NIV, NRSV, REB, TEV], 'non-Jewish sinners' [NCV].

QUESTION—Where does Paul's speech at Antioch end?
  1. It begins and ends in 2:14 [Herm, Mor, WBC; GW, NCV, NET, NRSV, REB, TEV].
  2. It continues on to the end of 2:21 [Alf, BNTC, Lns, NAC, NTC; CEV, NASB, NIV, NLT].

QUESTION—To whom does ἡμεῖς 'we' refer?
  1. It refers to Peter and Paul [Alf, BNTC, BST]: you and I are by nature Jews.
  2. It refers to all Jewish Christians [Herm, Lns, NCBC, NIBC, NIC, NIGTC, SSA, TNTC, WBC]: we Jews are by nature Jews.

QUESTION—How are the nouns related in the genitive construction ἐξ ἐθνῶν ἁμαρτωλοί 'sinners of the Gentiles' and why are they called sinners?

The term 'sinners' was used by the Jews as a synonym for the Gentiles [BNTC, Lns, Lt, NIC, TH, WBC]: we are not Gentiles, those who are sinners. 'Gentile' indicates the type of sinners they were [BNTC, Mor; all versions except GW, KJV, NASB]: Gentile sinners, sinners like the Gentiles. Gentiles were habitual transgressors of the law and therefore were as a class called sinners [ICC], they were people who were not restrained by the laws of Moses [TNTC]. Not having the Law of Moses, the Gentiles could not achieve righteousness [Herm]. What made the Gentiles sinners, according to the Jews, was not only that they did not observe the law but also that they did not even possess it and, therefore, lacked the possibility of obtaining righteousness through it [Mor, NIC]. The Jews referred to non-Jews who were without the law as 'sinners' [NIBC].

2:16 and knowing[a] that (a) person[b] is- not -justified[c] by[d] deeds[e] of-law[f]

TEXT—Some manuscripts omit δέ 'and'. GNT does not discuss this variant but includes it in brackets in the text, indicating that the Committee had difficulty deciding whether to include it.

LEXICON—a. perf. (with pres. meaning) act. participle of οἶδα (LN 28.1): 'to know' [BNTC, Herm, LN, Mor, SSA, WBC; all versions]. This term is usually used by Paul to introduce a dogmatic position as something commonly known [NIC]. Paul is talking about basic knowledge. The knowledge that he is talking about is not knowledge that all Jews know about, but is known only by those Jews who have come to salvation through Christ [Mor].
  b. ἄνθρωπος (LN 9.1, 9.24) (BAGD 3.a.γ. p. 69): 'person' [LN (9.1), SSA, WBC; GW, NCV, NRSV, TEV], 'man' [LN (9.24), Mor; KJV, NASB, NIV], 'human being' [BNTC, Herm], 'one' [BAGD; CEV, NET, REB], 'we' [NLT].

c. pres. pass. indic. of δικαιόω (LN 34.46) (BAGD 3.a. p. 197): 'to be justified' [BAGD, BNTC, Herm, Mor, SSA, WBC; KJV, NASB, NET, NIV, NRSV, REB], 'to be put right with (someone)' [LN], 'to be made right with God' [NCV], 'to become right with God' [NLT], 'to be put right with God' [TEV], 'to be pronounced and treated as righteous, to be acquitted' [BAGD], 'to be able to please God' [CEV], 'to receive God's approval' [GW]. The passive implies that God is the subject [Lns, TH].

d. ἐκ with genitive object (LN 89.77, 90.16) (BAGD 3.f. p. 235): 'by' [BNTC, Herm, LN (90.16), Mor, WBC; all versions except GW], 'by means of' [LN (89.77)], 'by reason of, as a result of' [BAGD], 'because of' [BAGD; GW], 'because' [SSA]. It indicates the source of justification [ICC, NCBC].

e. ἔργον (LN 42.11) (BAGD 1.c.β. p. 308): 'deed' [BAGD, LN], 'act' [LN], 'works' [BNTC, Herm, Mor, WBC; KJV, NASB, NET, NRSV]. The phrase ἔργων νόμου 'deeds of law' is translated 'obeying the law' [CEV], 'obeys the Mosaic law' [SSA], 'efforts to live according to a set of standards' [GW], 'following the law' [NCV], 'observing the law' [NIV], 'doing what the law commands' [NLT], 'doing what the law requires' [REB], 'doing what the Law requires' [TEV].

f. νόμος (LN 33.55, 33.333) (BAGD 3. p. 542): 'law' [BAGD, BNTC, LN (33.333), Mor, WBC; KJV, NCV, NET, NIV, NRSV], 'Law' [Herm, LN (33.55); CEV, NASB], 'Mosaic law' [SSA], 'a set of standards' [GW], 'what the law commands' [NLT], 'what the law requires' [REB, TEV].

QUESTION—How is this clause connected with the preceding verse?
1. It is a counter-expectation of the preceding verse [ICC, Lns, NTC, SSA; all versions except KJV, NIV]: we are Jews, *yet* we know that a person is not justified by works of the Law, but through faith in Christ.
2. The preceding verse identifies 'we' in this verse [BNTC, Herm; KJV, NIV]: we who are Jews, since we know that a person is not justified by works of the Law, but through faith in Christ, even we have believed.

QUESTION—What relationship is indicated by the use of the participle εἰδότες 'knowing'?
1. It indicates the reason for the 'we believed' in the following main clause [ICC, SSA; GW, NCV, NIV, NLT, REB]: we know that a person is not justified by works of the Law, but through faith in Christ, *therefore* we have believed in Christ.
2. It indicates the basis for being a Christian in distinction from being a Jew [Herm]: we who are Jews…know that a person is not justified by works of the Law but through faith in Christ.

QUESTION—To whom does ἄνθρωπος 'person' refer?
Paul doesn't have anyone in mind here [BST, ICC, Lns, WBC].

QUESTION—What relationship is indicated by ἐκ 'by'?
It indicates the source of justification [ICC]. However, since justification is an act of God, while ἔργων νόμου are deeds of men, the preposition in effect marks its object as a conditioning clause [ICC].

QUESTION—How are the nouns related in the genitive construction ἔργων νόμου 'deeds of law' and what law is referred to?

It means the deeds or actions that the law requires [BNTC, BST]. It refers to obeying certain rules and regulations in the law [TH].
1. The law refers to the commandments that were given by God in the Mosaic law [BST, Herm, ICC, Lns, Mor, NAC, SSA, TH; CEV, NASB].
2. The law is general, meaning that they are deeds of any law [Lns, NCBC].

if[a] not through[b] faith[c] of-Jesus Christ,

LEXICON—a. ἐάν (LN 89.67): 'if' [LN]. The phrase 'if not' is translated 'but' [Herm, Mor; all versions except REB, TEV], 'only' [TEV], 'but only' [BNTC, WBC; REB], 'unless' [SSA].
b. διά with genitive object (LN 89.76, 90.8) (BAGD A.III.1.d. p. 180): 'through' [BAGD, BNTC, Herm, LN (89.76, 90.8), Mor; NASB, NRSV, REB, TEV], 'by' [LN (89.76), WBC; GW, KJV, NCV, NET, NIV, NLT], 'by means of' [LN (89.76, 90.8)], not explicit [SSA; CEV].
c. πίστις (LN 31.102) (BAGD 2.b.β. p. 663): 'faith' [BAGD, BNTC, Herm, LN, Mor; all versions except GW, NCV, NET], 'trusts' [SSA], 'believing' [GW], 'trusting' [NCV]. This is translated as an adverb: 'faithfulness' [WBC; NET].

QUESTION—What relationship is indicated by ἐάν μή 'if not'?

It refers to οὐ δικαιοῦται 'he is not justified'. He is not justified from works of law, he is not justified except through faith [ICC, Lt, SSA, WBC]. He is not justified by works of the law, but through faith in Christ [NIGTC].

QUESTION—What relationship is indicated by διά 'through'?

It indicates the agent or means of justification [Herm, ICC, Lns, Mor, NCBC, NIC, TH].

QUESITON—How are the nouns related in the genitive construction πίστεως Ἰησοῦ Χριστοῦ 'faith of Jesus Christ'?
1. The genitive is objective. The faith of Jesus Christ means faith in Jesus Christ [Alf, BNTC, ICC, Lns, Mor, NAC, NCBC, NIC, NIGTC, TH; all versions except KJV, NET]. Believing in the message about Jesus Christ is accompanied by trusting in Jesus and committing oneself to him [TH].
2. The genitive is subjective. The faith of Jesus Christ means Jesus Christ's faith [NIBC, WBC].

even/also[a] we have-believed[b] in[c] Christ Jesus,

LEXICON—a. καί (LN 89.93): 'even' [LN, SSA, WBC; KJV, NASB], 'also' [LN, Mor], 'so' [Herm; CEV, GW, NCV, NIV, NLT, REB], 'too' [TEV], 'and' [BNTC; NET, NRSV].
b. aorist act. indic. of πιστεύω (LN 31.85, 31.102) (BAGD 2.a.β. p. 661): 'to believe' [BAGD, LN (31.85)], 'to be a believer, to be a Christian' [LN (31.102)]. This verb is translated 'have believed' [BNTC, WBC; KJV, NASB, NLT, TEV], 'believed' [Mor; GW], 'trusted' [SSA], 'put our faith' [CEV], 'have put our faith' [NCV, NIV, REB], 'have come to believe' [Herm; NET, NRSV].

c. εἰς with accusative object (LN 84.22, 90.23): 'in' [BNTC, Herm, LN (90.23), Mor, WBC; all versions], 'into' [LN (84.22)], not explicit [SSA].

QUESTION—What is meant by καί ἡμεῖς 'even we'?

1. It means even we who are Jews by birth [BST, ICC, Mor, NCBC, NIC, NIGTC, SSA, WBC; KJV, NASB]. It refers to Peter and Paul [BST].
2. It means we too as well as the Gentiles [Alf, Lns, Mor, TH; TEV].

QUESTION—What is meant by ἡμεῖς εἰς Χριστὸν Ἰησοῦν ἐπιστεύσαμεν 'we have believed in Christ Jesus'?

It is an act of commitment by running to Him for refuge and calling on Him for mercy [BST]. It means to entrust or commit oneself to Christ [BNTC, ICC, NCBC, WBC].

QUESTION—What is the significance in the change from 'Jesus Christ' in the previous phrase to 'Christ Jesus' in this phrase?

1. There is no significance in the change of order [NCBC, NIC, NIGTC, WBC].
2. There is a significance in the change of order. It puts an emphasis on Jesus' messiahship [Mor].

in-order-that we-might-be-justified by[a] faith[b] of-Christ

LEXICON—a. ἐκ with genitive object (LN 89.77, 90.16) (BAGD 3.f. p. 235): 'by' [BNTC, Herm, LN (90.16), Mor; KJV, NASB, NET, NIV, NRSV], 'by means of' [LN (89.77)], 'by reason of, as a result of' [BAGD], 'because of' [BAGD; CEV, GW, NLT], 'on the basis of' [WBC], 'because' [SSA; NCV], 'through' [REB, TEV].

b. πίστις (LN 31.102) (BAGD 2.b.β. p. 663): 'faith' [BAGD, BNTC, Herm, LN, Mor; all versions except NCV, NET], 'trusted' [SSA; NCV]. This is translated as an adverb: 'faithfulness' [WBC; NET].

QUESTION—What relationship is indicated by ἵνα 'in order that'?

It indicates purpose [Mor, WBC; all versions]: we have believed in Christ Jesus in order that we might be justified.

QUESTION—Who is the one who justifies in the verb δικαιωθῶμεν 'we might be justified'?

God is the one who justifies them [Lns, SSA].

QUESTION—What relationship is indicated by ἐκ 'by'?

1. It indicates the source of justification [NCBC]: that we might be justified by Christ.
2. It indicates the means of justification [Lt, SSA]: that we might be justified by means of faith in Christ.
3. It indicates grounds for being justified [Alf]: that we might be justified because of what Christ had done.

QUESTION—How are the nouns related in the genitive construction πίστεως Χριστοῦ 'faith of Christ'?

1. The genitive is objective. The faith of Christ means faith in Christ [Mor, NCBC, SSA; all versions except NET].

2. The genitive is subjective. The faith of Christ means the faithfulness of Christ [WBC; NET], Christ's faith [NIBC].
QUESTION—What is the significance in the change from 'Jesus Christ' and 'Christ Jesus' in the previous clauses to 'Christ' in this clause?
There is no significant difference [NIGTC, WBC].

and not by^a deeds^b of-law,^c

LEXICON—a. ἐκ with genitive object (LN 89.77, 90.16) (BAGD 3.f. p. 235): 'by' [BNTC, Herm, LN (90.16), Mor; KJV, NASB, NET, NIV, NRSV, TEV], 'by means of' [LN (89.77), SSA], 'by reason of, as a result of' [BAGD], 'because of' [BAGD; GW], 'because' [NCV, NLT], 'on the basis of' [WBC], 'through' [REB], not explicit [CEV].

b. ἔργον (LN 42.11) (BAGD 1.c.β. p. 308): 'deed' [BAGD, LN], 'act' [LN], 'works' [BNTC, Herm, Mor, WBC; KJV, NASB, NET, NRSV], not explicit [CEV]. The phrase ἔργων νόμου 'deeds of law' is translated 'obeying the Mosaic law' [SSA], 'our own efforts' [GW], 'followed the law' [NCV], 'observing the law' [NIV], 'actions dictated by law' [REB], 'doing what the Law requires' [TEV], 'obeyed the law' [NLT].

c. νόμος (LN 33.55, 33.333) (BAGD 3. p. 542): 'law' [BAGD, BNTC, LN (33.333), Mor, WBC; KJV, NCV, NET, NIV, NLT, NRSV, REB], 'Law' [Herm, LN (33.55); NASB, TEV], 'Mosaic law' [SSA], not explicit [CEV, GW].

because by deeds of-law all flesh^a not shall-be-justified.^b

LEXICON—a. σάρξ (LN 8.63, 9.11) (BAGD 3. p. 743): 'flesh' [BNTC, Herm, LN (8.63), Mor; KJV, NASB], 'human being' [LN (9.11); REB], 'people' [LN (9.11); GW]. The phrase οὐ...πᾶσα σάρξ 'not...all flesh' is translated 'no person, nobody' [BAGD], 'no one' [SSA, WBC; CEV, NCV, NET, NIV, NLT, NRSV, TEV].

b. fut. pass. indic. of δικαιόω (LN 34.46) (BAGD 3.a. p. 197): 'to be justified' [BAGD, BNTC, Herm, Mor, SSA, WBC; KJV, NASB, NET, NIV, NRSV, REB], 'to be pronounced and treated as righteous, to be acquitted' [BAGD], 'to please God' [CEV], 'to receive God's approval' [GW], 'to be made right with God' [NCV], 'to be put right with God' [LN; TEV], 'to be saved' [NLT].

QUESTION—What is meant by πᾶσα σάρξ 'all flesh'?
Flesh is practically equivalent to ἄνθρωπος 'person' in the first clause of this verse [ICC, Lns]. All flesh means all mankind [NIC, NIGTC], every living being [Herm, TH, WBC]. It is used here by metonymy for a materially conditioned being [ICC]. This emphasizes the frailty of people [Lns].

DISCOURSE UNIT: 2:17–21 [TNTC]. The topic is death and the new life.

2:17 But if seeking^a to-be-justified in^b Christ we-have-been-found^c (to be) sinners^d ourselves also^e

LEXICON—a. pres. act. participle of ζητέω (LN 57.59) (BAGD 2.b.γ. p. 339): 'to seek' [BNTC, Herm, LN, Mor, WBC; KJV, NASB, NET, NIV, NLT,

REB], 'to strive for, to aim at' [BAGD], 'to desire' [SSA], 'to look for a way' [CEV], 'to search' [GW], 'to try' [NCV, TEV], 'in our effort' [NRSV].

b. ἐν with dative object (LN 89.119, 90.6) (BAGD I.5.d. p. 259): 'in' [BNTC, Herm, LN (89.119), Mor; GW, NASB, NET, NIV, NRSV, REB], 'in union with' [LN (89.119)], 'through faith in' [NLT], 'by' [LN (90.6), WBC; KJV], 'because we are united with' [SSA], 'by our union with' [TEV], not explicit [CEV]. This preposition is also translated as a clause: 'we Jews came to (Christ)' [NCV]. It indicates a very close connection [BAGD].

c. aorist pass. indic. of εὑρίσκω (LN 27.1) (BAGD 2. p. 325): 'to be found' [BAGD, BNTC, Herm, Mor, WBC; KJV, NASB, NET, NRSV, TEV], 'to be discovered' [BAGD; CEV], 'to find out' [LN; NLT], 'to turn out to be' [REB], 'to become' [SSA], not explicit [GW]. This is also translated 'it became clear' [NCV], 'it becomes evident' [NIV].

d. ἁμαρτωλός (LN 88.295): 'sinner' [BNTC, Herm, LN, Mor, WBC; all versions], 'ones who did not observe the Mosaic law' [SSA]. It is a term to designate those who are not obeying the Mosaic Law [ICC, TH].

e. καί (LN 89.93): 'also' [Herm, LN, Mor; KJV, NASB, NET], 'too' [BNTC; CEV, NCV], 'even (we Jews)' [SSA], 'as much as' [TEV], not explicit [WBC; GW, NIV, NLT, NRSV, REB].

QUESTION—What relationship is indicated by εἰ 'if'?

It is a conditional particle [Lns, WBC]. It argues as though it is a fact, although it is not [Lns].

QUESTION—What relationship is indicated by the participle ζητοῦντες 'seeking'?

It means a desire to obtain [BNTC]. It means a desire that we be justified [SSA]. It means desiring fervently or hoping [TH].

QUESTION—What is the meaning of ἐν Χριστῷ 'in Christ'?

1. It indicates the sphere within which the believer lives. It expresses the intimate fellowship between Christ and the believer [ICC, TH, WBC]. It means to be united to Christ [BST; TEV].
2. Here it must imply *because of being* in Christ [ICC, Mor, SSA].
3. Christ is the location at which justification takes place and ἐν 'in' acts as the instrument. So that justification is the result of union with Christ through faith [NIC].

QUESTION—What is meant by 'we have been found to be sinners'?

The expression 'we have been found' is the equivalent to 'to become' [ICC, SSA, TH].

1. It means that they had acknowledged that they had sinned [Lt, NIGTC, WBC; CEV, NCV, NIV, NLT, REB]. As a result of yielding to Christ they have in logic, if not in consciousness, abandoned faith in the law, and have to take their place as sinners, utterly in need of God's justifying grace [NIGTC].

2. Paul uses the Jewish term 'sinner' for being outside the law as a permissible state for Christians [ICC, TH]. This is a reference to the disregard of the statutes of the law, especially those concerning clean and unclean meats. Paul maintained that those statutes should not be kept. Paul would admit that they had become violators of the law by seeking to be justified in Christ, but denied that this was equivalent to saying that they had become actual sinners [ICC]. Sinners could mean either in the ethical sense (wrongdoers, evildoers) or, as in 2:15, a term to designate those who are outside the Law. Most probably the latter is meant here. Therefore, one may translate the expression as "to be so-called 'sinners' as much as the Gentiles are" [TH].
3. Paul draws an implication from Peter's action without accepting it as fact [Lns, NTC, TNTC]. If at the very moment while we say that we ourselves are justified by faith alone, we turn out to be preaching to others that 'faith alone' is inadequate, but that they must keep the law as well. Does that not mean that trusting in Christ is only leading them into sin? Since it is teaching them not to trust the law [TNTC].

QUESTION—To whom does αὐτοί 'ourselves' refer?
1. It refers to Paul, Peter, and all the Jewish Christians [Lns, NCBC].
2. It refers to Paul and Peter [Alf, ICC, Mor].

QUESTION—What relationship is indicated by καί 'also'?
It indicates that the Jewish Christians were sinners like the Gentile Christians [Lns, WBC].

then[a] (is) Christ a minister[b] of-sin? may-it- not -come-to-be![c]

LEXICON—a. ἆρα (LN **69.14**) (BAGD p. 104): 'then' [BAGD, BNTC, Herm, LN, Mor; NASB, NET, NRSV], 'therefore' [SSA; KJV], not explicit [NLT]. This is translated 'does that mean that' [WBC; GW, NIV, REB], 'does this mean that' [CEV, NCV, TEV].

b. διάκονος (LN 35.20) (BAGD 1.b. p. 184): 'minister' [LN, Mor, WBC; KJV, NASB], 'servant' [BNTC, Herm, LN; NRSV], 'promoter' [REB]. This is translated as a verb: 'to promote' [NIV], 'to serve' [TEV]. The phrase ἁμαρτίας διάκονος 'minister of sin' is translated 'one who encourages sin' [BAGD; NET], 'one who causes sin' [SSA], 'one who makes us sinners' [CEV], 'encourages us to sin' [GW], 'encourages sin' [NCV], 'led us into sin' [NLT].

c. aorist mid. (deponent = act.) optative of γίνομαι (LN 13.3, 13.107) (BAGD I.3.a. p. 158): 'to come to be, to happen, to occur' [LN (13.107)], 'to be' [LN (13.3)]. The phrase μὴ γένοιτο 'not may it become' is translated 'by no means' [BAGD, Mor], 'far from it' [BAGD], 'God forbid' [BAGD; KJV], 'Impossible' [BNTC], 'No, it doesn't' [CEV], 'That's unthinkable' [GW], 'May it never be' [NASB], 'No' [NCV], 'Absolutely not' [WBC; NET, NIV], 'Of course not' [NLT, REB], 'Certainly not' [NRSV], 'By no means' [TEV], 'This can never be' [Herm], not explicit [SSA].

QUESTION—How are the nouns related in the genitive construction ἁμαρτίας διάκονος 'minister of sin'?

A minister of sin promotes the interests or the cause of sin [ICC, Lns, TH].

QUESTION—What is meant by ἆρα Χριστὸς ἁμαρτίας διάκονος 'then (is) Christ a minister of sin'?

This is a rhetorical question [ICC, WBC] for which Paul gives the obvious answer [TH].

2:18 For if (the) things-which I-destroyed[a] these-things I-am-building[b] again,[c]

LEXICON—a. aorist act. indic. of καταλύω (LN 20.54) (BAGD 1.b.β. p. 414): 'to destroy' [LN, Mor, WBC; KJV, NASB, NET, NIV], 'to tear down' [BAGD, LN; CEV, GW, NLT, NRSV, TEV], 'to demolish' [BNTC], 'to pull down' [REB], 'to dissolve' [Herm]. This is translated 'those things that I gave up' [NCV], 'things which I already distrusted' [SSA].

b. pres. act. indic. of οἰκοδομέω (LN 45.1) (BAGD 2. p. 558): 'to build' [BNTC, Mor, WBC; CEV, KJV], 'to build up' [NET, NRSV, REB], 'to begin teaching' [NCV], 'to establish' [Herm]. The phrase πάλιν οἰκοδομῶ 'to build again' is translated 'to rebuild' [BAGD; GW, NASB, NIV, NLT, TEV], 'again trust' [SSA].

c. πάλιν (LN 67.55) (BAGD 1.b. p. 606): 'again' [BAGD, BNTC, Herm, LN, Mor, SSA, WBC; CEV, KJV, NCV, NET, NRSV, REB]. The meaning is included in the verb 'rebuild' [GW, NASB, NIV, NLT, TEV].

QUESTION—What relationship is indicated by γάρ 'for'?

It is to be taken with μὴ γένοιτο 'Absolutely not!' from 2:17 and introduces the reason why Paul said 'Absolutely not!' [Alf, ICC, Lt, NIGTC, WBC].

QUESTION—What is the significance of the change from the plural 'we' in 2:17 to the singular 'I' in 2:18?

The singular in 2:18 is not mainly personal. Paul used the singular to refer to anyone who behaved in the manner that he describes in this verse [NIC, NIGTC, NTC, WBC]. He tactfully applies this to himself [ICC], thus softening the rebuke [Lns]. He would be as guilty as anyone else if he did this [NTC].

QUESTION—What relationship is indicated by εἰ 'if'?

This is presented as a hypothetical case, but he really has in mind Peter's conduct [ICC] and that of certain other Jewish Christians [WBC].

QUESTION—What is meant by the metaphors καρέλυσα 'I destroyed' and οἰκοδομῶ 'I am building'?

1. This refers to his obligation to obey all of the Jewish Law [Alf, BNTC, Herm, ICC, Lt]. Peter tore this obligation down by his associating with the Gentiles, which in effect declared this obligation to be invalid [ICC].
2. This refers to the system of justification by obedience to the law [Lns, NCBC, NIC, NIGTC, TH, TNTC, WBC]. The Judaizers were rebuilding the system of human merit that Paul had destroyed [TNTC].

I-show[a] myself (a) transgressor.[b]
LEXICON—a. pres. act. indic. of συνίστημι (LN 28.49) (BAGD I.1.c. p. 790): 'to show' [LN, Mor, WBC; TEV], 'to demonstrate' [BAGD, BNTC, LN; NET, NRSV], 'to prove' [SSA; CEV, NASB, NIV, REB], 'to admit' [GW], 'to make' [KJV, NLT], 'to really be' [NCV]. The phrase ἐμαυτὸν συνιστάνω 'I show myself' is translated 'I set myself up' [Herm].
  b. παραβάτης (LN 36.29) (BAGD p. 612): 'transgressor' [BAGD, Herm, LN, Mor; KJV, NASB, NRSV], 'wrong-doer' [BNTC], 'lawbreaker' [WBC; NIV], 'one who transgresses' [SSA], 'one who breaks God's law' [NET], 'guilty' [NLT], 'one who breaks the law' [REB], 'someone who breaks the law' [TEV], '(that I was) wrong' [CEV, GW], '(I would be) wrong' [NCV].
QUESTION—How would he show himself to be a transgressor?
  1. He would be a transgressor by tearing down those things [Alf, Lns, Lt]. If he now said they were obliged to keep the law, then his former act in setting it aside was sin [Alf, Lt].
  2. He committed sin by building up those things again [BNTC, Mor, NAC, NCBC, NIBC, NIC, NTC, WBC]. Since faith in Christ is the only means of salvation, it is sin to teach that a person must keep the law in order to be saved.
  3. He is convicted as a sinner by the very law that he wants to follow [BNTC, Herm, ICC, TH, TNTC]. When someone returns to the system of salvation by works of the law, he then becomes a sinner in terms of the law [TH]. The best the law can do is to show that a person is a lawbreaker [TNTC].

2:19 For I through[a] law[b] died[c] to-law
LEXICON—a. διά with genitive object (LN 89.76, 90.8) (BAGD A.III.1.d. p. 180): 'through' [BNTC, Herm, LN (89.76, 90.8), Mor, WBC; KJV, NASB, NET, NIV, NRSV, REB], 'by means of' [LN (89.76, 90.8)], 'by' [BAGD, LN (89.76)], not explicit [NLT]. This entire phrase is translated 'it was the Law itself that killed me and freed me from its power' [CEV], 'when I tried to obey the law's standards, those laws killed me' [GW], 'it was the law that put me to death' [NCV], 'so far as the Law is concerned, however, I am dead—killed by the Law itself' [TEV]. The phrase ἐγὼ γὰρ διὰ νόμου 'for I through law' is translated 'While I was observing Mosaic law, I learned that I should not trust it in order that I might be justified' [SSA].
  b. νόμος (LN 33.55, 33.333) (BAGD 3. p. 542): 'law' [BNTC, LN (33.333), Mor, WBC; KJV, NET, NIV, NRSV, REB], 'Law' [Herm, LN (33.55); NASB], not explicit [NLT]. It refers to the Mosaic law [BAGD, SSA]. See a. [CEV, GW, NCV, TEV].
  c. aorist act. indic. of ἀποθνῄσκω (LN 23.99) (BAGD 1.b.γ. p. 91): 'to die' [BAGD, BNTC, Herm, LN, Mor, SSA, WBC; NASB, NET, NIV, NLT, NRSV, REB], 'to be dead' [KJV]. Instead of 'I' as the subject, some

translate with 'the law' as the subject: 'to kill' [CEV, GW, TEV], 'to put to death' [NCV].

QUESTION—What relationship is indicated by γάρ 'for'?

It establishes the statement of the foregoing verse [Lt]. It adds as an explanation how he had used the law in order to be done with the law [Lns].

QUESTION—What relationship is indicated by διά 'through'?

It indicates the instrument of Paul's figurative death [TH].

QUESTION—What is meant by this phrase?

1. It refers to legal relationships. The law demanded death for sinners and, in union with Christ, believers are counted as dead [Alf, BST, Lt]. Paul died to the law by being united with Christ so that when Christ died, he also was involved in Christ's death [Alf].
2. It refers to a subjective evaluation by Paul. The law caused him to realize that he must depend on God's grace and so he does not feel that the law has any claim on him [ICC, Lns, NCBC, NIC, NIGTC, TH, TNTC]. Paul died to the law he lived under as a Pharisee in the sense that he no longer had any relation to it and it had no claim on him or control over him [ICC].

in-order-that I-might-live[a] to-God.

LEXICON—a. aorist act. subj. of ζάω (LN 23.88) (BAGD 2.a. p. 336; 3.b. p. 337): 'to live' [BAGD, LN, WBC; GW, KJV, NASB, NET, NRSV], 'to live for (someone)' [BAGD, BNTC, Herm, Mor, SSA; CEV, NCV, NIV, NLT, REB, TEV].

QUESTION—What relationship is indicated by ἵνα 'in order that'?

It indicates the purpose of his death to law [Herm, ICC, SSA, TH].

QUESTION—What is the meaning of θεῷ ζήσω 'I might live to God'?

It refers to a life under the control of God [NCBC]. It means to live in accordance with God's will [TH]. It means no longer living for self, but living as God wants a person to live [NTC].

I-am-crucified-together-with[a] Christ;

LEXICON—a. perf. pass. indic. of συσταυρόω (LN 20.78) (BAGD 2. p. 795): 'to be crucified together with' [BAGD, LN], 'to be crucified with' [BNTC, Herm, Mor, SSA, WBC; all versions except CEV, NCV, TEV], 'to be nailed to the cross with' [CEV], 'to be put to death on the cross with' [NCV], 'to be put to death with' [TEV]. Note: in the following versions this phrase occurs in 2:20 [KJV, NASB, NCV, NET, NIV, REB].

QUESTION—Who is the actor of συνεσταύρωμαι 'I have been crucified'?

It is implied that the Law put Christ to death [TH].

QUESTION—In what way was Paul crucified with Christ?

1. It refers to his objective relationship to the law [BNTC, NAC, WBC]. By his death, Christ brought the reign of Law to an end, and Paul's fellowship with Christ made him free from the law [ICC].

GALATIANS 2:19

2. It refers to his subjective relationship to his former life [Lns, NIGTC, NTC]. As Christ was crucified physically, so Paul was crucified spiritually and escaped from the dominion of law and sin [Lns].

2:20 **and I-live[a] no-longer[b] (as) I, but Christ lives in[c] me;**

LEXICON—a. pres. act. indic. of ζάω (LN 23.88) (BAGD 2.a. p. 336): 'to live' [BAGD, LN]. The phrase ζῶ δὲ οὐκέτι ἐγώ 'I live no longer as I' is translated 'I live, but no longer I' [Mor], 'No longer do I live' [WBC], 'I no longer live' [GW, NIV], 'I do not live anymore' [NCV], 'I myself no longer live' [NLT], 'I live; yet not I' [KJV], 'it is no longer I who live' [Herm; NASB, NET, NRSV, TEV], 'it is no longer I that lives' [BNTC], 'no longer am I controlling myself' [SSA], 'I have died' [CEV], 'the life I now live is not my life' [REB].
  b. οὐκέτι (LN 67.130) (BAGD 1. p. 592): 'no longer' [BAGD, BNTC, Herm, LN, Mor, SSA, WBC; GW, NASB, NET, NIV, NLT, NRSV, TEV], not explicit [KJV, REB]. See a. [CEV, NCV].
  c. ἐν with dative object (LN 83.13, **89.119**) (BAGD I.5.a, d. p. 259): 'in' [BAGD, BNTC, Herm, LN (83.13, **89.119**), Mor, WBC; all versions]. It indicates a close personal relationship [BAGD]. The phrase δὲ ἐν ἐμοὶ Χριστός 'but Christ lives in me' is translated 'but Christ is controlling me internally' [SSA].

QUESTION—What relationship is indicated by the initial δέ 'and'?
  It is continuative [ICC, Lns, NIC, TH, WBC]: I am crucified with Christ and I live no longer. It indicates that what follows is a further explanation of the previous verse [ICC].

QUESTION—In what sense does he no longer live?
  1. When it refers to his objective relationship to the law. Under the law it was 'I' who lived, and since he is no longer under law, that 'I' no longer lives [BNTC, ICC, TH].
  2. When it refers to his subjective relationship to his former life. He has dethroned his self so that he will not say that he lives any longer [NIGTC]. When he was crucified with Christ, he was crucified to the world and all the passions of the sinful 'I' [Herm]. He is no longer controlling his own life [SSA].

QUESTION—What relationship is indicated by δέ 'but' in the final clause?
  It is adversative. It contrasts the jurisdiction of Christ in a believer's life to that of one's ego [WBC]. It introduces the positive correlative to a preceding negative [ICC].

QUESTION—In what sense does Christ live ἐν 'in' him?
  Paul lives in such intimate fellowship with Christ that Paul considers Christ to be resident in him, imparting impulse and power, transforming him morally, and working through him [ICC]. Christ is controlling him internally [SSA].

and (that) which now I-live[a] in (the) flesh,[b]
> LEXICON—a. pres. act. indic. of ζάω (LN 23.88) (BAGD 2.a. p. 336): 'to live' [BAGD, LN]. The phrase ὃ δὲ νῦν ζῶ ἐν σαρκί 'that which now I live in the flesh' is translated 'the life which I now live in the flesh' [KJV, NASB], 'the life I now live in the flesh' [NRSV], 'the life I now live in the body' [WBC; NET], 'the life I live in the body' [NIV], 'I live my life in this earthly body' [NLT], 'the/this life I now live' [GW, TEV], 'I still live in my body' [NCV], 'now (I live)' [CEV], 'whatever I do now' [SSA], 'my present mortal life' [REB], 'the life I now live in the flesh' [BNTC], 'what I now live in the flesh' [Herm, Mor].
> b. σάρξ (LN 8.4, 8.63) (BAGD 5. p. 744): 'flesh' [BNTC, Herm, LN (8.63), Mor; KJV, NASB, NRSV], 'body' [LN (8.4), WBC; NCV, NET, NIV], 'earthly body' [NLT], 'physical body' [LN (8.4)], not explicit [CEV, GW, TEV]. This noun is also translated as an adjective 'mortal (life)' [REB]. It relates to human life [BAGD, SSA]. It has the sense of 'the mortal body' [NIGTC, WBC].

QUESTION—What relationship is indicated by δέ 'and'?
> It is continuative [ICC, WBC]. It explains why he could say that he was no longer living in that he did not have an independent life [ICC, TH]. He explains what he meant by 'Christ lives in me' [Herm].

QUESTION—What relationship is indicated by ὅ 'that/what'?
> It refers to 'life' [ICC, WBC; GW, KJV, NASB, NET, NIV, NRSV, TEV]. It limits and qualifies the idea of life [Lt].

QUESTION—What relationship is indicated by νῦν 'now'?
> It marks the transition from his old life [ICC, NCBC]. It points to the Christian existence in contrast to the pre-Christian existence [Alf, Herm, Lt, WBC].

QUESTION—What relationship is indicated by ἐν 'in'?
> It indicates the sphere in which the life is lived [ICC].

I-live[a] in/by[b] faith/faithfulness,[c] the-(faith/faithfulness) of-the Son of-God
TEXT—Instead of τοῦ υἱοῦ τοῦ θεοῦ 'of the Son of God' some manuscripts read τοῦ θεοῦ καὶ Χριστοῦ 'of God and Christ'. GNT reads τοῦ υἱοῦ τοῦ θεοῦ 'of the Son of God' with an A decision, indicating that the text is certain.
> LEXICON—a. pres. act. indic. of ζάω (LN 23.88) (BAGD 2.a. p. 336): 'to live' [BAGD, BNTC, Herm, LN, Mor, WBC; all versions except REB], '(my life) is lived' [REB], not explicit [SSA].
> b. ἐν with dative object (LN 13.8, 83.13, 89.76, 90.10): 'in' [Herm, LN (13.8, 83.13), Mor], 'by' [BNTC, LN (89.76, 90.10), WBC; all versions except NET], 'by means of' [LN (89.76)], 'because of' [NET], not explicit [SSA].
> c. πίστις (LN 31.85, 31.102) (BAGD 2.b.β. p. 663): 'faith' [BAGD, BNTC, Herm, LN (31.85, 31.102), Mor, WBC; all versions except GW, NET,

NLT], 'faithfulness' [NET]. This noun is also translated as a verb: 'to believe' [GW], 'to trust' [SSA; NLT].

QUESTION—How are the nouns related in the genitive construction τῇ τοῦ υἱοῦ 'the (faith/faithfulness) of the Son'?
1. The Son is the object of faith [NAC, SSA; all versions except NET]: faith directed toward the Son of God.
2. Faithfulness is an attribute of the Son [NET]: the faithfulness exercised by the Son of God.

QUESTION—What relationship is indicated by ἐν 'in/by'?
1. It indicates the means by which he lives [BNTC, NAC, WBC; all versions except NET]: I live by having faith in the Son of God.
2. It indicates the sphere in which he lives [Alf, ICC, Lt, NCBC]: I live in the element of faith in the Son of God.
3. It indicates the reason he lives [NET]: I live because of the faithfulness of the Son of God.

the (one) having-loved[a] **me and having-given-over**[b] **himself for**[c] **me.**

LEXICON—a. aorist act. participle of ἀγαπάω (LN 25.43) (BAGD 1.b.α. p. 4): 'to love' [BAGD, BNTC, Herm, LN, Mor, SSA, WBC; all versions].

b. aorist act. participle of παραδίδωμι (LN 57.77) (BAGD 1.b. p. 615): 'to give over' [LN], 'to hand over' [BAGD, LN], 'to give' [BNTC, Herm, Mor, WBC; all versions except GW], 'to die (voluntarily)' [SSA], 'to take the punishment (for my sins)' [GW].

c. ὑπέρ with genitive object (LN 90.36) (BAGD 1.a.ε. p. 838): 'for' [BAGD, BNTC, Herm, LN, Mor, WBC; all versions except NCV], 'for the sake of, on behalf of' [LN], 'instead of' [SSA]. The phrase ὑπὲρ ἐμοῦ 'for me' is translated 'to save me' [NCV].

QUESTION—Who is the subject of ἀγαπήσαντός 'having loved'?
All take the subject to be the Son of God [Herm, SSA, WBC; all versions]. Either God or Christ may be the subject [NIGTC].

QUESTION—What relationship is indicated by ὑπέρ 'for'?
1. It indicates substitution [Lns, SSA]: he gave himself to die in my place. He died instead of me [SSA].
2. It indicates for the benefit of the person [Herm, TH]: he gave himself to die for my sake.

2:21 **I-do- not -set-aside**[a] **the grace**[b] **of-God;**

LEXICON—a. pres. act. indic. of ἀθετέω (LN 31.100, 76.24) (BAGD 1.a. p. 21): 'to set aside' [BAGD, LN (31.100); NET, NIV], 'to reject' [LN (31.100, 76.24); GW, TEV], 'to declare invalid' [BAGD], 'to nullify' [BAGD, BNTC, Herm, Mor, WBC; NASB, NRSV, REB], 'to frustrate' [KJV], 'to ignore/dismiss' [SSA], 'to turn one's back on' [CEV], 'to go against' [NCV], 'to treat as meaningless' [NLT].

b. χάρις (LN 25.89, 88.66) (BAGD 3.b. p. 878): 'grace' [BAGD, BNTC, Herm, Mor, WBC; all versions except CEV, GW], 'favor, good will' [LN

(25.89)], 'kindness' [LN (88.66); CEV, GW]. The genitive χάριν τοῦ θεοῦ 'grace of God' is translated 'that which God graciously did' [SSA].

QUESTION—What is Paul denying when he said that he did not set aside the grace of God?

There is an implication that this charge was brought against Paul [Herm, ICC, NIC]. Paul denies that his teachings amount to setting aside God's grace in salvation [Herm]. He does not reject God's grace when he rejects the Law as the instrument of justification [NIC, TH]. He would be setting aside God's grace if he did follow the Jewish regulations concerning fellowship with the Gentiles in order to seek acceptance by God [NTC].

QUESTION—How are the nouns related in the genitive construction χάριν τοῦ θεοῦ 'grace of God'?

1. This refers to God's grace in connection with providing justification through faith in Christ [BST, Herm, Lns, Lt, Mor, TH, TNTC]. God's grace was shown in the death of Christ [Lt].
2. This refers to God's grace in giving the law to the Jews [ICC, WBC].

for if righteousness[a] (is) through[b] law,[c]

LEXICON—a. δικαιοσύνη (LN 34.46) (BAGD 3. p. 197): 'righteousness' [BAGD, BNTC, Mor, WBC; KJV, NASB, NET, NIV, REB], 'justification' [Herm; NRSV]. This is translated 'how God puts people right with himself' [LN], 'make us right with God' [NCV], 'God justifies a person' [SSA], 'be acceptable to God' [CEV], 'receive God's approval' [GW], 'be saved' [NLT], 'be put right with God' [TEV].

b. διά with genitive object (LN 89.76, 90.8): 'through' [BNTC, Herm, LN (89.76, 90.8), Mor, WBC; NASB, NET, NIV, NRSV, TEV], 'by means of' [LN (89.76, 90.8)], 'by' [KJV, REB], 'by obeying' [CEV, GW], 'by keeping' [NLT], 'because he obeys' [SSA], not explicit [NCV].

c. νόμος (LN 33.55, 33.333) (BAGD 3. p. 542): 'law' [BNTC, LN (33.333), Mor, SSA, WBC; KJV, NCV, NET, NIV, NLT, NRSV, REB], 'Law' [Herm, LN (33.55); CEV, NASB, TEV], 'laws' [GW]. It refers to the law of Moses [BAGD].

QUESTION—What relationship is indicated by γάρ 'for'?

It introduces an explanatory sentence that supports Paul's statement of denial [WBC]. It justifies his claim [Alf].

QUESTION—What relationship is indicated by εἰ 'if'?

This indicates a conditional clause which states the opposite of what Paul had written in 2:16 [Herm]. It makes a condition that is clearly what Paul regards as contrary to the truth [ICC, NTC].

QUESTION—Does δικαιοσύνη 'righteousness' refer to an ethical or forensic righteousness?

It is forensic righteousness [ICC]. It is both forensic and ethical righteousness [WBC].

QUESTION—What relationship is indicated by διά 'through'?

It indicates the means by which a person is justified [TH].

then[a] Christ died[b] in-vain.[c]

LEXICON—a. ἄρα (LN 89.46) (BAGD 3. p. 103): 'then' [BAGD, BNTC, LN, Mor, SSA, WBC; all versions except CEV, NIV, TEV], 'consequently' [LN], 'as a result' [BAGD, LN], 'it means that' [TEV], not explicit [Herm; CEV, NIV].
  b. aorist act. indic. of ἀποθνῄσκω (LN 23.99): 'to die' [LN; CEV, NLT], 'died' [BNTC, Herm, Mor, SSA, WBC; NASB, NET, NIV, NRSV, REB, TEV], 'to be dead' [KJV]. This is translated as a noun: '(Christ's) death' [GW, NCV].
  c. δωρεάν (LN **89.63**) (BAGD 3. p. 210): 'in vain' [BAGD, Herm; KJV], 'to no purpose' [BAGD, BNTC], 'for no purpose' [**LN**], 'without purpose' [LN], 'for nothing' [WBC; NET, NIV, NRSV, REB, TEV], 'needlessly' [Mor; NASB], 'unnecessarily' [SSA], 'useless' [CEV, NCV], 'pointless' [GW], 'no need' [NLT].

QUESTION—What relationship is indicated by ἄρα 'then'?

This indicates the result that would occur if righteousness was obtained through the law instead of through Christ's death [ICC]. In that case, Christ's death was needless [Alf, Lt].

DISCOURSE UNIT: 3:1–29 [REB]. The topic is the freedom of faith.

DISCOURSE UNIT: 3:1–18 [WBC]. The topic is righteousness apart from the law: against legalism.

DISCOURSE UNIT: 3:1–14 [GNT; CEV, GW, NASB, NCV, NET, NIV, NLT, NRSV, TEV]. The topic is law or faith [GNT; NRSV, TEV], faith is the only way [CEV], God approves of those who believe [GW], faith brings righteousness [NASB], blessings come through faith [NCV], justification by law or by faith? [NET], faith or observance of the law [NIV], the law and faith in Christ [NLT].

DISCOURSE UNIT: 3:1–9 [BST]. The topic is the folly of the Galatians.

DISCOURSE UNIT: 3:1–6 [NIC, NIGTC, TNTC]. The topic is introduction [TNTC], the primacy of faith over love [NIGTC], an appeal to experience [NIC].

DISCOURSE UNIT: 3:1–5 [Mor, NAC, NCBC]. The topic is the Galatians' own experience [Mor, NCBC], the argument from conversion [NAC].

3:1 Oh[a] foolish[b] Galatians,

LEXICON—a. ὦ (LN **91.14**) (BAGD 1. p. 895): 'O' [BAGD, **LN**, Mor; KJV], 'Oh' [NLT], not explicit [BNTC, Herm, **LN**, SSA, WBC; all versions except KJV, NLT].
  b. ἀνόητος (LN **32.50**) (BAGD 1. p. 70): 'foolish' [BAGD, BNTC, Herm, **LN,** Mor, WBC; all versions except CEV, GW, REB], 'without understanding' [LN], 'unintelligent' [BAGD], 'irrational' [SSA], 'stupid' [CEV, GW, REB]. They were not using their mental or spiritual powers

[TH]. It is not saying that they were naturally stupid, but that they failed to use their powers of perception [ICC]. They did not use their mental power as they should [NTC]. They acted thoughtlessly [Lns]. This means 'mindless' and refers to their lack of spiritual perception [Mor].

who has bewitched[a] you,
LEXICON—a. aorist act. indic. of βασκαίνω (LN **53.98, 88.159**) (BAGD 1. p. 137): 'to bewitch' [BAGD, BNTC, Herm, **LN** (53.98, 88.159), Mor, WBC; KJV, NASB, NET, NIV, NRSV, REB], 'to practice magic on' [LN (53.98)], 'to delude' [SSA], 'to put an evil spell on' [CEV], 'to put under an evil spell' [GW], 'to cast an evil spell on' [NLT], 'to put a spell on' [TEV], 'to trick' [NCV], 'to deceive' [**LN** (88.159)], 'to beguile' [LN (88.159)].

QUESTION—What is meant by ἐβάσκανεν 'bewitched'?
Paul's metaphor is taken from the popular belief in the power of the evil eye [Herm, Lt, NAC, NIBC, NIGTC, SSA, WBC]. In this verse Paul is using the word to mean 'to pervert', 'to confuse the mind', 'to lead astray' [ICC, TH, WBC]. Probably they were acting like they had been bewitched by a Judaizer who got them to believe that faith in Christ must be supplemented by Mosaic ritualism [NTC].

(you) to-whom in-front-of[a] (your) eyes[b] Jesus Christ has-been-portrayed[c] crucified?[d]
LEXICON—a. κατά with accusative object (LN **83.34**) (BAGD II.1.b. p. 406): 'in front of' [LN], 'before' [BAGD, BNTC, Herm, LN, Mor, WBC; KJV, NASB, NET, NIV, NRSV, REB, TEV]. The phrase οἷς κατ' ὀφθαλμούς 'to whom in front of the eyes' is translated 'before whom' [**LN**], 'before whose eyes' [BNTC, Herm, Mor, WBC; KJV, NASB], 'before your eyes' [NET], 'before your very eyes' [NIV, TEV], 'it was before your eyes that' [NRSV], 'you before whose eyes' [REB], not explicit [SSA; CEV, GW, NCV, NLT].
  b. ὀφθαλμός (LN 8.23) (BAGD 2. p. 600): 'eye' [BAGD, BNTC, Herm, LN, Mor, WBC; KJV, NASB, NET, NIV, NRSV, REB, TEV], not explicit [SSA; CEV, GW, NCV]. This noun is also translated as a verb: 'to see' [NLT].
  c. aorist pass. indic. of προγράφω (LN **33.191**) (BAGD 2. p. 704): 'to be portrayed' [BAGD, **LN**], 'to be described vividly' [LN], 'to be vividly portrayed' [Herm; NET], 'to be clearly portrayed' [WBC; NIV], 'to be openly portrayed' [BNTC], 'to be publicly portrayed' [NASB], 'to be placarded' [Mor], 'to be publicly exhibited' [NRSV], 'to be openly displayed' [REB], 'to be evidently set forth' [KJV], 'to be clearly described' [GW], 'to be told very clearly' [NCV]. The passive form is also translated actively with 'Paul' as the subject: 'I clearly explained to you' [SSA], 'I told you exactly how' [CEV]; with 'the Galatians' as the subject: 'you had a clear description of' [TEV], 'you used to see the

meaning of...as clearly as though I had shown you a signboard with a picture' [NLT].

d. perf. pass. participle of σταυρόω (LN 20.76) (BAGD 1. p. 765): 'to be crucified' [BAGD, BNTC, Herm, LN, Mor, WBC; KJV, NASB, NET, NIV, NRSV], 'to die on the cross' [SSA], 'to be nailed to a cross' [CEV], '(was openly displayed) on the cross' [REB], 'the death (of Jesus Christ) on the cross' [NCV, TEV], '(Christ) dying on the cross' [NLT]. This verb is also translated as a noun: '(Christ Jesus') crucifixion' [GW].

QUESTION—What is meant by Jesus being προεγράφη 'openly portrayed' before them?

1. This is a metaphor using the figure of posting a public announcement [ICC, Lns, Lt, Mor, NAC, NCBC, NIC, NIGTC, NTC, TH, WBC]. The expression is metaphorical and describes the practice of making public announcements by means of bills or posters [Lt, Mor]. In this case the announcement is 'the death of Jesus Christ on the cross' [TH].

2. This is a metaphor referring to the drawing of a picture in public [Herm; NASB, NET, NIV, NLT, NRSV]. One of the goals of the ancient orator was to deliver his speech so vividly and impressively that his listeners imagined the matter to have happened right before their eyes. Paul spoke in this way in his initial efforts to proclaim the gospel of Jesus Christ crucified to them [Herm].

QUESTION—What is indicated by the perfect participle ἐσταυρωμένος 'crucified'?

The perfect participle means literally 'having been crucified.' The perfect participle expresses an existing permanent result of the past fact of crucifixion [ICC, Lns, Mor, NAC, NCBC, TH, WBC]. The perfect participle indicates that Paul did not explain the process of Christ's crucifixion (the physical details) [SSA], but he explained its value [NTC], its benefits [BST], or its lasting results [ICC].

3:2 This only do-I-wish[a] to-learn[b] from[c] you:

LEXICON—a. pres. act. indic. of θέλω (LN 25.1) (BAGD 1. p. 355): 'to wish' [BAGD, LN, Mor], 'to want' [BAGD, BNTC, Herm, LN, WBC; CEV, GW, NASB, NET, NRSV], 'to desire' [BAGD, LN, SSA], 'would like' [NIV], 'would' [KJV]. This entire phrase is translated 'Tell me this one thing' [NCV, TEV], 'Let me ask you this one question' [NLT], 'Answer me one question' [REB].

b. aorist act. infin. of μανθάνω (LN **27.12**) (BAGD 3. p. 490): 'to learn' [BNTC, Herm, LN, Mor, WBC; GW, KJV, NET, NIV, NRSV], 'to find out' [BAGD; NASB], 'to know' [CEV], not explicit [SSA; NCV, NLT, REB, TEV].

c. ἀπό with genitive object (LN 90.15) (BAGD IV.2.b. p. 87): 'from' [BAGD, BNTC, Herm, LN, Mor, WBC; GW, NASB, NET, NIV, NRSV], 'of' [KJV], not explicit [SSA; CEV, NCV, NLT, REB, TEV].

QUESTION—What is meant by τοῦτο μόνον 'this only'?

The implication of 'only' is that an answer to the question about to be asked would itself be a decisive argument [ICC, NIC]. It indicates the one thing that is necessary for making his point [Mor, WBC]. If they conceded this point, they had conceded Paul's case. In view of their experience, they had no other choice but to agree that they had received the Spirit by faith and the ground would then be taken away from the judaizing argument [NIGTC]. Paul does not mention all the other grounds on which he might rest his argument [Alf].

by[a] deeds[b] of-law[c] did-you-receive[d] the Spirit[e]

LEXICON—a. ἐκ with genitive object (LN 89.77, 90.12) (BAGD 3.f. p. 235): 'by' [BNTC, Herm, LN (90.12); all versions], 'by means of' [LN (89.77)], 'by reason of' [BAGD], 'because of' [BAGD, SSA], 'as a result of' [BAGD, LN (90.12)], 'on the basis of' [WBC], 'from' [Mor].

b. ἔργον (LN 42.11) (BAGD 1.c.β. p. 308): 'deed' [BAGD, LN], 'act' [LN], 'works' [BNTC, Herm, Mor, WBC; KJV, NASB, NET, NRSV]. The phrase ἔργων νόμου 'deeds of law' is translated 'obeying the Law of Moses' [CEV], 'efforts to live according to a set of standards' [GW], 'following the law' [NCV], 'observing the law' [NIV], 'keeping the law' [NLT, REB], 'doing what the Law requires' [TEV], 'obeys the Mosaic law' [SSA].

c. νόμος (LN 33.55, 33.333) (BAGD 3. p. 542): 'law' [BAGD, BNTC, LN (33.333), Mor, WBC; KJV, NCV, NET, NIV, NLT, NRSV, REB], 'Law' [Herm, LN (33.55); NASB], 'Mosaic law' [SSA], 'Law of Moses' [CEV]. This is translated 'a set of standards' [GW], 'what the Law requires' [TEV]. See this word at 2:16.

d. aorist act. indic. of λαμβάνω (LN 57.125): 'to receive' [BNTC, Herm, LN, Mor, SSA, WBC; all versions except CEV], 'to be given' [CEV].

e. πνεῦμα (LN 12.18) (BAGD 5.d.α. p. 677): 'Spirit' [BAGD, BNTC, Herm, LN, Mor, WBC; all versions except CEV, NLT, TEV], 'Holy Spirit' [LN, SSA; NLT], 'Spirit of God' [LN], 'God's Spirit' [CEV, TEV].

QUESTION—What relationship is indicated by ἐξ 'by'?

It indicates the source or basis for justification [Lns, WBC]. It expresses the means [SSA, TH].

QUESTION—How are the nouns related in the genitive construction ἔργων νόμου 'deeds of law'?

It means doing what the law requires [BST, SSA, TH; CEV, NIV, NLT, REB, TEV].

QUESTION—To what does πνεῦμα ἐλάβετε 'did you receive the Spirit' refer?

Paul assumes they have all received the Holy Spirit [BST, NCBC, NIGTC, WBC]. The verb 'receive' points to the truth that the Spirit is given to believers, not acquired as a result of some merit they possessed [Mor]. They received the Spirit into their hearts at the beginning of their Christian lives

[ICC, Lns, SSA], when they heard and believed the gospel [NIGTC]. It refers both to their initiation into the Christian faith and to their reception of the gifts of the Spirit which were signs of the Spirit's presence in them [ICC, TH] as shown by the reference to mighty works in 3:5 [ICC].

or by[a] (the) hearing[b] of-faith?[c]

LEXICON—a. ἐκ with genitive object (LN 89.77, 90.12) (BAGD 3.f. p. 235): 'by' [BNTC, Herm, LN (90.12); all versions except NCV, NLT], 'by means of' [LN (89.77)], 'by reason of' [BAGD], 'because' [BAGD, SSA; NCV], 'as a result of' [BAGD, LN (90.12)], 'from' [Mor], 'on the basis of' [WBC], not explicit [NLT].

b. ἀκοή (LN 24.52) (BAGD 2.b. p. 31): '(the) hearing' [BNTC, LN, Mor; KJV, NASB]. This noun is also translated as a verb: 'to hear' [SSA, WBC], 'to hear (the Good News)' [NCV], 'to hear (the gospel)' [TEV], 'to hear (about Christ)' [CEV, NLT]. The phrase ἐξ ἀκοῆς πίστεως 'by the hearing of faith' is translated 'as the result of preaching which demanded only faith' [BAGD], 'by believing the gospel message' [REB], 'by believing what you heard' [GW, NET, NIV, NRSV], 'by the proclamation of faith' [Herm].

c. πίστις (LN 31.85, 31.102) (BAGD 2.d.α. p. 663): 'faith' [BAGD, BNTC, Herm, LN (31.85, 31.102), Mor; KJV, NASB]. This noun is also translated as a verb: 'to believe' [WBC; TEV], 'to trust' [SSA], 'to believe (what you heard)' [GW, NET, NIV, NRSV], 'to believe (the Good News)' [NCV], 'to believe (the gospel message)' [REB], 'to believe (the message about Christ)' [NLT], 'to have faith (in him)' [CEV].

QUESTION—What is meant by ἀκοῆς πίστεως 'the hearing of faith'?

1. 'Faith' refers to the Galatians' response in faith to what they heard preached [BST, ICC, Lt, Mor, NAC, NCBC, NIC, NTC, TH, TNTC; all versions except KJV].
2. 'Faith' refers to the content of what they heard preached [Alf, Herm, WBC].

3:3 Are-you so[a] foolish,[b]

LEXICON—a. οὕτως (LN 78.4) (BAGD 3. p. 598): 'so' [BAGD, BNTC, Herm, LN, Mor, SSA, WBC; all versions except GW, NCV, NLT], 'that' [GW]. This phrase is translated 'Have you lost your senses?' [NLT], 'That is foolish' [NCV].

b. ἀνόητος (LN 32.50) (BAGD 1. p. 70): 'foolish' [BAGD, BNTC, Herm, LN, Mor, WBC; KJV, NASB, NCV, NET, NIV, NRSV, TEV], 'without understanding' [LN], 'unintelligent' [BAGD], 'stupid' [CEV, GW, REB]. This adjective is also translated as an adverb: '(to act so) irrationally' [SSA]; as a verb phrase: 'to lose one's senses' [NLT].

QUESTION—What is meant by οὕτως ἀνόητοι 'so foolish'?

Οὕτως 'so' suggests the degree of foolishness and it points to that which follows in 3b-c [Lns, Lt]. They are so foolish because they would be contradicting themselves when they come under the Torah, as they are planning (see 4:21) [Herm]. The repetition of ἀνόητοι 'foolish' connects 3:1 and 3:3 and makes it clear that the Galatians' foolishness is not related to the past but to what they are doing now [SSA]. The question expresses unbelief on the part of Paul. He can't believe that the Galatians can be that foolish [TH].

having-begun[a] in-(the) Spirit[b]/spirit[b] are-you-ending[c]/are-you-being-completed[c] now[d] in-flesh?[e]

LEXICON—a. aorist mid. (deponent = act.) participle of ἐνάρχομαι (LN **68.3**) (BAGD p. 262): 'to begin' [BNTC, Herm, **LN**, WBC; GW, KJV, NASB, NCV, NET, NIV, TEV], 'to make a beginning' [BAGD, Mor], 'to commence' [LN], 'to start' [CEV, NLT, NRSV, REB], '(you were) first related to God' [SSA].

b. πνεῦμα (LN 12.18, 26.9) (BAGD 5.d.β. p. 677): 'Spirit' [BAGD, BNTC, Herm, LN (12.18), Mor, WBC; KJV, NASB, NCV, NET, NIV, NLT, NRSV], 'Holy Spirit, Spirit of God' [LN (12.18)], 'spirit' [LN (26.9)], 'God's Spirit' [CEV, TEV], not explicit [SSA]. This is translated 'a spiritual way' [GW], '(with) the spiritual' [REB].

c. pres. mid./pass. indic. of ἐπιτελέω (LN 68.22) (BAGD 1. p. 302): 'to end' [BAGD; NRSV], 'to end up' [GW], 'to finish' [Herm; NET, TEV], 'to continue' [SSA], 'to attain your goal' [NIV], 'to complete' [CEV], 'to be completed' [LN], 'to be made complete' [BAGD, BNTC], 'to be made perfect' [KJV], 'to be perfected' [Mor; NASB], 'to attain perfection' [WBC], 'to make it complete' [NCV], 'to become perfect' [NLT], '(look to the material) to make you perfect' [REB]

d. νῦν (LN 67.38): 'now' [BNTC, Herm, LN, Mor, SSA, WBC; all versions except CEV, GW], not explicit [CEV, GW].

e. σάρξ (LN 8.63, 26.7, 58.10) (BAGD 7. p. 744): 'flesh' [BAGD, BNTC, Herm, LN (8.63), Mor; KJV, NASB, NRSV], 'human nature' [LN (26.7, 58.10)], 'physical nature' [LN (58.10)], 'human way' [GW], 'the material' [REB]. This is translated 'by means of what you yourselves do' [SSA], 'by your own power' [NCV, TEV], 'by human effort' [WBC; NET, NIV], 'by your own human effort' [NLT], 'by yourself' [CEV].

QUESTION—To what does ἐναρξάμενοι 'having begun' refer?

It refers to the moment that the Galatians began their Christian lives [Alf, BNTC, Mor, NIC, NIGTC, SSA, TNTC, WBC; NCV, NLT].

QUESTION—What is meant by πνεύματι 'in the Spirit/spirit'?

1. It refers to the Holy Spirit [Alf, Herm, ICC, Mor, NIBC, NTC, TH, WBC; all versions except GW, REB].

2. It refers to the spiritual aspect of their experience [Lns; GW, REB].

QUESTION—What is meant by ἐπιτελεῖσθε νῦν 'are you ending/being completed now'?

1. It focuses on ending what was begun [Lns, TH, TNTC; GW, NRSV].

2. It focuses on reaching the goal that they started out with [Alf, Herm, ICC, Lt, NIC, NTC, WBC; all versions except GW, NRSV].

QUESTION—What is meant by σάρξ 'flesh'?

It refers to an independent reliance on one's own accomplishments over against a spirit of dependence upon and submission to the Spirit's rule [NAC]. It refers to human effort [WBC]. It refers to the outward deeds that belong to the bodily nature of man [Lns]. It means 'flesh' or 'body' as that which is circumcised [ICC]. It refers not only to the body where circumcision is carried out, but to human nature in its unregenerate weakness [NIGTC]. The flesh is the seat and vehicle of sinful desires [Mor]. It is the absence of Christ's indwelling. It indicates anything apart from Christ on which one bases his hope for salvation [NTC].

3:4 **Have-you-experienced**[a] **so-many**[b] **(things)/so-much**[b] **in-vain?**[c]

LEXICON—a. aorist act. indic. of πάσχω (LN 24.78, 90.66) (BAGD 1. p. 634): 'to experience' [BNTC, Herm, LN (90.66), Mor, WBC; NRSV, REB], 'to have (remarkable) experiences' [BAGD], 'to suffer' [LN (24.78, 90.66), SSA; GW, KJV, NASB, NET, NIV, NLT], 'to go through' [CEV]. This verb is also translated as a noun: 'experience' [TEV], 'experiences' [NCV].
  b. τοσοῦτος (LN 59.6, 59.18) (BAGD 2.a.β. p. 823): 'so many' [LN (59.6) Mor; KJV, NASB, NET], 'many' [SSA], 'all of this' [CEV], 'all (your experiences)' [NCV, TEV], 'all (you have experienced)' [REB], 'so much' [BNTC, LN (59.18), WBC; GW, NIV, NLT, NRSV], 'such things' [Herm]. The phrase τοσαῦτα ἐπάθετε 'have you experienced so many things' is translated 'have you had such remarkable experiences' [BAGD].
  c. εἰκῇ (LN 89.20, 89.63) (BAGD 2. p. 222): 'in vain' [BAGD, BNTC, Herm, Mor; KJV, NASB, NLT], 'to no avail' [BAGD], 'for no reason' [LN (89.20)], 'for no purpose' [LN (89.63)], 'needlessly' [SSA], 'for nothing' [WBC; CEV, GW, NET, NIV, NRSV], 'to come to nothing' [REB], 'to mean nothing' [TEV]. This adverb is also translated as a verb: 'to waste' [NCV].

QUESTION—What does ἐπάθετε 'have you experienced' refer to?

1. It refers to the spiritual benefits they have experienced [BST, Herm, ICC, NTC, TNTC]. A reference to the great experiences through which the Galatians had already passed in their life as Christians, and in effect an appeal to them not to let these experiences be of no avail [ICC]. They had experienced the preaching of the gospel, their reception of the Holy Spirit, and had seen miracles performed in their midst [NTC].
2. It refers to the persecution they suffered [Alf, ICC, Lt, NCBC, NIBC, NIGTC, SSA; GW, KJV, NASB, NET, NIV, NLT]. This refers to the persecutions endured by them. If we suppose that the Jews were the chief instigators in these persecutions, Paul's appeal becomes more significant [Lt].
3. It refers to everything they have experienced, both pleasant and painful [Mor].

QUESTION—What does εἰκῇ 'in vain' mean?
It means futility [WBC]. What they had experienced would be in vain if they had not profited spiritually from such blessings [NTC]. Or, it means that any kind of suffering for the gospel's sake would be pointless if salvation could be attained by keeping the law [NIGTC]. It can mean either 'ineffectively' or 'needlessly', it would mean the latter if the verb is understood to mean 'suffering' [NCBC].

if indeed^a (it is) even^b in-vain.^c

LEXICON—a. γέ (LN 91.6) (BAGD 3.a. p. 152): 'indeed' [BAGD, BNTC, LN, Mor, SSA, WBC; NASB, NET], 'then' [LN], 'really' [BAGD, WBC; CEV, NIV, NRSV], 'surely' [NLT, REB, TEV], 'so' [Herm], not explicit [LN; GW, KJV, NCV].
   b. καί (LN 89.93): 'even' [LN], 'yet' [KJV], 'really was' [Herm], not explicit [BNTC, Mor, SSA, WBC; all versions except KJV].
   c. εἰκῇ (LN 89.20, 89.63) (BAGD 2. p. 222): 'in vain' [BAGD, BNTC, Herm, Mor; KJV, NASB, NLT], 'to no avail' [BAGD], 'for no reason' [LN (89.20)], 'for no purpose' [LN (89.63)], 'for nothing' [WBC; CEV, GW, NET, NIV, NRSV], 'needlessly' [SSA], not explicit [NCV, REB, TEV].

QUESTION—What is meant by this clause?
   1. It indicates that Paul thinks it is not too late for them to avoid making their experience to be in vain [BNTC, Herm, ICC, Lns, Lt, Mor, NAC, NCBC, NIGTC, NTC, TH, TNTC, WBC; all versions except CEV, NCV]. It shows that the question whether these experiences are to be in vain is still in doubt, depending on whether the Galatians actually yield to the persuasion of the Judaizers or not. Γέ 'indeed' emphasizes the contingency and suggests that the condition does not need to be fulfilled [ICC]. It expresses doubt about its all being in vain and καί 'even' increases this [Lns]. Paul cannot believe that it has all been in vain, despite all that he has heard about the situation in Galatia, and despite the fact that many of his converts had followed the legalistic error [Mor]. It indicates that the situation in Galatia was not yet hopeless [NAC, WBC].
   2. It indicates that what they have experienced is already in vain [Alf].

3:5 Therefore^a the (one) supplying^b to-you the Spirit^c and working^d mighty-works^e among^f you,

LEXICON—a. οὖν (LN 89.50): 'therefore' [Herm, LN, Mor, SSA; KJV], 'so' [BNTC, LN], 'so then' [LN; NASB], 'then' [LN, WBC; NET, NRSV], not explicit [CEV, GW, NCV, NIV, NLT, REB, TEV].
   b. pres. act. participle of ἐπιχορηγέω (LN 35.31) (BAGD 2. p. 305): 'to supply' [BNTC, Herm, LN; GW, NRSV], 'to give' [BAGD, SSA, WBC; CEV, NCV, NET, NIV, NLT, REB, TEV], 'to provide' [Mor; NASB], 'to minister' [KJV].

GALATIANS 3:5

c. πνεῦμα (LN 12.18) (BAGD 5.d.α. p. 677): 'Spirit' [BAGD, BNTC, Herm, LN, Mor, WBC; all versions except NLT], 'Holy Spirit' [LN, SSA; NLT], 'Spirit of God' [LN].

d. pres. act. participle of ἐνεργέω (LN 42.3) (BAGD 2. p. 265): 'to work' [BAGD, BNTC, Herm, LN, Mor, SSA, WBC; all versions], 'to produce, to effect' [BAGD].

e. δύναμις (LN 76.7) (BAGD 4. p. 208): 'mighty deed' [LN], 'deed of power' [BAGD], 'miracle' [BAGD, BNTC, Herm, LN, Mor, WBC; all versions]. This noun is translated as an adverb modifying 'to work': 'powerfully' [SSA].

f. ἐν with dative object (LN 83.9, 83.13): 'among' [BNTC, Herm, LN (83.9), Mor, SSA, WBC; all versions except CEV], 'in' [LN (83.13); CEV].

QUESTION—What relationship is indicated by οὖν 'therefore'?

It signals the fact that Paul is concluding his arguments in the form of a summary [WBC]. It marks the resumption of the question in 3:2 [Lt] and asks it in another form [Alf]. It introduces a new question [Lns].

QUESTION—Who is the subject of the phrase ὁ ἐπιχορηγῶν 'the one supplying'?

It is God [Alf, BNTC, BST, Herm, ICC, Mor, NIBC, NIC, NIGTC, TH, WBC; all versions except KJV, NASB].

QUESTION—What is indicated by the present tense of the verbs ἐπιχορηγῶν 'supplying' and ἐνεργῶν 'working'?

1. The present tense verbs refer to what God has been doing up to the time that this was written [BNTC, Herm, NIC, NIGTC, TH]. The verb ἐπιχορηγῶν 'supplying' indicates that the experience of receiving the Spirit is not merely an experience in the past but can be thought of as being in progress, even up to the time of his writing this letter [TH]. It indicates a steady supply of the Holy Spirit [BNTC, Herm].

2. The present tense verbs refer to something that has already been accomplished [BST, ICC]. The two present tense verbs do not necessarily refer to a continuous activity of God. It is more probable that they are still referring to Paul's visit when they received the Spirit [BST]. The choice of the present tense shows that the apostle has in mind an experience extended enough to be thought of as in progress, but not that it is in progress at the time that this was written [ICC].

3. The present tense verbs characterize God without focusing on when he did these actions [Alf, Lns]. Both verbs refer to any and every furnishing and giving, whether it occurred at the time when the Galatians were converted or since then [Lns].

QUESTION—What is meant by the phrase ὠνεργῶν δυνάμεις ὢ ν ὑμῖν 'working mighty works among you'?

1. It means that God works miracles in their midst/among them [BST, Herm, ICC, Lns, NIC, WBC; all versions except CEV].

2. It means that God works miracles within individuals [Alf, Lt; CEV].

3. It means that God works miracles among them and within individuals [Mor, NTC]. The mighty works can be viewed either as outward manifestations such as healing, prophecy, and tongues or as inward moral and spiritual gifts such as faith, hope, and love [NTC].

(is it) by^a deeds^b of-law^c or by^d (the) hearing^e of-faith?^f

LEXICON—a. ἐκ with genitive object (LN 89.25, 89.77, 90.12) (BAGD 3.f. p. 235): 'by' [BNTC, Herm, LN (90.12), Mor; KJV, NASB, NET, NRSV], 'by means of' [LN (89.77)], 'through' [GW], 'as a result of' [BAGD, LN (90.12)], 'by reason of' [BAGD], 'because of' [BAGD, LN (89.25), SSA; CEV, NCV, NIV, NLT, REB, TEV], 'on the basis of' [WBC].

b. ἔργον (LN 42.11) (BAGD 1.c.β. p. 308): 'deed' [BAGD, LN], 'act' [LN], 'works' [BNTC, Herm, Mor, WBC; KJV, NASB, NET, NRSV]. This noun is also translated as a verb: 'to obey' [SSA; CEV, NLT], 'to follow' [NCV], 'to observe' [NIV], 'to keep' [REB]. The phrase ἔργων νόμου 'deeds of law' is translated 'deeds that the law commands you to do' [BAGD], 'what the Law requires' [TEV], 'your own efforts' [GW].

c. νόμος (LN 33.55, 33.333) (BAGD 3. p. 542): 'law' [BAGD, BNTC, LN (33.333), Mor, WBC; KJV, NCV, NET, NIV, NRSV, REB], 'Law' [Herm, LN (33.55); NASB, TEV], 'Law of Moses' [CEV], 'Mosaic law' [SSA], 'law of Moses' [NLT], not explicit [GW].

d. ἐκ with genitive object (LN 89.25, 89.77, 90.12) (BAGD 3.f. p. 235): 'by' [BNTC, Herm, LN (90.12), Mor; KJV, NASB, NET, NRSV], 'through' [GW], 'by means of' [LN (89.77)], 'as a result of' [BAGD, LN (90.12)], 'by reason of' [BAGD], 'because of' [BAGD, LN (89.25), SSA; CEV, NCV, NIV, NLT, REB, TEV], 'on the basis of' [WBC].

e. ἀκοή (LN 24.52, 24.57) (BAGD 2.b. p. 31): 'hearing' [BNTC, LN (24.52), Mor; KJV, NASB], 'what is heard' [LN (24.57); GW], 'what you heard' [WBC; NET, NIV, NRSV], 'preaching' [BAGD], 'message' [LN (24.57); REB], 'the message you heard' [NLT]. This noun is also translated as a verb with 'the Galatians' as the subject: 'to hear' [SSA; CEV, NCV, TEV]. The phrase ἀκοῆς πίστεως 'hearing of faith' is translated 'proclamation of faith' [Herm].

f. πίστις (LN 31.85) (BAGD 2.d.α. p. 663): 'faith' [BAGD, BNTC, Herm, LN, Mor; CEV, KJV, NASB, REB]. This noun is also translated as a verb: 'to believe' [WBC; GW, NCV, NET, NIV, NLT, NRSV, TEV], 'to trust' [SSA].

QUESTION—How are the nouns related in the genitive construction ἔργων νόμου 'deeds of law'?

See this question in 3:2.

QUESTION—What is meant by πίστεως 'of faith'?

See this question in 3:2.

DISCOURSE UNIT: 3:6–9 [Mor, NAC, NCBC]. The topic is Abraham [Mor], the case of Abraham [NAC, NCBC].

3:6 Just-as[a] Abraham "believed[b] God and it-was accounted[c] to-him for[d] righteousness."[e]

LEXICON—a. καθώς (LN 64.14) (BAGD 1. p. 391): 'just as' [BAGD, BNTC, LN; NET, NRSV], 'even as' [Mor; KJV], 'since' [SSA], 'even so' [NASB], 'in the same way' [NLT], 'as' [Herm], not explicit [WBC; CEV, GW, NCV, NIV, REB, TEV].

   b. aorist act. indic. of πιστεύω (LN 31.85) (BAGD 1.b. p. 661): 'to believe' [BAGD, BNTC, Herm, LN, Mor, WBC; all versions except CEV, REB], 'to trust' [LN, SSA], 'to trust in' [LN], 'to have faith' [CEV], 'to put (his) faith in' [REB].

   c. aorist pass. indic. of λογίζομαι (LN 57.227) (BAGD 1.a. p. 476): 'to be accounted' [LN; KJV], 'to be regarded' [LN; GW], 'to be credited' [BAGD, Herm, WBC; NET, NIV], 'to be put into (one's) account, to be charged to (one's) account' [LN], 'to be reckoned to' [BNTC, Mor; NASB, NRSV], 'to be counted to' [REB], not explicit [SSA; CEV, NCV]. This passive verb is also translated actively with 'God' as the subject: 'to declare' [NLT], 'to accept' [TEV].

   d. εἰς with accusative object (LN 89.57): 'for' [BNTC, LN; KJV], 'for the purpose of' [LN], 'as' [Herm, Mor, WBC; NASB, NET, NIV, NRSV, REB, TEV], '(regarded) to be' [GW], not explicit [SSA; CEV, NCV, NLT].

   e. δικαιοσύνη (LN 34.46, 88.13) (BAGD 3. p. 197): 'righteousness' [BAGD, BNTC, Herm, LN (88.13), Mor, WBC; KJV, NASB, NET, NIV, NRSV, REB], '(was regarded by God to be his) approval' [GW]. This noun is also translated as an adjective: 'righteous' [NLT, TEV]; as a verb phrase: 'to be in a right relationship with' [LN (34.46)]. The phrase ἐλογίσθη αὐτῷ εἰς δικαιοσύνην 'it was accounted to him for righteousness' is translated 'God accepted Abraham' [CEV], 'God justified him' [SSA], '(that faith) made him right with God' [NCV].

QUESTION—What relationship is indicated by καθώς 'just as'?

   It is an introductory formula [BNTC, Herm]. It introduces a new topic [TH]. It introduces an example, 'take Abraham for example' [WBC; GW, TEV]. It introduces a quotation from scripture [Mor; NCV]: 'The Scriptures say the same thing about Abraham' [NCV].

QUESTION—Who is the actor of ἐλογίσθη 'it was accounted'?

   The implied actor is God [BNTC, Lns, Mor, NIC, NTC, SSA, TH, TNTC; CEV, GW, NLT, TEV].

QUESTION—To what does ἐλογίσθη 'it was accounted' refer?

   It refers to his faith. It was his faith that was accounted as the ground of acceptance [BNTC, BST, ICC, Lns, NIBC, NIC, NTC; NCV, NLT, REB, TEV].

DISCOURSE UNIT: 3:7–14 [NIC]. The topic is from curse to blessing.

DISCOURSE UNIT: 3:7–9 [NIGTC, TNTC]. The topic is the blessing of Abraham [NIGTC], Abraham's faith [TNTC].

3:7 Know[a]/You-know[a] then[b] that the (ones) of[c] faith,[d] these[e] are sons[f] of-Abraham.

LEXICON—a. pres. act. indic./impera. of γινώσκω (LN 28.1, 32.16): 'to know' [BNTC, LN (28.1), Mor, WBC; KJV, NCV], 'to understand' [LN (32.16); CEV, GW, NET, NIV], 'to perceive, to comprehend' [LN (32.16)], 'to realize' [SSA; TEV], 'to be sure' [NASB], 'to see' [NRSV], 'to take it' [REB], 'to recognize' [Herm], not explicit [NLT].
- b. ἄρα (LN 89.46) (BAGD 1. p. 103): 'then' [BAGD, BNTC, LN, Mor, WBC; NIV, NLT, REB, TEV], 'consequently' [LN], 'therefore' [Herm, SSA; KJV, NASB], 'so then' [NET], 'so' [NCV, NRSV], 'and so' [CEV], not explicit [GW].
- c. ἐκ with genitive object (LN 89.77, 90.16) (BAGD 3.d. p. 235): 'from' [LN (89.77, 90.16)], 'by' [LN (90.16)], 'by means of' [LN (89.77)], 'of' [BNTC, Herm, Mor; KJV, NASB]. The phrase οἱ ἐκ πίστεως 'the ones of faith' is translated 'those who have faith' [BAGD; NCV, REB], 'everyone who has faith' [CEV], 'people who have faith' [GW, TEV], 'those who trust God' [SSA], 'those who rely on faith' [WBC], 'those who believe' [NET, NIV, NRSV], 'those who put their faith in God' [NLT].
- d. πίστις (LN 31.85, 31.102) (BAGD 2.d.α. p. 663): 'faith' [BAGD, BNTC, Herm, LN (31.85, 31.102), Mor, WBC; all versions except NET, NIV, NRSV]. This noun is also translated as a verb: 'to believe' [NET, NIV, NRSV], 'to trust' [SSA].
- e. οὗτος (LN 92.29) (BAGD 1.a.ε. p. 596): 'this' [BAGD, LN], 'they' [BNTC], 'these' [Herm, Mor], 'the same' [KJV], not explicit [SSA, WBC; all versions except KJV].
- f. υἱός (LN 10.30) (BAGD 1.c.γ. p. 834): 'male descendant' [LN]. The plural form is translated 'sons' [BNTC, Herm, Mor, WBC; NASB, NET, REB], 'children' [KJV, NCV, NIV, NLT], 'child' [CEV], 'descendants' [GW, NRSV, TEV], 'spiritual descendants' [SSA]. It refers to those who are bound to a personality by close, non-material ties [BAGD].

QUESTION—What is the form of γινώσκετε 'know/you know'?
1. It is the present imperative [BNTC, Herm, Lns, Mor, NIBC, NIC, NIGTC, NTC, SSA; CEV, GW, KJV, NASB, NET, NIV]: know (this). From the fact that Abraham believed, Paul draws a conclusion and states it as an imperative [Lns]. The Galatians have been acting foolishly and this imperative is appropriate [SSA].
2. It is the present indicative [Alf, Lt, NCBC, WBC; CEV, NCV, NRSV, TEV]: you know (this). The indicative better fits in the argument Paul is developing [Lt].

QUESTION—What relationship is indicated by ἄρα 'then'?
It marks the statement from 3:7 as the consequence of the quotation from 3:6 [ICC, Lns, WBC].

QUESTION—What is meant by οἱ ἐκ πίστεως 'the ones of faith'?
It indicates that they relied on faith [Mor, WBC]. Believing is their constant attitude. Faith is characteristic of them [Lns, Mor]. The preposition ἐκ 'of'

indicates the source of character and standing. The phrase means those who believe and whose standing and character are determined by that faith [ICC]. It means those who proceed from faith as their source [NCBC]. It means those whose existence before God is based upon faith [Herm]. The demonstrative οὗτοι 'these' indicates that it was those who had faith and none of those who did not have faith [Alf, Lns].

QUESTION—How are the nouns related in the genitive construction υἱοί εἰσιν Ἀβραάμ 'sons of Abraham'?

They are people who have the same characteristic of faith that Abraham had [TH]. In this reference 'sons' are those who rely on faith like Abraham did [BNTC, BST, Herm, ICC, Lns, Mor, NAC, NCBC, NIBC, NIC, NIGTC, NTC, TH, TNTC].

3:8 And the Scripture,[a] foreseeing[b] that by[c] faith[d] God justifies[e] the Gentiles,[f]

LEXICON—a. γραφή (LN 33.10, 33.53) (BAGD 2.b.β. p. 166): 'Scripture' [Herm, LN (33.53), Mor, WBC; GW, NASB, NIV], 'scripture' [BAGD, BNTC; KJV, NET, NRSV, REB, TEV], 'Scripture passage' [LN (33.53)], 'passage' [LN (33.10)]. This singular form of the noun is also translated as plural: 'Scriptures' [CEV, NCV, NLT]. The Scripture is personified in this passage and so this noun is also translated 'God' [SSA].

b. aorist act. participle of προοράω (LN 24.5, 28.6, **28.6 fn 4**) (BAGD 2. p. 709): 'to foresee' [BAGD, BNTC, Herm, Mor, WBC; KJV, NASB, NET, NIV, NRSV, REB], 'to see in advance' [BAGD], 'to see beforehand' [LN (24.5)], 'to say long ago' [CEV], 'to see ahead of time' [GW], 'to know beforehand or to cause something to be known ahead of time' [**LN** (28.6 fn 4)], 'to tell what would happen in the future' [NCV], 'to look forward' [NLT], 'to predict' [TEV], 'to plan beforehand' [SSA].

c. ἐκ with genitive object (LN 89.77): 'by means of' [LN], 'from' [BNTC, Mor], 'by' [WBC; NASB, NET, NIV, NRSV], 'because of' [SSA; CEV], 'through' [Herm; KJV, NCV, REB, TEV], 'on the basis of' [NLT], not explicit [GW].

d. πίστις (LN 31.85, 31.102) (BAGD 2.d.α. p. 663): 'faith' [BAGD, BNTC, Herm, LN (31.85, 31.102), Mor, WBC; all versions]. This noun is also translated as a verb: 'to trust' [SSA].

e. pres. act. indic. of δικαιόω (LN 34.46) (BAGD 3.b. p. 197): 'to justify' [BNTC, Herm, Mor, SSA, WBC; KJV, NASB, NET, NIV, NRSV, REB], 'to put right with' [LN; TEV], 'to cause to be in a right relationship with' [LN], 'to accept' [CEV, NLT], 'to make right' [NCV], 'to give approval to' [GW]. It refers to God's activity [BAGD].

f. ἔθνος (LN 11.55): 'nation' [LN]. The plural form is translated 'Gentiles' [BNTC, Herm, Mor, SSA, WBC; all versions except GW, KJV, NCV], 'non-Jewish people' [GW, NCV], 'the heathen' [LN; KJV], 'pagans' [LN].

QUESTION—What relationship is indicated by δέ 'and'?
It joins 3:8 to 3:7 [BNTC, ICC, WBC] as a deduction of 3:6 [ICC]. It is continuative and adds another important statement regarding Abraham and his real sons and brings the matter to the time of Paul and the Galatians [Lns].

QUESTION—What is meant by ἡ γραφὴ προϊδοῦσα 'the scripture having foreseen'?
Paul is using a normal Hebraic form of speech. 'Scripture foresaw' is the same as saying 'the Lord of scripture foresaw' [Alf, Lns, NAC, NIBC, NIC, NIGTC, NTC, TH, TNTC]. It is a personification of scripture [Lt, Mor, NIC, TH]. It is a figure of speech for God's foresight that is written in Scripture. It refers to the last part of the Abrahamic covenant in Genesis 12:3 [ICC, Mor, TH, WBC].

QUESTION—What relationship is indicated by ἐκ πίστεως 'by faith'?
It indicates that faith is the means that God uses to justify men [Mor]. It indicates that it was on the basis of faith [NAC]. It indicates that it was on the ground of (their) faith [NIGTC]. It indicates the result of faith [Lns, NTC]. As a result of faith, God would justify the Gentiles.

it-announced-the-gospel-in-advance[a] **to Abraham,** *quote* **"In**[b] **you all the nations/Gentiles**[c] **will-be-blessed";**[d]

LEXICON—a. aorist mid. (deponent = act.) indic. of προευαγγελίζομαι (LN **33.216**) (BAGD p. 705): 'to announce the gospel in advance' [NIV], 'to announce the good news ahead of time' [**LN**; GW], 'to proclaim good news in advance' [BAGD], 'to proclaim the gospel in advance' [WBC], 'to proclaim the gospel beforehand' [Herm], 'to tell the following good news' [SSA], 'to preach the gospel beforehand' [BNTC, Mor; NASB], 'to proclaim the gospel ahead of time' [NET], 'to promise this good news long ago' [NLT], 'to declare the gospel beforehand' [NRSV, REB], 'to announce the Good News' [TEV], 'to preach before the gospel' [KJV], 'to tell the good news' [CEV], 'to tell the Good News beforehand' [NCV].

b. ἐν with dative object (LN 83.13, 89.80, 89.119): 'in' [BNTC, Herm, LN (83.13, 89.119), Mor, WBC; KJV, NASB, NET, NRSV, REB], 'with' [LN (89.80)], 'in union with' [LN (89.119)], 'because of' [CEV], 'through' [GW, NCV, NIV, NLT, TEV]. This preposition is also translated as a verb phrase: 'I will use (you) in order that' [SSA].

c. ἔθνος (LN 11.55): 'nation' [LN]. The plural form is translated 'nations' [BNTC, Mor, WBC; CEV, KJV, NCV, NET, NIV, NLT, REB], 'all the people of the world' [GW], 'Gentiles' [Herm; NRSV], 'all people' [TEV], 'people in all nations' [SSA], 'Nations' [NASB].

d. fut. pass. indic. of ἐνευλογέω (LN **88.69**) (BAGD p. 265): 'to be blessed' [BAGD, BNTC, Herm, LN, Mor, WBC; all versions except REB, TEV], 'to find blessing' [REB]. This passive verb is also translated actively with 'God' as the subject: 'to bless' [SSA; TEV], 'to act kindly toward' [**LN**].

GALATIANS 3:8 97

QUESTION—Who is the subject of προευηγγελίσατο 'preached the good news before'?
  Scripture is the formal subject, but God is the actual subject [SSA, TNTC; CEV, NLT].
QUESTION—What relationship is indicated by ἐν 'in'?
  It indicates cause and means on the basis of what he is or has done [ICC]. Since this was to occur on a worldwide scale in the future, 'in you' really means 'in your descendant, the Messiah' [NTC].
QUESTION—Who will bless the nations?
  It is God [Herm, Lns, SSA; TEV]. God is the primary agent and Abraham is the secondary agent, so that Abraham will be the means by which God will bless all the nations [TH].
QUESTION—To whom does ἔθνη 'nations/Gentiles' refer?
  1. It refers to the Gentiles [Alf, Herm, ICC, Lns, NCBC, NIC, TNTC, WBC; NRSV].
  2. It refers to the nations, the Gentiles and the Jews [BNTC, NAC, SSA, TH; GW, TEV]. It means people in all nations because Jews were included in the promise [SSA].

3:9 therefore[a] the (ones) of[b] faith[c] are-blessed[d] together-with[e] the faithful[f] Abraham.
LEXICON—a. ὥστε (LN 89.52) (BAGD 1.a. p. 899): 'therefore' [BAGD, Herm, LN], 'so' [BAGD, LN, SSA, WBC; GW, NCV, NIV, NLT, TEV], 'so that' [LN], 'so then' [LN, Mor; KJV, NASB, NET], 'for this reason' [BAGD; NRSV], 'consequently' [BNTC], 'this means that' [CEV], 'thus' [REB].
  b. ἐκ with genitive object (LN 89.77, 90.16) (BAGD 3.d. p. 235): 'by means of' [LN (89.77)], 'by' [LN (90.16)], 'from' [LN (89.77, 90.16)], 'of' [BNTC, Herm, Mor; KJV, NASB]. The phrase οἱ ἐκ πίστεως 'the ones of faith' is translated 'those who have faith' [BAGD; NIV], 'everyone who has faith' [CEV], 'people who believe' [GW], 'all who believe' [NCV, TEV], 'those who believe' [NET, NRSV], 'all who put their faith in Christ' [NLT], 'those with faith' [REB], 'those who rely on faith' [WBC], 'Gentiles and Jews who trust (him)' [SSA].
  c. πίστις (LN 31.85, 31.102) (BAGD 2.d.α. p. 663): 'faith' [BAGD, BNTC, Herm, LN (31.85, 31.102), Mor, WBC; CEV, KJV, NASB, NIV, NLT, REB]. This noun is also translated as a verb: 'to believe' [GW, NCV, NET, NRSV, TEV], 'to trust' [SSA].
  d. pres. pass. indic. of εὐλογέω (LN 33.470) (BAGD 3. p. 322): 'to be blessed' [BNTC, Herm, LN, Mor, WBC; all versions except CEV, NLT, REB], 'to be provided with benefits' [BAGD], 'to share in the blessings' [CEV], 'to share the same blessing' [NLT], 'to share the blessing' [REB], '(God) blesses' [SSA].
  e. σύν with dative object (LN 89.107) (BAGD 2.b. p. 781): 'together with' [Herm, LN; GW], 'with' [BAGD, BNTC, LN, Mor, WBC; KJV, NASB,

NRSV, REB], 'along with' [SSA; NET, NIV], 'just as (Abraham was)' [NCV], 'as (he was)' [TEV], not explicit [CEV, NLT].
f. πιστός (LN **31.86**, 31.87) (BAGD 2. p. 665): 'faithful' [BAGD, BNTC, LN (31.87), Mor; KJV, REB], 'believing, full of faith' [BAGD], 'trusting' [LN (31.86)]. The phrase τῷ πιστῷ 'Αβραάμ 'the faithful Abraham' is translated 'Abraham, the one who trusted' [**LN** (31.86), SSA], 'Abraham, the man of faith' [WBC; GW, NIV], 'because of his faith' [CEV, NLT], 'Abraham the believer' [Herm; NASB, NET], 'Abraham who believed' [NRSV], 'Abraham believed' [NCV, TEV].

QUESTION—What relationship is indicated by ὥστε 'so'?
It introduces a final statement that stresses a result [Mor, NAC, WBC]. It indicates the conclusion [SSA].

QUESTION—What is meant by οἱ ἐκ πίστεως 'the ones of faith'?
See this question in 3:7.

QUESTION—What relationship is indicated by σύν 'with'?
It stresses the believer's connection with Abraham [WBC], in association with Abraham [Lns], in community with him [Alf]. It is used to interpret the relationship of believers to Abraham who is the prime example of a believing person [SSA]. Paul taught that those who inherit the blessing promised to Abraham must do so on the same basis on which he was blessed, that is, by faith, and in that sense 'with' him [ICC]. Abraham believed and was blessed; all who believe are blessed as he was [TH].

DISCOURSE UNIT: 3:10–14 [BST, Mor, NAC, NCBC, NIGTC, TNTC]. The topic is the alternative of faith and works [BST], the different results from faith and works [NCBC], who is under the curse? [TNTC], the curse of the law [NIGTC], no one is justified by the law [Mor], Christ and the curse [NAC].

3:10 For as-many-as[a] are of[b] deeds[c] of-law[d] are under[e] (a) curse;[f]
LEXICON—a. ὅσος (LN 59.7): 'as many as' [LN, Mor; KJV, NASB], 'all who' [BNTC, WBC; GW, NET, NIV, NRSV], 'all those who' [SSA], 'those who' [Herm; NCV, NLT, REB, TEV], 'anyone who' [CEV].
b. ἐκ with genitive object (LN 89.77, 90.16): 'by means of' [LN (89.77)], 'by' [LN (90.16); CEV], 'from' [LN (89.77, 90.16)], 'of' [Herm; KJV, NASB], 'to rely on' [BNTC, WBC; GW, NET, NIV, NRSV, REB], 'to depend on' [NCV, NLT, TEV], not explicit [Mor, SSA].
c. ἔργον (LN 42.11) (BAGD 1.c.β. p. 308): 'deed' [BAGD, LN], 'act' [LN], 'works' [BNTC, Herm, WBC; KJV, NASB, NET, NRSV], not explicit [NLT]. The phrase ἔργων νόμου 'deeds of law' is translated 'following the law' [NCV], 'their own efforts to live according to a set of standards' [GW], 'observing the law' [NIV], 'obeying the Law' [CEV, TEV], 'obey the Mosaic law' [SSA], 'obedience to the law' [REB], 'law-workers' [Mor].
d. νόμος (LN 33.55, 33.333) (BAGD 3. p. 542): 'law' [BAGD, BNTC, LN (33.333), Mor, WBC; KJV, NCV, NET, NIV, NLT, NRSV, REB], 'Law'

[Herm, LN (33.55); CEV, NASB, TEV], 'Mosaic law' [SSA], 'a set of standards' [GW].

e. ὑπό with accusative object (LN 37.7) (BAGD 2.b. p. 843): 'under' [BAGD, BNTC, Herm, LN, Mor, WBC; all versions except GW], 'under the control of' [LN]. The phrase ὑπὸ κατάραν 'under a curse' is translated 'there is a curse on' [GW], 'to be condemned' [SSA].

f. κατάρα (LN **33.473**) (BAGD p. 417): 'curse' [BAGD, BNTC, Herm, LN, Mor, WBC; all versions]. This clause is translated 'these who depend on obeying the Law live under a curse' [**LN**], 'all those who think that if they obey the Mosaic law they will be justified are condemned by God' [SSA].

QUESTION—What relationship is indicated by γάρ 'for'?

It marks another step in the argument [Herm]. What follows in 3:10-14 explains the implied dichotomy in 3:6-9 between relying on faith and relying on one's own observance of the law for righteousness [WBC]. What we learn from Abraham makes us conclude that we are all under the law's curse [Mor]. It indicates that what follows is an explanation of the theme in 3:8–9 [BNTC]. This supports the conclusion reached in 3:9 that those associated with Abraham also gained righteousness by faith [SSA].

QUESTION—What relationship is indicated by ἐξ 'of' in the phrase 'are of deeds of law'?

In this verse it means those whose main position originates in the law, thinking that keeping the law is the most important way to approach God [Mor]. It means that they are the ones who rely or depend on the law [BNTC, SSA, WBC; all versions except CEV, KJV, NASB]. They think that by obeying the law of Moses they will be justified [SSA]. See the question about the parallel phrase 'the ones of faith' in 3:7.

QUESTION—How are the nouns related in the genitive construction ἔργων νόμου 'deeds of law'?

It means doing what the law requires [NIC, SSA, TH; CEV, NCV, REB, TEV].

QUESTION—Which law is referred to by νόμου 'of law'?

It refers to the Jewish law [Herm, TH, WBC], the law from God written by Moses [SSA].

QUESTION—What is the meaning of ὑπὸ κατάραν 'under a curse'?

It has the idea of separation from God [NCBC]. This is literally 'cursed' with God being the implied agent 'cursed by God' [SSA, TH; NLT]. It is the curse of the law that is quoted in the following sentence [ICC, NIC, WBC]. They are under the threat of being condemned by God [SSA, TH].

for it-is-written,[a] *quote* **"Accursed**[b] **(is) every**[c] **(one) who not continues**[d] **in-all the-(things) written in**[e] **the scroll/book**[f] **of-the law**[g] **of-the to-do**[h] **them."**

LEXICON—a. perf. pass. indic. of γράφω (LN 33.61): 'to be written' [BNTC, Herm, LN, Mor, WBC; KJV, NASB, NET, NIV, NRSV]. This is translated 'The Scriptures say' [CEV, NCV, NLT], 'Scripture says' [GW], 'scripture says' [REB], 'the scripture says' [TEV], 'God has said' [SSA].

b. ἐπικατάρατος (LN **33.475**) (BAGD p. 294): 'to be accursed' [**LN**], 'to be cursed' [BAGD, BNTC, Herm, LN, Mor, WBC; all versions except CEV, TEV], 'to be under a curse' [CEV], 'to be under God's curse' [TEV], 'to be condemned' [SSA].

c. πᾶς (LN 59.23) (BAGD 1.c.γ. p. 632): 'every' [BAGD, LN], 'everyone' [BNTC, Herm, Mor, WBC; all versions except GW, NCV, TEV], 'anyone' [SSA; NCV], 'whoever' [GW, TEV].

d. pres. act. indic. of ἐμμένω (LN 68.11) (BAGD 2. p. 255): 'to continue' [LN, Mor, WBC; KJV, NIV], 'to abide' [BAGD, BNTC; NASB], 'to keep on' [NET], 'to persevere' [REB], 'to stay' [Herm], not explicit [CEV, GW, NLT, NRSV]. This verb is also translated as an adverb: 'continuously and completely (obey)' [SSA], 'always' [NCV, TEV].

e. ἐν with dative object (LN 83.13): 'in' [BNTC, Herm, LN, Mor, SSA, WBC; all versions].

f. βιβλίον (LN 6.64, 33.52) (BAGD 1. p. 141): 'scroll' [BAGD, LN (6.64)], 'roll' [LN (6.64)], 'book' [BAGD, BNTC, Herm, LN (6.64, 33.52), Mor, SSA, WBC; KJV, NET, NRSV, REB, TEV], 'Book' [NASB, NCV, NIV], 'God's Book' [NLT], not explicit [CEV, GW].

g. νόμος (LN 33.55, 33.333) (BAGD 4.a. p. 543): 'law' [BAGD, BNTC, LN (33.333), Mor, WBC; KJV, NET, NRSV, REB], 'Law' [Herm, LN (33.55); CEV, NASB, NCV, NIV, NLT, TEV], 'Moses Teachings' [GW], 'book by Moses' [SSA].

h. aorist act. infin. of ποιέω (LN 42.7, 90.45) (BAGD I.1.c.α. p. 682): 'to do' [BAGD, BNTC, Herm, LN (42.7, 90.45), Mor, WBC; KJV, NET, NIV, REB], 'to perform' [LN (42.7, 90.45); NASB], 'to practice' [LN (90.45)], 'to carry out' [LN (42.7)], 'to keep' [BAGD], 'to obey' [SSA; CEV, GW, NCV, TEV], 'to observe and obey' [NLT, NRSV].

QUESTION—What relationship is indicated by γάρ 'for'?

It introduces the reason that they are under the curse [Herm]. They are under the curse because no one is able to keep the law in its entirety [NIGTC].

QUESTION—Who is the implied actor of ἐπικατάρατος 'accursed'?

God is the implied actor [SSA, TH; TEV].

QUESTION—How are the nouns related in the genitive construction βιβλίῳ τοῦ νόμου 'book of the law'?

This refers to God's laws that were written in a book by Moses [SSA]. In this context, it does not focus on the book that contained the laws, but to a listing of all the laws [TH]. The entire law is considered as a unity [NTC].

3:11 But/and[a] that no-one is-justified[b] with[c] God by[d] law[e] (is) evident,[f]

LEXICON—a. δέ (LN 89.94, 89.124): 'and' [BNTC, LN (89.94)], 'but' [LN (89.124), Mor, SSA; KJV], 'on the other hand' [LN (89.124)], 'however' [WBC], 'consequently' [NLT], 'now' [NASB, NCV, NET, NRSV, TEV], 'it is, then' [Herm], not explicit [CEV, GW, NIV, REB].

b. pres. pass. indic. of δικαιόω (LN 34.46) (BAGD 3.a. p. 197): 'to be justified' [BAGD, BNTC, Herm, Mor, SSA, WBC; KJV, NASB, NET,

NIV, NRSV, REB], 'to be put right (with)' [LN; TEV], 'to receive God's approval' [GW], 'to be made right' [NCV], 'to be right' [NLT], 'to please God' [CEV].
  c. παρά with dative object (LN 89.111) (BAGD II.2.b. p. 610): 'with' [LN, Mor; NCV, NLT, TEV], 'in the sight of' [BAGD; KJV], 'before' [BNTC, Herm, WBC; NASB, NET, NIV, NRSV, REB], not explicit [CEV, GW]. The phrase οὐδεὶς δικαιοῦται παρὰ τῷ θεῷ 'no one is justified with God' is translated 'God has established that no person is justified by him' [SSA].
  d. ἐν with dative object (LN 89.76): 'by' [BNTC, Herm, LN, Mor, WBC; all versions except REB, TEV], 'by means of' [LN; REB, TEV], 'through' [LN], 'because of' [SSA].
  e. νόμος (LN 33.55, 33.333) (BAGD 3. p. 542): 'law' [BAGD, BNTC, LN (33.333), Mor, SSA, WBC; KJV, NCV, NET, NIV, NLT, NRSV, REB], 'Law' [Herm, LN (33.55); CEV, NASB, TEV]. This is translated 'the law's standards' [GW].
  f. δῆλος (LN **28.58**) (BAGD p. 178): 'evident' [**LN,** SSA; KJV, NASB, NRSV, REB], 'clear' [BAGD, LN; NCV, NET, NLT, TEV], 'plain' [BNTC], 'obvious' [Herm, Mor], not explicit [CEV, GW]. This adjective is also translated as an adverb: 'clearly' [WBC; NIV].
QUESTION—What relationship is indicated by δέ 'but/and'?
  1. It is adversative [Mor, SSA, WBC; KJV]. Not only does the Law pronounce a curse on those who do not obey it, but the Scriptures point to justification by faith [Mor].
  2. It introduces an additional argument for the position maintained in 3:10 [ICC]. It introduces a matter in addition to a previous one so that 3:11 is more than just a parallel to 3:10 [Herm].

because "The righteous[a] (person) by[b] faith[c] shall-live";[d]
LEXICON—a. δίκαιος (LN 34.47, 88.12) (BAGD 1.b. p. 195): 'righteous' [BAGD, BNTC, Herm, LN (88.12), WBC; NASB, NET, NIV, NLT, NRSV], 'just' [LN (88.12), Mor; KJV], 'in a right relationship with God' [LN (34.47)]. This noun is also translated as a verb: 'to be justified' [REB]. The phrase ὁ δίκαιος 'the righteous person' is translated 'that person whom God justifies' [SSA], 'the people God accepts' [CEV], 'the person who has God's approval' [GW], 'those who are right with God' [NCV], 'the person who is put right with God' [TEV].
  b. ἐκ with genitive object (LN 89.77, 90.12, 90.16): 'by' [Herm, LN (90.12, 90.16), Mor, WBC; KJV, NASB, NCV, NET, NIV, NRSV], 'by means of' [LN (89.77)], 'through' [NLT, REB, TEV], 'because of' [SSA; CEV, GW], 'as a result of' [LN (90.12)], 'from' [BNTC, LN (90.16)].
  c. πίστις (LN 31.85, 31.102) (BAGD 2.d.α. p. 663): 'faith' [BAGD, BNTC, Herm, LN (31.85, 31.102), Mor, WBC; all versions except NCV]. This noun is also translated as a verb: 'to trust' [SSA; NCV].

d. fut. mid. (deponent = act.) indic. of ζάω (LN 23.88) (BAGD 2.b.β. p. 336): 'to live' [BNTC, Herm, LN, Mor, SSA, WBC; all versions except NLT, REB], 'to have life' [BAGD; NLT], 'to gain life' [REB].

QUESTION—What relationship is indicated by ὅτι 'because'?

It indicates the grounds for the preceding statement [SSA].

QUESTION—Is this a direct quote?

This is introduced in translations with 'the Scriptures say' [CEV, NCV, NLT], 'the scripture says' [TEV], 'we read' [REB], 'God himself said' [SSA]. The words are enclosed by quotation marks [Mor, SSA; all versions except KJV, NET]. It is a direct quotation from Habakkuk 2:4 [SSA, TH].

QUESTION—Is ἐκ πίστεως 'by faith' connected to Ὁ δίκαιος 'the righteous' or is it connected to ζήσεται 'shall live'?

1. A person who is justified by means of his faith will have spiritual life [Alf, Mor, NCBC, NIC, NIGTC, SSA, TNTC; CEV, REB, TEV]. He is not seeking to show by what the righteous shall live, but the ground itself of that righteousness which shall issue in life [Alf]. Paul is writing about the way the sinner receives salvation, not the way he lives out the implications of his salvation [Mor].

2. A person who is justified is one who has spiritual life by means of faith [Herm, ICC, Lns; GW, KJV, NASB, NET, NIV, NLT, NRSV]. The one who is justified will ever live as a result of the faith by which he is justified [Lns].

3:12 but the law^a is not by^b faith,^c

LEXICON—a. νόμος (LN 33.55, 33.333) (BAGD 3. p. 542): 'law' [BAGD, BNTC, LN (33.333), Mor, WBC; all versions except CEV, NASB, TEV], 'Law' [Herm, LN (33.55); CEV, NASB, TEV], 'Mosaic law' [SSA].

b. ἐκ with genitive object (LN 90.16): 'by' [Herm, LN], 'from' [BNTC, LN], 'of' [Mor; KJV, NASB, NLT]. This preposition is also translated as a verb: 'to be based on' [WBC; CEV, NCV, NET, NIV], 'to rest on' [NRSV], 'to operate on the basis of' [REB]. This phrase is translated 'Laws have nothing to do with faith' [GW], 'How different from this way of faith is the way of law' [NLT], 'But the Law has nothing to do with faith' [TEV], 'and when God gave the Mosaic law to the Jews, he did not state that a person must trust him' [SSA].

c. πίστις (LN 31.85, 31.102) (BAGD 2.d.α. p. 663): 'faith' [BAGD, BNTC, Herm, LN (31.85, 31.102), Mor, WBC; all versions]. See b. [SSA].

QUESTION—What relationship is indicated by δέ 'but'?

It introduces the minor proposition of the syllogism [Alf, Lns]. Paul has built a regular negative syllogism. He put the conclusion in first: 'By the law no one is justified'. The major premise is 'The righteous one shall live by faith alone'. The minor premise is 'the law does not belong to faith' [Lns]. Δέ 'but' stands juxtaposed to ὅτι δέ 'now that' and can therefore be translated as 'also' [Herm]. It expresses the contrast between the Law and faith [TH]. It is adversative just as it is in 3:11. It sets 3:12 in sharp contrast to 3:11, just as 3:11 is in sharp contrast to 3:10 [NAC, WBC].

QUESTION—What is meant by ὁ νόμος οὐκ ἔστιν ἐκ πίστεως 'the law is not by faith'?

It means that the principles of legalism and the principles of faith are mutually exclusive as bases of justification [ICC]. Faith is not the starting point of the law. The law does not take faith as its fundamental principle [Lt]. The law and faith cannot be combined. Leaning on the law means leaning on self. Exercising faith means leaning on Christ [NTC]. Paul is referring to the law seen as a supposed means of obtaining God's favor by winning merit [TNTC]. The law in this context does not mainly refer to regulations as such but to a person's obedience to the law. Faith is not to be understood as an abstract term, but must be related to one's actual trust and confidence in God [TH]. There is no point of contact between law and faith. The law does not depend on faith for its basis [NCBC]. The law and faith are mutually exclusive as bases for righteousness [Mor, NIC, WBC].

but "The-(one) having-done[a] these-things shall-live[b] in[c] them."

LEXICON—a. aorist act. participle of ποιέω (LN 42.7, 90.45) (BAGD I.1.c.α. p. 682): 'to do' [BAGD, BNTC, Herm, LN (42.7, 90.45), Mor, WBC; KJV, NET, NIV, NRSV, REB, TEV], 'to practice' [BAGD, LN (90.45); NASB], 'to keep' [BAGD], 'to obey' [CEV, GW, NCV, NLT]. This clause is translated 'but God stated that a person must obey the many different laws continuously and completely' [SSA].

b. fut. mid. (deponent = act.) indic. of ζάω (LN 23.88) (BAGD 2.b.β. p. 336): 'to live' [BNTC, Herm, LN, Mor, WBC; all versions except CEV, NLT, REB], 'to have life' [BAGD; CEV, NLT, REB]. See a. [SSA].

c. ἐν with dative object (LN 13.8, 83.13, 89.76, 90.10): 'in' [LN (13.8, 83.13), Mor; KJV], 'by' [BNTC, Herm, LN (89.76, 90.10), WBC; NASB, NET, NIV, NLT, NRSV, REB], 'by means of, through' [LN (89.76)], 'because of' [GW, NCV], not explicit [CEV, TEV]. See a. [SSA].

QUESTION—What relationship is indicated by ἀλλά 'but'?

It is adversative [WBC]. It marks the antithesis between this statement of the OT (Lev. 18:5), which the apostle takes as a statement of the principle of legalism, and the possibility just denied that this principle and that of faith might somehow be reconciled or reduced to one [ICC].

QUESTION—What is referred to by αὐτά 'these things' and αὐτοῖς 'them'?

The plural αὐτά 'these things' is explained by the words which in the original text precede the passage quoted [Lt]. Paul quotes Leviticus 18:5, 'You shall therefore keep my statutes and my ordinances, by doing which a man shall live' [TNTC, WBC]. The plural αὐτοῖς 'them' does not refer to the Law (singular) in general, but to the requirements of the Law [TH].

QUESTION—What relationship is indicated by ἐν 'in' in the phrase 'in them'?

'In them' is a duplication of the preceding phrase 'having done these things': the one who practices these precepts will live having practiced these precepts [TH]. 'God stated that a person must obey the many different laws continuously and completely' [SSA]. 'Whoever obeys laws will live because of the laws he obeys' [GW]. 'A person who obeys these things will live because of them' [NCV]. 'Whoever does everything the Law requires will live' [TEV]. 'If you wish to find life by obeying the law, you must obey all of its commands' [NLT]. 'He who does this shall gain life by what he does' [REB].

3:13 Christ has-redeemed^a us from^b the curse^c of-the law,^d

LEXICON—a. aorist act. indic. of ἐξαγοράζω (LN **37.131**) (BAGD 1. p. 271): 'to redeem' [BAGD, BNTC, Herm, LN, Mor, SSA, WBC; KJV, NASB, NET, NIV, NRSV, TEV], 'to deliver' [BAGD], 'to buy' [BAGD; REB], 'to rescue' [CEV, NLT], 'to free' [GW], 'to take away (the curse the law put on us)' [NCV].

  b. ἐκ with genitive object (LN 84.4) (BAGD 1.c. p. 234): 'from' [BAGD, BNTC, Herm, LN, Mor, WBC; all versions except NCV], 'out from, out of' [LN], not explicit [NCV]. The phrase ἐκ τᾶς κατάρας τοῦ νόμου 'from the curse of the law' is translated 'in order that God might not condemn us(excl.) who have not continuously and completely obeyed God's law' [SSA].

  c. κατάρα (LN 33.473) (BAGD p. 417): 'curse' [BAGD, BNTC, Herm, LN, Mor, WBC; all versions]. See b. [SSA].

  d. νόμος (LN 33.55, 33.333) (BAGD 3. p. 542): 'law' [BAGD, BNTC, LN (33.333), Mor, WBC; KJV, NCV, NET, NIV, NLT, NRSV, REB], 'Law' [Herm, LN (33.55); CEV, NASB, TEV], 'God's laws' [GW], 'God's law' [SSA].

QUESTION—What is meant by ἐξηγόρασεν 'redeemed'?

It means that Christ has bought our freedom and he did it by giving away his life on the cross as the ransom that was paid to God the 'giver and maintainer of the law'. Through this he obtained for us the forgiveness of sins by his 'death for satisfaction' which was suffered according to God's gracious counsel in obedience thereto, so that now the curse of law does not apply to us [Lns, NIC]. It means that we have been bought with a price. Our redemption came at the cost of the sacrifice of Christ [NAC]. The verb translated redeemed (literally, 'to buy up') in this verse means 'to effect deliverance' or 'to secure the release of someone,' at some cost to the person who secures it in terms of effort, suffering, or loss [ICC, TH] and by speaking of Christ setting us free from the curse of the law it avoids questions such as asking how much did he pay and to whom did he pay the price [TH].

QUESTION—Who is referred to by ἡμᾶς 'us'?
1. It refers to both Jews and Gentiles [BNTC, Lns, NAC, NCBC, NIC, NIGTC, NTC]. This refers to the Gentiles and the Jews, since all who are under law are 'under a curse' (3:10) [Lns, NAC].
2. It refers specifically to the Jews [Alf, Herm, ICC, Lt, SSA]. From the context, Paul means those who through Christ were delivered from the 'curse of the law.' Those people are the Jewish Christians who were 'under the curse' in 3:10. The Gentile Christians were not under this curse because before they converted to Christianity they were not 'under the Torah' but 'under the elements of the world' [Herm].

QUESTION—What is meant by τῆς κατάρας τοῦ νόμου 'the curse of the law'?

The 'curse of the law' is the curse pronounced on the law-breaker in Deut. 27:26, and quoted in 3:10 [ICC, NAC, NIBC, NIC, NIGTC, WBC]. It is the curse that the Law brings [TH; GW, TEV] to those who try to live by all of its rules but who cannot fulfill everything that it requires [TH]. It is the curse the law put on us [NCV], the curse pronounced by the law [NLT].

having-become[a] (a) curse[b] for[c] us,

LEXICON—a. aorist mid. (deponent = act.) participle of γίνομαι (LN 13.48) (BAGD I.4.a. p. 159): 'to become' [BAGD, BNTC, Herm, LN, Mor, WBC; CEV, GW, NASB, NET, NIV, NRSV, TEV], 'to be made' [KJV]. This phrase is translated 'Christ redeemed us(excl.) by means of God's condemning him instead of condemning us(excl.)' [SSA], 'He changed places with us and put himself under that curse' [NCV], 'he took upon himself the curse for our wrongdoing' [NLT], 'by coming under the curse for our sake' [REB].

b. κατάρα (LN **33.474**) (BAGD p. 417): 'curse' [BAGD, BNTC, Herm, LN, Mor, WBC; all versions except GW, NCV], 'something accursed' [**LN**; GW], 'curse-offering' [BAGD], 'object of a curse' [BAGD]. See a. [SSA; NCV].

c. ὑπέρ with genitive object (LN 90.36) (BAGD 1.a.ε. p. 838): 'for' [BAGD, Herm, LN, Mor, WBC; KJV, NASB, NET, NIV, NRSV, TEV], 'on behalf of' [BNTC, LN], 'in behalf of' [BAGD], 'for the sake of' [LN]. The phrase ὑπὲρ ἡμῶν 'for us' is translated 'in our place' [CEV], 'instead of us' [GW], 'for our sake' [REB], 'for our wrongdoing' [NLT]. See a. [SSA; NCV].

QUESTION—What relationship is indicated by γενόμενος 'having become'?

It indicates the means by which Christ accomplished this deliverance from the curse of the Law [BST, ICC, TH]: by becoming a curse for us.

QUESTION—What relationship is indicated by ὑπέρ 'for'?
1. It means that Christ became a curse 'on our behalf' [BNTC, ICC, LN, Lt, NIGTC, TH; REB]. He did this for our sake [TH]. He took our place and became a curse for our sakes [Lt].

2. It means that Christ became a curse 'in our place' [Lns, Mor, NCBC, NTC; CEV, GW]. This refers to the substitution involved when we were under a curse and Christ took the curse on himself [Lns, Mor]. The preposition itself means 'on behalf of', however, the context implies that Christ took our place in becoming a curse. What should have come to us went to him [NCBC, NTC]. When Christ bore our curse upon himself, we must conclude that his curse-bearing was substitutionary [NTC].

because it-is-written,ª "Accursedᵇ (is) every the-(one) hanging/being-hangedᶜ uponᵈ (a) tree,"ᵉ

LEXICON—a. perf. pass. indic. of γράφω (LN 33.61): 'to be written' [BNTC, Herm, LN, Mor, WBC; KJV, NASB, NCV, NET, NIV, NLT, NRSV]. This is translated 'God has said' [SSA], 'the Scriptures say' [CEV], 'Scripture says' [GW], 'scripture says' [REB, TEV].

b. ἐπικατάρατος (LN 33.475) (BAGD p. 294): 'accursed' [LN], 'cursed' [BAGD, BNTC, Herm, LN, Mor, WBC; all versions except CEV, TEV], 'to condemn' [SSA]. This is translated 'under a curse' [CEV], 'under God's curse' [TEV].

c. pres. mid./pass. participle of κρεμάννυμι (LN 20.76) (BAGD 2.a. p. 450): as a middle voice: 'to hang' [BAGD, Herm, LN, Mor; KJV, NASB, NET, NRSV], as a passive voice: 'to be hanged' [BNTC, LN, WBC; GW, NIV, NLT, REB, TEV], 'to be displayed' [NCV]. The phrase πᾶς ὁ κρεμάμενος 'everyone having hung' is translated 'anyone whom people execute and whose body they attach' [SSA], 'anyone who is nailed' [CEV].

d. ἐπί with genitive object (LN 83.46) (BAGD I.1.a.β. p. 286): 'upon' [LN], 'on' [BAGD, BNTC, Herm, LN, Mor, WBC; all versions except CEV], 'to' [SSA; CEV].

e. ξύλον (LN 3.4) (BAGD 2.c. p. 549): 'tree' [BNTC, Herm, LN, Mor, SSA, WBC; all versions except REB], 'cross' [BAGD], 'gibbet' [REB].

QUESTION—What relationship is indicated by ὅτι 'because'?

This indicates the grounds for saying that Christ became a curse [NTC, SSA]. It gives the reason why Christ's crucifixion on the cross can be interpreted as his becoming accursed [ICC, Lns, TH].

QUESTION—Why does this talk about a tree instead of a cross?

When the OT was written, execution by crucifixion was unknown by the Jews and it was their custom to nail the corpse of a criminal to a wooden post or a tree after being executed [NTC, TH], in order that the body would not defile the land [TH]. Later, it was easy to apply the OT passage to the Roman practice of crucifixion [TH]. In NT times a cross was often called a tree [Mor]. Whether it was a corpse or a living person hanged to a 'tree', the principle of Deut. 21:22 is applicable [NIGTC].

QUESTION—Who is the one who curses the person hanging on a tree?

It is God [Lns, NAC, NIBC, TH, WBC; TEV]. He does not mean that a man is cursed by God just because he is hanged, but that death by hanging was the outward sign in Israel of being cursed by God [TNTC]. Christ crucified was described as having been 'hanged on a tree' and was recognized as having died under God's curse [BST].

3:14 **in-order-that to**[a] **the Gentiles**[b] **the blessing**[c] **of Abraham might-come-to-be**[d] **in**[e] **Christ Jesus,**

LEXICON—a. εἰς with accusative object (LN 84.22): 'to' [BNTC, LN, Mor, WBC; all versions except KJV, NLT], 'on' [KJV], 'upon' [Herm]. See c. [SSA; NLT].
  b. ἔθνος (LN 11.55): 'nation' [LN]. The plural form is translated 'Gentiles' [BNTC, Herm, Mor, SSA, WBC; all versions except GW, NCV], 'the people of the world' [GW], 'those who are not Jews' [NCV].
  c. εὐλογία (LN 33.470) (BAGD 3.b.α. p. 323): 'blessing' [BAGD, BNTC, Herm, LN, Mor, WBC; all versions except NLT]. The phrase εἰς τὰ ἔθνη ἡ εὐλογία τοῦ Ἀβραὰμ γένηται 'to the Gentiles the blessing of Abraham might come' is translated 'God might indeed bless the Gentiles through Abraham' [SSA], 'God has blessed the Gentiles with the same blessing he promised to Abraham' [NLT].
  d. aorist mid. (deponent = act.) subj. of γίνομαι (LN 13.107) (BAGD I.4.c.α. p. 159): 'to come to be, to happen, to occur' [LN], 'to come' [BAGD, BNTC, Herm, Mor, WBC; GW, KJV, NASB, NCV, NET, NIV, NRSV], 'to be extended to' [REB], 'to be given' [TEV], 'to be taken' [CEV]. See c. [SSA; NLT].
  e. ἐν with dative object (LN 83.13, 89.76, 90.6): 'in' [BNTC, LN (83.13), Mor; NASB, NET, NRSV, REB], 'by' [LN (89.76, 90.6)], 'by means of' [LN (89.76), SSA; TEV], 'through' [Herm, LN (89.76), WBC; GW, KJV, NCV, NIV, NLT], 'because of' [CEV].

QUESTION—What relationship is indicated by ἵνα 'in order that'?
  It introduces a purpose clause [WBC]. It introduces the positive purpose of God in all of this [Alf, ICC, Lns, Mor, NIGTC, NTC, TNTC]. It begins a clause that expresses the purpose of Christ's redemptive death [NIC, NIGTC]. It introduces either a purpose clause or a result clause [TH].

QUESTION—How are the nouns related in the genitive construction εὐλογία τοῦ Ἀβραὰμ 'blessing of Abraham'?
  It refers to the blessing promised to Abraham [Lns, TH]. However, it could also refer to the blessing which Abraham had received from God. Both aspects of the blessing could be present here. The blessing itself, when considering 3:8-9, is God's activity in putting the Gentiles into a right relationship with himself [TH]. This must be understood in view of 3:8-9, the blessing of justification by faith. According to Paul's interpretation of Genesis 12:3, this blessing was promised beforehand to the Gentiles and they shared it with Abraham [Alf, ICC, Lns]. The fact that the blessing was intended for the Jews as well is taken for granted [Lns].

QUESTION—What relationship is indicated by ἐν 'in'?
1. It indicates means [ICC, SSA; GW, KJV, NCV, NIV, NLT, TEV]: through Christ Jesus, by means of Christ Jesus. It was through Christ that God's purpose to accept us by faith was revealed and through faith in Christ we participate in that blessing [ICC].
2. It indicates reason [CEV]: because of what Christ Jesus has done.
3. It indicates union with Christ [Mor]. The blessing is received by the Gentiles only as they are in Christ [Mor].

in-order-that the promise[a] of-the Spirit[b] we-might-receive[c] through[d] the faith.[e]

TEXT—Instead of ἐπαγγελίαν 'promise' some manuscripts read εὐλογίαν 'blessing'. GNT reads ἐπαγγελίαν 'promise' with an A decision, indicating that the text is certain.

LEXICON—a. ἐπαγγελία (LN 33.288) (BAGD 2.b. p. 280): 'promise' [BNTC, Herm, LN, Mor, WBC; KJV, NASB, NET, NIV, NRSV], 'what was promised' [BAGD, SSA; CEV, GW, NCV, NLT, REB, TEV].
b. πνεῦμα (LN 12.18) (BAGD 5.d.α. p. 677): 'Spirit' [BNTC, Herm, LN, Mor, SSA, WBC; all versions except CEV, NLT], 'Holy Spirit' [LN; CEV, NLT], 'Spirit of God' [BAGD, LN].
c. aorist act. subj. of λαμβάνω (LN 57.125) (BAGD 2. p. 465): 'to receive' [BAGD, BNTC, Herm, LN, Mor, SSA, WBC; all versions except CEV], 'to be given' [CEV].
d. διά with genitive object (LN 90.8) (BAGD A.III.1.d. p. 180): 'through' [BAGD, BNTC, Herm, LN, Mor; GW, KJV, NASB, NLT, NRSV, REB, TEV], 'by means of' [LN, SSA], 'by' [WBC; CEV, NCV, NET, NIV].
e. πίστις (LN 31.85): 'faith' [BNTC, Herm, LN, Mor, WBC; all versions except NCV]. This noun is also translated as a verb: 'to trust' [SSA], 'to believe' [NCV].

QUESTION—What relationship is indicated by ἵνα 'that'?
It introduces a purpose clause [ICC, Lns, NAC, NCBC, NIGTC, WBC]. This second clause in 3:14 should be understood as coordinate with the first clause [Alf, Herm, ICC, Lns, NCBC, NIC, NTC, WBC], the second clause explains the first clause [NIGTC, NTC]. The second clause is attached to the first clause and expresses the moral dependence of the one on the other [Lt].

QUESTION—How are the nouns related in the genitive construction ἐπαγγελίαν τοῦ πνεύματος 'promise of the Spirit'?
It means the promised Spirit [ICC, NCBC, NTC, TH; CEV, GW, NLT, REB], the Spirit who has been promised [Herm; NCV, TEV]. It means the promise which has the Spirit for its object [Alf].

QUESTION—What relationship is indicated by διά 'through'?
It indicates the means by which we receive the Spirit [Lns, SSA].

QUESTION—Who is the first person plural referent of λάβωμεν 'we might receive'?

It refers to all Christians [Alf, BNTC, ICC, Lns, Lt, NAC, NCBC, TH, TNTC; NLT].

DISCOURSE UNIT: 3:15–29 [NCBC; GW, NASB]. The topic is the promise and law [NCBC], the relationship between law and promise [GW], the intent of the law [NASB].

DISCOURSE UNIT: 3:15–25 [NAC; NIV]. The topic is the law and the promise.

DISCOURSE UNIT: 3:15–23 [NLT]. The topic is the law and God's promises.

DISCOURSE UNIT: 3:15–22 [BST, Mor, NIC; NET]. The topic is Abraham, Moses, and Christ [BST], the covenant [Mor], the law and the promise [NIC], inheritance comes from promises and not law [NET].

DISCOURSE UNIT: 3:15–20 [GNT; CEV, NCV, TEV]. The topic is the law and the promise.

DISCOURSE UNIT: 3:15–18 [NIGTC, TNTC; NRSV]. The topic is the priority and permanence of the promise [NIGTC], does law annul promise? [TNTC], the promise to Abraham [NRSV].

3:15 Brothers,[a] I-speak[b] according-to[c] man;[d]

LEXICON—a. ἀδελφός (LN 11.23): 'brother, Christian brother, fellow believer' [LN]. The plural form is translated 'brothers' [BNTC, Herm, Mor, SSA, WBC; NIV], 'friends' [CEV, REB, TEV], 'brothers and sisters' [GW, NCV, NET, NLT, NRSV], 'brethren' [KJV, NASB].

b. pres. act. indic. of λέγω (LN 33.69) (BAGD I.5. p. 468): 'to speak' [BNTC, LN, Mor; KJV, NASB], 'to reason' [SSA], 'to illustrate' [NET], 'to say' [BAGD]. The phrase κατὰ ἄνθρωπον λέγω 'I speak according to man' is translated 'let me take an example from everyday life' [WBC; NIV], 'I will use an everyday example to explain what I mean' [CEV], 'let me use an example from everyday life' [GW], 'here's an example from everyday life' [NLT], 'I give an example from everyday life' [NRSV], 'I am going to use an everyday example' [TEV], 'let me give you an illustration' [REB], 'let us think in human terms' [NCV], 'I draw an example from common human life' [Herm].

c. κατά with accusative object (LN 89.4, 89.8): 'according to, in accordance with' [LN (89.8)], 'in relation to' [LN (89.4, 89.8)], 'with regard to' [LN (89.4)], 'in' [BNTC, SSA; NCV], 'as' [Mor], 'in terms of' [NASB], 'with' [NET], 'after the manner of' [KJV], 'from' [Herm]. See b. [WBC; CEV, GW, NIV, NLT, NRSV, REB, TEV].

d. ἄνθρωπος (LN 9.1) (BAGD 1.c. p. 68): 'man' [LN, Mor], 'person, human being' [LN]. The plural form is translated 'men' [KJV]. The phrase κατὰ ἄνθρωπον 'according to man' is translated 'from a human standpoint, in a human way' [BAGD], 'in human terms' [BNTC; NCV], 'in a human manner' [SSA], 'with a human analogy' [NET], 'in terms of human relations' [NASB], 'from common human life' [Herm]. See b. for translations of the clause [WBC; CEV, GW, NIV, NLT, NRSV, REB, TEV].

QUESTION—What is meant by ἀδελφοί 'brothers'?

In this reference brothers should be understood as 'fellow Christians' or 'fellow believers in Christ' [TH]. It refers to the male and female members of the Galatian churches [NIBC].

Likewise/although[a] (a) covenant[b] of-(a)-man[c] ratified[d] no-one sets-aside[e] or adds-to.[f]

LEXICON—a. ὅμως (LN **64.11, 89.74**) (BAGD p. 569 *twice*): 'likewise' [BAGD, Herm, LN (64.11)], 'similarly' [**LN (64.11)**], 'also' [BAGD], 'although' [**LN (89.74)**], 'though' [LN (89.74); KJV], 'all the same, yet' [BAGD], 'nevertheless' [BAGD, SSA], 'even' [BNTC, Mor; NCV], 'even though' [NASB, NET], not explicit [CEV, GW, NRSV, REB, TEV]. This is translated 'so it is in this case' [WBC; NIV, NLT]. This entire clause is translated 'even though it involves only a man's last will and testament, nevertheless no one annuls it' [BAGD].

b. διαθήκη (LN **34.44**, 57.124) (BAGD 1. p. 183): 'covenant' [**LN (34.44)**, Mor, WBC; KJV, NASB, NIV], 'pact' [LN (34.44)], 'testament' [Herm, LN (57.124)], 'will' [BAGD, BNTC, LN (57.124); GW, NRSV], 'will/covenant' [SSA], 'agreement' [CEV, NCV, NLT, TEV], 'contract' [NET], 'will and testament' [REB].

c. ἄνθρωπος (LN 9.1, 9.24): 'man' [Herm, LN (9.24)], 'person' [LN (9.1); GW, NRSV], 'human being' [LN (9.1)], 'human' [BNTC, Mor, SSA, WBC; NET, NIV], 'someone' [CEV], 'man' [KJV, NASB, REB], not explicit [NLT]. This singular form is also translated as plural: 'persons' [NCV], 'people' [TEV].

d. perf. pass. participle of κυρόω (LN **76.18**) (BAGD 1. p. 461): 'to be ratified' [BAGD, BNTC, Herm, Mor; NASB, NET, NRSV], 'to be validated' [**LN**, SSA], 'to be put into force' [**LN**], 'to be established' [WBC; NIV], 'to be accepted' [NCV], 'to be executed' [REB], 'to be confirmed' [KJV], 'to be put into effect' [GW], not explicit [NLT]. This passive voice is translated actively with 'the participants' as subjects: 'once someone agrees to something' [CEV], 'when two people agree on a matter' [TEV].

e. pres. act. indic. of ἀθετέω (LN 76.24) (BAGD 1.a. p. 21): 'to set aside' [BAGD, BNTC; NASB, NET, NIV, NLT, REB], 'to reject' [LN, SSA], 'to regard as invalid' [LN], 'to declare invalid' [BAGD], 'to nullify' [BAGD, Mor], 'to cancel' [CEV, GW], 'to stop' [NCV], 'to annul' [Herm, WBC; NRSV], 'to break' [TEV], 'to disannul' [KJV].

f. pres. mid. (deponent = act.) indic. of ἐπιδιατάσσομαι (LN **59.73**) (BAGD p. 292): 'to add to' [BNTC, **LN**, SSA, WBC; KJV, NIV, NRSV], 'to add a codicil' [BAGD, Herm; REB], 'to introduce something new' [LN], 'to alter' [Mor], 'to change' [CEV], 'to add conditions to' [GW, NASB], 'to add anything to' [NCV, NET, TEV], 'to amend' [NLT].

QUESTION—What sense of ὅμως 'likewise' is in focus here?
  1. It has the sense of 'equally, likewise'. Here this should be read in terms of comparative relations rather than antithetical relations [WBC].
  2. It has the sense of 'although' [Lns; KJV, NASB, NET]. It is purely concessive [Lns].

QUESTION—Does διαθήκη refer to a will which involves only one person or does it refer to a covenant which involves two individuals?
  1. It refers to a covenant [Alf, ICC, Lt, Mor, TH, WBC; KJV, NASB, NET, NIV, TEV]. The biblical usage of the term is in the sense of an agreement between two parties. The same word is used in 3:17 where it clearly means 'covenant,' since to translate it 'testament' or 'will' would imply the death of God before the testament goes into effect [TH]. The singular number of this noun (man) furnishes no argument against the meaning 'covenant' for two reasons: (1) the covenant, in Hebrew thought, though constituting a relation between two persons often proceeds from one person; (2) the noun is here most naturally understood as qualitative ('human') as in the phrase κατὰ ἄνθρωπον 'according to man' [ICC].
  2. It refers to a will or testament [BST, Lns, NIC, NIGTC, NTC, TNTC; GW, NRSV, REB]. The many legal terms in the passage clearly suggest that the word is being used in the sense of Hellenistic law and points to 'will, testament' as the correct interpretation [NIC]. 'Testament' is the meaning here where it is used with the singular; a man's testament is being referred to. If a human covenant were being referred to, we should have the plural [Lns].

3:16 Now[a] to-Abraham were-spoken[b] the promises,[c] and to his seed.[d]

LEXICON—a. δέ (LN 89.94, 89.124): 'now' [Herm, Mor, SSA; KJV, NASB, NET, NRSV, REB, TEV], 'and' [LN (89.94)], 'furthermore' [WBC], 'but' [BNTC, LN (89.124)], not explicit [CEV, GW, NCV, NIV, NLT].
  b. aorist pass. indic. of λέγω (LN 33.69): 'to be spoken' [BNTC, Herm, LN, Mor, WBC; GW, NASB, NET, NIV], 'to be announced' [SSA], 'to give' [NLT], 'to be made' [CEV, KJV, NCV, NRSV, TEV], 'to be pronounced' [REB].
  c. ἐπαγγελία (LN 33.288) (BAGD 2.a. p. 280): 'promise' [BAGD, LN; NLT], 'what he was promising' [SSA]. The plural form is translated 'promises' [BNTC, Herm, Mor, WBC; all versions except NLT].
  d. σπέρμα (LN 10.29) (BAGD 2.b. p. 762): 'seed' [BAGD, BNTC, Herm, LN, Mor, WBC; KJV, NASB, NIV], 'posterity, descendants' [BAGD, LN], 'children' [BAGD], 'offspring' [LN; NRSV], 'descendant' [SSA; CEV, GW, NCV, NET, TEV], 'child' [NLT], 'issue' [REB].

QUESTION—What relationship is indicated by δέ 'now'?
It is a coordinating conjunction which relates the two statements of 3:15–16 as complementary arguments [WBC]. It is transitional [TH].

QUESTION—Who is the subject of ἐρρέθησαν 'were spoken'?
It is God [Alf, BST, Herm, Lns, SSA].

QUESTION—What is the significance of the change from the singular ἐπαγγελίαν 'promise' in 3:14 to the plural ἐπαγγελίαι 'promises' in this verse?
There is no significance in the change [ICC, NCBC, TH, WBC]. This plural form is translated as singular [NLT]. It is plural because the promise was repeated many times (Gen. 12:7; 15:5, 18; 17:7, 8; 22:18) [Alf, ICC, Lns, Lt]. Since the promise was addressed to Abraham, the two occasions must be Gen. 13:15 and 17:8 [Lt]. It is plural in reference to the two promises spoken to Abraham and his seed, that of the final part of Gen. 12:3 where the tribes of the earth were to be blessed in Abraham and Gen. 22:18 where all the nations will be blessed in Abraham's seed and Paul is taking this blessing to be justification [SSA].

Not he/it-says,[a] "And to-the seeds,"[b] as a-reference-to[c] many,[d]

LEXICON—a. pres. act. indic. of λέγω (LN 33.69) (BAGD I.7. p. 468): 'to say' [BNTC, Herm, LN, Mor, WBC; all versions except CEV, TEV], 'it says' [BAGD]. The phrase οὐ λέγει 'not it says' is translated 'the words which God spoke were not' [SSA], 'the promises were not made to' [CEV], 'the Scripture does not use (the plural)' [TEV].

b. σπέρμα (LN 10.29) (BAGD 2.b. p. 762): 'seed, posterity' [BAGD, LN], 'descendant, offspring' [LN]. The plural form is translated 'seeds' [BNTC, Herm, Mor, WBC; KJV, NASB, NIV], 'descendants' [SSA; CEV, GW, NCV, NET, TEV], 'children' [BAGD; NLT], 'offsprings' [NRSV], 'issues' [REB].

c. ἐπί with genitive object (LN **90.23**) (BAGD I.1.b.γ. p. 286): 'a reference to' [**LN**], 'about' [BAGD, Herm, LN], 'of' [BAGD]. The phrase ὡς ἐπί 'as a reference to' is translated 'as referring to' [NASB], 'referring to' [SSA; GW, NET], 'as to' [BNTC, WBC], 'as in the case of' [Mor], 'as of' [KJV, NRSV], 'meaning' [NIV, TEV], 'as if it meant' [NLT], 'that would mean' [NCV], not explicit [CEV, REB].

d. πολύς (LN 59.1) (BAGD I.2.a.α. p. 688): 'many' [BAGD, BNTC, Herm, LN, Mor, SSA, WBC; CEV, GW, KJV, NASB, NCV, NET, NRSV], 'many people' [NIV, TEV], 'many descendants' [NLT]. The phrase ὡς ἐπὶ πολλῶν 'as to many' is translated 'in the plural' [REB].

QUESTION—Who is the speaker of λέγει 'it says'?
1. It is God [Alf, ICC, Lns, WBC; CEV, NCV].
2. It is Scripture [GW, NET, NIV, TEV].

but as a-reference-to one,[a] **"And to-your seed,"**[b] **who is Christ.**
LEXICON—a. εἰς (LN 60.10): 'one' [BNTC, Herm, LN, Mor, SSA, WBC; all versions except NLT, REB]. This is translated 'in the singular' [REB]. See b. [NLT].
b. σπέρμα (LN 10.29) (BAGD 2.b. p. 762): 'seed' [BNTC, Herm, LN, Mor, WBC; KJV, NASB, NIV], 'posterity, descendants' [LN], 'offspring' [LN; NRSV], 'descendant' [SSA; GW, NCV, NET, TEV], 'issue' [REB]. It is contrary to normal OT usage when one person, i.e., the Messiah, is called σπέρμα 'seed' [BAGD]. This entire phrase is translated 'But the promise was to his child and that, of course, means Christ' [NLT], 'but only to one, and that one is Christ' [CEV].
QUESTION—What is significant about the absence of the definite article with 'Christ'?
It indicates that Paul is using 'Christ' as a proper name and not as the title 'Messiah' [Mor].

3:17 **Now**[a] **this I-say:**[b] **the Law,**[c] **having-come-into-existence**[d] **after**[e] **four-hundred and thirty years,**
LEXICON—a. δέ (LN 89.87, 89.94): 'now' [Mor], 'and' [LN (89.87, 89.94); KJV], 'and then' [LN (89.87)], 'so' [WBC], 'but' [Herm], not explicit [BNTC, SSA; all versions except KJV].
b. pres. act. indic. of λέγω (LN 33.69, **33.140**) (BAGD I.2.b. p. 468): 'to say' [LN (33.69)], 'to mean' [LN (33.140)]. The phrase τοῦτο λέγω 'this I say' [Mor, WBC; KJV] is also translated 'this is what I mean' [BAGD, Herm, **LN** (33.140); GW, NCV], 'what I mean is this' [NIV], 'what I mean is that' [TEV], 'my point is this' [BNTC; NRSV, REB], 'I reason as follows' [SSA], 'what I am saying is that' [CEV], 'what I am saying is this' [NASB, NET], 'this is what I am trying to say' [NLT].
c. νόμος (LN 33.55, 33.333) (BAGD 3. p. 542): 'Law' [Herm, LN (33.55); CEV, NASB, TEV], 'law' [BNTC, LN (33.333), Mor, WBC; KJV, NCV, NET, NIV, NLT, NRSV, REB], the law which Moses received from God [BAGD], 'Mosaic law' [SSA], 'the laws given to Moses' [GW].
d. perf. act. participle of γίνομαι (LN 13.80, 85.7): 'to come into existence' [LN (13.80)], 'to come to be' [LN (85.7)], 'to come' [BNTC, Herm; NASB, NCV, NET, NRSV], 'to appear' [WBC], 'to be given' [CEV, GW, TEV], 'to be introduced' [NIV], 'to be made' [REB], 'to be' [KJV], '(God) gave' [SSA; NLT], not explicit [Mor].
e. μετά with accusative object (LN 67.48) (BAGD B.II.1. p. 510): 'after' [BAGD, LN, SSA; GW, KJV], 'later' [BNTC, Herm, Mor, WBC; all versions except CEV, GW, KJV], not explicit [CEV].
QUESTION—What relationship is indicated by δέ 'and'?
It is a transitional particle which in connection with τοῦτο λέγω· 'this I say' alerts the reader to an immediately following concluding statement [WBC].

GALATIANS 3:17

QUESTION—What is the function of the phrase τοῦτο δὲ λέγω 'and this I say'?

It alerts the reader to pay attention to what follows [Herm]. It indicates that what follows is significant [Mor]. It is to resume for further argument or explanation a thought already expressed [ICC, TH]. It draws attention to a further development of the argument that was started in 3:15 [NCBC]. It signals a concluding section [WBC].

QUESTION—What law is referred to here?

It refers to the Torah [Herm, TNTC], the Mosaic Law [SSA; GW].

(does) not void^a a-covenant^b previously-ratified^c by^d God,

TEXT—Following θεοῦ 'God', some manuscripts add εἰς Χριστόν 'in Christ'. GNT rejects this addition with an A decision, indicating that the text is certain. Εἰς Χριστόν 'in Christ' is added by KJV.

LEXICON—a. pres. act. indic. of ἀκυρόω (LN 76.25) (BAGD p. 34): 'to void' [BAGD, BNTC, Herm, Mor], 'to invalidate the authority of' [LN; NASB, REB], 'to reject' [LN], 'to do away with' [WBC], 'to change' [NCV], 'to cancel' [NET], 'to set aside' [NIV], 'to be cancelled' [NLT], 'to annul' [SSA; NRSV], 'to break' [TEV], 'to disannul' [KJV], not explicit [CEV, GW].

b. διαθήκη (LN 34.44, 57.124) (BAGD 1., 2. p. 183): 'covenant' [BAGD (2.), BNTC, LN (34.44), Mor, SSA, WBC; KJV, NASB, NET, NIV, NRSV, TEV], 'pact' [LN (34.44)], 'testament' [Herm, LN (57.124)], 'will' [BAGD (1.), LN (57.124)], 'promise' [CEV, GW], 'agreement' [NCV, NLT], 'testament or covenant' [REB].

c. perf. pass. participle of προκυρόω (LN **76.19**) (BAGD p. 708): 'to be previously ratified' [BAGD, Herm; NASB, NET, NRSV], 'to be validated in advance' [LN], 'to be established in advance' [**LN**], 'to be ratified beforehand' [BNTC, Mor], 'to be previously established' [WBC; NIV], 'to be previously validated' [SSA], 'to be put into effect' [GW], 'to be made' [CEV, NLT, TEV], 'to already have been validated' [REB], 'to be confirmed before' [KJV], not explicit [NCV].

d. ὑπό with genitive object (LN 90.1): 'by' [BNTC, Herm, LN, Mor, WBC; NASB, NET, NIV, NRSV, REB], 'of' [KJV], not explicit [SSA; CEV, GW, NCV, NLT, TEV].

QUESTION—What relationship is indicated by ὑπὸ τοῦ θεοῦ 'by God'?

The phrase ὑπὸ τοῦ θεοῦ 'by God' identifies God as the one who gave the Abrahamic covenant [WBC], the one who established it [Mor, WBC], or confirmed it [Lns]. God made the covenant and promised to keep it [TH; TEV].

so-as^a to-invalidate^b the promise.^c

a. εἰς with accusative object (LN 89.48): 'so as' [BNTC, Mor; NASB, NET, NRSV], 'with the result that, to cause' [LN], 'so that as a result' [LN, SSA], 'and so' [NCV, REB], 'and thus' [NIV], 'that it should' [KJV], 'in order' [Herm], not explicit [WBC; CEV, GW, NLT, TEV].

b. aorist act. infin. of καταργέω (LN 76.26) (BAGD 1.b. p. 417): 'to invalidate' [LN; NET], 'to make ineffective' [BAGD, BNTC; REB], 'to nullify' [BAGD, Herm, Mor; NASB, NRSV], 'to abolish' [LN], 'to annul' [WBC], 'to change or cancel' [CEV], 'to cancel' [SSA; GW, TEV], 'to destroy' [NCV], 'to do away with' [NIV], 'to break' [NLT], 'to make of none effect' [KJV].

c. ἐπαγγελία (LN 33.288) (BAGD 2.a. p. 280): 'promise' [BAGD, BNTC, Herm, LN, Mor, WBC; all versions except REB], 'what he promised' [SSA]. The singular form is also translated as plural: 'promises' [REB].

QUESTION—What relationship is indicated by εἰς 'so as to'?

It indicates the result that would occur if the covenant had been voided [Lns, WBC].

3:18 For if from[a] law (is) the inheritance,[b] no-longer[c] (is it) from[d] promise;[e]

LEXICON—a. ἐκ with genitive object (LN 90.16): 'from' [BNTC, LN], '(comes) from' [NRSV], '(comes) through' [Herm], 'by' [LN; REB], 'of' [Mor; KJV], '(is) based on' [WBC; NASB, NET], 'depends on' [NIV, TEV]. The phrase εἰ ἐκ νόμου 'if from law (is)' is translated 'if because persons obey a law God gives to them' [SSA], 'if we have to obey the Law in order to receive' [CEV], 'if (the inheritance) could be received only by keeping the law' [NLT], 'if we have to gain (the inheritance) by following those laws' [GW], 'if the law could give' [NCV].

b. κληρονομία (LN 57.140) (BAGD 3. p. 435): 'inheritance' [BNTC, Herm, LN, Mor, WBC; all versions except CEV, NCV, TEV], 'Abraham's blessing' [NCV], 'God's gift' [TEV], 'God's blessings' [CEV], 'what he has promised them' [SSA], 'salvation' [BAGD].

c. οὐκέτι (LN 67.130) (BAGD 2. p. 592): 'no longer' [BAGD, BNTC, Herm, LN, Mor, WBC; GW, NASB, NET, NIV, NRSV, TEV], 'no more' [KJV]. The clause οὐκέτι ἐξ ἐπαγγελίας 'no longer is it from promise' is translated 'then God gives to persons what he has promised them not just because God has promised that he would give it' [SSA], 'then it would not be the result of accepting God's promise' [NLT], 'then it is not by promise' [REB], 'those blessings don't really come to us because of God's promise' [CEV], 'then the promise would not be necessary' [NCV].

d. ἐκ with genitive object (LN 90.16): 'from' [BNTC, LN; NRSV], 'by' [LN; REB], 'of' [Mor; KJV], 'through' [Herm], 'based on' [WBC; NASB, NET], 'comes to us because of' [CEV, GW], 'depends on' [NIV, TEV], 'result of accepting' [NLT], not explicit [NCV]. See c. [SSA].

e. ἐπαγγελία (LN 33.288) (BAGD 2.a. p. 280): 'promise' [BAGD, BNTC, Herm, LN, Mor, WBC; all versions]. This noun is also translated as a verb with 'God' as the subject: 'to promise' [SSA].

QUESTION—What relationship is indicated by γάρ 'for'?
It is explanatory and sets up the real reason for Paul's conclusion of 3:17 that promise and law are opposed to one another when thought of in terms of acceptance before God [WBC]. It makes the fact clearer that the law does not alter the confirmation of the promise, it does not abolish the promise [Lns].

QUESTION—What relationship is indicated by εἰ 'if'?
It makes a condition that, as in 2:21, Paul clearly regards as contrary to the truth [ICC].

QUESTION—What relationship is indicated by ἐκ 'from' in ἐκ νόμου 'from law'?
It indicates that the inheritance is derived from the law [Lns], that is, by obeying the law [SSA; CEV, GW, NLT]. It is based on the law [WBC; NASB, NET].

QUESTION—What is meant by κληρονομία 'inheritance'?
By this term Paul means to include all the spiritual blessings promised to Abraham and his seed [Alf, NCBC]. It is the blessing promised by God and ratified to him and to his 'seed' by means of an unconditional covenant [NAC]. To a Jew, the word 'inheritance' would be a reminder of the promise of God to Israel concerning the possession of Canaan, the promised land, and of what God had done in order to fulfill that promise. Therefore, the word 'inheritance' was used figuratively to refer to spiritual favors and blessings from God. Paul may be referring to the content of God's promise to Abraham which is the gift of a right relationship with God (3:6) [TH]. It refers to the possession promised in the covenant, which was with Abraham and his seed [ICC]. It includes all the benefits of God's work of salvation [Herm]. Paul is thinking in the first place of God's great promise to Abraham. He is also thinking, in a New Testament sense, of the gift of the Spirit as in 3:14 [TNTC].

QUESTION—What relationship is indicated by ἐξ 'from' in ἐξ ἐπαγγελίας 'from promise'?
It indicates that the inheritance is derived from the promise [Lns].

but to-Abraham through[a] promise[b] God freely-gave[c] (it).

LEXICON—a. διά with genitive object (LN 90.8) (BAGD A.III.1.e. p. 180): 'through' [BNTC, LN (90.8), Mor; GW, NCV, NET, NIV, NRSV], 'by means of' [LN (90.8); NASB], 'by virtue of' [BAGD], 'by' [Herm, WBC; KJV, REB], 'as a' [NLT], 'because of' [TEV], not explicit [SSA; CEV].

b. ἐπαγγελία (LN 33.288) (BAGD 2.a. p. 280): 'promise' [BAGD, BNTC, Herm, LN, Mor, WBC; all versions], 'what he had promised' [SSA].

c. perf. mid. (deponent = act.) indic. of χαρίζομαι (LN **57.102**) (BAGD 1. p. 876; 3. p. 877): 'to give freely' [BAGD, BNTC; GW, NCV], 'to give graciously' [**LN**, WBC; NET, NIV], 'to give graciously as a favor' [BAGD], 'to bestow generously' [LN], 'to grant' [Herm, LN; NASB,

NRSV], 'to give' [LN, Mor, SSA; KJV, NLT, TEV], 'to make' [CEV], 'to bestow' [REB].

QUESTION—What relationship is indicated by διά 'through'?

It indicates the means through which God gave his good gift [Mor].

DISCOURSE UNIT: 3:19–4:7 [NRSV]. The topic is the purpose of the law.

DISCOURSE UNIT: 3:19–29 [TNTC]. The topic is what is the purpose of the law?

DISCOURSE UNIT: 3:19–25 [WBC]. The topic is the purpose and function of the law.

DISCOURSE UNIT: 3:19–22 [NIGTC]. The topic is the purpose of the law.

3:19 Why then (is) the Law?[a] For-the-sake-of[b] the transgressions[c] it-was-added,[d]

TEXT—Instead of νόμος; τῶν παραβάσεων χάριν προσετέθη 'Law? For the sake of the transgressions it was added' some manuscripts read νόμος; τῶν παραδόσεων χάριν ἐτέθη 'Law? For the sake of handing over it was placed'; others read νόμος τῶν πράξεων; ἐτέθη 'law of deeds? It was placed'; and one ancient manuscript reads νόμος τῶν πράξεων; 'law of deeds?' GNT reads νόμος; τῶν παραβάσεων χάριν προσετέθη 'Law? For the sake of the transgressions it was added' with a C decision, indicating that the Committee had difficulty in making the decision.

LEXICON—a. νόμος (LN 33.55, 33.333) (BAGD 3. p. 542): 'Law' [Herm, LN (33.55); CEV, NASB, TEV], 'law' [BNTC, LN (33.333), Mor, WBC; KJV, NCV, NET, NIV, NLT, NRSV, REB], the law which Moses received from God [BAGD], 'Mosaic law' [SSA]. The plural form is translated 'laws' [GW].

b. χάριν with a preceding genitive object (LN 89.29, **89.60**) (BAGD 1. p. 877): 'for the sake of' [BAGD, LN (89.60)], 'because of' [LN (89.29)], 'for the purpose of' [LN (89.60)]. The phrase τῶν παραβάσεων χάριν 'for the sake of the transgressions' [BAGD, BNTC] is also translated 'because of transgressions' [WBC; KJV, NASB, NET, NIV, NRSV], 'because of the transgressions' [Herm], 'on account of transgression' [Mor], 'in order to show what wrongdoing is' [**LN** (89.60); TEV], 'in order that he might affect sinful human beings' [SSA], 'to show people how guilty they are' [NLT], 'to make wrongdoing a legal offence' [REB], 'to show that we sin' [CEV], 'to show that the wrong things people do are against God's will' [NCV], 'to identify what wrongdoing is' [GW]. It means to bring about transgressions [BAGD].

c. παράβασις (LN 36.28) (BAGD p. 612): 'transgression' [BAGD, BNTC, Herm, LN, Mor, WBC; KJV, NASB, NET, NIV, NRSV], 'wrongdoing' [GW, REB, TEV], 'wrong things' [NCV]. This noun is also translated as a verb: 'that we sin' [CEV]; as an adjective: 'sinful (human beings)'

[SSA], 'how guilty (they are)' [NLT]. A transgression is a willful violation of an existing law [TH].
d. aorist pass. indic. of προστίθημι (LN 59.72) (BAGD 1.a. p. 719): 'to be added' [BAGD, BNTC, LN, Mor, WBC; all versions except CEV, NCV, NLT], 'to be given' [CEV, NCV, NLT]. The passive is also translated actively with 'God' as the subject: 'to give' [SSA]. This is translated 'it was given in addition' [Herm].

QUESTION—What relationship is indicated by οὖν 'then'?

It connects this question to what precedes it [ICC, WBC]. It gives the conclusion of an implied reason: 'Since God has blessed Abraham not because Abraham obeyed a law, someone may ask, "Why did God later give the Mosaic law?"' [SSA].

QUESTION—What relationship is indicated by χάριν 'for the sake of'?

It indicates the purpose for which the law was given [ICC, Lns, Lt, NIC, NIGTC, SSA; TEV]. The law was given in order to produce transgressions because with the law comes the conscious disobedience of definite commandments [NIGTC]. It was added to the transgressions in order to awaken a sense of guilt [NTC]. It indicates that the law was added in order to create transgressions, since where there is no law there is no transgression [Lt]. 'It made wrong doing a legal offense' [REB]. Its purpose was to define what transgressions were [Lns]. The law was given to bring about a sense of guilt [NTC] and showed us how much we need salvation [Mor]. Giving the law for some purpose that is related to sin is also giving law because of sin [SSA]. The law had shown men the right way to live and had made men aware when they deviated from it and it is in this sense that Paul means that the law came 'because' of transgressions [Alf, BST, NCBC, NTC, WBC; NASB, NET, NIV, NRSV].

QUESTION—What is meant by προσετέθη 'it was added'?

It was an addition to the promises [NTC]. It marks the law as supplementary, and therefore subordinate to the covenant [ICC, TH]. The law was added to accomplish some subordinate and supplementary purpose [NAC]. The law was simply a supplement to the promise [Mor]. Or, the law was not added as a supplement to the promise [Lns, NIGTC], it was added to the human situation [NIGTC]. It was added to bring out the fact of their transgressions [Lns].

QUESTION—Who added the Law?

It is God [Herm, Lns, Mor, NIBC, NTC, SSA, WBC].

until[a] when should-come[b] the seed[c] to/of-whom it-was-promised,[d]

LEXICON—a. ἄχρι (LN 67.119): 'until' [BNTC, Herm, LN, Mor, SSA, WBC; all versions except REB], 'pending' [REB].
b. aorist act. subj. of ἔρχομαι (LN 15.81): 'to come' [BNTC, Herm, LN, Mor, SSA, WBC; all versions except NET, REB], 'to arrive' [NET, REB].
c. σπέρμα (LN 10.29) (BAGD 2.b. p. 762): 'seed' [BNTC, LN, Mor; KJV, NASB], 'Seed' [WBC; NIV], 'posterity' [LN], 'offspring' [Herm, LN;

NRSV], 'descendant' [LN, SSA; CEV, GW, NCV, NET, TEV], 'child' [NLT], 'issue' [REB]. It is contrary to normal OT usage when one person, that is, the Messiah, is called σπέρμα 'seed' [BAGD].

d. perf. pass. indic. of ἐπαγγέλλομαι (LN 33.286) (BAGD 1.b. p. 281): 'to be promised' [LN, Mor, SSA]. The phrase ᾧ ἐπήγγελται 'to/of whom it was promised' is translated 'to whom it was promised' [Mor], 'to whom the promise was given' [GW], 'to whom the promise was/had-been made' [BNTC, Herm; KJV, NASB, NET, NRSV, REB, TEV], 'to whom God's promise was made' [NLT], 'for whom the promise was intended' [BAGD, WBC], 'who was given the promise' [CEV], 'who had been promised' [NCV], 'to whom God had announced what he was promising' [SSA], 'to whom the promise referred' [NIV].

QUESTION—What relationship is indicated by ἄχρις 'until'?

It has a temporal sense of 'until' [WBC; all versions except REB]. This whole clause sets the limit to the period during which the law continued [ICC].

QUESTION—Was the promise made to or about the seed?

1. The promise was made *to* Christ [ICC, Lns, Lt, Mor, NIGTC, NTC, SSA; all versions except NCV, NIV]. In 3:16 it says that the promise was made to both Abraham and his seed [TH]. Christ is the Seed of Abraham and the promise had been made to him so that he is the heir of the whole inheritance and those who are in Christ are joint heirs with him [Lns].
2. The promise was made *about* Christ [NCV, NIV]. 'It was added because of transgressions until the Seed to whom the promise referred had come' [NIV]. 'And it continued until the special descendant, who had been promised, came' [NCV].

having-been-put-into-effect^a through^b angels by^c (the) hand of-(a) mediator.^d

LEXICON—a. aorist pass. participle of διατάσσω (LN 62.8) (BAGD p. 189): 'to be put into effect' [LN; GW, NIV], 'to be arranged for' [LN], 'to be ordered' [BAGD, BNTC], 'to be appointed' [Mor], 'to be ordained' [Herm, SSA, WBC; KJV, NASB, NRSV], 'to be given' [NCV, NLT], 'to be administered' [NET], 'to be promulgated' [REB], 'to be handed down' [TEV]. The passive voice is also translated as active with 'the angels' as the subject: 'to give' [CEV].

b. διά with genitive object (LN 89.76, 90.4) (BAGD A.III.2.a. p. 180): 'through' [BNTC, Herm, LN (89.76, 90.4), Mor, WBC; GW, NASB, NCV, NET, NIV, NRSV, REB], 'by' [LN (90.4); KJV, TEV], 'by means of' [BAGD, LN (89.76), SSA]. The phrase διαταγεὶς δι' ἀγγέλων 'put into effect through angels' is translated 'God gave his laws to angels to give to Moses' [NLT], 'angels gave the law' [CEV].

c. ἐν with dative object (LN 83.13, 90.6, 90.10): 'by' [LN (90.6, 90.10)], 'in' [LN (83.13)], 'through' [Herm]. The phrase ἐν χειρ 'by the hand of' [BNTC] is also translated 'in the hand of' [Mor; KJV], 'by the agency of'

[NASB], 'by' [NET, NIV, NRSV], 'by means of' [WBC], 'using' [GW], 'with (a man)' [TEV], '(given through angels) who used Moses for' [NCV], 'and he gave it to' [CEV], 'Moses transmitted (the law to the people)' [SSA], not explicit [NLT, REB].
   d. μεσίτης (LN 31.22) (BAGD p. 507): 'mediator' [BAGD, Herm, LN, Mor, SSA, WBC; GW, KJV, NASB, NCV, NIV, NRSV], 'mediator between God and the people' [NLT], 'go-between' [LN], 'a man acting as a go-between' [TEV], 'intermediary' [BNTC; NET, REB], not explicit [CEV].
QUESTION—Who put the law into effect?
   It is God [Alf, NAC, NCBC, NIBC, NTC, SSA, TH; NLT].
QUESTION—What relationship is indicated by διά 'through'?
   'God gave his laws to angels to give to Moses' [NLT]. The angels were not the source of the Law, rather God used angels to pass the Law to Moses [TH]. The OT does not tell about this, but the giving of the law or message by angels is mentioned in Acts 7:53 and Heb. 2:2, and in Acts 7:38 it tells about an angel speaking to Moses [SSA].
QUESTION—What is meant by ἐν χειρὶ μεσίτου 'in the hand of a mediator'?
   It indicates the way the law was given to Israel [Mor]. 'In the hand of' is a Semitic idiom meaning 'through' [BNTC, Lt], 'by means of' [SSA]. Moses was the mediator and through him the Law was given to the people on Mt. Sinai [ICC, Lns, Mor, NIGTC, TH]. 'Angels gave the Law to Moses, and he gave it to the people' [CEV]. Moses was not the mediator between the angels and the people, but between God and the people [NTC, TH]. God acted through angels, yet not with Israel itself, but with Israel's representative who than took all the commandments to the people [Lns].

3:20 Now the mediator[a] is not of-one,[b] but God is one.[c]
LEXICON—a. μεσίτης (LN 31.22) (BAGD p. 507): 'mediator' [BAGD, Herm, LN, Mor, SSA, WBC; GW, KJV, NASB, NCV, NIV, NLT, NRSV], 'go-between' [LN; TEV], 'intermediary' [BNTC; NET, REB], not explicit [CEV]. This entire clause is translated 'an intermediary does not exist for one party alone', but this sense is disputed. It probably means that the activity of an intermediary implies the existence of more than one party, and hence it may be unsatisfactory because it must result in a compromise. The presence of an intermediary would prevent the one God from attaining his purpose in the law without any impediment [BAGD].
   b. εἷς (LN 60.10, 63.4) (BAGD 2.b. p. 231): 'one' [LN (60.10, 63.4)], 'one alone' [BAGD]. The phrase ὁ μεσίτης ἑνὸς οὐκ ἔστιν 'the mediator is not of one' [Herm] is also translated 'a mediator is not a mediator of one' [KJV], 'the mediator is not of one party' [Mor], 'a mediator is not for one party only' [NASB], 'a mediator, however, does not represent just one party' [WBC], 'an intermediary is not for one party alone' [NET], 'an intermediary means that there is not just one party' [BNTC], 'a mediator involves more than one party' [NRSV], 'a mediator does not represent just one party' [NIV], 'a mediator is not used when there is only one

person involved' [GW], 'a mediator is not needed when there is only one side' [NCV], 'a go-between is not needed when only one person is involved' [TEV], 'an intermediary is not needed for one party acting alone' [REB], 'a mediator is needed if two people enter into an argument' [NLT], 'when a mediator functions, one party or person is not communicating with another directly' [SSA], 'and the law did not come directly from him' [CEV].
  c. εἷς (LN 60.10, **63.4**) (BAGD 2.b. p. 231): 'one' [LN (60.10, 63.4)], 'only one, single' [BAGD]. The clause θεὸς εἷς ἐστιν 'God is one' [BNTC, Herm, Mor, WBC; KJV, NET, NIV, NRSV, REB, TEV] is also translated 'God is only one' [NASB, NCV], 'there is only one God' [CEV], 'God has acted on his own' [GW], 'God acted on his own when he made his promise to Abraham' [NLT], 'many times God has communicated with another directly' [SSA]. This phrase refers to the fact that God is defined as a unit and not characterized by numerous manifestations [**LN** (63.4)].
QUESTION—What is meant by 'the mediator is not of one'?
A mediator does not mediate on behalf of one party alone [NIGTC]. The existence of a mediator implies that there is more than just one party involved and the mediator is a third party [SSA]. There has to be two parties in a dispute before there is need of a mediator and sin had brought a gap between God and people so that a mediator was needed [Mor].
QUESTION—What is meant by 'God is one'?
The relationship between the two clauses in this verse is a problem that is said to have 300 [ICC, Lt, NIGTC], or 430 [NTC] solutions.
  1. There is only one God and there is no other deity to go to when confronted by God's demands [Mor]. God's true redemptive activity is always direct and unilateral in nature [WBC]. The law was given through deputies and that law divided Jews from the Gentiles. But the one God is God of Jews and Gentiles alike and therefore it is fitting that God should provide one way of salvation through faith for both [NIGTC].
  2. Although at Mt. Sinai there were two parties with a mediator, God is able to act alone without a mediator as a third party, and this happened when God gave his promise to Abraham [SSA]. God appeared to Abraham to give him his promise and that promise concerned the one heir, Christ. But the law was intended for the whole nation of Israel and their representative Moses brought it to them [Lns]. The promise is superior to the Law since the promise was not given through a mediator, but came directly from God [TH]. A mediator lacks independent authority, but when God made his promise to Abraham, and to all believers, Jews and Gentiles, he did this on his own sovereign account [NTC].

DISCOURSE UNIT: 3:21–4:7 [GNT; CEV, NCV, TEV]. The topic is slaves and children [CEV], slaves and sons [GNT], the purpose of the law of Moses [NCV], the purpose of the law [TEV].

3:21 (Is) therefore[a] the Law[b] in-opposition-to[c] the promises[d] of God?
TEXT—Some manuscripts omit the phrase τοῦ θεοῦ 'of God'. GNT includes this phrase in the text in brackets, indicating that the Committee had difficulty making the decision. Τοῦ θεοῦ 'of God' is omitted by REB.
LEXICON—a. οὖν (LN 89.50) (BAGD 1.c.α. p. 593): 'therefore' [BAGD, LN; NET, NIV], 'then' [BAGD, BNTC, Herm, LN, Mor, WBC; GW, KJV, NASB, NRSV, REB], 'so then, so' [LN], 'well then' [NLT], not explicit [SSA; CEV, NCV, TEV].
  b. νόμος (LN 33.55, 33.333) (BAGD 3. p. 542): 'Law' [Herm, LN (33.55); CEV, NASB, TEV], 'law' [BNTC, LN (33.333), Mor, WBC; KJV, NCV, NET, NIV, NLT, NRSV, REB], the law which Moses received from God [BAGD], 'Mosaic law' [SSA]. This is also translated with a plural form: 'laws' [GW].
  c. κατά with genitive object (LN 90.31): 'in opposition to, in conflict with' [LN], 'against' [BNTC, LN; KJV, NCV, TEV], 'opposed to' [WBC; NET, NIV, NRSV], 'contrary to' [Herm, Mor; NASB]. This preposition is also translated as a noun: '(is there a) conflict' [NLT]; as a verb: 'to contradict' [SSA; GW, REB], 'to disagree' [CEV].
  d. ἐπαγγελία (LN **33.288**) (BAGD 2.a. p. 280): 'promise' [BAGD, BNTC, Herm, LN, Mor, WBC; all versions]. This noun is also translated as a verb with 'God' as the subject: 'to promise' [SSA].
QUESTION—What relationship is indicated by οὖν 'therefore'?
  It indicates a false conclusion that someone might draw [Herm, NTC, SSA]. The preceding argument might suggest an affirmative answer that Paul must repudiate [NIGTC].

Not may-it-happen.[a]
LEXICON—a. aorist mid. (deponent = act.) optative of γίνομαι (LN 13.107) (BAGD I.3.a. p. 158): 'to happen, to occur, to come to be' [LN]. The phrase μὴ γένοιτο 'not may it happen' is translated 'by no means' [BAGD, Herm, Mor, WBC], 'far from it' [BAGD], 'God forbid' [BAGD; KJV], 'Not at all' [BNTC], 'God certainly did not contradict himself when he ordained the Mosaic law' [SSA], 'No, it doesn't' [CEV], 'That's unthinkable' [GW], 'May it never be' [NASB], 'Never' [NCV], 'Absolutely not' [NET, NIV, NLT], 'Certainly not' [NRSV], 'Of course not' [REB], 'No, not at all' [TEV].

For if (a) law[a] **had-been-given**[b] **the (one) being-able**[c] **to-give-life,**[d]
LEXICON—a. νόμος (LN 33.55, 33.333) (BAGD 3. p. 542): 'law' [BNTC, Herm, LN (33.333), Mor, SSA, WBC; all versions except GW], 'Law' [LN (33.55)], the law which Moses received from God [BAGD], 'laws' [GW].
  b. aorist pass. indic. of δίδωμι (LN 57.71): 'to be given' [BNTC, Herm, LN, Mor, SSA, WBC; KJV, NASB, NET, NIV, NRSV, REB], not explicit [CEV, GW, NCV, NLT]. This passive form is also translated actively with 'human beings' as the subject: 'to receive' [TEV].

c. pres. mid. (deponent = act.) participle of δύναμαι (LN 74.5): 'to be able' [LN; NASB, NET], 'to be capable' [Herm], 'can' [LN], 'could' [BNTC, Mor, SSA, WBC; all versions except NASB, NET, REB], 'to have power' [REB].

d. aorist act. infin. of ζῳοποιέω (LN 23.92) (BAGD 1. p. 341): 'to give life' [BAGD, LN, Mor, WBC; CEV, GW, KJV, NET, NLT], 'to make live' [BAGD, BNTC, Herm, LN, SSA; NRSV], 'to impart life' [NASB, NIV], 'to bestow life' [REB], 'to bring life' [NCV, TEV].

QUESTION—What relationship is indicated by γάρ 'for'?

It sets off this sentence and the next sentence as the explanatory reason for Paul's strong negative exclamation [NIGTC, WBC]. This explains why the charge contained in the question cannot be true [SSA].

QUESTION—What law is indicated by νόμος 'law' here?

Since in the Greek 'law' is not preceded by the article, many exegetes have argued that Paul is referring to any divine law [ICC, TH]. It refers to any God-given law [WBC]. 'Law' without the article refers to the Jewish Torah [Herm]. It means 'law' in general since there is no article [Lns].

QUESTION—What is meant by ζῳοποιῆσαι 'to give life'?

It refers to spiritual life [Lns, NTC, WBC]. It refers to the spiritual life in the present and the glorified life in the future [Lt]. It refers to eternal life [Herm, SSA].

really[a] righteousness[b] would-have-been[c] by/because-of[d] law;

LEXICON—a. ὄντως (LN 70.2) (BAGD 1. p. 574): 'really' [BAGD, LN], 'certainly' [BAGD, BNTC, LN, WBC; GW, NET, NIV], 'truly' [LN], 'in truth' [BAGD], 'actually' [SSA], 'indeed' [Herm; NASB, NRSV, REB], 'verily' [KJV], 'surely' [Mor], not explicit [CEV, NCV, NLT, TEV].

b. δικαιοσύνη (LN 88.13) (BAGD 3. p. 197): 'righteousness' [BAGD, BNTC, Herm, LN (88.13), Mor, WBC; KJV, NASB, NET, NIV, NRSV, REB]. This noun is also translated as a verb phrase: 'God would justify persons' [SSA], 'to become acceptable to God' [CEV], 'to receive God's approval' [GW], 'to be made right with God' [NLT], 'to be put right with God' [TEV], 'to make right' [NCV].

c. imperf. indic. of εἰμί (LN 13.1): 'to be' [BNTC, LN, Mor, WBC; KJV, NASB], 'to come' [Herm; NET, NIV, NRSV, REB], not explicit [SSA; CEV, GW, NCV, NLT, TEV].

d. ἐκ with genitive object (LN 89.77, 90.12, 90.16): 'by' [LN (90.12, 90.16), Mor; CEV, KJV, NET, NIV, NLT, TEV], 'by means of' [LN (89.77)], 'from' [BNTC, Herm, LN (89.77, 90.16); REB], 'because of' [SSA], 'because' [GW], 'based on' [NASB], 'through' [NRSV], 'on the basis of' [WBC], not explicit [NCV].

QUESTION—What relationship is indicated by ἐκ 'by'?

1. It indicates the source of righteousness [Lns, Mor, WBC]: righteousness would be given by law.

2. It indicates the means of obtaining righteousness [CEV, NLT, REB, TEV]: righteousness would be obtained by obeying the law [CEV].
3. It indicates the reason they would obtain righteousness [GW]: righteousness would be obtained because we obeyed the law.

3:22 **But the Scripture[a] has-shut-up[b] all[c] under[d] sin,**

LEXICON—a. γραφή (LN 33.53) (BAGD 2.b.β. p. 166): 'Scripture' [Herm, LN, Mor, WBC; GW, NASB, NIV], 'scripture' [BAGD, BNTC; KJV, NET, NRSV, REB, TEV], 'Scripture passage' [LN], 'Scriptures' [CEV, NCV, NLT]. This entire phrase is translated 'But God had previously determined that he would justify no sinful persons because they obey any law' [SSA].
b. aorist act. indic. of συγκλείω (LN 13.125) (BAGD 2. p. 774): 'to shut up' [LN, Mor; NASB], 'to restrict' [LN], 'to imprison' [BAGD; NET, NRSV], 'to confine' [BNTC, Herm, WBC], 'to bind' [NCV], not explicit [CEV, GW, KJV, TEV]. This verb is also translated as a noun: 'prisoner' [NIV], 'prisoners' [NLT, REB]. See a. [SSA].
c. πᾶς (LN 59.23, 63.2) (BAGD 2.b.β. p. 633): 'all' [BAGD, LN (59.23); KJV], 'every' [LN (59.23)], 'entire, total' [LN (63.2)], 'we...all' [NLT], 'everyone' [WBC; CEV, NASB], 'the whole world' [GW, NCV, NIV, REB, TEV], 'everything and everyone' [NET], 'all things' [Mor; NRSV], 'everything' [BNTC, Herm]. This is translated to express it negatively: 'no sinful persons' [SSA]. The neuter τὰ πάντα 'the all' can be used of persons here in Gal. 3:22 [BAGD].
d. ὑπό with accusative object (LN **37.7**) (BAGD 2.b. p. 843): 'under' [BAGD, Herm, LN, Mor, WBC; KJV, NASB, NET], 'under the power of' [BNTC, **LN**; NRSV, TEV], 'under the control of' [LN], 'to control' [CEV], 'to control by the power of' [GW], 'by' [NCV], 'of' [NIV, NLT], 'in subjection to' [REB]. See a. [SSA].

QUESTION—What relationship is indicated by ἀλλά 'but'?
It is the strong adversative [Mor], which marks a contrast between the unreal hypothesis of 3:21 and the actual situation stated here [ICC, Lns, NCBC, WBC]. It separates Paul's negative argument against a false conclusion in 3:21 from his positive statement of the law's function in 3:22 [ICC, NAC]. Paul now summarizes God's actual plan for imparting life [SSA].

QUESTION—To what is referred by ἡ γραφή 'the scripture'?
1. It refers to a particular passage [ICC, Lt, WBC]. Paul is referring to Deut. 27:26 [ICC, Lt, WBC], or Psalm 143:2 [Lt].
2. It refers to more than one passage in the Old Testament [Lns, NTC, TNTC]. Paul is thinking of the scriptures of the law [TNTC].
3. It refers to all of scripture [Mor, NIC].
4. It is a metonymy for God himself who speaks in Scripture [Alf, NAC, NIBC, NIGTC, SSA]. The OT reveals God's plan in relation to sin and so God is the ultimate agent who confines sinful people [SSA].

QUESTION—What is meant by πάντα 'all'?
Paul means 'all people' [NTC, SSA, TH, TNTC, WBC; CEV, NASB, NLT, NRSV, and probably those who translate 'the whole world': GW, NCV, NIV, REB, TEV]. He refers to sin's universality rather than to its cosmic aspect [TNTC]. It refers to the Jews, the ones who were under the Law [ICC]. Or, it refers to 'all things' [BNTC, Lns] and refers to all that pertains to men: their thoughts, words, deeds, their whole characters and lives [Lns].

QUESTION—What is meant by συνέκλεισεν τὰ πάντα ὑπὸ ἁμαρτίαν 'has shut up all under sin'?
Scripture is personified as the official who puts the law-breaker in the prison house where sin is the jailer [NIGTC]. 'Under sin' is a personification of sin and this speaks of sin as a jailer in control of sinners so that they cannot break free from evil [Mor]. It means being under the power and bondage of sin with no possibility of escape [NTC, TH]. It means that Scripture shows the true state of mankind before God, with the result that no-one is free of guilt. It therefore shuts up everyone to the consequences of sin [NCBC].

in-order-that the promise[a] from[b] faith[c] of-Jesus Christ might-be-given[d] to-the (ones) believing.[e]

LEXICON—a. ἐπαγγελία (LN 33.288) (BAGD 2.c. p. 280): 'promise' [BAGD, BNTC, Herm, LN, WBC; GW, KJV, NASB, NCV, NET, NLT], 'what was promised' [Mor; NIV, NRSV], 'what he promised' [SSA], 'the gift which is promised' [TEV], 'the promised blessing' [REB]. This singular form of the noun is also translated as plural: 'promises' [CEV].
  b. ἐκ with genitive object (LN 89.25, 89.77, 90.16): 'from' [BNTC, LN (89.77, 90.16)], 'by' [Herm, LN (90.16); KJV, NASB], 'through' [Mor; NCV, NIV, NRSV], 'by means of' [LN (89.77)], 'because of' [LN (89.25); NET], 'because (they trust him)' [SSA], 'based on' [WBC; GW], 'on the basis of' [TEV], '(faith) should be the ground' [REB], not explicit [CEV, NLT].
  c. πίστις (LN 31.85, 31.102) (BAGD 2.b.β. p. 633): 'faith' [BAGD, BNTC, Herm, LN (31.85, 31.102), Mor; all versions except NET, NLT], 'faithfulness' [WBC; NET]. This noun is also translated as a verb: 'to trust' [SSA], 'to believe in' [NLT].
  d. aorist pass. subj. of δίδωμι (LN 57.71): 'to be given' [BNTC, Herm, LN, Mor, WBC; all versions except CEV, NLT], 'to give' [SSA], 'to be for' [CEV], 'to receive' [NLT].
  e. pres. act. participle of πιστεύω (LN 31.85, 31.102) (BAGD 2.b. p. 661): 'to believe' [BAGD, BNTC, Herm, LN (31.85), Mor, WBC; all versions except CEV, NCV, NLT], 'to believe in' [BAGD, LN (31.85); NCV], 'to have faith in' [LN (31.85)], 'to trust' [BAGD, LN (31.85), SSA], 'to be a believer, to be a Christian' [LN (31.102)], not explicit [CEV, NLT].

QUESTION—What relationship is indicated by ἵνα 'in order that'?
It indicates the purpose of shutting up all under sin [ICC, Mor, TH; all versions except GW, NCV, NLT, TEV]. This is God's purpose [Mor].

QUESTION—What is referred to by ἡ ἐπαγγελία 'the promise'?
It is the promise that was given to Abraham [BNTC, Lns, TH].
QUESTION—What relationship is indicated by ἐκ 'from'?
It indicates the ground on which the giving of the promise takes place [ICC, TH]. The promise was given as a result of faith in Christ Jesus [Lns].
QUESTION—How are the nouns related in the genitive construction πίστεως Ἰησοῦ Χριστοῦ 'faith of Jesus Christ'?
1. It means faith in Jesus Christ [BNTC, ICC, Lns, Lt, Mor, NIGTC, NTC, SSA; all versions except KJV, NET]. Jesus Christ is the object of this faith [ICC, Lns, Mor, NIGTC]. The promise was given to the ones believing in Christ, not because they did works of the law, but because they had faith in Christ [Lt].
2. It means the faithfulness of Christ [WBC; NET]. The promise could be given to those who believe (in Christ) because the object of our faith is reliable and worthy of our faith [NET].
QUESTION—Who is the actor of δοθῇ 'might be given'?
It is God who gives what he has promised [Lns, SSA].

DISCOURSE UNIT: 3:23–4:7 [NET]. The topic is the sons of God are heirs of promise.

DISCOURSE UNIT: 3:23–29 [BST, Mor, NIC]. The topic is being under the law and in Christ [BST], the law our tutor [Mor], the coming of faith: sonship to God [NIC].

DISCOURSE UNIT: 3:23–25 [NIGTC]. The topic is liberation from the law.

3:23 Now/but[a] before[b] the faith[c] came[d] we-were-being-guarded[e] under[f] law,[g]

LEXICON—a. δέ (LN 89.124) (BAGD 2. p. 171): 'now' [BAGD; NET, NRSV], 'but' [LN, Mor; KJV, NASB, TEV], 'however' [BNTC], not explicit [Herm, SSA, WBC; CEV, GW, NCV, NIV, NLT, REB].
b. πρό with genitive object (LN 67.17) (BAGD 2. p. 702): 'before' [BAGD, BNTC, Herm, LN, Mor, SSA, WBC; all versions except CEV, GW, NLT], not explicit [CEV, GW, NLT].
c. πίστις (LN 31.85, 31.102) (BAGD 3. p. 664): 'faith' [BNTC, Herm, LN (31.85, 31.102), Mor, WBC; all versions except GW], 'this faith' [GW], 'body of faith, body of belief, body of doctrine' [BAGD], 'good news concerning Christ' [SSA].
d. aorist act. infin. of ἔρχομαι (LN 15.81) (BAGD I.2.b. p. 311): 'to come' [BAGD, BNTC, Herm, LN, Mor, WBC; all versions except NLT], 'to appear' [BAGD], 'to be revealed' [SSA], 'to be shown' [NLT].
e. imperf. pass. indic. of φρουρέω (LN 37.119) (BAGD 2. p. 867): 'to be guarded' [LN; NLT], 'to be kept under watch' [LN], 'to be held under custody' [BAGD], 'to be supervised' [SSA], 'to be kept under control' [GW], 'to be kept in custody' [Herm, WBC; NASB], 'to be held prisoners' [NCV, NIV], 'to be held in custody' [BNTC, Mor; NET], 'to

be guarded' [NRSV], 'to be close prisoners' [REB], '(to be locked up) as prisoners' [TEV], 'to be kept' [KJV]. This passive verb is also translated actively with 'the Law' as the subject: 'to control' [CEV].
  f. ὑπό with accusative object (LN 37.7) (BAGD 2.b. p. 843): 'under' [BAGD, BNTC, Herm, LN, WBC; CEV, KJV, NASB, NET, NRSV], 'under the control of' [LN], 'by' [Mor; GW, NCV, NIV, NLT], 'by means of' [SSA], 'in the custody of' [REB], not explicit [TEV].
  g. νόμος (LN 33.55, 33.333) (BAGD 3. p. 542): 'law' [BAGD, BNTC, LN (33.333), Mor, WBC; all versions except CEV, GW, TEV], 'the Law' [Herm, LN (33.55); CEV, TEV], 'the Mosaic law' [SSA], 'Moses' laws' [GW].

QUESTION—What relationship is indicated by δέ 'but'?
  It means 'moreover', adding the new point as to how the Mosaic law functioned during this period with reference to Christ [Lns]. It carries us on to a further account of the rationale and office of the law [Alf]. It points to the next step of the argument [Herm]. Or, some translate it as being adversative: 'but' [Mor; KJV, NASB, TEV], 'however' [BNTC].

QUESTION—What is meant by Πρὸ ἐλθεῖν τὴν πίστιν 'before the faith came'?
  1. Faith refers to the act of faith in Jesus Christ [Alf, BNTC, ICC, Mor, NCBC, NIC, NIGTC, NTC, TH; CEV, NLT, and probably those who translate 'this faith' [GW, NCV, NIV, REB]. It is the faith in Christ that is spoken of in 3:22 [ICC, NIGTC]. The coming of faith is identical with the coming of Christ, who is the object of faith. It is the coming of Christ, making possible the coming of faith in him, which is the decisive point in salvation history [NIC]. It was not faith as the content of what was taught, but faith as a principle of religious life [Mor]. What the coming of the faith means we see from the phrase 'for the faith about to be revealed.' The coming refers to this revelation [Lns]. This was 'when the time came when we would have faith' [CEV], when 'faith in Christ was shown to us as the way of becoming right with God' [NLT].
  2. The faith is the doctrine that is believed [Lt, SSA]. It was the Good News concerning Christ that was revealed by God [SSA].

QUESTION—Who is the 'we' of ἐφρουρούμεθα 'we were being kept'?
  The 'we' means 'we Jews' [BNTC, Herm, Lns, NTC]. Properly it means 'we Jewish believers', however, this should not be used since Paul is speaking of the divine dealings with men generally. The Law was for all mankind [Alf, Mor, NAC, NIC, NIGTC].

QUESTION—To what law is referred by νόμον 'law'?
  It is the law that was given in the Old Testament [Mor], the Jewish law [TH]. It is the Mosaic law [Lns, WBC; GW]. It is the Torah [Herm].

being-shut-up[a] for[b] the being-about[c] to-be-revealed[d] faith,[e]
LEXICON—a. pres. pass. participle of συγκλείω (LN 13.125) (BAGD 2. p. 774): 'to be shut up' [BAGD, Mor; KJV, NASB], 'to be imprisoned'

[BAGD], 'to be restricted' [LN], 'to be confined' [BNTC, Herm, WBC], 'to be under (their) control' [GW], 'to have no freedom' [NCV], 'to be locked up' [NIV], 'to be kept in protective custody' [NLT], 'to be imprisoned' [NRSV], 'to be close prisoners' [REB], 'to be locked up as prisoners' [TEV], 'to be kept as prisoners' [NET]. This passive verb is also translated actively with 'the Law' as the subject: 'to keep under its power' [CEV]. This is translated 'and we(excl.) were not being justified by means of our(excl.) obeying the Mosaic law' [SSA].
- b. εἰς with accusative object (LN 67.119, 84.16): 'to' [LN (67.119, 84.16), Mor; NASB], 'until' [BNTC, Herm, LN (67.119), WBC; all versions except KJV, NASB, REB], 'pending' [REB], 'unto' [KJV], 'in order that' [SSA].
- c. pres. act. participle of μέλλω (LN 67.62, 71.36) (BAGD 1.b.β. p. 501): 'to be about to' [LN (67.62); GW], 'to be destined' [BAGD], 'must be, has to be' [LN (71.36)], 'should be' [BNTC, WBC; KJV, NIV, TEV], 'was to be' [Mor; NASB], 'would be' [NET, NRSV], 'to intend to' [SSA], not explicit [Herm; CEV, NCV, NLT, REB].
- d. aorist pass. infin. of ἀποκαλύπτω (LN 28.38) (BAGD 4. p. 92): 'to be revealed' [BAGD, BNTC, Herm, LN, Mor, SSA, WBC; all versions except CEV, NCV, NLT], not explicit [CEV, NLT]. The passive voice is also translated actively with 'God' as the subject: 'to show' [NCV].
- e. πίστις (LN 31.85, 31.102) (BAGD 3. p. 664): 'faith' [BNTC, Herm, LN (31.85, 31.102), Mor, WBC; all versions except CEV, NCV], 'body of faith' [BAGD], 'body of belief, body of doctrine' [BAGD], 'way of faith' [NCV]. This noun is also translated as a verb with 'we' as the subject: 'to believe' [SSA], 'to have faith' [CEV].

QUESTION—What relationship is indicated by εἰς 'until'?
1. It indicates purpose [Alf, ICC, Lns, Lt, NTC, SSA]: we were carefully guarded in order that we might be ready for it.
2. It indicates time [NCBC; all versions except KJV, NASB]: until the time that we would have faith.
3. It defines the participle συγκλειόμενοι 'being shut up' [KJV, NASB]: being shut up to faith.

QUESTION—What is the meaning of πίστιν 'faith' here?
1. It is faith in Jesus Christ [Mor, NIC, NIGTC, TH].
2. It is the faithfulness of Jesus Christ [WBC].

DISCOURSE UNIT: 3:24–4:7 [NLT]. The topic is God's children through faith.

3:24 Therefore[a] the Law[b] became[c] our guardian[d] to[e] Christ,

LEXICON—a. ὥστε (LN 89.52) (BAGD 1.a. p. 899): 'therefore' [BAGD, Herm, LN, WBC; KJV, NASB, NRSV], 'as a result, so then' [LN], 'so that' [BNTC, LN, Mor], 'so' [BAGD, LN; NIV], 'in other words' [NCV], 'thus' [NET, REB], 'and so' [TEV], not explicit [SSA; CEV, GW, NLT].

b. νόμος (LN 33.55, 33.333) (BAGD 3. p. 542): 'law' [BNTC, LN (33.333), Mor, WBC; KJV, NCV, NET, NIV, NLT, NRSV, REB], 'the Law' [Herm, LN (33.55); CEV, NASB, TEV], the law which Moses received from God [BAGD], 'the Mosaic law' [SSA], 'Moses' laws' [GW].
c. perf. act. indic. of γίνομαι (LN 13.3, 13.48): 'to become' [BNTC, LN (13.48); NASB, NET], 'to be' [Herm, LN (13.3), Mor, WBC; CEV, KJV, NCV, NLT, NRSV, TEV], 'to serve as' [GW], not explicit [SSA; NIV, REB].
d. παιδαγωγός (LN **36.5**) (BAGD p. 603): 'guardian' [Herm, LN, WBC; GW, NCV, NET], 'guide' [BAGD, **LN**], 'custodian' [BAGD, BNTC, Mor], 'teacher' [CEV], 'tutor' [NASB], 'guardian and teacher' [NLT], 'disciplinarian' [NRSV], 'schoolmaster' [KJV]. This noun is also translated as a verb: 'to supervise' [SSA], 'to be put in charge' [NIV, REB], 'to be in charge' [TEV].
e. εἰς with accusative object (LN 67.119, 84.16) (BAGD 2.a.α. p. 228): 'to' [BNTC, LN (84.16), Mor; NASB, NCV, NIV], 'until' [Herm, LN (67.119); NET, NLT], 'unto' [KJV], not explicit [CEV, GW]. The phrase εἰς Χριστόν 'to Christ' is translated 'until the coming of the Messiah' [BAGD], 'until Christ came' [WBC; NRSV, TEV], 'until Christ should come' [REB], 'in order that we(excl.) might trust Christ' [SSA].

QUESTION—What relationship is indicated by ὥστε 'therefore'?
It signals the result or consequence of what has just been stated [WBC]. It is in the concluding sense [Herm].

QUESTION—What relationship is indicated by εἰς 'to'?
1. This is temporal [BNTC, BST, Herm, NAC, NCBC, NIC, NIGTC, WBC; NET, NLT, NRSV, REB, TEV]: until Christ came.
2. It indicates purpose [ICC, Lns, Mor, NTC, SSA, TNTC; KJV, NASB, NCV, NIV]: in order to lead us to Christ.

in-order-that we-might-be-justified[a] by[b] faith;[c]

LEXICON—a. aorist pass. subj. of δικαίοω (LN 34.46) (BAGD 3.a. p. 197): 'to be justified' [BNTC, Herm, Mor, SSA, WBC; KJV, NASB, NIV, NRSV, REB], 'to be put right' [LN], 'to be acquitted, to be pronounced and treated as righteous' [BAGD], 'to be declared righteous' [NET], 'to be acceptable to God' [CEV], 'to receive God's approval' [GW], 'to be made right with God' [NCV, NLT], 'to be put right with God' [TEV].
b. ἐκ with genitive object (LN 89.77, 90.12) (BAGD 3.f. p. 235): 'by' [Herm, LN (90.12), Mor, SSA, WBC; KJV, NASB, NET, NIV, NRSV], 'by means of' [LN (89.77)], 'by reason of' [BAGD], 'because of' [BAGD; GW], 'as a result of' [BAGD, LN (90.12)], 'through' [NCV, NLT, REB, TEV], 'from' [BNTC], not explicit [CEV].
c. πίστις (LN 31.85, 31.102): 'faith' [BNTC, Herm, LN (31.85, 31.102), Mor, WBC; all versions]. This noun is also translated as a verb: 'to trust (Christ)' [SSA].

QUESTION—What relationship is indicated by ἐκ 'by'?

It indicates that faith is the source of God's act of justification [Lns]. When a sinner is justified it is because of faith, not because of keeping the law. [Lns].

3:25 But the faith[a] having-come[b] no-longer[c] are-we under[d] (a) guardian.[e]

LEXICON—a. πίστις (LN 31.85, 31.102) (BAGD 3. p. 664): 'faith' [BNTC, Herm, LN (31.85, 31.102), Mor, WBC; all versions except NCV, NLT, TEV], 'the way of faith' [NCV], 'faith in Christ' [NLT], 'time for faith' [TEV], 'body of faith, body of belief, body of doctrine' [BAGD], 'the good news concerning Christ' [SSA].

b. aorist act. participle of ἔρχομαι (LN 15.81) (BAGD I.2.b. p. 311): 'to come' [BAGD, BNTC, Herm, LN, Mor, WBC; all versions except CEV, TEV], 'to appear' [BAGD], 'to be here' [TEV], 'to be revealed' [SSA]. The phrase ἐλθούσης τῆς πίστεως 'the faith having come' is translated 'once a person has learned to have faith' [CEV].

c. οὐκέτι (LN 67.130): 'no longer' [BNTC, Herm, LN, Mor, SSA, WBC; all versions except CEV, REB], 'no more (need)' [CEV], not explicit [REB].

d. ὑπό with accusative object (LN 37.7) (BAGD 2.b. p. 843): 'under' [BNTC, Herm, LN, Mor, WBC; KJV, NASB, NCV, NET, NIV], 'under the control of' [LN; GW], 'under (someone's) power' [BAGD], 'subject to' [NRSV], 'to be in charge of' [REB, TEV], 'to be supervised' [SSA]. The clause οὐκέτι ὑπὸ παιδαγωγόν ἐσμεν 'no longer are we under a guardian' is translated 'its charge is at an end' [REB], 'the Law is no longer in charge of us' [TEV], 'there is no more need to have the Law as a teacher' [CEV], 'we no longer need the law as our guardian' [NLT].

e. παιδαγωγός (LN **36.5**) (BAGD p. 603): 'guardian' [Herm, LN; GW, NCV, NET, NLT], 'supervisory guardian' [WBC], 'guide' [BAGD, **LN**], 'custodian' [BAGD, BNTC, Mor], 'tutor' [NASB], 'schoolmaster' [KJV], 'disciplinarian' [NRSV], 'its charge' [REB], 'the Law' [TEV], 'the Mosaic law' [SSA], '(under) the supervision of the law' [NIV], 'teacher' [CEV].

QUESTION—What relationship is indicated by δέ 'but'?

It is adversative [Alf] and emphasizes that what we are is quite different from what we were [BST].

QUESTION—What faith is referred to here?

It should be understood again as 'faith in Jesus Christ' [Alf, BNTC, ICC, Mor, NCBC, TH; NLT].

QUESTION—What relationship is indicated by οὐκέτι 'no longer'?

It is temporal and contrasts the two periods of time [ICC].

QUESTION—Who are referred to by the verb ἐσμεν 'we are'?

It refers to the Jews [Lns, SSA], the Jewish Christians [ICC]. Or, it is to be taken as an inclusive 'we', the Gentile and Jewish believers, the same as the 'you' in 3:26 since Gentiles and Jews alike are confined under the law [NIGTC].

GALATIANS 3:26

DISCOURSE UNIT: 3:26–4:11 [NAC]. The topic is sons and servants.

DISCOURSE UNIT: 3:26–4:7 [NIV]. The topic is sons of God.

DISCOURSE UNIT: 3:26–29 [NIGTC, WBC]. The topic is Jews and Gentiles one in Christ [NIGTC], new relationships 'in Christ' [WBC].

3:26 For[a] you-are all sons[b] of-God through[c] the faith[d] in[e] Christ Jesus;

LEXICON—a. γάρ (LN 89.23): 'for' [BNTC, Herm, LN, Mor, WBC; KJV, NASB, NET, NRSV], 'because' [LN], 'now' [SSA], 'so' [NLT], not explicit [CEV, GW, NIV, REB, TEV]. This is translated 'this means that' [NCV].

b. υἱός (LN 9.4, 9.46) (BAGD 1.c.γ. p. 834): 'son' [BAGD, LN (9.4, 9.46)], 'child' [LN (9.46)]. The plural form is translated 'sons' [BNTC, Herm, Mor, WBC; NASB, NET, NIV, REB], 'children' [SSA; CEV, GW, KJV, NCV, NLT, NRSV, TEV].

c. διά with genitive object (LN 89.76, 90.8) (BAGD A.III.1.d. p. 180): 'through' [BAGD, BNTC, Herm, LN (89.76, 90.8), Mor, WBC; all versions except CEV, GW, KJV], 'by means of' [LN (89.76, 90.8)], 'by' [LN (89.76); GW, KJV], 'because of' [SSA; CEV].

d. πίστις (LN 31.85, 31.102): 'faith' [BNTC, Herm, LN (31.85, 31.102), Mor, WBC; all versions except GW]. This noun is also translated as a verb: 'to trust' [SSA], 'to believe' [GW].

e. ἐν with dative object (LN 83.13, 89.119): 'in' [BNTC, Herm, LN (83.13, 89.119), Mor, SSA, WBC; all versions except REB, TEV], 'in union with' [LN (89.119); REB, TEV].

QUESTION—What relationship is indicated by γάρ 'for'?

It introduces the reason we are no longer under a guardian [Alf, Mor, NIC]. It indicates that the following assertion is as much the basis of the argument just completed (3:23-25) as its conclusion [BNTC]. It means, 'that you may understand what this means for you, note what you are' [Lns].

QUESTION—Who is referred to in the phrase πάντες ἐστε 'you are all'?

It refers to all Christians [BNTC, NAC, NIBC, NIC, WBC], both Jews and Gentiles [Alf, Lns, Lt, NCBC, NIGTC, SSA]. 'All' is emphatic [ICC, TH] and includes all Christians [BNTC, NAC, WBC]. The present tense of ἐστε 'you are' really refers to an event in the past to which Paul reminds his readers [Herm]. Paul transfers from 'we' in 3:25 to 'you' in 3:26 to bring out more clearly his appeal to these readers [NCBC]. Those addressed as 'you' in 3:26 are identical with those indicated by the inclusive 'we' in 3:23–25 [NIGTC]. 'All' means all without distinction. This word is meant to emphasize strongly the power of faith. Anyone who has faith becomes a son of God and free from the schoolmaster [Mor].

QUESTION—What is meant by the genitive construction υἱοὶ θεοῦ 'sons of God'?

It means that they are now members of the heavenly family [Mor]. It is Paul's description of the redeemed, those who have been purchased with the blood of Christ [NAC]. In contrast to the minor child under the supervision of a pedagogue, God's sons have reached the age of maturity and therefore now enjoy the privileges and rights of mature men [TH]. It means mature, full-grown sons who are in possession of the inheritance, the fulfillment of the promise (3:18). The word υἱοί 'sons' suggests the idea of their independent standing free from any mentor such as children would have [Lns].

QUESTION—What relationship is indicated by διά 'through'?

It indicates that the objective means of the sonship of the Galatians is through faith [Lns].

QUESTION—What relationship is indicated by ἐν Χριστῷ Ἰησοῦ 'in Christ Jesus'?

1. It indicates their position as being 'in Christ Jesus' [BST, Herm, ICC, Lt, NCBC, NIC, NIGTC, NTC, TH, TNTC, WBC; NET, NRSV, REB, TEV]: in union with Christ Jesus.
2. It indicates the goal of their faith [Alf, Lns, Mor; CEV, GW, KJV, NASB, NCV, NIV, NLT]: by faith in Christ Jesus.

3:27 for[a] as-many-as[b] have-been-baptized[c] into[d] Christ have-put-on[e] Christ.

LEXICON—a. γάρ (LN 89.23): 'for' [BNTC, Herm, LN, Mor, WBC; KJV, NASB, NET, NIV], 'because' [LN], 'clearly' [GW], 'and' [CEV, NLT], 'that is' [SSA], not explicit [NCV, NRSV, REB, TEV].

b. ὅσος (LN 59.7): 'as many as' [BNTC, Herm, LN, Mor, WBC; KJV, NRSV], 'all who' [GW, NASB, NET, NIV, NLT], 'you were all' [NCV], not explicit [SSA; CEV, REB, TEV].

c. aorist pass. indic. of βαπτίζω (LN 53.41) (BAGD 2.b.β. p. 132): 'to be baptized' [BAGD, BNTC, Herm, LN, Mor, WBC; all versions except NLT]. The phrase εἰς Χριστὸν ἐβαπτίσθητε 'have been baptized into Christ' is translated 'have been united with Christ in baptism' [NLT], 'you who were united with Christ by means of his Spirit' [SSA].

d. εἰς with accusative object (LN 84.22, 90.23): 'into' [BNTC, Herm, LN (84.22), Mor, WBC; all versions except CEV, GW, NLT], 'in' [LN (90.23); GW], not explicit [CEV]. The phrase εἰς Χριστὸν 'into Christ' is translated 'united with Christ' [SSA; NLT].

e. aorist mid. indic. of ἐνδύω (LN 49.1) (BAGD 2.b. p. 264): 'to put on' [BNTC, Herm, LN; CEV, KJV, REB], 'to clothe oneself in' [BAGD, LN, Mor, WBC; GW, NASB, NET, NIV, NRSV], 'to be clothed with' [NCV]. The phrase Χριστὸν ἐνεδύσασθε 'have put on Christ' is translated 'you are clothed, so to speak, with the life of Christ' [TEV], 'have been made like him' [NLT], 'identified yourselves with Christ' [SSA].

QUESTION—What relationship is indicated by γάρ 'for'?

It introduces evidence to support what Paul has just said in 3:26 [Mor, WBC]. This explains 'in Christ Jesus' as it is used in 3:26 [BNTC, Lns, Lt, TNTC].

QUESTION—To whom does ὅσοι 'as many as' refer?
   It refers to all those who had been baptized [Mor]. It refers to 'all of you' in 3:26 [NTC, SSA, TH, WBC]. It is not intended to limit the 'all' of 3:26, but identifies what is meant by 'all' [Herm].
QUESTION—What is meant by εἰς Χριστὸν ἐβαπτίσθητε 'have been baptized into Christ'?
   This baptism is certainly water baptism [NIC] and the phrase should be understood in the sense of 'with reference to Christ' [ICC, WBC]. It means to be incorporated into Christ by baptism and as a result to be 'in Christ' [NIGTC]. This phrase is possibly a metaphor. It has the sense of 'into' so as to become 'in' describing when, by means of their being baptized, their lives and destinies and very identities became bound up with Christ [BNTC]. It involves mainly a change of state signaled by the rite of baptism [TH]. If this refers to water baptism at all, it implies that associated with it there is a spiritual transaction that is effected through faith [SSA].
QUESTION—What is meant by Χριστὸν ἐνεδύσασθε 'have put on Christ'?
   This is a metaphor. It suggests the closeness that exists between Christ and the believer [NCBC]. It means putting on Christ's character which is that of righteousness [NIBC]. It is figurative and means taking on Christ's characteristics, virtues, and intentions, and so becoming like him [WBC]. Baptism is regarded as 'putting on' Christ, who is thought of as a garment enveloping the believer and symbolizing his new spiritual existence [NIC; all versions except KJV, NLT]. It means that they have identified themselves with their Savior. It indicates not only the external, but the habitual association and identification with Christ [Mor]. It is another way for Paul to express incorporation into Christ [NIGTC]. To put on Christ is to become like Christ, to take upon oneself his character and his standing before God [ICC, TH]. He who puts on Christ becomes a partaker of his salvation [Lns].

3:28 There-is[a] not Jew nor Greek,[b]
LEXICON—a. ἔνι (LN **13.70**) (BAGD p. 266): 'to be' [LN], 'to exist' [**LN**], 'there is' [BNTC, Herm, Mor, WBC; all versions except CEV, GW], 'are' [CEV], 'there are' [GW], not explicit [SSA]. This entire clause is translated 'there is neither Jew nor Gentile' [BAGD].
   b. Ἕλλην (LN 11.40, 11.90) (BAGD 2.a. p. 252): 'Greek' [BNTC, Herm, LN (11.40, 11.90), Mor, WBC; all versions except NLT], 'Gentile' [BAGD, LN (11.40), SSA; NLT], 'non-Jew' [LN (11.40)].
QUESTION—What is meant by οὐκ ἔνι 'there is not'?
   It is an emphatic negation [NIGTC, WBC]. God does not identify a person according to the different categories listed [SSA]. It makes no difference to their status in Christ [NIGTC]. The distinctions still exist, but they are no longer important and they can become children of God whatever they are [TH].

there-is[a] not slave[b] nor free[c] (person),
LEXICON—a. ἔνι (LN 13.70): 'to be, to exist' [LN], 'there is' [BNTC, Herm, Mor; KJV, NASB, NET, NRSV], not explicit [SSA, WBC; CEV, GW, NCV, NIV, NLT, REB, TEV].
  b. δοῦλος (LN 87.76) (BAGD 1.b. p. 205): 'slave' [BAGD, BNTC, Herm, LN, Mor, SSA, WBC; all versions except KJV], 'bondservant' [LN], 'bond' [KJV].
  c. ἐλεύθερος (LN 87.84) (BAGD 1. p. 250): 'free' [BAGD, BNTC, Mor, SSA, WBC; KJV, NET, NIV, NLT, NRSV], 'free person' [LN; CEV, GW, NCV, TEV], 'free man' [Herm, LN; NASB, REB].

there-is[a] not male[b] and female;[c]
LEXICON—a. ἔνι (LN 13.70): 'to be, to exist' [LN], 'there is' [BNTC, Herm, Mor; KJV, NASB, NET, NRSV], not explicit [SSA, WBC; CEV, GW, NCV, NIV, NLT, REB, TEV].
  b. ἄρσην (LN 79.102) (BAGD p. 109): 'male' [BAGD, BNTC, Herm, LN, Mor, SSA, WBC; all versions except CEV, TEV], 'man' [LN; CEV, TEV].
  c. θῆλυς (LN 79.103) (BAGD p. 360): 'female' [BAGD, BNTC, Herm, LN, Mor, SSA, WBC; all versions except CEV, TEV], 'woman' [LN; CEV, TEV].

for[a] you all are one[b] in Christ Jesus.
TEXT—Instead of εἷς ἐστε ἐν Χριστῷ Ἰησοῦ 'you are one in Christ Jesus', some manuscripts read ἐστε ἐν Χριστῷ 'you are in Christ'; others read ἕν ἐστε ἐν Χριστῷ 'you are one thing in Christ'; others read ἐστε ἕν (or ἐν) Χριστοῦ 'you are one thing (or in) of Christ'; and still others read ἐστε Χριστοῦ 'you are Christ's'. GNT reads εἷς ἐστε ἐν Χριστῷ Ἰησοῦ 'you are one in Christ Jesus' with an A decision, indicating that the text is certain.
LEXICON—a. γάρ (LN 89.23): 'for' [BNTC, Herm, LN, Mor, WBC; KJV, NASB, NET, NIV, NLT, NRSV, REB], 'because' [LN], not explicit [SSA; CEV, GW, NCV, TEV].
  b. εἷς (LN 60.10, 63.4) (BAGD 1.b. p. 230): 'one' [BAGD, BNTC, Herm, LN (60.10, 63.4), Mor, WBC; KJV, NASB, NET, NIV, NLT, NRSV, TEV], 'one person' [REB], 'one sort of person' [SSA], 'the same' [GW, NCV], 'equal with each other' [CEV].
QUESTION—What relationship is indicated by γάρ 'for'?
  It introduces the reason for the statements Paul has made [Alf, Mor].
QUESTION—What is meant by ὑμεῖς εἷς ἐστε 'you all are one'?
  Christ has abolished the distinctions of race, rank, and sex so that they do not matter. They are still there but they no longer create any barriers to fellowship. We recognize each other as equals, brothers and sisters in Christ [BST]. His 'all' is important. All believers are one in Christ Jesus and the unity is the important thing. It doesn't matter if a believer is Jew, Greek, slave, free, male, or female. It is the unity that counts [Mor]. The distinctions which exist are no longer important and present no hindrance to any of these

persons becoming children of God. The emphasis of 'you all are one' is on being united in the fellowship of Christ [TH]. In their union with Christ they are all 'one person' (masculine, not neuter), not just 'one thing or one body.' What union with Christ signifies for Jew, Greek, slave, etc., is that they are all alike in their spiritual standing, everyone has been baptized, declared righteous. None are higher, lower, richer, poorer, better, worse, with more, with less, in every respect they are exactly as 'one person in Christ Jesus' [Lns]. All those in Jesus Christ merge into one personality [ICC].

QUESTION—What relationship is indicated by ἐν 'in'?

In Christ we belong not only to God as His sons, but to each other as brothers and sisters. We belong to each other in such a way as to render of no account the things which normally distinguish us, such as race, rank, and sex [BST]. Paul is saying that when people are saved by Jesus Christ they are brought into a unity between the saved and the Savior and a unity that binds together all the saved [Mor].

3:29 And if you (are) Christ's, then[a] you-are seed[b] of-Abraham,

LEXICON—a. ἄρα (LN 89.46) (BAGD 3. p. 103): 'then' [BAGD, BNTC, Herm, LN, Mor, WBC; GW, KJV, NASB, NET, NIV, NRSV, TEV], 'consequently' [LN], 'as a result' [BAGD, LN], 'therefore' [SSA], 'so' [NCV], not explicit [CEV, NLT, REB].

b. σπέρμα (LN 10.29) (BAGD 2.b. p. 762): 'seed' [BAGD, BNTC, LN, Mor, WBC; KJV, NIV], 'descendants' [BAGD, LN, SSA; NASB, NCV, NET, TEV], 'children' [BAGD; NLT], 'offspring' [Herm, LN; NRSV], 'posterity' [BAGD, LN], 'descendants and heirs' [GW], 'issue' [REB]. The phrase ἄρα τοῦ Ἀβραὰμ σπέρμα ἐστέ 'then you are seed of Abraham' is translated 'you are now part of Abraham's family' [CEV].

QUESTION—What relationship is indicated by δέ 'and'?

It is continuative. The new sentence adds fresh inferences to what has already been said [ICC].

QUESTION—What is meant by εἰ ὑμεῖς Χριστοῦ 'if you are Christ's'?

The 'if' does not introduce a mere hypothesis, rather it suggests that what follows is true and certain [NCBC, NTC, TH]. 'You' in the phrase is emphatic. He is making a comment that had special relevance for Galatian Christians [Mor]. Paul states this phrase with some emphasis [BNTC]. 'To be of Christ' is a Greek idiom: to be his, to belong to him. This defines what 'being in Christ Jesus' means [Lns]. This is a conditional clause that expresses itself in a simple supposition. It refers to something that is assumed to be true [ICC].

QUESTION—What relationship is indicated by ἄρα 'then'?

It introduces the self-evident deduction: 'then you are Abraham's seed,' his true spiritual descendants [Lns]. They were spiritual descendants [Mor]. Christ is Abraham's physical descendant and by their union and identification with Christ, the believers have the standing of being Abraham's physical descendants [SSA].

heirs[a] **in-accordance-with**[b] **promise.**[c]
LEXICON—a. κληρονόμος (LN 57.133, 57.139) (BAGD 2.b. p. 435): 'heir' [BAGD, BNTC, Herm, LN (57.133, 57.139), Mor, SSA, WBC; GW, KJV, NASB, NET, NIV, NRSV, REB]. This entire phrase is translated 'and you will be given what God has promised' [CEV], 'You will inherit all of God's blessings because of the promise God made to Abraham' [NCV], 'You are his heirs, and now all the promises God gave to him belong to you' [NLT], 'and will receive what God has promised' [TEV].
  b. κατά with accusative object (LN 89.8): 'in accordance with' [LN], 'according to' [BNTC, Herm, Mor, WBC; KJV, NASB, NET, NIV, NRSV], 'by virtue of' [REB]. The phrase κατ' ἐπαγγελίαν 'in accordance with promise' is translated 'God promised' [SSA], 'as God promised' [GW]. See a. [CEV, NCV, NLT, TEV].
  c. ἐπαγγελία (LN 33.288) (BAGD 2.a. p. 280): 'promise' [BAGD, BNTC, Herm, LN, Mor, WBC; KJV, NASB, NET, NIV, NRSV, REB]. See a. [CEV, NCV, NLT, TEV]. See b. [SSA; GW].
QUESTION—What relationship is indicated by κατά 'in accordance with'?
God had made promises to Abraham and those promises are fulfilled in the believers, not those who were physical descendants [Mor]. They were heirs by promise, not by law [Lt].

DISCOURSE UNIT: 4:1–20 [NASB, REB]. The topic is sonship in Christ [NASB], life under the law [REB].

DISCOURSE UNIT: 4:1–11 [BST, TNTC; GW]. The topic is once slaves, but now sons [BST], the difference between son and infant [TNTC], you are God's children [GW].

DISCOURSE UNIT: 4:1–7 [Mor, NAC, NCBC, NIC, NIGTC, WBC]. The topic is emerging into sonship [NCBC], an illustration of relationships [WBC], sons of God [Mor], from slavery to sonship [NIGTC], the coming of Christ: spiritual maturity [NIC], the radical change: from slavery to sonship [NAC].

4:1 Now[a] I-say,[b] for as-long[c] a-time the heir[d] is (a) minor,[e]
LEXICON—a. δέ (LN 89.87, 89.94): 'and' [LN (89.87, 89.94)], 'and then' [LN (89.87)], 'now' [SSA; KJV, NASB, NET], 'but' [Mor], 'but now' [TEV], not explicit [BNTC, Herm, WBC; CEV, GW, NCV, NIV]. See b. [NLT, NRSV, REB].
  b. pres. act. indic. of λέγω (LN 33.69, 33.140) (BAGD II.1.e. p. 469; II.3. p. 470): 'to say' [LN (33.69), Mor, WBC; KJV, NASB, NIV], 'to mean' [BAGD, LN (33.140); NET], 'to declare, to proclaim' [BAGD], 'to tell' [BNTC, Herm; NCV], 'to explain' [GW], not explicit [CEV]. The phrase λέγω δέ 'now I say' is translated 'Now to continue' [TEV], 'Think of it this way' [NLT], 'My point is this' [NRSV], 'This is what I mean' [REB], 'Now I will further discuss (children and heirs)' [SSA].
  c. ὅσος (LN 67.139) (BAGD 1. p. 586): 'as long as' [BAGD, LN]. The phrase ἐφ' ὅσον χρόνον 'for as long a time' is translated 'for as long a

time as' [Mor], 'as long as' [BNTC, Herm, SSA, WBC; GW, KJV, NASB, NET, NIV, NRSV], 'so long as' [REB], 'while' [TEV], 'while still' [NCV], not explicit [CEV]. The phrase ἐφ' ὅσον χρόνον... νήπιός ἐστιν 'for as long a time...is a minor' is translated 'until they grow up' [NLT].

d. κληρονόμος (LN 57.133, 57.139) (BAGD 1. p. 435): 'heir' [BAGD, BNTC, LN (57.133, 57.139), Mor, SSA, WBC; GW, KJV, NASB, NET, NIV, NRSV, REB], 'he' [Herm]. This noun is also translated 'the son who will receive his father's property' [TEV], 'those who will inherit their fathers' property' [NCV], 'everything their parents own will someday be theirs' [CEV], 'If a father dies and leaves great wealth for his young children' [NLT].

e. νήπιος (LN 9.43) (BAGD 2. p. 537): 'minor' [BAGD, Herm, Mor, SSA, WBC; NET, NRSV, REB], 'small child' [LN], 'young child' [NLT], 'child' [BNTC; GW, KJV, NASB, NCV, NIV], 'children who are under age' [CEV]. This noun is also translated as an adjective: '(he is) young' [TEV].

QUESTION—What is the function of the phrase λέγω δέ 'now I say'?

It is an expression which Paul uses to introduce an expansion or explanation of a previous argument [Lt, TH]. Now he takes up the thought of the inferior state of being under the law [ICC]. It intends to emphasize what is said [BNTC, Lns]. It moves us to a different aspect of the topic [Mor]. This introduces a new phase of the argument rather than explaining his previous statements [Alf]. It is resumptive. Paul begins an analogy meant to illustrate what he said in 3:23–25 about living 'under the law' and in 3:26–29 about new relationships 'in Christ' [WBC].

he-differs[a] nothing-from a-slave,[b]

LEXICON—a. pres. act. indic. of διαφέρω (LN 58.41) (BAGD 2.a. p. 190): 'to differ from' [LN], 'to be different from' [BAGD, LN], 'to differ' [BAGD]. The phrase οὐδὲν διαφέρει 'he differs nothing from' [KJV] is also translated 'he does not differ at all from' [NASB], 'they are no different from' [NCV], 'he is no different from' [BNTC, Mor, WBC; NET, NIV], 'he is no better off than' [GW, REB], 'are no better off than' [CEV], 'are not much better off than' [NLT], 'are no better than' [NRSV], 'he is just like' [SSA], 'is treated just like' [TEV], 'the heir is no different than' [Herm].

b. δοῦλος (LN 87.76) (BAGD 1.b. p. 205): 'slave' [BAGD, BNTC, Herm, Mor, SSA, WBC; all versions except KJV], 'bondservant' [LN], 'servant' [KJV].

QUESTION—What is the meaning of this phrase?

This is a hyperbole for the sake of the illustration and what Paul means is that the minor and the slave are alike in that they both live under rules and regulations [WBC]. The minor and the slave lack the capacity of self-determination [Herm, Mor]. A minor who is in a state of legal infancy is no different from a slave as far as freedom of action is concerned. The minor has no power of disposition over the estate. He is under the supervision of guardians and trustees [BST, NAC, NIC, NIGTC]. The comparison refers to freedom of action not to status. The minor son and the slave are under the father's authority [NCBC]. The main point is that the minor is not yet old enough to fulfill the terms of his father's will [TNTC]. The phrase refers mainly to legal status. The child, who is a minor, can't perform any legal act except through his legal representatives [Lt, TH]. The child, who is a minor, is fed, nourished, and sheltered in the house. He also does not have any control of the property. All of this is true of a slave in the house [Lns].

being owner[a] of-all[b] (things);
LEXICON—a. κύριος (LN **57.12**): 'owner' [**LN**; NASB, NET, NRSV], 'lord' [Herm, LN, Mor; KJV], 'master' [LN], 'young master' [WBC]. This noun is also translated as a verb with 'the heir' as the subject: 'to control' [SSA], 'to own' [BNTC; GW, NCV, NIV, NLT, TEV]. This entire phrase is translated 'everything their parents own will someday be theirs' [CEV], 'the whole estate is his' [REB].

b. πᾶς (LN 59.23) (BAGD 2.a.δ. p. 633): 'all' [BAGD, Herm, LN, Mor, SSA, WBC; KJV, NRSV], 'every' [BAGD, LN], 'everything' [BNTC; GW, NASB, NCV, NET, NLT, TEV], 'the whole estate' [NIV, REB], 'everything their parents own' [CEV].

QUESTION—What is the function of the participle ὤν 'being'?
It expresses a concession [ICC, SSA, WBC; all versions except NCV]: although he is owner of all.

QUESTION—What is referred to by πάντων 'of all'?
It refers to the inheritance [BNTC, Herm, Mor, NAC, NCBC, NIC, NTC, TH; CEV, NIV, NLT, NRSV, REB], all that his father has [SSA].

4:2 but he-is under[a] guardians[b] and stewards[c] until[d] the designated-time[e] set by the father.
LEXICON—a. ὑπό with accusative object (LN 37.7) (BAGD 2.b. p. 843): 'under' [BAGD, BNTC, Herm, LN, Mor, WBC; KJV, NASB, NET, NRSV], 'under the control of' [LN; GW], 'in the care of' [CEV]. This is also translated as a verb: 'to be subject to' [NIV, REB], 'to have to obey' [NCV, NLT], not explicit [SSA; TEV].

b. ἐπίτροπος (LN **36.5**) (BAGD 3. p. 303): 'guardian' [BAGD, BNTC, Herm, LN, Mor, WBC; CEV, GW, NASB, NET, NIV, NRSV, REB], 'tutor' [KJV], 'men/those who take care of him' [**LN**; TEV]. This noun is also translated as a verb with 'other persons' as the subject: 'to supervise' [SSA]. The phrase ἐπιτρόπους καὶ οἰκονόμους 'guardians and stewards' is translated 'guardians' [NLT], 'those who are chosen to care for them' [NCV].

c. οἰκονόμος (LN **36.5**, 37.39, 46.4) (BAGD 1.a. p. 560): 'steward' [BNTC, LN (46.4)], 'administrator' [Herm, LN (37.39), WBC], 'manager' [BAGD, LN (37.39), Mor; NASB, NET], 'governor' [KJV], 'teacher'

[CEV], 'trustee' [GW, NIV, NRSV, REB], 'men/those who manage his affairs' [**LN** (36.5); TEV]. This noun is also translated as a verb phrase: 'to manage (his) property' [SSA]. See b. [NCV, NLT].
   d. ἄχρι with genitive object (LN 67.119) (BAGD 1.a. p. 128): 'until' [BAGD, BNTC, Herm, LN, Mor, SSA, WBC; all versions except NCV], not explicit [NCV].
   e. προθεσμία (LN **67.2**) (BAGD p. 706): 'designated time, set time' [LN], 'time set' [BAGD, BNTC, **LN**, Mor, WBC; CEV, GW, NIV, TEV], 'time appointed' [KJV], 'time fixed' [Herm], 'date set' [NASB, NET, NRSV, REB], 'age set' [NCV, NLT], 'day previously determined' [SSA].
QUESTION—What is the difference between the functions of a guardian and a steward?
   The guardian is in charge of the minor's personal life [NIGTC]. It is a general term for someone who has charge of the total care of a child and instructs him in what to do [BNTC, SSA, TH], the person responsible for the child's welfare [Alf, Lns, Lt, NTC]. The steward is in charge of the property that someday will come under control of the child [Alf, Lns, Lt, NIGTC, NTC, TH], one who takes care of the finances [TH]. Some note the differences between the terms but consider them practically synonyms in this case [ICC, Mor, NIC, WBC]. The different function could be performed by the same person [ICC]. The administrators and managers referred to here control the property and finances of the minor [NAC]. Only one designation is given in some translations: 'guardians' [NLT], 'those who are chosen to care for them' [NCV].
QUESTION—What is meant by 'the designated time'?
   This refers to the previously appointed time [Alf, Mor] when the son would come of age and inherit the property [BNTC, TNTC]. The son was heir all the time, but the appointed time was when the control of a guardian and steward came to an end [Lt].

4:3 Thus[a] we also, when we-were minors,[b]
LEXICON—a. οὕτως (LN 61.9): 'thus' [BNTC, LN], 'so' [Herm, LN, Mor, WBC; KJV, NASB, NET, NIV, NRSV, REB]. The phrase οὕτως καὶ ἡμεῖς 'thus we also' is translated 'It was the same way with us' [GW], 'likewise' [SSA], 'It is the same for us' [NCV], 'And that's the way it was with us' [NLT], 'In the same way' [TEV], 'That is how it was with us' [CEV].
   b. νήπιος (LN 9.43) (BAGD 2. p. 537): 'minor' [BAGD, Herm, SSA, WBC; NET, NRSV], 'child' [BNTC; CEV, GW, KJV, NASB, NCV, NIV], 'small child' [LN], 'infant' [Mor], not explicit [NLT]. The phrase ὅτε μεν νήπιοι 'when we were minors' is translated 'during our minority' [REB], 'before we reached spiritual maturity' [TEV].
QUESTION—To whom is referred by οὕτως καὶ ἡμεῖς 'thus we also'?
   1. This refers to all Christians, both Jews and Gentiles [Alf, Herm, ICC, Lt, Mor, NCBC, NTC, TH]. The change to the first person plural now applies

to all Christians [Herm]. The Jews were referred to in the preceding illustration of being under God's revelation, but in this application all people are freed in Christ [Alf].
2. This refers to only the Jews [Lns, NIGTC, SSA, WBC]. This refers to the time before Christ came when the Jews were treated as minor heirs who would come to freedom after Christ came [Lns]. Before Christ came, the Jews as a people already had a relationship with God and were regarded as heirs [SSA].

QUESTION—What is meant by ὅτε ἦμεν νήπιοι 'when we were minors'?
It refers to the pre-Christian condition [Herm, ICC, NCBC, NIBC, TH]. It refers to religious infancy [NIGTC], spiritual infancy [NIC, TH; TEV].

we-were enslaved[a] under[b] the basic-principles/elemental-spirits[c] of-the world;[d]

LEXICON—a. perf. pass. participle of δουλόω (LN 37.27, 87.82) (BAGD 2. p. 206): 'to be enslaved' [BAGD, BNTC, Herm, LN (87.82), Mor, WBC; NET, NRSV], 'to be made a slave of' [LN (37.27)], 'to be made subjected to' [**LN** (37.27)], 'to be in bondage' [KJV], 'to be ruled' [CEV], 'to be slaves' [GW, NCV, NLT, REB, TEV], 'to be held in bondage' [NASB], 'to be in slavery' [NIV]. The phrase ὑπὸ τὰ στοιχεῖα τοῦ κόσμου ἤμεθα δεδουλωμένοι 'we were enslaved under the basic principles/elemental spirits of the world' is translated 'to be subject to rudimentary knowledge' [BAGD]. The phrase ἤμεθα δεδουλωμένοι 'we were enslaved' is translated 'we were like slaves' [SSA].
b. ὑπό with accusative object (LN 37.7) (BAGD 2.b. p. 843): 'under' [BAGD, BNTC, Herm, LN, Mor, WBC; KJV, NASB, NET, NIV], 'to' [GW, NCV, NLT, NRSV], 'under the control of' [LN], 'subject to' [REB], 'of' [TEV], '(ruled) by' [CEV]. See c. [SSA].
c. στοιχεῖον (LN 12.43, 58.19) (BAGD 3., 4. p. 769): 'basic principles, elementary concepts' [LN (58.19)], 'supernatural powers over the world' [LN (12.43)], 'heavenly bodies' [BAGD (4.)]. The meaning is much disputed, referring either to elementary forms of religion or to 'elemental spirits' [BAGD (3.)]. The plural form is translated 'basic principles' [WBC; NIV], 'elemental principles' [Mor], 'elemental things' [NASB], 'principles' [GW], 'useless rules' [NCV], 'elements' [Herm; KJV], 'elemental forces' [BNTC], 'elemental spirits' [NRSV, REB], 'basic forces' [NET], 'powers' [CEV], 'spiritual powers' [NLT], 'ruling spirits' [TEV]. The phrase ὑπὸ τὰ στοιχεῖα τοῦ κόσμου 'under the basic principles of the world' is translated 'we Jews had to comply with the Mosaic rules and rites which concerned external and material things' [SSA].
d. κόσμος (LN 1.1, 1.39): 'world' [BNTC, Herm, LN (1.39), Mor, WBC; all versions except REB, TEV], 'universe' [LN (1.1); REB, TEV], 'cosmos' [LN (1.1)], 'earth' [LN (1.39)]. See c. [SSA].

QUESTION—Who is the implied actor of ἤμεθα δεδουλωμένοι 'we were enslaved'?

People were enslaved by surrendering themselves to the ordinances they thought would bring them redemption [NIC]. People are enslaved by the elements of the world [NTC]. Or, God is the implied actor since he imposed this condition on the people by giving them the Mosaic law [Lns]. Instead of implying an agent who enslaved people, many translations focus on the state of being slaves [CEV, GW, KJV, NASB, NCV, NIV, NLT, REB, TEV].

QUESTION—What is meant by στοιχεῖα τοῦ κόσμου 'elements of this world'?

1. This refers to elementary knowledge possessed by all people [ICC, NIC, NTC]. These are elementary teachings regarding rules and regulations which Jews and Gentiles attempted to use to achieve salvation before Christ came [NTC].
2. This refers specifically to the Jewish religion [Alf, Lns, Lt, NIC, NIGTC, SSA, WBC]. This condition of slavery had been imposed by means of the Mosaic law. Their enslavement began at Sinai and ended with Christ [Lns]. These were elementary teachings of the law which had reference to material things in the world [Lt]. Or, these things were not the law itself but the earthly things the law had to do with [Lns].
3. This refers to spiritual beings [BST, Herm, NCBC, TH; CEV, NET, NLT, NRSV, REB, TEV]. It was thought that spirits controlled the universe, both demonic spirits and the 'spirits' of the celestial bodies [TH].

4:4 but when the fullness^a of-the time^b came,

LEXICON—a. πλήρωμα (LN **67.69**) (BAGD 5. p. 672): 'fullness' [BAGD, BNTC, Herm, Mor, WBC; KJV, NASB, NRSV], 'completion, end' [LN]. The phrase τὸ πλήρωμα τοῦ χρόνου 'the fullness of the time' is translated 'the complete time' [LN], 'the right time' [GW, NCV, NLT, TEV], 'the appropriate time' [NET], 'appointed time' [REB]. This entire phrase is translated 'But exactly at the time which God had previously determined to send his Son' [SSA], 'But when the time was right' [CEV]. This noun is also translated as an adverb and modifies 'come': 'fully come' [NIV].

b. χρόνος (LN 67.1, 67.78) (BAGD p. 888): 'time' [BAGD, BNTC, Herm, LN (67.1, 67.78), Mor, WBC; KJV, NASB, NIV, NRSV], 'period of time' [BAGD, LN (67.78)]. See a. [SSA; CEV, GW, NCV, NET, NLT, REB, TEV].

QUESTION—How are the nouns related in the genitive construction τὸ πλήρωμα τοῦ χρόνου 'the fullness of the time'?

The phrase marks the completion of the old era and the dawn of the new [NCBC]. The noun 'fullness' indicates that God has been working his purposes out through history, and it was only when the right time came that he sent his Son [Mor]. It probably means the end of the reign of the Law and the beginning of a new era when the decisive aspect is not what man does or attempts to do, but what God does on behalf of man. The emphasis is on a time designated by God when he assured man's deliverance from helplessness and subservience to the Law and also to those forces that are opposed to God [TH]. God alone judged and determined when the right time was for the Son of God to be revealed to the world [NAC, NIC]. Christ arrived at the time previously determined by the Father [NTC, SSA]. The Gospel was withheld by God until the world had arrived at a mature age in which the law had completed its educational purpose and it was superseded by the Messiah's coming [Lt].

God sent-forth[a] his Son,
LEXICON—a. aorist act. indic. of ἐξαποστέλλω (LN 15.68) (BAGD 1.b. p. 273): 'to send forth' [LN; KJV, NASB], 'to send out' [BAGD, LN, SSA; NET], 'to send' [BNTC, Herm, LN, Mor, WBC; all versions except KJV, NASB, NET].
QUESTION—What is meant by this phrase?
It is God's commissioning of Christ to bring about the redemption of humanity [WBC]. The form of the verb involves more than just a commissioning. It involves a sending out from a previous state and implies the pre-existence of the Son [ICC, Lns, Lt, NCBC, TH]. It means that God sent Christ out from himself [Alf, Lt, NAC, NTC, SSA].

having-come-into-being[a] from[b] (a) woman,[c]
LEXICON—a. aorist mid. (deponent = act.) participle of γίνομαι (LN 13.80, 85.7) (BAGD I.1.a. p. 158): 'to come into being, to come to be, to appear' [LN (85.7)], 'to be born' [BAGD, BNTC, Herm, Mor, SSA, WBC; NASB, NCV, NET, NIV, NLT, NRSV, REB], 'to be begotten' [BAGD], 'to be formed, to come to exist, to come into existence' [LN (13.80)], 'to be made' [KJV]. This verb is also translated with 'woman' as its subject: 'to give birth to' [CEV, GW]. This entire phrase is translated 'He came as the son of a human mother' [TEV].
b. ἐκ with genitive object (LN 90.16) (BAGD 3.a. p. 234): 'from' [LN], 'by' [BAGD, Herm, LN], 'of' [BNTC, Mor, WBC; all versions except CEV, GW, TEV], '(was born) to' [SSA], not explicit [CEV, GW]. See a. [TEV].
c. γυνή (LN 9.34): 'woman' [BNTC, Herm, LN, Mor, WBC; all versions except TEV], 'human mother' [SSA; TEV].
QUESTION—What is meant by γενόμενον 'having become' in this phrase?
It is often used in the sense of passing from one state to another and in this phrase it is Jesus' transition from the womb to the world [Mor]. The phrase γενόμενον ἐκ γυναικός 'having come into being from a woman' probably refers to his full humanity rather than to the virgin birth, though this could be included as well [TNTC]. The phrase is used in other scripture passages as a common Jewish expression meaning simply one's status as a human being [BNTC, NAC, TH], having the sense 'born of a woman' [Mor, NIGTC]. The phrase includes the entire human nature of the Son as this was obtained from

his human mother [Lns]. The phrase identified him with all of mankind [Alf]. He took upon himself our human nature [Lt].

having-come-into-being[a] under[b] law[c]/(the) Law,[c]
LEXICON—a. aorist mid. (deponent = act.) participle of γίνομαι (LN 13.48, 13.80, 85.7) (BAGD II.4.a. p. 160): 'to come into being, to come to be' [LN (85.7)], 'to become' [LN (13.48)], 'to be formed, to come to exist, to come into existence' [LN (13.80)], 'to be born' [BNTC, Mor, SSA, WBC; NASB, NET, NIV, NRSV, REB], 'to be made' [KJV], 'to be put' [Herm], 'to come' [GW], 'to live' [NCV, TEV]. This entire phrase is translated 'His Son obeyed the Law' [CEV]. Not explicit [NLT].
  b. ὑπό with accusative object (LN 37.7) (BAGD 2.b. p. 843): 'under' [BAGD, BNTC, Herm, LN, Mor, WBC; all versions except CEV, GW, NLT], 'under the control of' [LN; GW]. This preposition is also translated as a verb: 'to be subject to' [SSA; NLT]. See a. [CEV].
  c. νόμος (LN 33.55, 33.333) (BAGD 3. p. 542): 'Law' [Herm, LN (33.55); CEV, NASB], the law which Moses received from God [BAGD], 'law' [BNTC, LN (33.333), Mor, WBC; KJV, NCV, NET, NIV, NLT, NRSV, REB], 'Mosaic law' [SSA], 'Jewish Law' [TEV]. This singular form is also translated as plural: 'God's laws' [GW].
QUESTION—What is the meaning of the participle γενόμενον 'having become' in this phrase?
  The phrase γενόμενον ὑπὸ νόμον 'having come under law' is probably a reference to his birth into the Jewish race [TNTC]. Since he was born of a Jewish mother, Jesus was born a Jew and therefore was under the law [BST, NIGTC]. Or, Jesus was made subject to the Law [ICC, TH]. The Son of God took upon himself human form and was subject to all the requirements of the Jewish law [TH]. 'Under law' implies that Jesus was to fulfill law and thereby purchase our Christian freedom [Lns].

4:5 in-order-that he-might-redeem[a] the-(ones) under[b] (the) Law/law,[c]
LEXICON—a. aorist act. subj. of ἐξαγοράζω (LN 37.131) (BAGD 1. p. 271): 'to redeem' [BAGD, BNTC, Herm, LN, Mor, SSA, WBC; KJV, NASB, NET, NIV, NRSV, TEV], 'to set free' [LN; CEV], 'to deliver' [BAGD], 'to pay for the freedom' [GW], 'to buy freedom for' [NCV, NLT, REB]. See this word at 3:13.
  b. ὑπό with accusative object (LN **37.7**) (BAGD 2.b. p. 843): 'under' [BAGD, BNTC, Herm, **LN,** Mor, WBC; all versions except CEV, GW, NLT], 'under the control of' [LN], 'under the power of' [BAGD], 'to be controlled by' [GW], 'to be slaves to' [NLT], 'to be subject to' [SSA]. The phrase ὑπὸ νόμον 'under the Law' is translated 'under obligation to abide by the regulations of the Law' [**LN**]. Not explicit [CEV].
  c. νόμος (LN 33.55, 33.333) (BAGD 3. p. 542): 'Law' [Herm, LN (33.55); CEV, NASB, TEV], the law which Moses received from God [BAGD], 'Mosaic law' [SSA], 'law' [BNTC, LN (33.333), Mor, WBC; KJV, NCV,

NET, NIV, NLT, NRSV, REB]. This singular form is also translated as plural: 'God's laws' [GW].

QUESTION—What is meant by ἐξαγοράσῃ 'he might redeem'?

It means deliverance from the law itself [ICC, Lns, NCBC, NIGTC, SSA, TH, TNTC]. They were redeemed from the curse of the law (3:13) [Lns, NIGTC, NTC]. This deliverance is from the enslaving power of the law so that neither Jews nor Gentiles would continue to live under a system of legalism [ICC]. They are delivered from strict obedience to the law being necessary for salvation [NTC]. Or, since sinners are slaves to sin, they must be rescued by the price Jesus paid on the cross [Mor].

QUESTION—What relationship is indicated by ἵνα 'in order that'?

It indicates purpose [BNTC, Mor, NIC, NIGTC, SSA, WBC]: he was born under the Law/law in order that he might redeem those who were under the Law/law.

QUESTION—Who are τοὺς ὑπὸ νόμον 'the ones under the law'?

1. This refers to both Jews and Gentiles [ICC, Lns, Lt, NAC, NCBC, NIC, NIGTC, NTC]. This anarthrous form 'law' includes the specific Law the Jews were under and also the general law written in the hearts of all people [Lns].
2. This refers to only the Jews who were under the Law of Moses [BNTC, Herm, Mor, TH, WBC].

in-order-that we-might-receive the adoption.[a]

LEXICON—a. υἱοθεσία (LN 35.53) (BAGD 2. p. 833): 'adoption' [BAGD, LN]. The phrase τὴν υἱοθεσίαν ἀπολάβωμεν 'we might receive the adoption' [BNTC] is also translated 'we could become God's children' [CEV], 'we would be adopted as his children' [GW], 'we might receive the adoption as sons' [Herm; NASB], 'we could become his children' [NCV], 'we may be adopted as sons with full rights' [NET], 'we might receive the full rights of sons' [NIV], 'we might receive adoption as children' [NRSV], 'we might attain the status of sons' [REB], 'we might become God's children' [TEV], 'we might receive the adoption of sons' [KJV], 'we might receive adoption' [Mor], 'we might receive the sonship' [WBC], 'we(excl.) Jews might receive from God what he promised that he would give to his children/might be God's heirs' [SSA], 'he could adopt us as his very own children' [NLT].

QUESTION—What relationship is indicated by ἵνα 'in order that'?

1. This is coordinate with the first clause. Both clauses give the purposes God had in sending his son [NCBC, NTC, TH, WBC]. God had two purposes in sending his son to become a human being and to live under the Jewish law. The first was to redeem those who were under the law and the second was so that we might become God's sons [NCBC, TH].
2. This specifies what is meant by redemption [Mor, NIC, NIGTC]: in order that we might receive the adoption as sons.

3. This connects chiastically with the last two phrases of the preceding verse [Herm, Lt]. The two clauses correspond to those of the preceding verse in an inverted order by the grammatical figure called chiasm [Lt].

QUESTION—Who is referred to by the verb ἀπολάβωμεν 'we might receive'?
1. This refers to all Christians, both Jews and Gentiles [BNTC, Herm, ICC, Lt, Mor, NAC, NIBC, NIC, NIGTC, NTC, TH].
2. This refers only to the Jewish Christians [Lns, WBC].

4:6 And because[a] you-are sons,[b]

LEXICON—a. ὅτι (LN 89.33): 'because' [LN, Mor, WBC; GW, KJV, NASB, NET, NIV, NLT, NRSV], 'since' [Herm, LN; NCV], 'in view of the fact that' [LN], 'in that' [BNTC], 'This shows that' [SSA], 'Now that' [CEV], 'To prove that' [REB], 'To show that' [TEV].
b. υἱός (LN 36.39) (BAGD 1.c.γ. p. 834): 'son' [BAGD], 'disciple, follower' [LN]. It refers to the devout, the believers [BAGD]. The plural form is translated 'sons' [BNTC, Herm, Mor, WBC; KJV, NASB, NET, NIV, REB], 'children' [SSA; CEV, GW, NCV, NLT, NRSV, TEV].

QUESTION—What relationship is indicated by ὅτι 'because'?
1. It indicates the reason God sent his Spirit [Alf, BST, Herm, ICC, Lns, Lt, Mor, NAC, NIC, NIGTC, NTC, TNTC, WBC; GW, KJV, NASB, NET, NIV, NLT, NRSV]: because you are sons, God sent the Spirit into our hearts.
2. It is demonstrative 'that' [BNTC, NCBC, SSA; REB, TEV]: that you are sons is proven by the fact that God sent the Spirit into your hearts. The Galatian believers are to realize that having the Holy Spirit in their hearts was proof that they were already sons of God without having undergone circumcision [SSA].

QUESTION—What is the significance of Paul switching from the first person pronoun ἀπολάβωμεν 'we might receive' in 4:5 to the second person pronoun ἐστε 'you are' in this phrase?

It indicates that Paul is making a more direct appeal to his Galatian readers [NCBC, TH].

God sent-forth[a] the Spirit[b] of-his Son into[c] our hearts[d]

TEXT—Instead of ἡμῶν 'our' some manuscripts read ὑμῶν 'your'. GNT reads ἡμῶν 'our' with an A decision, indicating that the text is certain. The pronoun ὑμῶν 'your' is read by KJV, NCV, NLT.
LEXICON—a. aorist act. indic. of ἐξαποστέλλω (LN 15.68) (BAGD 1.b. p. 273): 'to send forth' [LN; KJV, NASB], 'to send out' [BAGD, LN], 'to send' [BNTC, Herm, LN, Mor, SSA, WBC; all versions except KJV, NASB].
b. πνεῦμα (LN 12.18) (BAGD 5.b. p. 676): 'Spirit' [BNTC, LN, Mor, SSA, WBC; all versions], 'spirit' [Herm]. It refers to the Spirit of Christ [BAGD].
c. εἰς with accusative object (LN 84.22): 'into' [BNTC, Herm, LN, Mor, SSA, WBC; all versions].

d. καρδία (LN 26.3) (BAGD 1.b.θ. p. 404): 'heart' [BAGD, LN], 'inner self, mind' [LN]. The plural form is translated 'hearts' [BNTC, Herm, Mor, WBC; all versions except GW], 'us' [SSA; GW].

QUESTION—How are the nouns related in the genitive construction τὸ πνεῦμα τοῦ υἱοῦ 'the Spirit of his Son'?

'The Spirit' refers to the Holy Spirit [Herm, Mor, NAC, NTC, TH, TNTC]. All three members of the Trinity are closely linked and since the emphasis is on the Son redeeming believers and bringing them into the divine family, with the resultant gift of the Holy Spirit, it is natural to link the Spirit with the Son [Mor]. The Spirit is intimately linked to God's Son [SSA]. The Holy Spirit was promised by the Son as well as by the Father and it is this Spirit who rested on Christ in all his fullness [TNTC]. The same Spirit who indwelt the Son also indwelt the believers [NIGTC].

QUESTION—What is meant by εἰς τὰς καρδίας ἡμῶν 'into our hearts'?

Heart is used as the seat of a person's intellectual and emotional life generally and as the center of a person's moral and spiritual life in particular [ICC, WBC]. The heart stands for the seat of the inner life [BNTC], the whole of the inner being of man [NIC]. The heart is the center of intellectual, moral and spiritual life [TH]. The heart controls the entire personality and it is the core and center of man's being [NTC]. The heart was considered the organ responsible for the control of the will and therefore the appropriate place for the indwelling of the Spirit [Herm]. The presence of the Spirit in believers is in their hearts. It is something that happens in their innermost being and is not a minor disturbance on the surface of life [Mor].

QUESTION—What is the significance of changing to first person plural 'our hearts'?

Paul identifies himself with the Galatians in the fact of receiving the Holy Spirit [Lns, Mor, TH, WBC]. It is such a wonderful reality, Paul did not want to write in a detached manner [NTC]. Paul changes pronouns from 'you' plural to 'our' here, and to 'you' singular in 4:7 to turn the thought in every direction, not to stress significant changes of referents [Lns].

crying,[a] "Abba,[b] Father."

LEXICON—a. pres. act. participle of κράζω (LN 33.83) (BAGD 2.b.α. p. 448): 'to cry' [BAGD, BNTC, Mor, WBC; KJV, NASB, NRSV, REB], 'to call out' [BAGD; GW, NIV], 'to call' [BAGD; NET], 'to shout' [LN], 'to pray/exclaim' [SSA], 'to cry out' [Herm; NCV, TEV]. This entire phrase is translated 'And his Spirit tells us that God is our Father' [CEV], 'and now you can call God your dear Father' [NLT].

b. ἀββά (LN 12.12) (BAGD p. 1): 'Abba' [BAGD, BNTC, Herm, LN, Mor, WBC; GW, KJV, NASB, NET, NIV, NRSV, REB]. The phrase Αββα ὁ πατήρ 'Abba, Father' is translated 'dear Father' [SSA; NLT], 'Father, my Father' [TEV], 'Father' [CEV, NCV].

QUESTION—Who utters the words 'Abba, Father'?

The Spirit is sent into our hearts and the Spirit cries out 'Abba, Father' [Alf, BNTC, ICC, Lns, NIGTC, NTC, TH, WBC; NASB, NCV, NET, NIV, NRSV, REB, TEV]. The Spirit is the main subject and believers are regarded merely as the organs of the Spirit [Alf]. The Spirit cries out to God on behalf of the believer [ICC]. However, it is to be understood that the Spirit energizes the believers to cry out to God the Father, 'Abba, Father' [BST, ICC, Lns, NTC, SSA, TH, WBC]. This outcry is ascribed to the Spirit, but this is to be understood that it is the mediation of the Spirit 'whereby we cry, Abba! Father!' [NTC]. Some directly say that the believers cry out 'Abba, Father' [Mor, NIBC, NIC; NLT].

4:7 Therefore[a] no-longer are-you (a) slave[b] but (a) son;

LEXICON—a. ὥστε (LN 89.52) (BAGD 1.a. p. 899): 'therefore' [BAGD, Herm, LN, SSA, WBC; NASB, REB], 'for this reason' [BAGD], 'so' [BAGD, LN; GW, NET, NIV, NRSV], 'so that, and so' [LN], 'so then' [LN, Mor; TEV], 'consequently' [BNTC], 'wherefore' [KJV], 'so now' [NCV], 'now' [NLT], not explicit [CEV].

b. δοῦλος (LN 87.76) (BAGD 1.c. p. 205): 'slave' [BAGD, BNTC, Herm, LN, Mor, SSA, WBC; all versions except CEV, GW, KJV], 'bondservant' [LN], 'servant' [KJV]. This singular form is also translated as plural: 'slaves' [CEV, GW].

QUESTION—What relationship is indicated by ὥστε 'therefore'?

It introduces a conclusion [Mor, SSA]. The ground for this conclusion is 4:6 where it states that they are sons [Mor, SSA], or it is everything through 4:1-6 [Lt, TH]. The grounds are that their minority has come to an end and they have direct proof of it in the gift of the Spirit [Lt].

QUESTION—What is the significance about the change from the second person plural in 4:6 to the second person singular εἶ 'are you' in this phrase?

It has the effect of bringing matters home to each individual reader [Alf, ICC, Lns, TH, WBC]. Paul makes it personal by using the singular [Mor].

and if (a) son, also (an) heir[a] through[b] God.

LEXICON—a. κληρονόμος (LN 57.133, 57.139) (BAGD 2.b. p. 435): 'heir' [BAGD, BNTC, Herm, LN (57.133, 57.139), Mor, SSA, WBC; GW, KJV, NASB, NET, NIV, NRSV, REB]. The phrase κληρονόμος διὰ θεοῦ 'an heir through God' is translated 'you will be given what he has promised' [CEV], 'God will give you the blessing he promised' [NCV], 'everything he has belongs to you' [NLT], 'God will give you all that he has for his children' [TEV].

b. διά with genitive object (LN 90.4): 'through' [BNTC, Herm, LN, Mor, WBC; KJV, NASB, NET, NRSV], 'by' [LN; REB], 'by means of (what God has done)' [SSA]. The phrase διὰ θεοῦ 'through God' is translated 'God has made (you heirs)' [GW, NIV]. See a. [CEV, NCV, NLT, TEV]. God has made them so [ICC].

QUESTION—What relationship is indicated by δέ 'and'?

It is continuative and signals a further explanation of Paul's conclusion [WBC].

QUESTION—What relationship is indicated by εἰ 'if'?

There is no doubt that this is so [TNTC] and it is translated 'since' [SSA, TH, WBC; GW, NIV, NLT, TEV], 'because' [NCV].

QUESTION—What relationship is indicated by the prepositional phrase διὰ θεοῦ 'through God'?

The prepositional phrase διὰ θεοῦ 'through God' reminds Paul's readers that their status as heirs is entirely the result of God's grace. The phrase also assures them of the certainty of their possession of that status, since it is the result of God's work on their behalf and not their own efforts [ICC, Lns, Lt, Mor, TH, WBC]. The redeemed are heirs through the Trinity, not through the law or through fleshly efforts [Alf]. The prepositional phrase διὰ θεοῦ 'through God' is a reminder that the entire process of redemption is the work of God [Herm].

DISCOURSE UNIT: 4:8–20 [GNT; CEV, NCV, NIV, NLT, NRSV, TEV]. The topic is Paul's concern for the Galatians [GNT; CEV, NIV, NLT, TEV], Paul's love for the Christians [NCV], Paul reproves the Galatians [NRSV].

DISCOURSE UNIT: 4:8–12 [NET]. The topic is heirs of promise are not to return to law.

DISCOURSE UNIT: 4:8–11 [Mor, NAC, NCBC, NIC, NIGTC, WBC]. The topic is returning to beggarliness [NCBC], the beggarly elements [Mor], Paul's concern for the Galatians [WBC], no turning back! [NIGTC], cultic observance: relapse into slavery [NIC], the danger of turning back [NAC].

4:8 But then[a] on-the-one-hand[b] not knowing[c] God

LEXICON—a. τότε (LN 67.47) (BAGD 1.a. p. 823): 'then' [BAGD, LN, Mor; KJV], 'formerly when' [BNTC, Herm, WBC; NET, NIV, NRSV, REB], 'when' [SSA; GW], 'at that time' [NASB], 'in the past' [NCV, TEV], 'before' [NLT], not explicit [CEV].

    b. μέν (LN 89.136): 'on the one hand' [LN], not explicit [BNTC, Herm, Mor, SSA, WBC; all versions].

    c. perf. (with pres. meaning) act. participle of οἶδα (LN 28.1) (BAGD 1.a. p. 555): 'to know' [BNTC, Herm, LN, Mor, WBC; all versions]. The phrase οὐκ εἰδότες θεόν 'not knowing God' is translated 'to know nothing about God' [BAGD], 'you were not related to God' [SSA].

QUESTION—What relationship is indicated by ἀλλά 'but'?

It is the strong adversative [Mor, NAC, NTC]. It highlights the contrast between their status in 4:6–7 and 4:8 [ICC, Mor, WBC]. In the Greek the verse starts with 'but then,' and while most translations omit the connective, it is possible to interpret it to mean that the previous description of the Galatians as being children of God is in direct contrast with the description of their former state of apostasy in this verse [TH]. It marks the turning point

[Herm]. Or, it is merely copulative, not adversative, and adds a further fact. [Lns].

QUESTION—What relationship is indicated by τότε 'then'?

It refers to the period before conversion [Alf, Herm, SSA] and corresponds to οὐκέτι 'no longer' (Gal. 2:20, 3:25, 4:7) [Alf, Herm]. Τότε μὲν 'then' is in contrast with νῦν δὲ 'but now' in 4:9 [Lns].

QUESTION—What is meant by εἰδότες 'knowing' God?

It means to have knowledge about God [ICC], a knowledge of facts about God [TH]. They didn't even know the true God [Lns]. Far more than merely knowing about God, it indicates intimate relationship with God [SSA, TH]. Along with all people, they had a certain kind of knowledge about God's attributes, but they didn't have a saving knowledge of him [NTC].

you-were-slaves[a] to-the-(ones) by-nature[b] not being gods;

LEXICON—a. aorist act. indic. of δουλεύω (LN 35.27, 37.25, 87.79) (BAGD 2.b. p. 205): 'to be a slave' [LN (37.25, 87.79)], 'to be slaves to' [Mor; all versions except KJV, NET, NRSV], 'to serve' [BAGD, LN (35.27); KJV], 'to slavishly serve' [SSA], 'to be in slavery' [BNTC], 'to be enslaved' [Herm, WBC; NET, NRSV], 'to be controlled by' [LN (37.25)].

b. φύσις (LN **58.8**) (BAGD 2. p. 869): 'nature' [BAGD, LN]. The phrase τοῖς φύσει μὴ οὖσιν θεοῖς 'to the ones by nature not being gods' is translated 'to those who by nature are not gods' [Mor; NIV], 'to beings that by nature are not gods' [NRSV], 'to beings that by nature are no gods' [BNTC], 'to beings that in nature are no gods' [Herm], 'to those which by nature are no gods' [NASB], 'to beings that by nature are not gods at all' [NET], 'unto them which by nature are no gods' [KJV], 'to those who in reality are not gods' [WBC], 'to things which are really not gods at all' [GW], 'to gods who are not gods at all' [REB], 'of beings who are not gods' [TEV], 'to gods that were not real' [NCV], 'of gods that are not real' [CEV], 'to so-called gods that do not even exist' [NLT], 'gods who actually did not exist/who were not actually divine' [SSA].

QUESTION—What is referred to by τοῖς φύσει μὴ οὖσιν θεοῖς 'the ones by nature not being gods'?

The phrase φύσει 'by nature' refers to their essential character [ICC, NCBC, TH]. He was probably thinking of these beings as spiritual agencies such as demons [NCBC]. The beings which they had served during their pagan days were considered by them to be gods, but they were not really gods [NIGTC]. There were spirit beings who essentially were not gods [Mor]. This refers to the idols of paganism [NIGTC, NTC].

4:9 but/on-the-other-hand now having-come-to-know[a] God,

LEXICON—a. aorist act. participle of γινώσκω (LN 28.1) (BAGD 1.b. p. 160): 'to come to know' [BAGD, BNTC, Herm, Mor; NASB, NET, NRSV], 'to know' [BAGD, LN, WBC; CEV, GW, KJV, NCV, NIV, TEV], 'to become related to' [SSA], 'to find' [NLT], 'to acknowledge' [REB].

QUESTION—What relationship is indicated by the phrase νῦν δὲ 'but now'?
The phrase νῦν δὲ 'but now' introduces a contrast [Mor]. The phrase νῦν δὲ 'but now' in 4:9 contrasts with τότε μὲν 'then' in 4:8 [ICC] and sets out the Galatians' present condition [WBC]. 'But now' relates 4:9 with 4:8 and emphasizes the strong contrast between their pre-Christian and Christian states [Herm, TH].

QUESTION—What is meant by γνόντες 'to know'?
It is used in the Biblical sense of 'to experience' [NAC] and not in the sense of 'to perceive' or 'to acquire knowledge about' [WBC]. The word οἶδα used for 'know' in 4:8 implies mainly knowledge of facts while the word used for 'know' here in 4:9 is often used in the deeper sense of recognition or acknowledgment of facts and of persons. It involves personal knowledge or experience [TH].

but rather[a] having-become-known[b] by[c] God,
LEXICON—a. μᾶλλον (LN **89.126**) (BAGD 3.d. p. 489): 'rather' [BAGD, BNTC, Herm, **LN**, Mor, SSA, WBC; GW, KJV, NASB, NET, NIV, NRSV, REB], 'instead' [LN], 'better still' [CEV], 'really' [NCV], 'should I say' [NLT, TEV].
  b. aorist pass. participle of γινώσκω (LN 28.1, 31.27) (BAGD 7. p. 161): 'to become known' [LN (28.1), Mor], 'to be known' [BNTC, Herm, LN (28.1), WBC; KJV, NASB, NET, NIV, NRSV], 'to be acknowledged' [BAGD, LN (31.27); REB], 'to become related to' [SSA]. The phrase γνωσθέντες ὑπὸ θεοῦ 'having become known by God' is translated 'God knows you' [CEV, GW], 'it is God who knows you' [NCV], 'now that God has found you' [NLT], 'now that God knows you' [TEV].
  c. ὑπό with genitive object (LN 90.1): 'by' [BNTC, Herm, LN, Mor, WBC; NASB, NET, NIV, NRSV], 'to' [SSA], 'of' [KJV], not explicit [REB]. See b. [CEV, GW, NCV, NLT, TEV].

QUESTION—What relationship is indicated by the phrase μᾶλλον δὲ 'but rather'?
The phrase μᾶλλον δὲ 'but rather' introduces a statement that supplements and corrects what has just been said. It transfers the emphasis from what has just been said to the superior significance of what is now being said [WBC].

QUESTION—What is meant by γνωσθέντες 'having become known' by God?
It cannot refer simply to knowledge in a purely theoretic or intellectual sense because such knowledge was always possessed by God, so here it means to become objects of his favorable attention [ICC]. God had acknowledged them as his sons and revealed himself to them [Alf].

how are-you-returning[a] back[b] to[c] the weak[d] and beggarly[e] basic-principles[f]
LEXICON—a. pres. act. indic. of ἐπιστρέφω (LN **31.60**) (BAGD 1.b.β. p. 301): 'to return' [BAGD, Mor], 'to turn back' [BAGD, BNTC, Herm, WBC; GW, NASB, NET, NRSV], 'to want to turn back' [**LN**], 'to turn to' [LN], 'to turn' [CEV, KJV, NCV, NIV, REB, TEV], 'to go back' [NLT], not explicit [SSA].

b. πάλιν (LN **67.55**) (BAGD 1.a. p. 606): 'back' [BAGD; CEV, NCV, NIV, REB, TEV], 'again' [BNTC, Herm, **LN**, Mor, SSA, WBC; GW, KJV, NASB, NET, NLT, NRSV].
c. ἐπί with accusative object (LN 84.17) (BAGD III.1.b.δ. p. 289): 'to' [BAGD, BNTC, Herm, LN, Mor, WBC; all versions except CEV], not explicit [SSA; CEV].
d. ἀσθενής (LN 74.25, 79.69) (BAGD 1.b. p. 115): 'weak' [BAGD, BNTC, Herm, LN (74.25, 79.69), Mor, WBC; all versions except GW, REB], 'ineffective' [SSA], 'powerless' [GW], 'feeble' [REB].
e. πτωχός (LN **65.16**) (BAGD 2. p. 728): 'beggarly' [BAGD, BNTC, Mor; KJV, NRSV], 'poor' [BAGD], 'worthless' [**LN**; NASB, NET], 'miserable' [BAGD, WBC; NIV], 'inadequate' [SSA], 'pitiful' [CEV, TEV], 'bankrupt' [GW, REB], 'useless' [NCV, NLT], 'impotent' [Herm].
f. στοιχεῖον (LN 12.43, 58.19) (BAGD 3., 4. p. 769): This plural form is translated 'basic principles' [LN (58.19), WBC], 'elementary concepts' [LN (58.19)], 'supernatural powers over the world' [LN (12.43)], 'heavenly bodies' [BAGD], 'elemental forces' [BNTC], 'elemental principles' [Mor], 'rules and rites' [SSA], 'elements' [Herm; KJV], 'powers' [CEV], 'principles' [GW, NIV], 'elemental things' [NASB], 'rules' [NCV], 'basic forces' [NET], 'spiritual powers' [NLT], 'elemental spirits' [NRSV, REB], 'ruling spirits' [TEV]. The meaning is much disputed, referring either to elementary forms of religion or to 'elemental spirits' [BAGD].

QUESTION—What is the purpose of the question in this verse?

It is a rhetorical question [ICC, SSA, TH, WBC]. It puts a dilemma before the Galatian Christians. Now that they know God the Father, why would they want any other relationship? [NCBC, WBC]. It is intended to state that the action is absurd [ICC], or irrational [SSA]. It expresses both Paul's unbelief and dismay [TH], his shock [NTC].

QUESTION—What is meant by στοιχεῖα 'basic principles'?
1. This refers to elemental things in both Gentile and Jewish religion [Alf, ICC, Lns, Lt, NTC, WBC; GW, NASB, NCV, NIV].
2. This refers to spirit beings [BST, Herm, TH; CEV, NET, NLT, NRSV, REB, TEV].

to-which again[a] anew you-wish[b] to-be-slaves?[c]

LEXICON—a. πάλιν (LN **67.55**) (BAGD 2. p. 606): 'again' [BAGD, LN], 'anew, once more' [BAGD]. The phrase πάλιν ἄνωθεν 'again anew' is translated 'all over again' [**LN**, WBC; GW, NASB, NET, NIV, REB, TEV], 'again' [Mor, SSA; KJV, NCV, NRSV], 'once more' [Herm; NLT], 'once again' [BNTC], not explicit [CEV]. The word πάλιν 'again' strengthens the force of ἄνωθεν 'anew' [BAGD, ICC] and the two words are nearly synonymous [ICC]. This is a strong expression to indicate the completeness of their relapse [Lt].

b. pres. act. indic. of θέλω (LN **25.1**) (BAGD 2. p. 355): 'to wish' [BAGD, **LN**, Mor; NIV], 'to desire' [LN; KJV, NASB], 'to want' [BAGD, BNTC, Herm, LN, WBC; GW, NCV, NET, NLT, NRSV, TEV], 'to be minded' [BAGD], 'to propose' [REB], 'to choose' [SSA], not explicit [CEV].

c. pres. act. infin. of δουλεύω (LN 35.27, 37.25, 87.79) (BAGD 2.b. p. 205): 'to be a slave' [LN (37.25, 87.79), SSA], 'to become (their) slaves' [GW, TEV], 'to enter (their) service' [REB], 'to enslave (yourselves)' [Mor], 'to be in bondage' [KJV], 'to become the slaves of' [CEV], 'to be slaves to' [NCV], 'to become slaves to' [NLT], 'to be in slavery to' [BNTC], 'to be enslaved to' [NASB, NET, NRSV], 'to be enslaved by' [NIV], 'to serve' [BAGD, LN (35.27), WBC], 'to be controlled by' [LN (37.25)], 'whose slave to become' [Herm].

QUESTION—What is the function of this clause?

It is a supplementary question to the main rhetorical question. It extends the impact of the main question [WBC]. It brings out that they are doing this by their own choice [NTC]. It is not a conscious choice, but this is the consequence of their actions [TNTC].

4:10 **You-observe[a] days and months and seasons[b] and years;**

LEXICON—a. pres. mid. indic. of παρατηρέω (LN **41.27**) (BAGD 3. p. 622): 'to observe' [BNTC, Herm, **LN**, Mor, WBC; KJV, NASB, NET, NIV, NRSV], 'to observe religiously' [BAGD; GW], 'to celebrate' [CEV], 'to keep' [REB], 'to pay special attention to' [TEV], 'to follow (teachings about)' [NCV], 'to carefully observe' [SSA], 'to try to find favor with God by what you do or don't do (on certain days or months or seasons or years)' [NLT].

b. καιρός (LN **67.1**) (BAGD 2.b. p. 395): 'season' [BAGD, Herm, Mor, WBC; all versions except KJV], 'special season' [SSA], 'festal season' [BAGD], 'occasion' [LN], 'time' [LN; KJV], 'special time' [BNTC].

QUESTION—What are the days, months, seasons, and years?

It is most likely that, as used here, the four terms are not mutually exclusive and cover all kinds of celebrations of days and periods observed by the Jews [ICC, NAC, NIC, WBC]. Taken together they simply refer to the total system of celebrations observed by the Jews at that time [TH]. 'Days' refers to the days determined by the Mosaic law. 'Months' refers to entire months such as Tisri, which is called the Sabbath month. 'Seasons' refers to seasons of prayer and fasting required by the law. 'Years' refers to the sabbatical year and the interval of years [Lns]. The 'days' are the days recurring weekly, the Sabbaths. The 'months' are the monthly celebrations. The 'seasons' are the annual festivals such as the Passover. The 'years' are the sacred years such as the sabbatical year and the year of jubilee [Lt]. The 'days' are the Sabbaths, new moons and feast days. The 'months' are any months that were distinguished by great feasts. The 'seasons' are any festal seasons [Alf]. Paul is referring to the Sabbath days, days of the new moon, festival seasons, and the Sabbath and jubilee years or the New Year [NTC].

4:11 I-am-afraid[a] for-you lest[b] in-vain[c] I-have-toiled[d] for[e] you.

LEXICON—a. pres. mid. (deponent = act.) indic. of φοβέομαι (LN 25.252) (BAGD 1.a. p. 863): 'to be afraid' [BAGD, BNTC, Herm, LN, Mor; CEV, GW, KJV, NCV, NRSV, REB], 'to fear' [LN, SSA, WBC; NASB, NET, NIV, NLT], 'to be worried' [TEV].

b. μή πως (LN 89.62), μήπως (BAGD 1.b. p. 519): The phrase μή πως (or μήπως) 'lest' [Herm, LN; KJV] is also translated 'that perhaps' [BAGD, BNTC, SSA, WBC; NASB], 'lest somehow' [BAGD], 'lest by any chance' [Mor], 'maybe' [GW], 'may have' [NET, NRSV, REB], 'that somehow' [NIV], 'can it be' [TEV], not explicit [CEV, NCV, NLT].

c. εἰκῇ (LN **89.54**) (BAGD 2. p. 222): 'in vain' [BAGD, Herm, LN, Mor; KJV, NASB, NET], 'to no avail' [BAGD, BNTC, LN, WBC], 'without results' [**LN**], 'futilely' [SSA]. This adjective is also translated as a verb phrase: 'to waste (my time)' [CEV], 'to waste (my efforts)' [NIV], 'to be wasted' [GW, NCV, NRSV, REB], 'to be worth nothing' [NLT], 'to be for nothing' [TEV].

d. perf. act. indic. of κοπιάω (LN 42.47) (BAGD 2. p. 443): 'to toil' [LN], 'to labor' [BNTC, LN, Mor; NASB], 'to work' [CEV], 'to work hard' [BAGD, LN, WBC], 'to spend hard work' [GW], 'to spend my labor' [Herm], 'to bestow labor' [KJV], 'to strenuously serve' [SSA]. This verb is also translated as a noun: 'my work' [NCV, NET, NRSV, TEV], 'my hard work' [NLT, REB], 'my efforts' [NIV].

e. εἰς with accusative object (LN 83.9, 90.41): 'for' [BNTC, LN (90.41), Mor, WBC; NCV, NET, NLT, NRSV, TEV], 'on behalf of' [LN (90.41)], 'among' [LN (83.9)], 'with' [CEV], 'on' [Herm; GW, NIV, REB], 'over' [NASB], 'upon' [KJV], not explicit [SSA].

QUESTION—What is the object of φοβοῦμαι 'I am afraid' in this clause?
1. The object of 'fear' is their welfare: 'I fear for you'. Paul is afraid about what will happen to his readers [Alf, Lns, NAC, NIBC, NIGTC, NTC, TH; GW, NASB, NCV, NET, NIV, NLT, TEV].
2. The object of 'fear' is the whole clause. Paul is afraid about what the results of his labor will be [BNTC, BST, ICC, Mor, NIC, WBC; CEV, NRSV, REB].

QUESTION—What is meant by μή πως 'lest'?
Πως 'somehow' or 'perhaps' indicates that Paul has not definitely decided that all of his efforts have been a waste of time [NTC]. He fears this, yet he is not yet in despair [Mor].

DISCOURSE UNIT: 4:12–20 [BST, Mor, NAC, NCBC, NIC, NIGTC, TNTC, WBC; GW]. The topic is a personal appeal [NCBC, NIC, NIGTC], the relation between Paul and the Galatians [BST], a personal appeal for better relations [TNTC], personal appeals [WBC], Paul's personal appeal [NAC], Paul's perplexity [Mor], what happened to your positive attitude? [GW].

4:12 Becomeᵃ asᵇ I, because I-also (am) as you, brothers,ᶜ I-beseechᵈ you.
LEXICON—a. pres. mid. (deponent = act.) impera. of γίνομαι (LN 13.3, 13.48) (BAGD II.1. p. 160): 'to become' [BAGD, BNTC, LN (13.48), SSA, WBC; GW, NASB, NCV, NET, NIV, NRSV], 'to be' [BAGD, LN (13.3), Mor; CEV, KJV, TEV], 'to show (oneself) like' [BAGD], 'to live' [NLT], 'to remain' [Herm]. The phrase Γίνεσθε ὡς ἐγώ ὅτι κἀγὼ ὡς ὑμεῖς 'Become as I because I also am as you' is translated 'Put yourselves in my place as I put myself in yours' [REB].
  b. ὡς (LN 64.12): 'as' [BNTC, Herm, LN, Mor; KJV, NASB, NRSV], 'like' [LN, SSA, WBC; CEV, GW, NCV, NET, NIV, TEV]. See a. [NLT, REB].
  c. ἀδελφός (LN 11.23): 'Christian brother, fellow believer' [LN]. The plural form is translated 'brothers' [BNTC, Herm, Mor, SSA, WBC; NIV], 'brethren' [KJV, NASB], 'friends' [CEV, NRSV, REB, TEV], 'brothers and sisters' [GW, NCV, NET, NLT].
  d. pres. mid. (deponent = act.) indic. of δέομαι (LN 33.170) (BAGD 3. p. 175): 'to beg' [BAGD, BNTC, Herm, LN, Mor; all versions except KJV, NIV, NLT], 'to plead' [LN, WBC; NIV, NLT], 'to strongly urge/implore' [SSA], 'to beseech' [KJV], 'please' [BAGD].
QUESTION—What relationship is indicated by ὅτι 'because'?
  It introduces the reason or grounds that they should become like Paul [Herm, ICC, Mor].
  1. This pertains to their relationship with the Law [Alf, BNTC, Herm, Lns, Lt, Mor, NIBC, NIC, NTC, SSA, TH, WBC]. Paul points out that he has become like them in that he is free from the restrictions of Jewish laws [Alf, BNTC, NAC], without the Jewish legal system [Lns]. He pleads with his converts not to try to become like Jews [Mor]. Paul pleads that the Gentiles remain as he himself has become in that both he and they were at the present outside the Jewish Torah [Herm]. Paul had abandoned the Jewish Law as a means of being reconciled to God and like the Gentiles was free from the Law [TH]. Paul had given up the Jewish customs in order to live like a Gentile [Lt]. Paul still thinks of them as Gentile Christians who have not as yet apostatized, as his reference to his having become like them suggests [WBC]. In exchanging adherence to the law for faith in Christ, Paul became a "Gentile sinner," as the Gentiles were (2:15, 17). He now pleads with them to become free as he is from legal bondage and to know the liberty that is in Christ [NIC]. He refers to the fact that, after understanding that salvation came only through Christ, he had become like a Gentile. So he now directs the Galatians to reject law observance and remain Gentiles just as he had rejected law observance to become as a Gentile [NIBC].
  2. This pertains to their mutual relationships [NIGTC, TNTC]. It means 'Be as frank and loving with me as I have always been with you' and he wants them to resume this relationship which had been ruptured by the Judaizers

Nothing[a] you-have-wronged[b] me;
LEXICON—a. οὐδείς (LN 92.23) (BAGD 2.b.γ. p. 592): (as a neuter): 'nothing' [LN], 'in no respect, in no way' [BAGD], 'did not' [WBC; NLT], 'no' [BNTC, Herm, Mor; NASB, NET, NIV, NRSV], 'have not' [KJV], 'didn't do anything' [GW], 'never did any' [REB], 'have not done any' [TEV], 'no you didn't' [CEV]. This entire phrase is translated 'Then you treated me entirely justly' [SSA], 'You were very good to me before' [NCV].
  b. aorist act. indic. of ἀδικέω (LN 88.22, 88.128) (BAGD 2.a. p. 17): 'to wrong' [BAGD, WBC], 'to do wrong' [BAGD, BNTC, Herm, Mor; GW, NASB, NET, NIV, NRSV, REB, TEV], 'to do what is wrong, to act unjustly' [LN (88.22)], 'to mistreat' [LN (88.128); CEV, NLT], 'to act unjustly toward' [LN (88.128)], 'to injure' [KJV]. See a. [SSA; NCV].
QUESTION—What is meant by this phrase?
  1. It means you have not done me any wrong in the past, but now you do [Alf, ICC, NCBC, NTC].
  2. It means I have no ground for complaining about your conduct [BST, Herm, Lns, Lt, NIC].

DISCOURSE UNIT: 4:13–20 [NET]. The topic is personal appeal of Paul.

4:13 **and/but[a] you-know[b] that on-account-of[c] illness[d] of-the flesh**
LEXICON—a. δέ (LN 89.94, 89.124): 'and' [LN (89.94)], 'but' [LN (89.124), Mor; NASB, NET], 'for' [BNTC], not explicit [Herm, SSA, WBC; all versions except NASB, NET].
  b. perf. (with pres. meaning) act. indic. of οἶδα (LN 28.1, 29.6): 'to know' [BNTC, LN (28.1), Mor, WBC; CEV, GW, KJV, NASB, NET, NIV, NRSV], 'to remember' [Herm, LN (29.6); NCV, NLT, REB, TEV], 'to recall' [LN (29.6), SSA], 'to recollect' [LN (29.6)].
  c. διά with accusative object (LN 90.44) (BAGD B.II.1. p. 181): 'on account of' [BNTC, LN, Mor], 'because of' [BAGD, Herm, LN, WBC; NASB, NCV, NET, NIV, NRSV], 'because' [SSA; CEV, TEV], 'through' [KJV], not explicit [GW, NLT, REB].
  d. ἀσθένεια (LN 23.143) (BAGD 1.a. p. 115): 'illness, disability, weakness' [LN]. The phrase ἀσθένειαν τῆς σαρκός 'illness of the flesh' [Herm] is also translated 'bodily ailment' [BAGD], 'infirmity of the flesh' [Mor; KJV], 'weakness of the flesh' [BNTC], 'bodily illness' [NASB, REB], 'physical illness' [NET], 'physical infirmity' [NRSV], 'illness' [WBC; NCV, NIV], 'I was physically weak' [SSA], 'I was sick' [CEV, NLT, TEV], 'I was ill' [GW].
QUESTION—What is indicated by οἴδατε 'you know'?
The Galatians are reminded of the close relationship that they and Paul enjoyed when Paul was first with them [WBC]. Paul wanted to remind the

Galatians of the past experience they have had with him [Herm]. It implies that the circumstances that led to Paul's visit to Galatia are common knowledge among the Galatian Christians [NCBC, TH].

QUESTION—What relationship is indicated by διά 'on account of'?
1. It indicates that the ailment was the cause of his preaching to them [Alf, BNTC, BST, Herm, ICC, Lns, Lt, Mor, NCBC, NIBC, NIC, NIGTC, SSA, TH, WBC; all versions except GW, KJV, NLT]: He preached the gospel to them because he was sick. It was for this reason that he was detained, otherwise he would not have stayed there and preached [Alf, BNTC, Lt, Mor, NIC]. It was a bodily ailment that gave Paul the opportunity to preach to the Galatians. This occurred either by detaining him in Galatia longer than he had planned or by leading him to go there contrary to his previous plan [ICC, NIGTC]. Perhaps Paul had become ill while in the unhealthy costal regions and went to Antioch to recuperate in its higher elevation [Lns, SSA].
2. It indicates that the ailment was an accompanying circumstance of his preaching [GW, KJV, NLT]: He preached the gospel to them when he was sick.

I-preached-the-gospel[a] to-you the-former[b] (time),

LEXICON—a. aorist mid. (deponent = act.) indic. of εὐαγγελίζω (LN 33.215) (BAGD 2.a.γ. p. 317): 'to preach the gospel' [Herm, Mor, WBC; KJV, NASB, NIV, TEV], 'to preach the good news' [BNTC; NCV], 'to announce the gospel' [LN; NRSV], 'to tell the good news' [LN, SSA], 'to bring the Good News' [GW, NLT], 'to proclaim the gospel' [NET], 'to bring the gospel' [REB], 'to preach' [BAGD; CEV], 'to proclaim' [BAGD].

b. πρότερος (LN **60.47**, 67.18) (BAGD 1.b.β. p. 722): 'former' [LN (67.18)], 'formerly' [LN (67.18), Mor], 'first' [SSA, WBC; CEV, NET, NIV, NLT, NRSV], 'earlier' [BNTC], 'at the first' [KJV], 'originally' [Herm; REB]. The phrase τὸ πρότερον 'the former time' is translated 'the first time' [BAGD, **LN** (60.47); GW, NASB, NCV, TEV], 'once' [BAGD].

QUESTION—What is implied by τὸ πρότερον 'the former time'?
1. This implies that Paul had been there a second time [Alf, ICC, Lns, Lt, NTC, SSA; GW, NASB, NCV, TEV]. The phrase τὸ πρότερον is a comparative form and implies 'the first of two' [SSA].
2. This does not imply a later visit [Herm, NCBC, NIC, TNTC, WBC]. Τὸ πρότερον should be contrasted with the implied νῦν 'now' in 4:16. The contrast in 4:13–16 would then be understood as being between the Galatians' reception of Paul when he first preached the gospel to them and their response to him now after the Judaizers intruded [WBC]. It refers here only to an early visit in comparison with his present dealings with them [NCBC].

4:14 and your testing[a] in my flesh not you-despised[b] nor spit-out,[c]

TEXT—Instead of τὸν πειρασμὸν ὑμῶν ἐν 'your testing in' some manuscripts read τὸν πειρασμὸν ὑμῶν τόν ἐν 'your testing the one in (i.e., 'which was in')'; other manuscripts read τὸν πειρασμόν μου ἐν 'my testing in'; other manuscripts read τὸν πειρασμόν μου τόν ἐν 'my testing the one in'; and other manuscripts read τὸν πειρασμὸν τόν ἐν 'the testing the one in'. GNT reads τὸν πειρασμὸν ὑμῶν ἐν 'your testing in' with an A decision, indicating that the text is certain. 'My temptation which was in' is read by KJV.

LEXICON—a. πειρασμός (LN 27.46, 88.308) (BAGD 2.b. p. 641): 'testing' [LN (27.46)], 'temptation' [BAGD, LN (88.308)]. The phrase τὸν πειρασμὸν ὑμῶν ἐν τῇ σαρκί μου 'your testing in my flesh' is translated 'what was a trial to you in my flesh' [Mor], 'what was a provocation to you in my flesh' [BNTC], 'that which was a trial to you in my bodily condition' [NASB], 'though my condition put you to the test' [NRSV], 'even though my illness was a trial to you' [NIV], 'though my sickness was a trouble for you' [NCV], 'my illness must have caused you some trouble' [CEV], 'even though my illness was difficult for you' [GW], 'even though my sickness was revolting to you' [NLT], 'though my physical condition put you to the test' [NET], 'even though my physical condition was a great trial to you' [TEV], 'although I was physically weak so that you might have despised me' [SSA], 'you resisted any temptation to (show scorn...) at my physical condition' [REB], 'you resisted any temptation through my flesh' [Herm], 'though my illness was a temptation for you to reject me' [WBC], 'my temptation which was in my flesh' [KJV].

b. aorist act. indic. of ἐξουθενέω (LN 88.195) (BAGD 1., 2. p. 277): 'to despise' [BAGD, BNTC, Herm, LN, Mor, SSA, WBC; GW, KJV, NASB, NET, TEV], 'to reject' [BAGD; NLT], 'to hate' [CEV, NCV], 'to scorn' [NRSV], 'to treat with contempt' [NIV], 'to show scorn' [REB].

c. aorist act. indic. of ἐκπτύω (LN **34.37**) (BAGD p. 244): 'to spit out' [BNTC, LN], 'to reject' [Herm, **LN**; GW, KJV, NET, TEV], 'to disdain' [BAGD, Mor, WBC], 'to have disdain for' [LN], 'to loathe' [NASB], 'to be made to leave' [NCV], 'to turn away' [CEV, NLT], 'to despise' [NRSV], 'to treat with scorn' [NIV], 'to show disgust' [REB]. This verb is also translated as an adverb: 'to act contemptuously toward' [SSA].

QUESTION—Does the phrase πειρασμὸν ὑμῶν mean 'your testing' or 'your temptation'?

1. This refers to the trial or testing they endured because of Paul's condition [Mor, NCBC, SSA, TH; all versions except KJV, REB]: even though my physical condition was a great trial to you. Paul had some distressing physical condition, but they had not rejected him or his message because of that [Mor]. Whether the problem was caused by the nature of the sickness or the problem of taking care of such a sick man they did not turn away from him [TH].

2. This refers to the temptation they had to despise and reject Paul [Herm, ICC, Lns, Lt, NIBC, NIC, NIGTC, NTC, TNTC, WBC; REB]: you resisted any temptation to show scorn or disgust at my physical condition. They had not yielded to the temptation to loath Paul because of his physical condition [NTC].

but as (an) angel of-God you-received[a] me, as Christ Jesus.
LEXICON—a. aorist mid. (deponent = act.) indic. of δέχομαι (LN 34.53) (BAGD 1. p. 177): 'to receive' [BAGD, LN, Mor; KJV, NASB, TEV], 'to welcome' [BNTC, Herm, LN, SSA, WBC; CEV, GW, NCV, NET, NIV, NRSV, REB]. This is translated 'you took me in and cared for me' [NLT].
QUESTION—What relationship is indicated by ἀλλά 'but'?
It introduces a strong contrast between how the Galatians could have received Paul and how they actually did [WBC].
QUESTION—What relationship is indicated by the two occurrences of ὡς 'as'?
This appears twice to introduce two exaggerated comparisons that compare how the Galatians received Paul earlier to how they would have received an angel of God or even Christ Jesus himself [WBC]. The manner in which the Galatians received Paul is what is being compared. They gave him the same respect and honor as they would have given to an angel of God or even Jesus Christ [ICC, TH]. The two occurrences of ὡς 'as' shows that the two are comparisons and not identifications [SSA].

4:15 Where then (is) your blessing?[a]
LEXICON—a. μακαρισμός (LN **25.118**) (BAGD p. 487): 'blessing' [BAGD, BNTC; NASB], 'blessedness' [Mor, WBC; KJV], 'happiness' [**LN**; NET, REB], 'good feeling' [CEV], 'positive attitude' [GW], 'joy' [NCV, NIV], 'goodwill' [NRSV], 'praise' [Herm]. This noun is also translated as a verb: 'to be blessed' [SSA]. The clause ποῦ οὖν ὁ μακαρισμὸς ὑμῶν 'Where then is your blessing?' is translated 'where is that joyful spirit we felt together then?' [NLT], 'You were so happy! What has happened?' [TEV].
QUESTION—What is meant by this question?
This is a rhetorical question and implies that when Paul was asking the question the Galatians no longer felt the same way as they did when Paul was with them [NCBC, NIC, TH]. The Galatians rejoiced when Paul arrived among them. They congratulated themselves that this messenger of God had come with such good news. Where was that sense of congratulation now? [NIC, NIGTC]. The question is rhetorical, implying that the congratulation has ceased, but without any good reason [ICC]. By this rhetorical question Paul says that the Galatians had a sense of blessing in response to him and his message and that this is now lost or forgotten [SSA].

For I-bear-witness[a] **to-you that if possible**[b] **having-dug-out**[c] **your eyes you-would-have-given**[d] **(them) to-me.**

LEXICON—a. pres. act. indic. of μαρτυρέω (LN 33.262) (BAGD 1.a. p. 492): 'to bear witness' [BAGD, Herm; NASB], 'to witness' [LN], 'to testify' [BNTC, Mor, SSA, WBC; NCV, NET, NIV, NRSV], 'to bear record' [KJV]. This is translated 'It's a fact' [GW], 'I am sure' [CEV], 'I know' [NLT], 'I believe' [REB], 'I myself can say' [TEV].
  b. δυνατός (LN 71.2) (BAGD 2.a. p. 208): 'possible' [BAGD, BNTC, Herm, LN, Mor; all versions except NIV, TEV]. The phrase εἰ δυνατὸν 'if possible' is translated 'if you could have done so' [WBC; NIV], 'if you could have' [SSA], 'if you could' [TEV].
  c. aorist act. participle of ἐξορύσσω (LN 19.42) (BAGD p. 277): 'to dig out' [BAGD, LN], 'to tear out' [BAGD, BNTC, WBC; GW, NIV, NRSV, REB], 'to take out' [LN; CEV, NCV, NLT, TEV], 'to pluck out' [Herm, Mor; KJV, NASB], 'to gouge out' [SSA], 'to pull out' [NET].
  d. aorist act. indic. of δίδωμι (LN 57.71): 'to give' [BNTC, Herm, LN, Mor, SSA, WBC; all versions].

QUESTION—What relationship is indicated by γάρ 'for'?
  It signals that Paul will now give confirmation of the Galatians' former sense of blessing [ICC, SSA].
QUESTION—What relationship is indicated by εἰ δυνατὸν 'if possible'?
  It expresses a contrary to fact condition [NIC, WBC]: you would have given me your eyes (but you couldn't). It indicates that Paul is only speaking hypothetically [Lns]. It saves what follows from being a hyperbole [ICC, WBC].
QUESTION—What is meant by τοὺς ὀφθαλμοὺς ὑμῶν ἐξορύξαντες ἐδώκατέ μοι 'you would have dug out your eyes and given them to me'?
  This statement should be interpreted as a metaphor meaning that they would even have given Paul that which they valued the most [TH]. This statement is proverbial for making a sacrifice of something that is priceless [Alf, Herm, Lns, Lt, NIC, NTC]. It is probably an idiom that speaks of going to the extreme to provide for someone's needs. In ancient times the eyes were considered to be the most precious of the body's parts [TH, WBC]. So 'to dig out one's eyes for someone' is a graphic and significant idiom for going to the extreme for another's welfare [WBC]. This statement should be interpreted as just extravagant devotion of convert to teacher [TH, TNTC]. Or, this statement implies that Paul had some eye disease and the Galatians were showing deep sympathy for him because of it [NCBC].

4:16 Therefore[a] **have-I-become your enemy, being-truthful**[b] **to-you?**

LEXICON—a. ὥστε (LN 89.52) (BAGD 1.a. p. 899): 'therefore' [BAGD, LN; KJV], 'for this reason' [BAGD], 'so' [BAGD, LN, WBC; NASB], 'so then' [LN, Mor; NET], 'so now' [BNTC], 'now (you wrongly believe)' [SSA], 'now' [CEV, NCV, NIV, NLT, NRSV, REB, TEV], not explicit [GW]. This is translated 'is the result of it all that' [Herm].

b. pres. act. participle of ἀληθεύω (LN **33.251**) (BAGD p. 36): 'to be truthful' [BAGD], 'to speak the truth' [LN], 'to tell the truth' [BAGD, BNTC, Herm, **LN**, Mor, WBC; all versions except REB], 'to speak truthfully' [SSA], 'to be frank' [REB].

QUESTION—Is this a question or a statement?

1. It is a rhetorical question [BNTC, Lns, Lt, Mor, NIGTC, NTC; all versions]: because I am being truthful to you, have I therefore become your enemy? The Galatians do not appear to be able to tolerate the truth [NTC]. Paul wants them to face the reality of what they were doing. Paul was not their enemy when he initially preached the gospel to them, and as he continued to do so, and they should see it as a friendly gesture, not as a hostile one [Mor]. Paul wanted them to realize that he was truly their friend even though he had to use strong language in this letter and possibly in the previous letter [NTC].
2. It is a statement [ICC, NCBC, NIBC, NIC, SSA, WBC]: therefore it appears that I have become your enemy because I am being truthful to you! The idea is 'So I have become your enemy!' and this reflects the Judaizers' view of Paul, not Paul's [NCBC]. The conjunction ὥστε 'therefore' indicates a conclusion from the facts stated in 4:14–15: Since they once regarded Paul with such great affection and now consider him as an enemy, this could only come about because he had been telling them the truth [ICC, WBC].

4:17 They-are-zealous[a] (for) you not well,[b]

LEXICON—a. pres. act. indic. of ζηλόω (LN **25.46**) (BAGD 1.b. p. 338): 'to be zealous' [BNTC, LN, Mor; NIV], 'to have a deep concern for' [**L N** (25.46)], 'to be deeply concerned about (someone), to court (someone's) favor' [BAGD], 'to pay a lot of attention to' [CEV], 'to pay zealous court to' [Herm], 'to be devoted to' [GW], 'to work hard' [NCV], 'to be anxious' [NLT], 'to make much of' [NRSV], 'to lavish attention on' [REB], 'to show a deep interest in' [TEV]. This verb is also translated as an adverb: 'to zealously affect' [KJV], 'to be eagerly interested in' [SSA], 'to eagerly seek' [NASB], 'to seek eagerly' [NET], 'to earnestly court' [WBC].

b. καλῶς (LN **88.4**) (BAGD 2. p. 401): 'good' [LN], 'well' [BAGD]. The phrase οὐ καλῶς 'not well' is translated 'but not well' [KJV], 'but their intentions are not good' [**LN**; TEV], 'but it isn't for your good' [CEV], 'but not in a good way' [GW], 'not in a good way' [Herm], 'but for no good purpose' [NET, NRSV], 'but this is not good for you' [NCV], 'but for no good' [WBC; NIV], 'but without sincerity' [REB], 'for no good purpose' [BNTC], 'in no good way' [Mor], 'not doing it for your good' [NLT], 'not commendably' [NASB], 'but not honorably' [SSA].

QUESTION—Who is referred to when he said ζηλοῦσιν 'they are zealous' and what do they want to do?
They are introduced obscurely in the third person [NCBC, SSA], and this is an intentional slight [Lns]. It refers to the false teachers [BST, Lt, Mor, TH], rival teachers [SSA]. They were the Judaizers [Lns, NTC, TH, TNTC, WBC]. They are zealous to win them over to their teachings [Mor].
QUESTION—What is the impact of adding 'not well'?
They were zealous, but not in the right way [NTC]. Instead of helping the Galatians, it would harm them [Mor]. Their goals were not honorable and unselfish, rather they were selfish [ICC].

but they-want[a] to-exclude[b] you,
LEXICON—a. pres. act. indic. of θέλω (LN 25.1): 'to want' [LN, SSA; all versions except KJV, NASB, NLT], 'to wish' [BNTC, LN, Mor; NASB], 'to desire' [LN, WBC], 'to intend' [Herm], not explicit [KJV, NLT].
b. aorist act. infin. of ἐκκλείω (LN **34.36**) (BAGD 1. p. 240): 'to exclude' [BAGD, Herm; KJV], 'to shut out' [BAGD], 'to separate' [LN]. The phrase ἐκκλεῖσαι ὑμᾶς 'to exclude you' [Herm; KJV, NET, NRSV] is also translated 'to shut you out' [BNTC, Mor; NASB], 'to isolate you' [REB]. The phrase ἐκκλεῖσαι ὑμᾶς θέλουσιν 'they want to exclude you' is translated 'what they desire is to exclude you from us' [WBC], 'they no longer want you to relate to me', or 'they want you no longer to belong to me', or 'they want you to exclude me from your company' [**LN**], 'all they want is to separate you from me' [TEV], 'they don't want you to associate with me' [GW], 'they only want to keep you away from me' [CEV], 'they want to persuade you to turn against us' [NCV], 'what they want is to alienate you from us' [NIV], 'they are trying to shut you off from me' [NLT], 'they even want to disassociate you from me and other genuine brothers' [SSA].
QUESTION—What relationship is indicated by ἀλλά 'but'?
This is a contrast with 'not well' [Lt, SSA]. This indicates a move from a mild and general evaluation to a strong and direct one [SSA].
QUESTION—From what do they want 'to exclude them'?
1. They want to separate them from other Christians. They want to separate them from Paul, or from Paul and his assistants [Lns, Mor, NAC, NCBC, NIGTC, WBC; CEV, GW, NCV, NIV, NLT, TEV]. They want to separate them from all other influences including Paul and all other churches and teachers who might agree with Paul [Alf, NTC]. They want to keep them away from what Paul taught and didn't want them to realize that others believed the same as Paul [Mor].
2. They want to shut them out from Christ [BST, Lt].
3. They want to shut them out from the benefits of faith in Christ [BST, ICC, NIC].

in-order-that you-may-be-zealous[a] **(for) them;**
LEXICON—a. pres. act. subj. of ζηλόω (LN 25.46, 88.163) (BAGD 1.b. p. 338): 'to be zealous' [BNTC, LN (88.163), Mor; NIV], 'to have a deep concern' [LN (25.46)], 'to be deeply concerned about (someone), to court (someone's) favor' [BAGD], 'to earnestly court' [WBC], 'to pay a lot of attention to' [CEV], 'to be devoted to' [GW], 'to pay more attention to' [NLT], 'to make much of' [NRSV], 'to lavish attention on' [REB], 'to have the same interest in' [TEV], 'to affect' [KJV], 'to seek' [NASB], 'to seek eagerly' [NET], 'to follow' [NCV], 'to be eagerly interested in' [SSA], 'to court' [Herm].

4:18 **But/Now**[a] **(it is) good**[b] **to-be-zealous**[c] **in**[d] **(a) good**[e] **(thing) always**[f]
LEXICON—a. δέ (LN 89.94, 89.124): 'but' [LN (89.124), SSA, WBC; KJV, NASB, NCV], 'however' [NET], 'yet' [Herm], 'and' [LN (89.94)], 'now' [LN (89.124); NLT, TEV], not explicit [BNTC, Mor; CEV, GW, NIV, NRSV, REB].
  b. καλός (LN 66.2, 88.4) (BAGD 3.c. p. 400): 'good' [BAGD, BNTC, Herm, LN (66.2, 88.4), Mor, WBC; all versions except NIV, NLT], 'fine' [LN (88.4); NIV], 'praiseworthy' [LN (88.4)], 'fitting' [LN (66.2)], 'wonderful' [NLT], not explicit [SSA].
  c. pres. mid./pass. infin. of ζηλόω (LN 25.46) (BAGD 1.c. p. 338): This is taken as a middle voice: 'to be zealous' [Mor; NIV], 'to display zeal' [BNTC], 'to show zeal' [BAGD], 'to have a deep concern for' [LN (25.46)], 'to show interest (in you)' [NCV], 'to have a deep interest' [TEV], 'to be eagerly and honorably interested in' [SSA], 'to be zealously affected' [KJV], 'to give attention to' [CEV], 'to be devoted' [GW]; taken as the passive voice: 'to be eagerly sought' [NASB], 'to be sought eagerly' [NET], 'to be eager' [NLT], 'to be courted' [Herm, WBC], 'to be made much of' [NRSV], 'to be the object of sincere attentions' [REB].
  d. ἐν with dative object (LN 83.13, 89.5): 'in' [BNTC, Herm, LN (83.13, 89.5), Mor, WBC; KJV, NASB], 'with regard to, in the case of, about' [LN (89.5)], 'to' [CEV, GW, NLT], 'for' [NET, NRSV], not explicit [SSA; NCV, NIV, REB, TEV].
  e. καλός (LN 65.22, 88.4) (BAGD 2.b. p. 400): 'good' [BNTC, Herm, LN (65.22, 88.4), Mor, WBC; all versions except CEV, NASB, REB], 'fine' [LN (65.22, 88.4)], 'praiseworthy' [BAGD, LN (88.4)], 'morally good' [BAGD], 'worthwhile' [CEV], 'commendable' [NASB], not explicit [SSA; REB].
  f. πάντοτε (LN 67.88): 'always' [BNTC, Herm, LN, Mor, SSA, WBC; all versions except NET, NLT, NRSV], 'at all times' [NET, NRSV], not explicit [NLT].
QUESTION—What relationship is indicated by δέ 'but/now'?
  1. It is adversative [ICC, SSA, WBC; KJV, NASB, NCV, NET]. It marks an antithesis between the ζηλόω 'making much of' of the Judaizers, which Paul disapproves, and his own, which he justifies [ICC].

GALATIANS 4:18

2. It is an added comment [Lns, Mor, NTC; NLT, TEV]. This is treated abstractly, a general principle [Lns]. It isn't that Paul objects to people being zealous since zeal is an important part of Christian life [Mor].

QUESTION—What is meant by ζηλοῦσθαι 'to be made much of'?
1. The passive voice is intended [Alf, Herm, ICC, Lns, Lt, NIC, NTC, WBC; NASB, NCV, NET, NRSV, REB]: to be made much of.
2. The middle voice, having an active sense is intended [CEV, GW, NIV, NLT, TEV]: to make much of.

and not only when^a I-am-present^b with^c you.
LEXICON—a. ἐν with dative object (LN 67.33): 'when' [BNTC, Herm, LN, Mor, WBC; all versions], 'when/while' [SSA].
   b. pres. infin. of πάρειμι (LN 85.23) (BAGD 1.a. p. 624): 'to be present' [BAGD, BNTC, Herm, LN, Mor; KJV, NASB, NET, NRSV], 'to be there' [LN], 'to be' [SSA, WBC; CEV, GW, NCV, NIV, NLT, REB, TEV].
   c. πρός with accusative object (LN 83.9, 89.112) (BAGD III.7. p. 711): 'with' [BAGD, BNTC, Herm, LN (89.112), Mor, SSA, WBC; all versions], 'among' [LN (83.9)].

QUESTION—What is meant by this phrase?
1. It is good for the Galatians to be made much of by anyone who has good intentions and not only by Paul alone when he is there [Alf, WBC]. Paul did not believe that the Judaizers courted his converts in a good way. The Galatians were supposed to make sure that the courting was done in a way that was honest, sincere and for the good of the recipients. This was to be done when Paul was courting them and during his absence when others would court them [WBC].
2. It is good for Paul to be made much of by the Galatians always and not only when he was with them [Herm, Lns, Lt, NIC, NTC]. Paul wanted the Galatians to always treat him as they did when he was present with them [Lt, NIC, NTC].
3. It is good for the Galatians to be made much of and Paul had done so always, not only when he was with them [ICC].

4:19 My children, for/with-whom^a again I-suffer-birth-pangs^b until^c when Christ is-formed^d in you;
TEXT—Instead of τέκνα 'children' some manuscripts read τεκνία 'little children'. GNT does not mention this variant. Τεκνία 'little children' is read by KJV, NCV, NRSV.
   LEXICON—a. ὅς (LN 92.27) (BAGD I.3.b.γ. p. 584): 'who' [BAGD, LN], 'whom' [BNTC, Herm, Mor, WBC; KJV, NASB, NIV, NRSV], 'you' [SSA; GW, NCV, NLT, REB, TEV], not explicit [CEV, NET]. This relative pronoun conforms to the (masculine) sense of the natural gender (i.e., 'persons') rather than to the grammatical gender (neuter) of its antecedent τέκνα 'children' [BAGD].

b. pres. act. indic. of ὠδίνω (LN 23.54, **24.87**) (BAGD p. 895): 'to suffer birth-pangs' [BAGD], 'to have birth pains' [LN (23.54)], 'to suffer birth pains' [GW], 'to be in labor' [NASB], 'to feel the pain of childbirth' [NCV], 'to undergo birth pains' [NET], 'to go through labor pains' [NLT], 'to be in the pain of childbirth' [BNTC; NRSV], 'to be in labor' [REB], 'to be in the pains of childbirth' [Mor, WBC; NIV], 'to travail in birth' [KJV], 'to suffer greatly' [LN (24.87)], 'to suffer' [**LN** (24.87)], 'to experience anguish' [SSA], 'to be in terrible pain' [CEV], 'to be in travail' [Herm]. The metaphor is made explicit: 'just like a mother in childbirth, I feel the same kind of pain' [TEV].

c. μέχρι with genitive object (LN 67.119) (BAGD 2. p. 515): 'until' [BAGD]. The phrase μέχρις οὗ 'until when' is translated 'until' [BAGD, BNTC, Herm, LN, Mor, SSA, WBC; all versions].

d. aorist pass. subj. of μορφόω (LN **58.4**) (BAGD p. 528): 'to be formed' [BAGD, BNTC, Mor, WBC; GW, KJV, NASB, NET, NIV, NRSV, TEV], 'to be fully developed' [NLT]. The phrase μορφωθῇ Χριστὸς ἐν ὑμῖν 'Christ is formed in you' is translated 'Christ's nature is formed in you, you become like Christ was/is' [**LN**], 'Christ may be seen living in you' [CEV], 'you truly become like Christ' [NCV], 'you trust Christ exclusively and wholeheartedly' [SSA], 'you come to have the form of Christ' [REB], 'Christ takes shape in you' [Herm].

QUESTION—What is meant by τέκνα μου 'my children'?

This is a metaphor and points to the fact that it was through him that they had been born into the Christian faith [Mor]. They were the fruit of his labor in Christ [TNTC]. This shows that Paul regards the Galatians as his children since he had brought them to faith in Christ [NIC]. It is an address of endearment and tender affection [TH].

QUESTION—What is meant by the phrase οὓς πάλιν ὠδίνω 'for whom again I suffer birth pangs'?

This is a metaphor and illustrates his travail for them by comparing his pain with the pain of childbirth [BST, TH]. Paul shows how deeply invested he was in their spiritual struggles by using a metaphor in which he compares himself to a mother who must go through the pains of childbirth for the sake of her children [NAC]. Paul compared the anguish and worry which he was feeling for the Galatians to the pain of childbirth [BNTC].

QUESTION—What is meant by Paul suffering birth pangs until Christ is formed in them?

1. Paul is pictured as again suffering birth-pangs because of the incomplete spiritual birth of the Galatians. Πάλιν 'again' points to the fact that he had been through this once before when he brought them the gospel and they had been born into the Christian faith [BST, Lt, Mor, NIC, NIGTC, NTC, TH]. Now Paul is in labor again because they are backsliding [BST], they are turning from the true gospel to the counterfeit gospel offered by the heretics [NIC, NTC]. Now the Galatians need spiritual rebirth [ICC, TH]. The whole act would have to be done again because of

the Galatians' apostasy [Herm]. The Galatians are pictured as again being in the womb while Christ is being formed in them [ICC, Lt, Mor, TH]. Their relapse has renewed a mother's birth-pangs in Paul until they will have taken the form of Christ [Lt]. This is a way to refer to being truly Christian. The believer not only professes faith, but is transformed into the likeness of Christ. Christ dwells in the believer and brings about a complete change [Mor]. Paul is illustrating the need for growth 'in Christ' [TNTC]. Or, Paul does not say that he is giving birth to them a second time, but leaves that figure to indicate that he is unnaturally suffering the pains all over again to the end that they fully embrace Christ alone in their lives [Lns]. The situation in Galatia is almost unbearable to Paul and he will be in anguish until they establish a permanent relationship with Christ [SSA].

2. The metaphor is reversed so that the Galatians are now pictured as expectant mothers who must wait while Christ is formed in them. Christ is pictured as the embryo being formed in the lives of the Galatians and this birth involves birth-pangs, but instead of Paul's converts enduring the pains, it is Paul who endures the pain on their behalf [NIGTC].

4:20 and/but I-was-wishing[a] to-be-present[b] with[c] you now[d] and to-alter[e] my voice,

LEXICON—a. imperf. act. indic. of θέλω (LN 25.1) (BAGD 1. p. 354): 'to wish' [BAGD, BNTC, Herm, LN, Mor, SSA, WBC; all versions except KJV], 'to want' [LN], 'to desire' [LN; KJV].

b. pres. infin. of πάρειμι (LN 85.23) (BAGD 1.a. p. 624): 'to be present' [BAGD, BNTC, Herm, LN, Mor; KJV, NASB, NRSV], 'to be there' [LN; NLT], 'to be' [SSA, WBC; CEV, GW, NCV, NET, NIV, REB, TEV].

c. πρός with accusative object (LN 83.9, 89.112) (BAGD III.7. p. 711): 'with' [BAGD, BNTC, Herm, LN (83.9, 89.112), Mor, SSA, WBC; all versions], 'among' [LN (83.9)].

d. ἄρτι (LN 67.38, 67.39) (BAGD 3. p. 110): 'now' [BAGD, BNTC, Herm, LN (67.38), Mor, SSA, WBC; all versions except GW, NLT], 'just now' [LN (67.39)], 'at the present time' [BAGD], 'right now' [GW, NLT]. It means 'at this very moment' [ICC, WBC].

e. aorist act. infin. of ἀλλάσσω (LN 58.43) (BAGD 1. p. 39): 'to alter, to change' [LN]. The phrase ἀλλάξαι τὴν φωνήν μου 'to alter my voice' [Herm] is also translated 'to change my voice' [KJV], 'to change my tone' [BAGD, BNTC, Mor; NASB, NIV, NRSV], 'change my tone of voice' [NET], 'change the tone of my voice' [GW], 'to exchange my voice for this letter' [WBC], 'change the way I am talking to you' [NCV], 'that I might communicate better with you' [SSA]. The phrase καὶ ἀλλάξαι τὴν φωνήν μου 'and to alter my voice' is translated 'Then I would not have to talk this way' [CEV], 'so that I could be more gentle with you' [NLT], 'for then I could modify my tone' [REB], 'so that I could take a different attitude toward you' [TEV].

QUESTION—What relationship is indicated by δέ 'and/but'?
>It is a connective [WBC] and also signals a conclusion [Herm, WBC]. It is slightly adversative [ICC].

QUESTION—What is meant by the phrase ἀλλάξαι τὴν φωνήν μου 'to alter my voice'?
>1. Paul wants to be able to change the manner in which he speaks to them from a severe manner to a gentler one [BST, ICC, Lt, NCBC, NIC, NTC, TH; NLT]. If he could only be with them, then maybe by hearing and seeing them and talking with them, the change that he wanted in them might take place more quickly. Then he would not have to rebuke them as he had done in this letter, so that he would change the tone of his voice [NTC].
>2. Paul wants to change the manner in which he speaks to them to a manner that better matches their condition. If he were with them, he would not have to get his information about them second-hand and could speak to them in the best way that would meet their need [Lns].
>3. Paul wants to change the form of communication from a written form to an oral form [Herm, NAC, WBC]. Paul could communicate better with them orally than with a letter [Herm].

QUESTION—What is the function of the imperfect tense of the verb ἤθελον 'I was wishing'?
>The imperfect is the tense of politeness and refers to a strong present desire [Lns]. It replaces the potential optative and gives a modest assertion [SSA]. The function of the imperfect tense here is to express a hesitant, impractical, or impossible wish [Herm, ICC, NCBC, NTC, TH, WBC; NASB]: I could wish...(but that is not possible).

because I-am-perplexed[a] in[b] you.

LEXICON—a. pres. mid. indic. of ἀπορέω (LN 32.9) (BAGD p. 97): 'to be perplexed' [Herm, LN, Mor, SSA, WBC; NASB, NET, NIV, NRSV], 'to be at a loss' [BAGD, BNTC, LN], 'to be uncertain' [BAGD, LN], 'to be anxious' [LN], 'to be in doubt' [BAGD, LN; KJV], 'to be at wits' end' [REB], 'to be worried' [TEV]. This is translated 'I do not know what to think' [NCV]. This entire phrase is translated 'You really have me puzzled' [CEV], 'I'm completely puzzled by what you've done' [GW], 'But at this distance I frankly don't know what else to do' [NLT].
>b. ἐν with dative object (LN 83.13, 89.5): 'in' [BNTC, LN (83.13, 89.5)], 'about' [Herm, LN (89.5), Mor, SSA, WBC; NASB, NCV, NET, NIV, NRSV, REB, TEV], 'with regard to' [LN (89.5)], 'of' [KJV]. See a. [CEV, GW, NLT].

QUESTION—What is meant by this clause?
>He doesn't know how to deal with them [Lt]. He doesn't know why they have yielded to temptation [NTC]. The verb ἀπορoῦμαι 'I am perplexed' reflects the tension in Paul's mind. His strong desire is to be warm-hearted towards them. He doesn't want the Galatians to regard him as their enemy.

However, in the present situation he is perplexed in knowing how to avoid that possibility [NCBC]. Paul couldn't understand how his Galatian converts could so soon be tempted to go off into some form of legalism after the way they had responded to the gospel [Mor].

DISCOURSE UNIT: 4:21–5:12 [REB]. The topic is freedom through Christ.

DISCOURSE UNIT: 4:21–5:1 [GNT, NIC, NIGTC, TNTC; NRSV]. The topic is an argument from rabbinics [TNTC], a lesson from scripture [NIGTC], the analogy of Hagar and Sarah [NIC], the allegory of Hagar and Sarah [GNT; NRSV].

DISCOURSE UNIT: 4:21–31 [BST, Mor, NAC, NCBC, WBC; CEV, GW, NASB, NCV, NET, NIV, NLT, TEV]. The topic is an allegorical appeal [NCBC], Isaac and Ishmael [BST], Abraham's two children [NLT], Hagar and Sarah [CEV, NIV], the Hagar-Sarah allegory [WBC], the analogy of Hagar and Sarah [NAC], the example of Hagar and Sarah [NCV, TEV], bond and free [NASB], an appeal from allegory [NET], two covenants [Mor], you are children of the promise [GW].

4:21 **Tell[a] me, the-(ones) wishing[b] to-be under[c] (the) Law,[d]**
LEXICON—a. pres. act. impera. of λέγω (LN 33.69): 'to tell' [BNTC, Herm, LN, Mor, WBC; all versions except CEV, NLT, TEV], not explicit [SSA; CEV]. The phrase λέγετέ μοι 'tell me' is translated 'let me ask' [TEV], 'listen to me' [NLT].
- b. pres. act. participle of θέλω (LN 25.1): 'to wish' [LN, Mor], 'to want' [BNTC, Herm, LN, WBC; GW, NASB, NCV, NET, NIV, NLT, TEV], 'to desire' [LN, SSA; KJV, NRSV], 'to like' [CEV], 'to be anxious' [REB].
- c. ὑπό with accusative object (LN 37.7) (BAGD 2.b. p. 843): 'under' [BAGD, BNTC, Herm, LN, Mor, WBC; all versions except GW, NRSV, TEV], 'under the control of' [LN]. The phrase ὑπὸ εἶναι 'to be under' is translated 'to comply with' [SSA], 'to be controlled by' [GW], 'to be subject to' [NRSV, TEV].
- d. νόμος (LN 33.55, 33.333) (BAGD 3. p. 542): 'Law' [Herm, LN (33.55); TEV], 'law' [BNTC, LN (33.333), Mor, WBC; all versions except CEV, GW, TEV], the law which Moses received from God [BAGD], 'the Mosaic law' [SSA], 'Law of Moses' [CEV]. This singular form is also translated as plural: 'Moses' laws' [GW].

QUESTION—What law is referred to in this phrase?
It refers to the Jewish law [TH], the Mosaic law [Mor, NAC, NIC, SSA, WBC; CEV, GW], the Pentateuch [Lns].

not do-you-hear[a] the Law?[b]
LEXICON—a. pres. act. indic. of ἀκούω (LN 24.52, 31.56) (BAGD 7. p. 32): 'to hear' [Herm, LN (24.52), Mor, WBC; KJV, TEV], 'to listen to' [BNTC, LN (31.56); GW, NASB, NRSV, REB], 'to heed, to pay attention

(to)' [LN (31.56)], 'to understand' [BAGD; NET], 'to consider' [SSA], 'to know' [CEV, NCV, NLT], 'to be aware of' [NIV]. It means to comprehend or realize what the law really means [TH].

b. νόμος (LN 33.55, 33.333) (BAGD 4.a. p. 543): 'Law' [LN (33.55); CEV, TEV], 'law' [BNTC, Herm, LN (33.333), Mor, WBC; all versions except CEV, GW, TEV]. This singular form is also translated as plural: 'Moses' Teachings' [GW]. It refers to the Pentateuch [BAGD]. This is translated 'what God caused that Moses write in the books which the Jews name "law"' [SSA].

4:22 For^a it-is-written^b that Abraham had two sons,

LEXICON—a. γάρ (LN 89.23): 'for' [BNTC, Herm, LN, Mor, WBC; KJV, NASB, NET, NIV, NRSV], 'because' [LN], not explicit [REB]. The phrase γέγραπται γάρ 'for it is written' is translated 'God caused that Moses write' [SSA], 'In the Scriptures we learn' [CEV], 'Scripture says' [GW], 'The Scriptures say' [NCV, NLT], 'It says' [TEV].

b. perf. pass. indic. of γράφω (LN 33.61): 'to be written' [BNTC, Herm, LN, Mor, WBC; KJV, NASB, NET, NIV, NRSV, REB]. See a. [SSA; CEV, GW, NCV, NLT, TEV].

QUESTION—What relationship is indicated by γάρ 'for'?

It introduces the reason for Paul's doubts about their understanding of the Law [Mor]. It introduces the section that Paul has in mind [Lns].

QUESTION—What is the purpose of γέγραπται 'it is written'?

It is the normal formula for introducing a scriptural reference [BNTC, Lt]. Paul usually used these words when he was going to quote a specific text from the Old Testament, but in this instance he gave a summary of the narrative concerning the birth of Abraham's two sons [NAC]. Γέγραπται γάρ 'for it is written' signals an indirect quotation from the law or Pentateuch [SSA]. It is used to introduce a summary of certain things contained in Scripture [Mor, TH]. It introduces a statement summarizing the stories about Abraham that are found in Genesis [Herm, WBC].

one from^a the slave-woman^b and one from^a the free^c (woman).

LEXICON—a. ἐκ with genitive object (LN 90.16) (BAGD 3.a. p. 234): 'from' [BAGD, Herm, LN, Mor; NLT], 'by' [BAGD, BNTC, LN, SSA, WBC; all versions except CEV, NCV, NLT], 'of' [CEV, NCV].

b. παιδίσκη (LN 87.83) (BAGD p. 604): 'slave woman' [Herm, LN, WBC; NCV, NET, NIV, NRSV, TEV], 'slave girl' [BNTC, Mor], 'slave-wife' [NLT], 'female slave' [BAGD, SSA], 'slave' [CEV, REB], 'servant-girl' [BAGD], 'maid' [BAGD], 'bondmaid' [KJV], 'bondwoman' [NASB]. This is translated 'a woman who was a slave' [GW].

c. ἐλεύθερος (LN 37.134, 87.84) (BAGD 1. p. 250): 'free' [BAGD, LN (37.134); CEV], 'free woman' [BNTC, Herm, WBC; all versions except CEV, NLT, REB], 'free person' [LN (87.84)], 'free one' [Mor], 'free wife' [SSA], 'freeborn wife' [NLT], 'free-born woman' [REB].

4:23 But the-(one) on-the-one-hand[a] from[b] the slave-woman was-born according-to flesh,[c]

LEXICON—a. μέν (LN 89.136) (BAGD 1.c. p. 503): 'on the one hand' [LN], 'indeed' [WBC], not explicit [BNTC, Herm, Mor, SSA; all versions except NET, NRSV]. The phrase ὁ μέν 'the one on the one hand' is translated 'the one' [BAGD; NET, NRSV].
- b. ἐκ with genitive object (LN 90.16) (BAGD 3.a. p. 234): 'from, by' [BAGD, LN], 'of' [BAGD]. The phrase ὁ μὲν ἐκ τῆς παιδίσκης 'the one from the slave woman' [Herm] is also translated 'the son of the slave girl' [BNTC], 'the one by the slave woman' [WBC], 'he who was born of the slave girl' [Mor], 'the son who was borne by the female slave' [SSA], 'he (who was) of the bondwoman' [KJV], 'the son of the slave woman' [CEV, GW], 'the son of the bondwoman' [NASB], 'Abraham's son from the slave woman' [NCV], 'the son by the slave woman' [NET], 'his son by the slave woman' [NIV, TEV], 'the son of the slave-wife' [NLT], 'the child of the slave' [NRSV], 'the slave's son' [REB].
- c. σάρξ (LN **58.10**) (BAGD 4. p. 743): 'flesh, human nature' [BAGD, LN], 'physical nature of people' [LN], 'the physical aspect of human nature' [**LN**]. The phrase κατὰ σάρκα γεγέννηται 'was born according to flesh' [Herm] is also translated 'was born according to the flesh' [Mor, WBC; NASB, NRSV], 'was born after the flesh' [KJV], 'was born in accordance with the flesh' [BNTC], 'was born in the usual way' [CEV, TEV], 'was conceived in a natural way' [GW], 'was born in the normal human way' [NCV], 'was born by natural descent' [NET], 'was born in the ordinary way' [NIV], 'was born in the ordinary course of nature' [REB], 'was conceived/fathered by Abraham naturally/normally' [SSA], 'was born in a human attempt to bring about the fulfillment of God's promise' [NLT].

QUESTION—What relationship is indicated by ἀλλά 'but'?
It is adversative [WBC] and is intended to bring out a deeper contrast between the sons of Abraham [Mor, NCBC]. It doesn't introduce a point different from the preceding verse, but it marks the transition to the following phrase [Herm]. Or, instead of being adversative, it carries the sketch forward [Lns].

QUESTION—What is meant by κατὰ σάρκα 'according to the flesh'?
It means that Ishmael was born according to the natural process and this didn't involve any divine intervention [TH]. What Paul means is that no miracle or special promise of God was involved [TNTC]. It means that his birth took place in the ordinary course of nature [Alf, ICC, NIGTC, SSA].

on-the-other-hand/but[a] the-(one) from the free[b] (woman) through[c] promise.[d]

LEXICON—a. δέ (LN 89.124, 89.136) (BAGD 1.c. p. 503 under μέν): 'on the other hand' [LN (89.124)], 'but' [LN (89.124), Mor, SSA, WBC; all versions except NASB, NET, NRSV], 'but on the other hand' [LN

(89.136)], 'whereas' [BNTC], 'and' [NASB], 'while' [Herm; NET]. The phrase ὁ δέ 'on the other hand' is translated 'the other' [BAGD; NRSV].
- b. ἐλεύθερος (LN 37.134, 87.84) (BAGD 1. p. 250): 'free' [BAGD, LN (37.134)]. This is also translated as a noun phrase: 'free person' [LN (87.84)], 'free one' [Mor], 'free woman' [BNTC, Herm, WBC; all versions except NLT], 'free wife' [SSA], 'freeborn wife' [NLT].
- c. διά with genitive object (LN 89.76, 90.8) (BAGD A.III.1.e. p. 180): 'through' [BAGD, LN (89.76, 90.8)], 'by means of' [BAGD, LN (89.76, 90.8)], 'by' [LN (89.76)], 'with' [BAGD]. The phrase δι' ἐπαγγελίας 'through promise' [BNTC, Mor] is also translated 'through the promise' [Herm; NASB, NET, NRSV], 'through God's promise' [REB], 'through a promise made to Abraham' [GW], 'as a result of promise' [WBC], 'as the result of a promise' [NIV], 'as a result of God's promise' [TEV], 'by promise' [KJV], 'because of God's promise' [CEV], 'because of the promise God made to Abraham' [NCV], 'as God's own fulfillment of his promise' [NLT], 'because God had promised that he would be conceived/fathered by Abraham' [SSA].
- d. ἐπαγγελία (LN 33.288) (BAGD 2.a. p. 280): 'promise' [BAGD, BNTC, Herm, LN, Mor, WBC; all versions]. This noun is also translated as a verb with 'God' as the subject: 'to promise' [SSA].

QUESTION—What relationship is indicated by διά 'through'?
It indicates the cause [Alf, Herm, WBC]. It indicates the instrument [NIC] or the means, the means being God's promise [Lns].

4:24 Which-things[a] are being-spoken-allegorically;[b]

LEXICON—a. ὅστις (LN 92.18): 'which things' [Mor; KJV], 'such things' [BNTC], 'these things' [Herm, WBC; NET, NIV, TEV], 'this' [NASB, NRSV, REB], 'these (historical facts in 23a–b)' [SSA], 'these historical events' [GW], 'all of this' [CEV], 'this story' [NCV], 'these two women' [NLT], 'this incident' [LN (33.18)], 'whatever' [LN].
- b. pres. pass. participle of ἀλληγορέω (LN **33.18**) (BAGD p. 39): 'to be spoken allegorically' [BAGD, LN], 'to be employed as an analogy, to be used as a likeness' [LN]. The phrase ἐστιν ἀλληγορούμενα 'are being spoken allegorically' is translated 'are/is an allegory' [KJV, NRSV, REB], 'are allegories' [Mor], 'are now being used by me as an allegory' [SSA], 'may be treated as an allegory' [NET], 'is allegorically speaking' [NASB], 'are to be interpreted allegorically' [BNTC], 'are now being interpreted allegorically' [WBC], 'can be taken as a kind of likeness' [**LN**], 'may be taken figuratively' [NIV], 'can be understood as a figure' [TEV], 'has another meaning as well' [CEV], 'teaches something else' [NCV], 'serve as an illustration' [NLT], 'I'm going to use as an illustration' [GW], 'have an allegorical meaning' [Herm].

QUESTION—What is referred to by ἅτινά 'which things'?
It refers in a summary way to all that had been said about Abraham, Sarah, Hagar, and their sons in 4:22–23 [Herm, NAC, WBC]. It refers to the

conception and birth of the two sons [TH]. It refers to all of the circumstances related to the births of the two sons [Alf]. It means the things of this nature or character [Lns].

QUESTION—What is the meaning of the participle ἀλληγορούμενα 'being spoken allegorically'?

It means to base an allegorical interpretation or application upon fact [WBC]. It means to take a historical event or a statement and draw from it a meaning quite different from its original significance [TH]. For something to be allegorical it is to be understood other than in its literal sense [Alf]. Its meaning does not lie on the surface [Lns]. The present participle form brings out the significance in the present circumstances, not in the historical context [NCBC].

for[a] these (women) are[b] two covenants,[c]

LEXICON—a. γάρ (LN 89.23): 'for' [BNTC, Herm, LN, Mor; KJV, NASB, NET, NIV], 'because' [LN], 'now' [NLT], not explicit [SSA, WBC; CEV, GW, NCV, NRSV, REB, TEV].

b. pres. indic. of εἰμί (LN 13.1, 58.68): 'to be' [BNTC, Herm, LN (13.1), Mor; KJV, NASB, NRSV], 'to represent' [LN (58.68), WBC; NET, NIV, TEV], 'to stand for' [LN (58.68); CEV, REB], 'to symbolize' [SSA], 'to illustrate' [GW], 'to serve as an illustration' [NLT], 'to be like' [NCV]. Here it means to stand for, to signify [NIGTC], to represent [NTC].

c. διαθήκη (LN 34.44) (BAGD 2. p. 183): 'covenant' [BAGD, BNTC, Herm, LN, Mor, SSA, WBC; all versions except CEV, GW, NCV], 'agreement' [CEV, NCV], 'arrangement' [GW].

QUESTION—What relationship is indicated by γάρ 'for'?

This introduces the allegorical interpretation of the people and events referred to in 4:22–23 [ICC]. It explains how the Scriptures have another, added meaning in the account of the two sons of Abraham [Lns].

QUESTION—Who does αὗται 'these' refer to?

This feminine pronoun refers to the two women mentioned in 4:22–23 [Alf, BNTC, Herm, ICC, Lns, Lt, NCBC, NIBC, NIC, NTC, SSA, TNTC, WBC; all versions except KJV]: the two women represent the two covenants.

QUESTION—What covenants are referred to here?

1. The covenants referred to are the old covenant and the new covenant [BST, Herm, Lt, Mor, WBC]. The old covenant is Torah centered. The new covenant is Christ centered [WBC]. The old covenant is based on law. The new covenant is based on promises [BST].
2. The covenants referred to are the covenant made with Abraham and the covenant made with Moses [ICC, NIC, NTC, SSA, TH, TNTC]. There is a continuity of the Abrahamic covenant with the new covenant so that it both precedes and follows the Mosaic Law [SSA].

one on-the-one-hand[a] from[b] Mount Sinai bearing[c] into[d] slavery,[e] which is Hagar.

LEXICON—a. μέν (LN 89.136) (BAGD 1.c. p. 503): 'on the one hand' [BAGD, LN], 'indeed' [WBC], 'that is' [SSA], 'in fact' [NRSV], not explicit [BNTC, Herm, Mor; all versions except CEV, NLT, NRSV]. This entire clause is translated 'Hagar, the slave woman, stands for the agreement that was made at Mount Sinai. Everyone born into her family is a slave' [CEV], 'Hagar, the slave-wife, represents Mount Sinai where people first became enslaved to the law' [NLT].
   b. ἀπό with genitive object (LN 90.15): 'from' [BNTC, Herm, LN, Mor, WBC; KJV, NASB, NET, NIV, NRSV, REB], 'to originate at' [SSA], 'on' [GW, NCV], 'at' [TEV]. See a. [CEV, NLT].
   c. pres. act. participle of γεννάω (LN 23.52) (BAGD 2. p. 155): 'to bear' [BAGD, LN, Mor, SSA, WBC; NASB, NET, NIV, NRSV], 'to give birth' [BNTC, Herm, LN], 'to gender' [KJV], not explicit [NCV]. Instead of the one woman or covenant being the subject, some make her children the subject of this verb: 'the one whose children are born' [TEV], 'her children are born' [GW, REB]. See a. [CEV, NLT].
   d. εἰς with accusative object (LN 84.22, 89.57): 'into' [BNTC, Herm, LN (84.22), WBC; GW, REB], 'for the purpose of' [LN (89.57)], 'for' [Mor; NET, NRSV], 'to' [KJV], 'in' [TEV], not explicit [SSA; NASB, NCV, NIV]. See a. [CEV, NLT].
   e. δουλεία (LN 37.26) (BAGD 2. p. 205): 'slavery' [BAGD, BNTC, Herm, LN, Mor, WBC; GW, NET, NRSV, REB, TEV], 'bondage' [KJV]. The phrase εἰς δουλείαν γεννῶσα 'bearing into slavery' is translated 'bears slaves' [SSA], 'born into her family is a slave' [CEV], 'bearing children who are to be slaves' [NASB], 'bears children who are to be slaves' [NIV], 'are like slaves' [NCV], See a. [NLT].

QUESTION—What is referred to by μία 'one'?
   1. It refers to the covenant that was from Mount Sinai. This covenant bore children for slavery. This covenant is represented by Hagar [Alf, Herm, ICC, Lns, Mor, SSA, TNTC; KJV, NCV, NET, NIV].
   2. It refers to one of the women who was from Mount Sinai. She bore children for slavery. This woman is Hagar [Lt, NCBC, NIC, WBC; NASB]. The connection between Hagar and Sinai is not obvious in this verse. In the next verse Paul defines Hagar as the one from Mount Sinai [NCBC].
   3. It refers to Hagar, who bore children for slavery. She represents the covenant from Mount Sinai [CEV, GW, NLT, NRSV, REB, TEV].

QUESTION—What is meant by εἰς δουλείαν γεννῶσα 'born into slavery'?
   It refers to the fact that those who came under the Sinai covenant were slaves to the bondage of the law [Mor, NIC]. This phrase designates Hagar, who is a slave, as one who bears children who are also slaves. This phrase as applied to the Sinai covenant refers to the fact that everyone who came under the Sinai covenant were slaves to the bondage of the law [ICC, NCBC].

4:25 Now[a] the (word) "Hagar" is Mount Sinai in[b] Arabia;
TEXT—Instead of δὲ Ἀγάρ 'now…Hagar', some manuscripts read γὰρ Ἀγάρ 'for…Hagar'; other manuscripts read only δέ 'now'; and other manuscripts read only γάρ 'for'. GNT reads δὲ Ἀγάρ 'now…Hagar' with a C decision, indicating that the Committee had difficulty making the decision. Γὰρ Ἀγάρ 'for…Hagar' is read by KJV. Δὲ Ἀγάρ 'now…Hagar' is read by NASB, NET, NIV, NRSV.
LEXICON—a. δέ (LN 89.94): 'now' [Herm, LN, Mor, WBC; NASB, NET, NIV, NRSV], 'and' [LN], 'also/even' [SSA], 'for' [KJV], 'and now' [NLT], not explicit [BNTC; CEV, GW, NCV, REB, TEV].
  b. ἐν with dative object (LN 83.13): 'in' [BNTC, Herm, LN, Mor, SSA, WBC; all versions].
QUESTION—What does Ἀγάρ 'Hagar' refer to?
  1. Hagar represents Mount Sinai [NAC, NIC, NIGTC, NTC, TH, TNTC; CEV, NET, NIV, TEV]. Identifying Hagar with Sinai simply means that she and her descendants represent the law which holds people in bondage [NIGTC].
  2. Hagar is connected in some way with Mount Sinai [NCBC]. Hagar not only represents the covenant of law given on Mount Sinai, but she is also to be identified with Mount Sinai itself. However it is impossible to be certain what Paul had in mind by this statement [NCBC].
  3. The name 'Hagar' is the Arabian name for Mount Sinai [Alf, Herm, ICC]. The statement does not refer to the woman Hagar. Instead, either the word ἐστίν 'is' affirms the equivalence of the two expressions Hagar and Σινᾶ ὄρος 'Mount Sinai' or by association of ὄρος 'mountain' after Σινᾶ 'Sinai' with both Hagar and Σινᾶ, the mountain [ICC].
  4. 'Hagar' should not be in the text [Lns, Lt; NLT, REB]. Hagar went to Beersheba and her son Ishmael lived in Paran near Sinai, so the place where the Law was given connected it with the slave woman Hagar and her descendants [Lns].
QUESTION—What is indicated by the neuter definite article τό 'the'?
It indicates that Paul is not speaking of the woman Hagar, but of the word 'Hagar' [Alf, Herm, Mor, SSA].

and it-corresponds[a] to-the present[b] Jerusalem,
LEXICON—a. pres. act. indic. of συστοιχέω (LN **58.68**) (BAGD p. 795): 'to correspond to' [BAGD, Herm, **LN**, Mor, SSA, WBC; NASB, NET, NIV, NRSV], 'to be a figure of' [**LN**; TEV], 'to represent' [LN; REB], 'to stand for' [LN], 'to belong to' [BNTC], 'to be like' [GW], 'to be a picture of' [NCV], 'to be just like' [NLT], 'to answer to' [KJV], not explicit [CEV].
  b. νῦν (LN 67.38) (BAGD 3.a. p. 546): 'present' [BAGD, BNTC, Herm, Mor, WBC; NASB, NET, NRSV], 'now' [LN; NLT], 'today' [GW]. This is translated 'as it is today' [SSA], 'which now is' [KJV]. The phrase τῇ νῦν Ἰερουσαλήμ 'the present Jerusalem' is translated 'the earthly Jewish

city of Jerusalem' [NCV], 'the present city of Jerusalem' [CEV, NIV, TEV], 'the Jerusalem of today' [REB].

QUESTION—What relationship is indicated by δέ 'and'?

It is resumptive [SSA]. It connects the previous equation with this one and, therefore, should be translated as 'also' [Herm].

QUESTION—Who is the implied actor of συστοιχεῖ 'corresponds'?

1. The actor is Hagar [Alf, ICC, NAC, NCBC, NIC, NIGTC, NTC, SSA, TH, WBC; CEV, GW, NASB, NCV, NET, NIV, NRSV, TEV]. Hagar stands for Mount Sinai and she also is a figure of the present city of Jerusalem [NAC, SSA, TH].
2. The actor is Mount Sinai [Herm, Lns, Lt; NLT, REB]. The present Jerusalem can be associated with 'Sinai/Hagar' since it is based on the Sinai covenant [Herm].

QUESTION—What is meant by τῇ νῦν Ἰερουσαλήμ 'the present Jerusalem'?

It is Paul's description of contemporary Judaism with Jerusalem being its capital [NCBC]. Jerusalem stands for the whole Jewish nation with Jerusalem as its center [TH]. Paul emphasizes the religious significance of the city. The Judaizers looked to Jerusalem as the source and support of their gospel [WBC]. It does not mean the literal city as much as the whole legal system of Judaism which had its center in Jerusalem [NIGTC]. Jerusalem stands as a symbol of the political and religious institution of Judaism [Herm].

for[a] she-is-in-bondage[b] with[c] her children.

TEXT—Instead of γάρ 'for' some manuscripts apparently read δέ 'and', although GNT does not mention this variant. Δέ 'and' is read by KJV.

LEXICON—a. γάρ (LN 89.23): 'for' [BNTC, Herm, LN, Mor; NASB, NET, NRSV, REB], 'because' [LN, WBC; GW, NIV, NLT], 'and' [KJV], 'since' [SSA], not explicit [CEV, NCV, TEV].

b. pres. act. indic. of δουλεύω (LN 87.79) (BAGD 1.a. p. 205): 'to be in bondage' [WBC; KJV], 'to be in slavery' [BNTC, Mor; NASB, NET, NIV, NLT, NRSV, REB, TEV], 'to be a slave' [BAGD, LN; CEV, GW, NCV], 'to live in slavery' [Herm]. The phrase δουλεύει μετὰ τῶν τέκνων αὐτῆς 'she is in bondage with her children' is translated 'Jerusalem city today is like a slave mother, and those who live there are like her slave children in that she and they must comply with the Mosaic law' [SSA].

c. μετά with genitive object (LN 89.108) (BAGD A.II.2. p. 509): 'with' [BAGD, BNTC, LN, Mor, WBC; KJV, NASB, NET, NIV, NRSV, TEV], 'together with' [Herm, LN], 'and' [CEV, GW, NCV, NLT, REB]. See b. [SSA].

QUESTION—Who is referred to by τέκνων 'children'?

It refers to all those who followed the way taught by the Judaizers [Mor]. It refers to all those who followed the law as the means of justification [NAC, NIC]. It refers to all Jewish people and not only to the inhabitants of

Jerusalem [TH]. It refers to all those Jews who followed the law [Lns]. It refers to all those who followed legalistic Judaism which has its center in Jerusalem [ICC].

4:26 But the Jerusalem above[a] is free,[b]

LEXICON—a. ἄνω (LN 83.48) (BAGD 1. p. 77): 'above' [BAGD, BNTC, Herm, LN, Mor, WBC; all versions except NLT, REB, TEV]. This preposition is also translated as an adjective: 'heavenly' [BAGD; NLT, REB, TEV], 'spiritual' [SSA].

b. ἐλεύθερος (LN 37.134, 87.84) (BAGD 3. p. 250): 'free' [BAGD, BNTC, Herm, LN (37.134), Mor, WBC; GW, KJV, NASB, NET, NIV, NRSV, TEV]. This is also translated as a noun phrase: 'free person' [LN (87.84)], 'free mother' [SSA], 'free woman' [NLT, REB]. The phrase ἐλευθέρα ἐστίν 'is free' is translated 'isn't a slave' [CEV], 'is like the free woman' [NCV], 'is like a free mother' [SSA].

QUESTION—What relationship is indicated by δέ 'but'?

By the use of δέ 'but' 4:26a, the heavenly Jerusalem that is free, is directly contrasted with 4:25b–c, the present Jerusalem that is in bondage [SSA, TH].

QUESTION—What is meant by ἡ ἄνω Ἰερουσαλὴμ 'the Jerusalem above'?

Since Paul is speaking allegorically, he is not speaking of the Jerusalem in Palestine, but of the holy city, where God's people delight to worship [Mor]. It represents the Christian church [BST, Lns, NCBC, TNTC]. It refers to the church, those who have put their faith and trust in Jesus Christ [TH].

QUESTION—What is meant by ἐλευθέρα 'free'?

In this community of believers there is freedom from bondage to law and freedom to become children of God [TH]. This probably means more than that the heavenly Jerusalem is not subject to human bondage. Paul is probably also suggesting that sin has no power there. Those who belong to the heavenly Jerusalem have victory over the forces of evil through Christ [Mor].

which[a] is mother of us;

TEXT—Instead of ἡμῶν 'of us' some manuscripts read πάντων ἡμῶν 'of us all'. GNT reads ἡμῶν 'of us' with an A decision, indicating that the text is certain. Πάντων ἡμῶν 'of us all' is read by KJV.

LEXICON—a. ὅστις (LN 92.18): 'who' [LN], 'which' [Mor; KJV], 'such' [BNTC], 'she/it' [SSA], 'she' [WBC; all versions except CEV, KJV], 'this' [Herm], not explicit [CEV].

QUESTION—How are the nouns related in the genitive construction μήτηρ ἡμῶν 'mother of us'?

The possessive pronoun ἡμῶν 'of us' refers to all believers in Christ [NCBC, NIC, TH, WBC]. Paul includes himself plus the Galatians [Lns]. Paul is claiming that all Jewish and Gentile believers belong to the one heavenly family [Mor]. It means to be members of the community of believers in Christ [ICC]. The idea of motherhood includes membership in the Christian community which provides the opportunity for spiritual growth [TH].

4:27 for it-is-written,ᵃ

LEXICON—a. perf. pass. indic. of γράφω (LN 33.61): 'to be written' [BNTC, Herm, LN, Mor, WBC; KJV, NASB, NCV, NET, NIV, NRSV]. This entire phrase is translated 'For scripture says' [REB], 'For the scripture says' [TEV], 'Scripture says' [GW], 'The Scriptures say about her' [CEV], 'since God has said through Isaiah' [SSA], 'That is what Isaiah meant when he prophesied' [NLT]. The quotation is from Isaiah 54:1 [BST, Herm, ICC, Lns, Mor, NAC, NCBC, NIBC, NIC, NIGTC, NTC, TH, TNTC, WBC].

QUESTION—What relationship is indicated by γάρ 'for'?

It is used to confirm that Sarah is to be identified with 'the Jerusalem that is above' and to confirm that all Christians have Sarah and the heavenly Jerusalem as their mother [WBC]. It is confirmatory and connects the whole statement in this verse with ἥτις ἐστὶν μήτηρ ἡμῶν 'who is the mother of us' in 4:26 [ICC]. It links the quotation with μήτηρ ἡμῶν 'the mother of us' in 4:26 [Lt].

"Be-gladdened,ᵃ barrenᵇ (woman) the-(one) not giving-birth,ᶜ

LEXICON—a. aorist pass. impera. of εὐφραίνω (LN 25.131) (BAGD 2. p. 327): 'to be gladdened' [BAGD], 'to be glad' [LN, WBC; CEV, NIV], 'to be happy' [LN; NCV, TEV], 'to rejoice' [BNTC, Herm, Mor, SSA; GW, KJV, NASB, NET, NLT, NRSV, REB].

b. στεῖρα (LN 23.56) (BAGD p. 766): 'barren' [BAGD, BNTC, Herm, LN, Mor, SSA, WBC; KJV, NASB, NET, NIV, REB], 'childless' [NLT, NRSV, TEV], not explicit [NCV]. This adjective is also translated as a verb phrase: 'not able to bear children' [LN], 'incapable of bearing children' [BAGD], 'not have children' [CEV], 'not able to get pregnant' [GW].

c. pres. act. participle of τίκτω (LN 23.52) (BAGD 1. p. 816): 'to give birth' [BAGD, LN; CEV, GW, NCV, NLT], 'to bear' [BAGD, BNTC, Herm, LN, Mor, SSA, WBC; KJV, NASB, NET, NIV, NRSV, REB], 'to feel the pains of childbirth' [TEV].

shoutᵃ and cry-out,ᵇ the-(one) not having-birth-pains;ᶜ

LEXICON—a. aorist act. impera. of ῥήγνυμι (LN **33.85, 68.81**) (BAGD 2. p. 735): 'to shout, to begin to shout' [LN (33.85)], 'to break forth with, to burst into' [LN (68.81)]. The phrase ῥῆξον καὶ βόησον 'shout and cry out' is translated 'break forth with shouts' [**LN** (68.81)], 'shout and cry with joy' [**LN** (33.85)], 'break forth and shout' [Herm; NASB, NET], 'break forth and cry' [KJV], 'break forth and cry out' [Mor], 'break forth and cry aloud' [BNTC, WBC; NIV], 'break into shouting' [GW], 'break into a shout of joy' [REB], 'shout and cry with joy' [TEV], 'burst into song and shout' [NRSV], 'break forth into loud and joyful song' [NLT],

'start singing and shout for joy' [NCV], 'now you can shout' [CEV], 'you will not restrain yourself but will cry out' [SSA].
b. aorist act. impera. of βοάω (LN 33.81) (BAGD 1. p. 144): 'to cry out' [LN], 'to shout' [BAGD, LN]. See above for the clause 'shout and cry out'.
c. pres. act. participle of ὠδίνω (LN 23.54) (BAGD p. 895): 'to have birth pains' [BAGD, LN; NET], 'to suffer birth-pangs' [BAGD; NRSV], 'to give birth' [Mor; NLT], 'to have labor pains' [BNTC, WBC; NIV], 'to painfully deliver children' [SSA], 'to travail' [KJV], 'to have pains of childbirth' [GW, TEV], 'to be in labor' [NASB, REB], 'to be in travail' [Herm], 'to have the pain of giving birth' [NCV], not explicit [CEV].

because many[a] (are) the children of-the desolate[b] (woman) more[c] than[d] the-(one) having[e] the husband."[f]
LEXICON—a. πολύς (LN 59.1) (BAGD I.1.a.α. p. 687): 'many' [BAGD, BNTC, LN, Mor, SSA], 'more' [WBC; all versions except KJV], 'many more' [KJV], not explicit [Herm].
b. ἔρημος (LN **35.55**) (BAGD 1.b. p. 309): 'desolate' [BAGD, Herm, Mor, WBC; KJV, NASB, NET, NIV, NRSV], 'deserted' [BAGD, BNTC, **LN**, SSA; GW, REB, TEV], 'forsaken' [LN], 'the woman who could bear no children' [NLT], not explicit [CEV, NCV].
c. μᾶλλον (LN 78.28) (BAGD 1. p. 489): 'more' [BNTC, Herm, LN, Mor], 'rather/more' [SSA], not explicit [WBC; all versions]. The phrase πολλὰ...μᾶλλον 'many...more' is translated 'numerous to a higher degree' [BAGD].
d. ἤ (LN 64.18): 'than' [BNTC, Herm, LN, Mor, SSA, WBC; all versions].
e. pres. act. participle of ἔχω (LN 57.1) (BAGD I.2.b.α, p. 332): 'to have' [BNTC, Herm, LN, Mor, SSA, WBC; GW, KJV, NASB, NCV, NET, NIV], 'to live with' [REB], not explicit [NLT]. The phrase ἐχούσης τὸν ἄνδρα 'having the husband' is translated 'to be married' [BAGD], 'has been married' [CEV], 'is married' [NRSV], 'whose husband never left' [TEV].
f. ἀνήρ (LN 10.53) (BAGD 1. p. 66): 'husband' [BAGD, BNTC, Herm, LN, Mor, SSA, WBC; all versions except CEV, NLT, NRSV], not explicit [NLT]. See e. [CEV, NRSV].

4:28 **And you, brothers,[a] like[b] Isaac are children[c] of-promise.[d]**
TEXT—Instead of ὑμεῖς...ἐστέ 'you...are' some manuscripts read ἡμεῖς...ἐσμέν 'we...are.' GNT reads ὑμεῖς...ἐστέ 'you...are' with a B decision, indicating that the text is almost certain. Ἡμεῖς...ἐσμέν 'we...are' is read by KJV.
LEXICON—a. ἀδελφός (LN 11.23): 'brother, Christian brother, fellow believer' [LN]. The plural form is translated 'brothers' [BNTC, Herm, Mor, SSA, WBC; NIV], 'brethren' [KJV, NASB], 'friends' [CEV, NRSV, REB, TEV], 'brothers and sisters' [GW, NCV, NET, NLT].

b. κατά with accusative object (LN 89.8) (BAGD II.5.b.α. p. 407): 'like' [BNTC, Herm, Mor, WBC; GW, NASB, NET, NIV, NRSV, REB], 'in accordance with' [LN], 'just as' [BAGD; CEV, TEV], 'just like' [NLT], 'as' [KJV, NCV]. The phrase κατὰ Ἰσαὰκ 'like Isaac' is translated 'because you/we (incl.) are united with Christ who is Isaac's descendant, and Isaac was promised to Abraham by God' [SSA].
c. τέκνον (LN 10.36): 'child' [BNTC, Herm, LN, Mor, WBC; all versions except CEV], 'descendant' [SSA], not explicit [CEV].
d. ἐπαγγελία (LN 33.288) (BAGD 2 a. p. 280): 'promise' [BAGD, BNTC, Herm, LN, Mor, WBC; all versions]. This noun is also translated as a verb phrase: 'whom God promised' [SSA].

QUESTION—What relationship is indicated by δέ 'and'?
It is continuative 'and' [ICC, NIC] or 'now' [TH]. It is explanatory 'now' [NIC]. It functions as a consequential connective 'so' [WBC].

QUESTION—How are the nouns related in the genitive construction ἐπαγγελίας τέκνα 'children of promise'?
They are the children God promised Abraham [SSA]. They are children who were born because of the preceding promise [CEV, NCV], as a result of God's promise [TEV]. They became God's children in fulfillment of God's promise to Abraham [TH]. The promise is the one already referred to in 3:16, 18, 21, and 22 [ICC].

QUESTION—Whose children are they?
1. They are God's children [Mor, TH; NCV, TEV]. When people put their trust in Christ, they are born into the heavenly family and become children of God [Mor].
2. They are Abraham's children [BST, ICC, NTC].
3. This is an idiom which does not imply any parent [Lns]. 'Children of promise' is a practical compound like 'children of light' and similar combinations, the genitive being ethically qualitative [Lns].

4:29 But just-as[a] then the (one) having-been-born[b] in-accordance-with[c] flesh[d] was-persecuting[e] the-(one) in-accordance-with[f] Spirit/spirit,[g]

LEXICON—a. ὥσπερ (LN 64.13): 'just as' [BNTC, Herm, LN, SSA, WBC; NET, NRSV, REB], 'as' [LN, Mor; KJV, NASB], not explicit [CEV, GW, NCV, NIV, NLT, TEV].
b. aorist pass. participle of γεννάω (LN 13.56) (BAGD 1.a. p. 155): 'to be born' [BNTC, Herm, LN, Mor, WBC; all versions except GW, NLT, REB], 'to be begotten' [BAGD], 'to be conceived' [SSA; GW], '(the natural) born (son)' [REB], not explicit [NLT].
c. κατά with accusative object (LN 89.8): 'in accordance with' [BNTC, LN], 'according to' [Herm, Mor, WBC; NASB, NRSV], 'after' [KJV], 'by' [NET], 'in' [CEV, NCV, NIV, TEV], not explicit [SSA; GW, NLT, REB].
d. σάρξ (LN 8.63, 26.7, 58.10) (BAGD 4. p. 743): 'flesh' [BNTC, Herm, LN (8.63), Mor, WBC; KJV, NASB, NRSV], 'human nature' [BAGD,

LN (26.7, 58.10)], 'mortal nature, earthly descent' [BAGD], 'physical nature of people' [LN (58.10)], 'natural descent' [NET], 'natural-born' [REB], not explicit [NLT]. This noun is also translated as an adverb: 'naturally/normally' [SSA]. This noun is also translated as an adjective: 'the natural way' [CEV], 'a natural way' [GW], 'the normal way' [NCV], 'the ordinary way' [NIV], 'the usual way' [TEV].

e. imperf. act. indic. of διώκω (LN 39.45) (BAGD 2. p. 201): 'to persecute' [BAGD, BNTC, Herm, LN, Mor, SSA, WBC; all versions except CEV, NCV, NLT], 'to harass' [LN], 'to make trouble for' [CEV], 'to treat badly' [NCV]. The active verb is also translated passively: 'to be persecuted' [NLT].

f. κατά with accusative object (LN 89.8): 'in accordance with' [BNTC, LN], 'according to' [Herm, Mor, WBC; NASB, NET, NRSV], 'after' [KJV], 'because of' [CEV, TEV], 'by' [NIV], 'of' [NLT], 'in' [GW], not explicit [SSA; NCV, REB].

g. πνεῦμα (LN 12.18, 26.9) (BAGD 5.d.β. p. 677): 'Spirit' [BAGD, BNTC, Herm, LN (12.18), Mor, WBC; CEV, KJV, NASB, NET, NIV, NRSV, TEV], 'Holy Spirit' [LN (12.18); NLT], 'spirit' [LN (26.9)], not explicit [NCV]. This noun is also translated as an adjective: 'spiritual' [LN (26.9); REB], 'a spiritual way' [GW]. This noun is also translated as an adverb: 'supernaturally' [SSA].

QUESTION—What relationship is indicated by ἀλλά 'but'?
It introduces a fact that is in contrast with the preceding statement [ICC]. Or, it provides a transition to the sentence of 4:29 rather than a contrast with 4:28 [Herm, WBC].

QUESTION—What is meant by κατὰ σάρκα 'in accordance with the flesh'?
See 4:23.

thus[a] now also.

LEXICON—a. οὕτως (LN 61.9): 'thus, in this way' [LN], 'so' [BNTC, LN, Mor, SSA, WBC; KJV, NASB, NET, NRSV, REB], not explicit [NLT]. This entire phrase is translated 'The same thing is happening today' [CEV], 'That's exactly what's happening now' [GW], 'It is the same today' [NCV], 'It is the same now' [NIV], 'and it is the same now' [TEV], 'so it is today' [Herm].

QUESTION—To what does this phrase refer?
Paul has identified his readers with Isaac and states that they are being persecuted by Ishmael. He likens Ishmael mainly to the Jewish Christian troublemakers and secondarily to the Jews in general [NIBC]. According to Paul, this persecution repeats itself in the present persecution of Christians by the Jews [Herm]. The persecution of the true church, of Christian believers, is not always by the world, but also by religious people, the nominal church [BST].

4:30 But what says the Scripture[a]?
LEXICON—a. γραφή (LN 33.53) (BAGD 2.b.β. p. 166): 'Scripture' [Herm, LN (33.53), Mor, WBC; GW, NASB, NCV, NIV], 'scripture' [BNTC; KJV, NET, NRSV, REB, TEV], 'Scriptures' [CEV, NLT], 'Scripture passage' [LN (33.53)], 'the words which God caused that Moses wrote' [SSA]. It designates Scripture as a whole [BAGD].
QUESTION—What relationship is indicated by ἀλλά 'but'?
It marks Paul's alternative to the persecution mentioned in 4:29 [TH]. It introduces this rhetorical question [NCBC].

"Drive-out[a] the slave-woman[b] and her son;
LEXICON—a. aorist act. impera. of ἐκβάλλω (LN 15.44) (BAGD 1. p. 237): 'to drive out' [Herm, LN; NRSV, REB], 'to send away' [LN, SSA; TEV], 'to expel' [BAGD, LN], 'to repudiate' [BAGD], 'to cast out' [Mor, WBC; KJV, NASB], 'to throw out' [BNTC; NCV, NET], 'to get rid of' [CEV, GW, NIV, NLT].
  b. παιδίσκη (LN 87.83) (BAGD p. 604): 'slave woman' [Herm, LN, Mor, WBC; CEV, GW, NCV, NET, NIV, TEV], 'slave girl' [BNTC, LN], 'female slave' [BAGD, SSA], 'servant-girl' [BAGD], 'maid' [BAGD], 'bondwoman' [KJV, NASB], 'slave' [NLT, NRSV, REB].

for by no means[a] the son of-the slave-woman[b] shall-inherit[c] with[d] the son of-the free[e] (woman)."
LEXICON—a. οὐ μή (LN 69.5) (BAGD D.2. p. 517). The phrase οὐ μή 'not not' is translated 'by no means' [LN], 'certainly not' [LN, SSA], 'never' [BNTC, WBC; GW, NIV], 'not' [Herm, Mor; all versions except CEV, GW, NIV], 'won't' [CEV]. It is the most decisive way of negating something in the future [BAGD].
  b. παιδίσκη (LN 87.83) (BAGD p. 604): 'slave woman' [Herm, LN, Mor, WBC; GW, NCV, NET, NIV, NLT, TEV], 'slave girl' [BNTC, LN], 'female slave' [BAGD, SSA], 'servant-girl' [BAGD], 'maid' [BAGD], 'bondwoman' [KJV, NASB], 'slave' [NRSV, REB], not explicit [CEV].
  c. fut. act. indic. of κληρονομέω (LN **57.138**) (BAGD 1. p. 434): 'to inherit' [BAGD, BNTC, LN, Mor; NCV], 'to inherit/share' [SSA], 'to inherit the father's property' [**LN**], 'to be an heir' [BAGD; KJV, NASB], 'to have a part of the father's property' [TEV], 'to receive everything' [CEV], 'to share in the inheritance' [WBC; NIV], 'to share the inheritance' [Herm; GW, NET, NRSV, REB], 'to share the family inheritance' [NLT].
  d. μετά with genitive object (LN 89.108) (BAGD A.II.2. p. 509): 'with' [BAGD, BNTC, Herm, LN, Mor, SSA, WBC; all versions except CEV, NCV, TEV], 'together with' [LN], 'along with' [TEV], not explicit [CEV, NCV].
  e. ἐλεύθερος (LN 37.134, 87.84) (BAGD 1. p. 250): 'free' [BAGD, LN (37.134)], 'free person' [LN (87.84)], 'free woman' [BNTC, Herm, WBC; all versions], 'free one' [Mor], 'free wife' [SSA].

4:31 Therefore[a], brothers,[b] we-are not children[c] of-a-slave-woman[d] but of-the free[e] (woman).

LEXICON—a. διό (LN 89.47): 'therefore' [LN, Mor, WBC; NET, NIV], 'wherefore' [BNTC], 'so then' [KJV, NASB, NRSV, TEV], 'then' [REB], 'so' [NCV, NLT], 'in conclusion' [Herm], not explicit [SSA; CEV, GW].

b. ἀδελφός (LN 11.23): 'Christian brother, fellow believer' [LN]. The plural form is translated 'brothers' [BNTC, Herm, Mor, SSA, WBC; NIV], 'brethren' [KJV, NASB], 'friends' [CEV, NRSV, REB, TEV], 'brothers and sisters' [GW, NCV, NET, NLT].

c. τέκνον (LN 10.36) (BAGD 2.c. p. 808): 'child' [BAGD, BNTC, Herm, LN, Mor, WBC; all versions], 'offspring' [LN], 'descendant' [SSA].

d. παιδίσκη (LN **87.83**) (BAGD p. 604): 'slave woman' [Herm, **LN**, Mor, WBC; GW, NCV, NET, NIV, NLT, TEV], 'slave girl' [BNTC, LN], 'female slave' [BAGD, SSA], 'servant-girl, maid' [BAGD], 'bondwoman' [KJV, NASB], 'slave' [CEV, NRSV, REB].

e. ἐλεύθερος (LN 37.134, 87.84) (BAGD 1. p. 250): 'free' [BAGD, LN (37.134); KJV], 'free person' [LN (87.84)], 'free one' [Mor], 'free woman' [BNTC, Herm, WBC; all versions except KJV], 'free wife' [SSA].

QUESTION—What relationship is indicated by διό 'therefore'?

It indicates a summary of the whole argument [TNTC]. It indicates the conclusion of what has been said [Alf, NIC, TH]. The conclusion stated in this verse is derived from what has been said about persecution in 4:29 [NIC]. Paul gives a summary of his allegorical argument in this verse [Herm, ICC, NAC, NCBC].

QUESTION—Who are the ἀδελφοί 'brothers' in this verse?

By using the word 'brothers' Paul includes all true believers and excludes those whom he thinks of as children of Hagar [NCBC].

QUESTION—Who is the referent of ἐσμὲν 'we-are' in this verse?

It refers to Paul and the Gentile believers [Mor, SSA, WBC]. It refers to Paul and all true believers [BNTC, Herm, NTC, TH]. The shift from the second person plural 'you' in 4:28 to the first person plural in this verse indicates Paul's desire to identify himself with the Galatian believers [NAC].

QUESTION—What is significant about the absence of the definite article before παιδίσκης 'of slave woman'?

It emphasizes the fact that slavery is not controlled solely by the Jewish system [TH]. The article is omitted to emphasize her slavish quality [NTC]. However, the article is added by many [BNTC, SSA, WBC; CEV, KJV, NCV, NET, NIV, NLT, NRSV].

DISCOURSE UNIT: 5:1–26 [GW, NASB]. The topic is live in the freedom that Christ gives you [GW], walk by the Spirit [NASB].

DISCOURSE UNIT: 5:1–15 [NCBC; CEV, NCV, NIV, NLT, TEV]. The topic is Christian life as a life of freedom [NCBC], Christ gives freedom [CEV], keep your freedom [NCV], freedom in Christ [NIV, NLT], preserve your freedom [TEV].

DISCOURSE UNIT: 5:1–12 [BST, Mor, NAC, WBC; NET]. The topic is false and true religion [BST], freedom and the bondage of circumcision [Mor], freedom in Christ [NAC], holding fast to freedom [WBC], freedom of the believer [NET].

5:1 **(For/in) the freedom[a] Christ has-freed[b] us; stand[c] therefore**

TEXT—Instead of τῇ ἐλευθερίᾳ ἡμᾶς Χριστὸς ἠλευθέρωσεν· στήκετε οὖν 'for/in freedom Christ has freed us; stand therefore' (some manuscripts change the word order to Χριστὸς ἡμᾶς 'Christ...us'). GW reads 'Christ has freed us...freedom. Therefore, be firm'. Some manuscripts read the aorist tense στῆτε 'stand' instead of the present tense στήκετε 'stand', some manuscripts read τῇ ἐλευθερίᾳ ᾗ Χριστὸς ἡμᾶς ἠλευθέρωσεν, στήκετε 'for/in the freedom for/in which Christ has freed us, stand' (some manuscripts add οὖν 'therefore' following τῇ ἐλευθερίᾳ 'for/in the freedom'), and some manuscripts read ᾗ ἐλευθερίᾳ ἡμᾶς Χριστὸς ἠλευθέρωσεν, στήκετε οὖν 'for/in which freedom (*i.e.,* for/in the freedom for/in which) Christ has freed us, stand therefore'. GNT reads τῇ ἐλευθερίᾳ ἡμᾶς Χριστὸς ἠλευθέρωσεν· στήκετε οὖν 'for/in freedom Christ has freed us; stand therefore' with a B decision, indicating that the text is almost certain.

LEXICON—a. ἐλευθερία (LN 37.133) (BAGD p. 250): 'freedom' [BAGD, BNTC, Herm, LN, Mor, WBC; all versions except CEV, KJV, NLT], 'liberty' [BAGD; KJV], not explicit [NLT]. This noun is also translated as an adverb: 'freely' [SSA]; as an adjective: 'free' [CEV].

b. aorist act. indic. of ἐλευθερόω (LN 37.135) (BAGD 2. p. 251): 'to free' [BAGD, SSA; GW], 'to set free' [BAGD, BNTC, Herm, LN, Mor, WBC; all versions except GW, KJV, NCV], 'to make free' [KJV, NCV].

c. pres. act. impera. of στήκω (LN 17.1) (BAGD 2. p. 768): 'to stand' [LN; TEV], 'to stand firm' [BAGD, BNTC, Herm, Mor; NASB, NET, NIV, NRSV, REB], 'to be steadfast' [BAGD], 'to stand fast' [WBC; KJV], 'to hold on to' [CEV], 'to be firm' [GW], 'to stand strong' [NCV]. This is translated 'Now make sure that you stay free' [NLT], 'resist/reject the false message that you must be circumcised by someone' [SSA].

QUESTION—What is meant by ἐλευθερίᾳ 'freedom'?

It means freedom from the Jewish law [BST, Mor, NIC, NTC, TH]. It means freedom from bondage to the law, to the evil elements dominating the world, to sin, the flesh and the devil [NAC]. It means freedom from the law. In setting us free Christ has not so much set our will free from the bondage of sin as to set our conscience free from the guilt of sin. The Christian freedom Paul describes is freedom of conscience and freedom from the struggle to keep the law [BST]. Paul is thinking of deliverance from the curse which the law puts on the sinner who had been trying to achieve his own righteousness

[NTC]. It means being released from any legal system or not being placed under one, specifically the Mosaic law [SSA].

QUESTION—What is the function of τῇ ἐλευθερίᾳ 'the freedom' in the clause τῇ ἐλευθερίᾳ ἡμᾶς Χριστὸς ἠλευθέρωσεν 'the freedom Christ has freed us'?

1. It gives the purpose of setting us free [BST, Herm, Lns, Mor, NAC, NCBC, NIBC, NTC, SSA, WBC; GW, NASB, NET, NIV, NRSV, REB]: Christ set us free in order for us to be free. He freed us in order that we should have this freedom and maintain, exercise, and enjoy it, not lose it [Lns]. The article τῇ 'the (freedom)' specifies the Christian freedom which Christ died to bring about, not just an abstract concept of freedom [Mor]. The clause is translated 'For freedom Christ has set us free' [NET, NRSV], 'It was for freedom that Christ set us free' [NASB, NIV, REB], 'Christ has freed us so that we may enjoy the benefits of freedom' [GW], 'In order that we might live freely, Christ freed us (that is, he justified us)' [SSA].
2. It gives the means by which we are set free [NIC, NIGTC; KJV]: Christ set us free by means of this freedom. The article τῇ 'the (freedom)' specifies the Christian freedom he has been speaking about, that freedom with which he set us free [NIC, NIGTC]. The clause is translated 'in the liberty wherewith Christ hath made us free' [KJV].
3. It emphasizes the verb [ICC, TNTC; CEV, NLT, TEV]: Christ set us free with freedom. The exclamation, 'Christ has freed us with freedom' illustrates Hebraic repetition [TNTC]. The article τῇ 'the (freedom)' refers to that freedom from the law the whole letter has been dealing with: 'With this freedom Christ has set us free' [ICC]. The clause is translated 'Christ has set us free!' [CEV], 'So Christ has really set us free' [NLT], 'Freedom is what we have—Christ has set us free!' [TEV].

QUESTION—Who is referred to by the pronoun ἡμᾶς 'us'?

It refers to Paul and the Galatians [Lns, SSA, TH].

QUESTION—What relationship is indicated by οὖν 'therefore'?

It introduces an exhortation based on the fact that Christ has set us free [Mor, NIC, TH; all versions except KJV, NIV, TEV].

and (do) not again be-subject-to[a] (a/the)-yoke[b] of-slavery.

LEXICON—a. pres. mid. (deponent = act.) impera. of ἐνέχω (LN **37.4**) (BAGD 2. p. 265): 'to be subject to' [BAGD, BNTC, **LN**; NASB, NET], 'to be under the control of' [LN], 'to be loaded down with' [BAGD, Mor], 'to be burdened by' [WBC; NIV], 'to be entangled with' [KJV], 'to submit to' [NRSV, REB], 'to be tied up in' [NLT], 'to get loaded with' [Herm]. This entire clause is translated 'and do not live like slaves again, that is, do not comply with rules and rites again' [SSA], 'and don't ever become slaves of the Law again' [CEV], 'and don't become slaves again' [GW], 'Do not change and go back into the slavery of the law' [NCV], 'and do not allow yourselves to become slaves again' [TEV].

b. ζυγός (LN 6.8) (BAGD 1. p. 339): 'yoke' [BAGD, BNTC, Herm, LN, Mor, WBC; KJV, NASB, NET, NIV, NRSV, REB]. The phrase ζυγῷ δουλείας 'yoke of slavery' is translated 'slavery of the law' [NCV], 'slaves of the Law' [CEV], 'slavery to the law' [NLT], not explicit [GW, TEV]. See a. [SSA].

QUESTION—What relationship is indicated by καί 'and'?

Along with the preceding exhortation comes this warning [TH]. Paul's positive command is accompanied by this negative command [Lns].

QUESTION—What is meant by πάλιν 'again'?

It means that as Gentiles they had been in slavery and equates the burden of Jewish legalism with that of heathenism [ICC]. It makes an implied reference to the pagan practices that controlled the Galatians before [SSA]. It means that before the Galatians were, like pagans, under the yoke of the 'elements of the world' [Herm]. It refers to their former state and, since this word is applied to Jews and Gentiles, Paul considers all pre-Christian states as slavery in some respect [NCBC]. The use of the word means that before the Galatians had become believers in Christ they had been under the basic principles of the world, which for them meant paganism. In Paul's view, from the perspective of being 'in Christ,' Judaism and paganism could be lumped together under 'the basic principles of the world' [WBC]. Paul is referring to their former state of slavery to either the Jewish system or the pagan system before they became believers in Christ [TH]. They had escaped from the slavery of Heathenism only to consider becoming slaves of Judaism [Lt, NTC].

QUESTION—What is meant by the metaphor ζυγῷ δουλείας 'yoke of slavery'?

The figure of a yoke is a metaphor for bondage [NCBC, TH]. It could refer to the pagan practices that controlled the Galatians before [SSA]. Paul refers to 'a' yoke of slavery, not 'the' yoke, and so addresses both Jews and Gentiles [TH]. Paul refers to slavery of any kind, including slavery to Judaism and paganism [Lns]. Any legalistic system can make slaves of people [TH]. The omission of the article with 'yoke of slavery' gives the phrase a qualitative force, and even though the reference is clearly to the yoke of legalism, it is appropriate after 'again' because the new yoke which he wants them to avoid is not identical with the one they previously carried [ICC].

DISCOURSE UNIT: 5:2–15 [GNT; NRSV]. The topic is Christian freedom [GNT], the nature of Christian freedom [NRSV].

DISCOURSE UNIT: 5:2–6 [NIC, NIGTC, TNTC]. The topic is faith versus works [NIC], the law demands total commitment [NIGTC], the goal of the gospel [TNTC].

5:2 Listen,[a] I Paul tell[b] you that if you-become-circumcised,[c]

LEXICON—a. ἴδε (LN **91.13**) (BAGD 1. p. 369): 'listen' [**LN**; NCV, NET, NLT, NRSV, TEV], 'see' [BAGD], 'look' [BNTC, Herm, Mor], 'mark my words' [WBC; NIV, REB], 'consider' [SSA], 'behold' [KJV, NASB], not explicit [CEV, GW].

b. pres. act. indic. of λέγω (LN 33.69) (BAGD II.1.f. p. 469): 'to tell' [BAGD, Herm, LN, Mor, SSA, WBC; NCV, NET, NIV, NLT, NRSV, TEV], 'to say' [BAGD, BNTC, LN; KJV, NASB, REB], 'to promise' [CEV], 'to guarantee' [GW].

c. pres. pass. subj. of περιτέμνω (LN 53.51) (BAGD 1. p. 652): 'to become circumcised' [BAGD, Herm, LN], 'to be circumcised' [BAGD, BNTC, LN, SSA, WBC; GW, KJV, NCV, NET, NIV, NRSV, TEV], 'to receive circumcision' [NASB], 'to have (oneself) circumcised' [BAGD], 'to get circumcised' [Mor; CEV, REB]. This verb is also translated as a noun: '(to count on) circumcision' [NLT].

QUESTION—What is the function of the phrase Ἴδε ἐγὼ Παῦλος λέγω 'listen, I Paul tell'?

Ἴδε 'listen' draws attention to what follows [Alf, BNTC, TH]. Paul wants the Galatians to pay special attention to what he is about to say [BNTC]. It emphasizes the importance of what follows in the verse [ICC, WBC]. Paul uses ἴδε 'listen' to draw attention to something that is really important [NCBC]. By using ἐγὼ Παῦλος 'I Paul' Paul is accenting the fact that this information is coming from him, therefore, it is authoritative in two ways: he is an apostle and he knows what he is talking about [TH]. The intent of the words was to give all the weight of his personal influence to what he was about to say [ICC]. Paul accents his personal apostolic authority [NAC]. Paul asserts all the authority at his command [Lns].

QUESTION—What is meant by the conditional clause ἐὰν περιτέμνησθε 'if you become circumcised'?

It indicates that the Galatians have not yet decided to become circumcised [BNTC, ICC, NAC, NCBC]. It implies that the thing which Paul fears is possible, not that it has already occurred [NTC]. It suggests that the Galatians have not become circumcised yet, but they are considering it [TH]. Paul uses ἐὰν 'if' to confront the Galatians with the actual results in case they allow themselves to be circumcised [Lns].

Christ will-benefit[a] you nothing.[b]

LEXICON—a. fut. act. indic. of ὠφελέω (LN 35.2) (BAGD 2. p. 900): 'to benefit' [BAGD, BNTC, Herm, SSA; GW, NASB, NET, NRSV, REB], 'to be of use (to)' [BAGD, WBC; TEV], 'to help' [BAGD, LN; NLT], 'to profit' [Mor; KJV], 'to be of value' [NIV]. This clause is translated 'Christ won't do you any good' [CEV], 'Christ does you no good' [NCV].

b. οὐδείς (LN 92.23): This neuter form οὐδέν is translated 'nothing' [LN, Mor; KJV], 'not at all' [BNTC], 'not even slightly' [SSA], 'no' [Herm, WBC; GW, NASB, NCV, NET, NIV, NRSV, TEV], 'no more' [REB].

The phrase ὑμᾶς οὐδὲν ὠφελήσει 'will benefit you nothing' is translated 'cannot help you' [NLT], 'won't do you any good' [CEV].

QUESTION—Why won't circumcision benefit them?

Paul means that if it is necessary to be circumcised in order to receive salvation, then all that Christ has done for our salvation is for nothing [NCBC, NTC, TH]. No one can be justified by their own efforts. No one can add circumcision to Christ as necessary for salvation. Christ has done everything necessary to obtain salvation [BST]. Paul means that Jesus Christ is all or nothing. If the Galatians reject him now, then he won't be of any use to them at all on the Day of Judgment. For the Galatians to reject the cross of Christ by accepting circumcision as a means of salvation would be the same as their sliding back into the paganism of their former life [NAC]. No one can be justified in two ways at once. No one can be justified by faith in Christ and at the same time by their own efforts [TNTC].

5:3 And I-testify[a] again to-every man circumcised[b]

LEXICON—a. pres. mid. (deponent = act.) indic. of μαρτύρομαι (LN 33.223, 33.319) (BAGD 1. p. 494): 'to testify' [BAGD, BNTC, Herm, LN (33.223), Mor, WBC; KJV, NASB, NET, NRSV], 'to bear witness' [BAGD], 'to assert' [LN (33.223)], 'to declare' [LN (33.223), SSA; NIV], 'to insist' [LN (33.319); GW], 'to warn' [NCV, TEV], 'to say' [NLT], 'to impress (on you)' [REB], not explicit [CEV].

b. pres. pass. participle of περιτέμνω (LN 53.51) (BAGD 1. p. 652): 'to be circumcised' [BAGD, BNTC, LN, Mor, SSA, WBC; all versions except CEV, NASB, REB], 'to become circumcised' [BAGD, Herm, LN], 'to receive circumcision' [NASB], 'to accept circumcision' [REB] not explicit [CEV].

QUESTION—What relationship is indicated by δέ 'and'?

It is not adversative but connective. It introduces a coordinate reason why the Galatians shouldn't even think of letting themselves become circumcised [WBC]. It introduces an addition and a slight contrast 'not only will Christ not profit…but…' [Alf]. Paul adds another supporting fact with the use of δέ 'and' [Lns].

QUESTION—What is meant by πάλιν 'again'?

It indicates that it is something that Paul said before [SSA]. It can be interpreted to refer either to an earlier statement of Paul, possibly made on the occasion referred to in 4:16 and 1:9, or to the verse immediately preceding. The close relation between the two verses tends to give more weight to the latter of these [TH]. It introduces another consideration that should keep the Galatians from becoming circumcised [NCBC]. It refers to 5:2 [NIC]. It repeats and reinforces the warning given in 5:2. It does not imply that Paul had already given them this warning when he was with them [NIGTC]. Or, it may refer to a statement that Paul previously made to the Galatians when he was with them [WBC]. It must refer to a statement that Paul previously made to the Galatians (see 4:16 and 1:9) [ICC]. It states that

Paul has testified to the Galatians at a previous time. It happened during Paul's second tour through Galatia when he brought with him the resolution from the Jerusalem conference which asked the Galatian Christians to abstain from certain things for their own good and the good of their Jewish fellow Christians [Lns].

QUESTION—Who is referred to by παντὶ ἀνθρώπῳ περιτεμνομένῳ 'every man circumcised'?

It refers to every Gentile Christian who is about to be circumcised to fulfill a legal obligation to be saved [NIC]. As in 5:2, it suggests that Paul is speaking to someone who has not become circumcised, but is considering it [TH]. It is addressed to every man who is considering circumcision [ICC]. It is not limited to those in Galatia or to those in Christian churches and is directed to individual men [SSA].

that he-is (a) debtor[a] to-do[b] all[c] the law.[d]

LEXICON—a. ὀφειλέτης (LN **71.27**) (BAGD 2.b. p. 598): 'debtor, one who is obligated to do something' [BAGD], 'one who is obliged or obligated to do something, one who must' [LN]. The phrase ὀφειλέτης ἐστίν 'he is a debtor' [KJV] is also translated 'he is under obligation' [Mor; NASB, REB], 'he is obligated' [BNTC, WBC; NET, NIV], 'he is obliged' [Herm; NRSV, TEV], 'he obligates himself' [GW], 'he/you must' [SSA; CEV, NCV, NLT].

b. aorist act. infin. of ποιέω (LN 42.7, 90.45) (BAGD I.1.c.α. p. 682): 'to do' [BAGD, BNTC, Herm, LN (42.7, 90.45); GW, KJV], 'to perform' [LN (42.7, 90.45)], 'to practice' [BAGD, LN (90.45)], 'to carry out' [BAGD, LN (42.7)], 'to keep' [BAGD, Mor; NASB, REB], 'to obey' [WBC; CEV, NET, NIV, NLT, NRSV, TEV], 'to follow' [NCV], 'to comply with' [SSA].

c. ὅλος (LN 63.1): 'all' [LN; NCV], 'whole' [BNTC, Herm, LN, Mor, SSA, WBC; CEV, KJV, NASB, NET, NIV, NLT, TEV], 'entire' [LN; NRSV, REB], 'everything (Moses' Teachings demand)' [GW].

d. νόμος (LN 33.55, 33.333) (BAGD 3. p. 542 *twice*): 'Law' [Herm, LN (33.55); CEV, NASB, TEV], 'law' [BNTC, LN (33.333), Mor, WBC; KJV, NCV, NET, NIV, NRSV, REB], 'Mosaic law' [SSA], 'Moses' Teachings' [GW], 'law of Moses' [NLT]. It refers to the law which Moses received from God [BAGD].

QUESTION—What law is meant by νόμος here?

It refers to the Mosaic law [SSA, WBC; GW, NLT]. It refers to the Torah [Herm]. It refers to the whole body of Old Testament statutes interpreted legalistically [ICC]. It means everything that is written in the book of the law [BNTC].

5:4 You-have-been-estranged[a] from[b] Christ,

LEXICON—a. aorist pass. indic. of καταργέω (LN 13.100) (BAGD 3. p. 417): 'to be estranged' [BAGD, BNTC], 'to become estranged' [Herm], 'to come to an end' [LN], 'to be separated' [SSA], 'to be alienated' [Mor,

WBC; NET, NIV], 'to be cut off' [GW, NLT, REB], 'to be severed' [NASB]. This passive verb is also translated actively with 'you' as the subject: 'to cut off' [CEV, NRSV, TEV]. This entire clause is translated 'Christ is become of no effect unto you' [KJV], 'your life with Christ is over' [NCV].

  b. ἀπό with genitive object (LN 89.122): 'from' [BNTC, Herm, LN, Mor, SSA, WBC; all versions except KJV, NCV]. See a. [KJV, NCV].

QUESTION—What is meant by this clause?

Paul is saying that justification can only come about because of what Christ has done. Attempting to be justified by the law is the same as rejecting God's way of justification and this will result in alienation from Christ [Mor]. It means that they have been removed from Christ's area of operation and, therefore, completely cut off from relations with him [NIC]. It means that they are no longer in union and fellowship with Christ [TH]. Paul had spoken before as if the matter was a possibility. Here he speaks to those affected as if it has already happened. This was to make the consequences of their proposed action more vivid [NCBC].

you-who are-trying-to-be-justified[a] by[b] (the) Law,[c]

LEXICON—a. pres. pass. indic. of δικαιόω (LN 34.46) (BAGD 3.a. p. 197): 'to be justified' [BAGD, BNTC, Herm, Mor, SSA; KJV, NASB, NIV, NRSV, REB], 'to be put right with' [LN; TEV], 'to be acquitted' [BAGD], 'to be made righteous' [WBC], 'to be made right with' [NCV], 'to be declared righteous' [NET]. This passive verb is also translated actively with 'you' as the subject: 'try to please God' [CEV], 'try to earn God's approval' [GW], 'try to make right with' [NLT].

  b. ἐν with dative object (LN 89.76, 90.10): 'by' [BNTC, Herm, LN (89.76, 90.10), Mor, SSA, WBC; GW, KJV, NASB, NET, NIV, NRSV], 'by keeping' [NLT], 'by obeying' [CEV, TEV], 'by way of' [REB], 'by means of' [LN (89.76)], 'through' [LN (89.76); NCV].

  c. νόμος (LN 33.55, 33.333): 'Law' [Herm, LN (33.55); CEV, TEV], 'law' [BNTC, LN (33.333), Mor, WBC; all versions except CEV, GW, TEV]. This singular form of the noun is also translated as plural: 'laws' [GW]. The phrase ἐν νόμῳ 'by law' is translated 'by God because you comply with the Mosaic law' [SSA].

QUESTION—Who is Paul writing to in this clause?

He is writing to those Galatians who have accepted the legalistic principle and were seeking justification by following the law [ICC, SSA, TH; GW, KJV, NASB, NET, NIV, NRSV, TEV].

QUESTION—What relationship is indicated by ἐν 'by'?

  It means 'by way of the law' [NIC, NTC; REB], that is, 'by doing what the law demands' [NIC]. They seek to be justified by obeying the Law, or because they do what the Law says [TH]. It means 'in the sphere of the law' [ICC, NCBC]. It means 'in connection with', the connection being the fact that we drop Christ and grace by starting to do works of law [Lns].

QUESTION—What is the use of the present indicative verb δικαιοῦσθε 'you who are trying to be justified'?

It is the conative present, stating a tendency or attempt in present time [BNTC, ICC, Lns, NIC, NIGTC, NTC, WBC; GW, NASB, NET, NIV, NRSV, REB, TEV]: you are attempting to be justified. It is the subjective present and has the force 'endeavoring to be justified', 'seeking justification' [Alf].

you-have-fallen-from[a] the grace.[b]
LEXICON—a. aorist act. indic. of ἐκπίπτω (LN **34.26, 90.72**) (BAGD 3.a. p. 244): 'to fall from' [LN (34.26), Mor; KJV, NASB], 'to turn away from' [**LN** (34.26)], 'to be outside of' [LN (90.72); REB, TEV], 'to no longer experience' [**LN** (90.72)], 'to lose' [BAGD], 'to leave' [NCV], 'to fall out of' [GW], 'to fall away from' [BNTC, WBC; NET, NIV, NLT, NRSV], 'to drop out of' [Herm]. This clause is translated 'You disbelieved that God freely and fully justifies persons' [SSA], 'you have cut yourself off (from Christ) and his wonderful kindness' [CEV].

b. χάρις (LN 25.89, 88.66) (BAGD 3.b. p. 878): 'grace' [BAGD, BNTC, Herm, Mor, WBC; all versions except CEV, GW], 'favor' [LN (25.89); GW], 'good will' [LN (25.89)], 'kindness' [LN (88.66); CEV]. See a. [SSA].

QUESTION—What is meant by ἐξεπέσατε 'you have fallen from' grace?

It should not be understood as though grace has been taken away from them, but rather that they have turned their backs on it [ICC, TH]. They are hoping to save themselves by what they do, so they have left the region where grace is operating [TNTC].

QUESTION—What is meant by χάρις 'grace'?

It is the grace of God or of Christ [ICC, WBC]. It is all that Christ has done for them. It involves God's free favor towards them [NCBC]. Most translators prefer to interpret it as God's grace [TH].

5:5 For[a] we by-(the)-Spirit/spirit by[b] faith[c] await-expectantly[d] (the) hope[e] of-righteousness.[f]

LEXICON—a. γάρ (LN 89.23): 'for' [BNTC, Herm, LN, Mor, WBC; KJV, NASB, NET, NRSV, REB], 'because' [LN], 'since' [SSA], 'but' [CEV, NCV, NIV, NLT], 'however' [GW], 'as for us' [TEV].

b. ἐκ with genitive object (LN 89.77, 90.12): 'by' [Herm, LN (90.12), Mor; KJV, NASB, NET, NIV, NRSV], 'by means of' [LN (89.77)], 'as a result of' [LN (90.12)], 'from' [BNTC], 'through' [WBC; NLT, REB, TEV], 'because of' [CEV], not explicit [NCV]. The phrase ἐκ πίστεως 'by faith' is translated 'and because we(excl.) trust Christ' [SSA], 'faith causes' [GW].

c. πίστις (LN 31.85, 31.102) (BAGD 2.d.α. p. 663): 'faith' [BAGD, BNTC, Herm, LN (31.85, 31.102), Mor, WBC; all versions except NCV], not explicit [NCV]. See b. [SSA].

d. pres. mid. (deponent = act.) indic. of ἀπεκδέχομαι (LN 25.63) (BAGD p. 83): 'to await expectantly, to look forward eagerly, to expect eagerly' [LN], 'to await eagerly' [BAGD, BNTC], 'to eagerly await' [Mor, SSA, WBC; NIV, REB], 'to wait' [KJV, NASB, TEV], 'to wait eagerly' [GW, NCV], 'to wait expectantly' [NET], 'to eagerly wait' [NLT, NRSV], 'to expect' [Herm]. The phrase 'we by the Spirit by faith await expectantly the hope' is translated 'the Spirit makes us sure' [CEV].

e. ἐλπίς (LN 25.59, 25.61, 25.62) (BAGD 2.b. p. 253): 'hope' [BAGD, BNTC, Herm, LN (25.59, 25.61), Mor; KJV, NASB, NCV, NET, NRSV, TEV], 'the basis for hope, the reason for hope' [LN (25.62)], 'confidence' [GW], not explicit [CEV]. This noun is also translated as a verb with 'we' as the subject: 'to hope' [WBC; NIV, REB], 'to expect' [SSA]. This is translated 'to receive everything promised to us' [NLT].

f. δικαιοσύνη (LN 34.46) (BAGD 3. p. 197): 'righteousness' [BAGD, BNTC, Herm, Mor, WBC; KJV, NASB, NET, NIV, NRSV, REB], 'put right, in a right relationship' [LN], 'God's approval' [GW]. This noun is also translated as a verb with 'God' as the subject: 'to accept' [CEV], 'to put right with' [TEV]; as a passive verb: 'to be made right with' [NCV], 'to be right with' [NLT], 'to be justified' [SSA].

QUESTION—What relationship is indicated by γάρ 'for'?

It introduces a reason for what Paul has just said in 5:4 [Mor, NTC]. Paul presents an argument that in a sense explains the previous verse by pointing out the contrasts involved [TH]. It introduces the proof based on a contrary experience [Alf, Lt].

QUESTION—To whom does the pronoun ἡμεῖς 'we' refer?

The pronoun is emphatic, we Christians in contrast to others who hold to some form of legalism [Alf, ICC, Mor, NAC, TH, TNTC]. The change of person from second to first emphasizes the contrast between Paul, along with those who have his point of view, and those who are following some form of legalism [NCBC]. This refers to Paul and others who do not depend on the Law but on Christ, in contrast to those who depend on the Law [SSA, TH]. By changing to 'we' Paul includes himself and the Galatians. He does not divide the Galatians into two classes, those who are with him and those who have fallen from grace. Instead he includes all of the Galatians with himself [Lns].

QUESTION—Does πνεύματι refer to the Holy Spirit or a person's spirit?

1. This refers to God's Holy Spirit [Alf, BNTC, BST, Herm, ICC, Mor, NAC, NCBC, NIBC, NIC, NIGTC, NTC, SSA, TH, TNTC, WBC; all versions except GW]. Salvation is a miracle that takes place only by the actions of the divine Spirit [Mor]. Their hope is not vague or uncertain, it is kept alive by the indwelling Spirit of God [NIGTC]. Πνεύματι 'spirit' is used without the article, therefore qualitatively, but undoubtedly with reference to the Spirit of God [ICC].

2. This refers to a person's own spirit [Lns; GW]. This is simply 'spirit.' 'Law' deals with outward works; all of our waiting is inward, spiritual. It

is done by means of that in us which has spirit quality [Lns]. It refers to our spiritual nature [GW].

QUESTION—To what is ἐκ πίστεως 'by faith' connected?

1. It is connected with 'we wait for' [BST, ICC, Lns, NTC; GW, NASB, NET, NIV, NRSV]: but by faith we eagerly await. Our waiting grows out of faith. Faith is the source of our eager waiting [Lns].
2. It is connected with 'righteousness' [Lt, Mor; REB]: it is by the Spirit and through faith that we hope to attain that righteousness.
3. It is connected with 'through the Spirit' [TEV]: the power of God's Spirit working through our faith.

QUESTION—How are the nouns related in the genitive construction ἐλπίδα δικαιοσύνης 'hope of righteousness'?

1. We wait for what we hope for, i.e., righteousness. It is clear that 'righteousness' is the object of the hope [ICC, NCBC]. Hope here is not simply some pious wish as it has come to mean in today's English usage. Instead it is a strong assurance. Paul means that he was eagerly looking forward to the full possession of that righteousness which he had inherited by faith [NCBC].
    1.1 'Righteousness' is one's legal standing, justification [Alf, BNTC, Herm, Lns, Lt, NIGTC, NTC, TH, TNTC; TEV]. The hope of righteousness is the hope of a favorable verdict in the last judgment [NIGTC, NTC]. The future tense of justification is expressed here. To be justified/counted acceptable to God not only at conversion, but in a continuing relationship with God that results in being accepted by God in the final judgment [BNTC]. 'Righteousness' means God's activity of putting men right with himself. This is what we hope for. Hope includes the elements of assurance and expectation which is also what we wait for. Righteousness here is in the future. However, no one should conclude that Paul did not believe in having a right relationship with God in the present [TH]. This genitive is objective. The hope whose object is perfect righteousness [Alf]. Righteousness before God will be granted only at the Last Judgment. Now it is a matter of hope. It is not visible and obtainable now, but because of the gift of the Spirit which the Galatians have experienced, and the 'arguments' which the readers have read in chapters 3 and 4, this hope could and should be a matter of certainty even in this life [Herm].
    1.2 'Righteousness' consists of legal standing and ethical behavior [ICC]. The word δικαιοσύνη 'righteousness' is best understood in its inclusive sense, having reference both to ethical character and to forensic standing [ICC].
2. We wait for what we as righteous people can hope for, i.e., future blessedness [BST]. We are waiting for 'the hope of righteousness' which is the expectation for the future which our justification brings. We are waiting to spend eternity with Christ in heaven [BST].

5:6 For in[a] Christ Jesus neither circumcision[b] avails[c] anything nor uncircumcision[d]

LEXICON—a. ἐν with dative object (LN 89.119): 'in' [BNTC, Herm, LN, Mor, WBC; KJV, NASB, NCV, NET, NIV, NLT, NRSV], 'in union with' [LN; REB, TEV], 'united with' [SSA]. The phrase ἐν Χριστῷ Ἰησοῦ 'in Christ Jesus' is translated 'If you are a follower of Christ Jesus' [CEV], 'As far as our relationship to Christ Jesus is concerned' [GW].

b. περιτομή (LN 53.51) (BAGD 2. p. 652): 'circumcision' [BNTC, Herm, LN, Mor, WBC; KJV, NASB, NET, NIV, NRSV, REB, TEV], 'the state of having been circumcised' [BAGD, SSA; CEV, GW, NCV, NLT]. The phrase οὔτε περιτομή τι ἰσχύει οὔτε ἀκροβυστία 'neither circumcision avails anything nor uncircumcision' is translated 'it makes no difference whether you are circumcised or not' [CEV], 'it doesn't matter whether we are circumcised or not' [GW], 'it is not important if we are circumcised or not' [NCV], 'it makes no difference to God whether we are circumcised or not circumcised' [NLT], 'circumcision makes no difference at all, nor does the lack of it' [REB], 'neither circumcision nor the lack of it makes any difference at all' [TEV].

c. pres. act. indic. of ἰσχύω (LN 74.9) (BAGD 4. p. 384): 'to avail' [KJV], 'to be valid' [BAGD], 'to have meaning' [BNTC, Herm; NASB], 'to be able to, to be capable of' [LN], 'to have any value' [WBC; NIV], 'to count for anything' [BNTC; NRSV], not explicit [SSA]. This is translated 'is of any force' [Mor], 'carries any weight' [NET]. See b. [CEV, GW, NCV, NLT, REB, TEV].

d. ἀκροβυστία (LN 11.52) (BAGD 2. p. 33): 'uncircumcision' [BAGD, BNTC, Herm, Mor, WBC; KJV, NASB, NET, NIV, NRSV], 'being uncircumcised' [LN, SSA; NLT]. See b. [CEV, GW, NCV, REB, TEV].

QUESTION—What relationship is indicated by γάρ 'for'?

It introduces a reason for what Paul has just said [Mor, NTC]. It explains why it is through faith [NIC], or through the Spirit [Lt].

QUESTION—What is meant by ἐν Χριστῷ Ἰησοῦ 'in Christ Jesus'?

It indicates being a real Christian. It emphasizes the importance of vital fellowship with the Savior. The Christian is not someone who has heard about Christ and is loosely attached to him. The Christian is wholly committed to Christ [Mor]. It means to be united with him in faith and in fellowship [TH]. It means on that basis which is created by Christ Jesus [ICC]. In union with Christ is being in the state of a Christian [Alf]. It describes those persons who are in Christ Jesus [SSA]. Paul defines clearly whom he was referring to by the 'we' in 5:5 with this phrase. The phrase 'in Christ Jesus' is more expressive than the adjective 'Christian', since there is a sense of 'abiding in', which is particularly relevant to Paul's purpose here [NCBC].

but faith[a] working[b] through[c] love.
LEXICON—a. πίστις (LN 31.85, 31.102) (BAGD 2.d.α. p. 663): 'faith' [BAGD, BNTC, Herm, LN (31.85, 31.102), Mor, WBC; all versions]. This phrase is translated 'but God investigates whether a person trusts Christ truly, that is, whether a person trusts Christ so that the person loves other persons' [SSA], 'All that matters is your faith that makes you love others' [CEV].
  b. pres. mid./pass. (deponent = act.) participle of ἐνεργέω (LN 42.3, 42.4) (BAGD 1.b. p. 265): 'to work' [BAGD, Herm, LN (42.3), Mor; KJV, NASB, NCV, NET, NRSV, TEV], 'to be at work' [LN (42.3)], 'to function' [LN (42.3)], 'to cause to function' [LN (42.4)], 'to express' [WBC; GW, NIV, NLT, REB], 'to operate' [BNTC]. See a. [SSA; CEV].
  c. διά with genitive object (LN 89.76, 90.8) (BAGD A.III.1.d. p. 180): 'through' [BAGD, BNTC, Herm, LN (89.76, 90.8), Mor, WBC; all versions except CEV, KJV, NLT], 'by means of' [LN (89.76, 90.8)], 'by' [LN (89.76); KJV], 'in' [NLT]. See a. [SSA; CEV].
QUESTION—What relationship is indicated by ἀλλά 'but'?
  It is the strong adversative [Mor].
QUESTION—What relationship is indicated by διά 'through'?
  It indicates the means through which faith works. Paul makes 'love' the means through which faith works [Lns]. It indicates mediate agency. Faith in Christ generates love and through it becomes effective in conduct [ICC]. Faith must work through the agency of love [NCBC]. Faith is trust in, submission to, and commitment of oneself to Christ. Love should be understood mainly as care and concern for people and not God's love for man or man's love for God [TH].

DISCOURSE UNIT: 5:7–12 [NIC, NIGTC, TNTC]. The topic is the cross versus circumcision [NIC], stern words for the trouble-makers [NIGTC], a personal aside [TNTC].

5:7 You-were-running[a] well;[b]
LEXICON—a. imperf. act. indic. of τρέχω (LN 15.230, **41.14**) (BAGD 2.a. p. 825): 'to run' [BNTC, Herm, LN (15.230), Mor, WBC; KJV, NASB, NCV, NET, NIV, NRSV, REB], 'to progress, to do better and better' [**LN** (41.14)], 'to behave' [LN (41.14)], 'to do' [CEV, GW, TEV], 'to get along' [NLT]. This clause is translated 'you were making such fine progress' [BAGD], 'You were believing the true message' [SSA].
  b. καλῶς (LN 72.12) (BAGD 1. p. 401): 'well' [BAGD, BNTC, Herm, Mor, WBC; KJV, NASB, NET, NRSV, REB], 'so well' [BAGD; CEV, GW, NLT, TEV], 'correctly' [LN]. This adverb is also translated as an adjective: 'good' [NCV, NIV]. See a. [SSA].
QUESTION—What is meant by running well?
  Paul uses an athletic metaphor for their spiritual progress [BNTC, NIBC, NIGTC, TH]. Paul reminds the Galatians of their former conduct before they were influenced by the Judaizers. It is to this time that the imperfect

ἐτρέχετε 'you were running' refers [ICC]. Paul compares the past performance of the Galatians with the runners in the stadium [Herm]. This clause refers to the Galatians' responses to the gospel in the past, implying that their present response was not that good [WBC]. Paul uses the athletic metaphor to describe the former Christian state of his readers [NCBC]. Paul uses the metaphor of running to express how the Christian life as a whole is directed towards a goal [NIC]. Paul compared the Christian life to the running of a race [BST, NAC].

who has-hindered[a] you not to-obey[b]/to-be-persuaded[b] by-the truth?[c]
TEXT—Some manuscripts omit τῇ 'the'. GNT does not deal with this variant in the apparatus but brackets it in the text, indicating that the Committee had difficulty making the decision.
LEXICON—a. aorist act. indic. of ἐγκόπτω (LN 13.147) (BAGD p. 216): 'to hinder' [BAGD, BNTC, LN, Mor; KJV, NASB, REB], 'to prevent' [LN; NET, NRSV], 'to cut in on' [WBC; NIV], 'to confuse' [SSA], 'to make (you) turn' [CEV], 'to stop' [GW, NCV, TEV], 'to interfere' [NLT]. The phrase τίς ὑμᾶς ἐνέκοψεν 'who has hindered you' is translated 'who got in your path' [Herm].
   b. pres. pass. (deponent = act.)/pass. infin. of πείθω (LN 33.301) (BAGD 3.b. p. 639): as a deponent: 'to obey' [BAGD, Herm, Mor, WBC; KJV, NASB, NET, NIV, NRSV, TEV], 'to follow' [BAGD; NCV, NLT, REB], 'to believe' [SSA]; as a passive: 'to be persuaded' [BNTC, LN], 'to be convinced' [LN], 'to be influenced' [GW], not explicit [CEV].
   c. ἀλήθεια (LN 72.2) (BAGD 2.b. p. 36): 'truth' [BAGD, BNTC, Herm, LN, Mor, WBC; all versions except NCV]. This noun is also translated as an adjective: 'true (message)' [SSA], 'true (way)' [NCV].
QUESTION—What is the function of the infinitive πείθεσθαι 'to obey'?
   1. It is progressive. This makes the meaning of the clause 'who has succeeded in preventing you from continuing to obey the truth?' [ICC]. It signifies 'to be keeping you from obeying' [WBC].
   2. It indicates the beginning of an action 'for you to start not to obey the truth' [Lns].
QUESTION—What is meant by τῇ ἀληθείᾳ 'the truth'?
   It means the gospel [BNTC, Herm, ICC, Lns, NAC, NIC, NIGTC, NTC, SSA]. It is the message which Paul had proclaimed to the Galatians [TH]. It is the true Gospel of Christ [Alf].

5:8 The persuasion[a] (is) not from[b] the-(one) calling[c] you.
LEXICON—a. πεισμονή (LN **33.303**) (BAGD p. 641): 'persuasion' [BAGD, BNTC, Herm, Mor; KJV, NASB, NET, NIV, NRSV, REB], 'that which persuades' [LN], 'persuasiveness' [WBC], 'arguments' [GW], 'change' [NCV]. The phrase ἡ πεισμονή 'the persuasion' is translated 'that which persuaded (you)' [**LN**], 'You are thinking like this' [SSA]. This entire clause is translated 'And that person was certainly not sent by the one who

chose you' [CEV], 'It certainly isn't God, for he is the one who called you to freedom' [NLT], 'It was not done by God, who calls you' [TEV].

b. ἐκ with genitive object (LN 90.16) (BAGD 3.c. p. 235): 'from' [BAGD, BNTC, Herm, LN, Mor, WBC; GW, NASB, NCV, NET, NIV, NRSV, REB], 'by' [LN; CEV], 'of' [KJV]. The phrase οὐκ ἐκ τοῦ καλοῦντος ὑμᾶς '(is) not from the one calling you' is translated 'not because God who is calling you is causing that you think like this' [SSA]. See a. [NLT, TEV].

c. pres. act. participle of καλέω (LN 33.307, 33.312) (BAGD 2. p. 399): 'to call' [BAGD, BNTC, Herm, LN (33.307, 33.312), Mor, SSA, WBC; all versions except CEV, NCV, NLT], 'to choose' [CEV, NCV], 'to call to a task' [LN (33.312)], 'to call to freedom' [NLT]. It means that God invited them to become his own people [TH]. Since there is no emphasis on the time of the calling, the present tense is used [NIGTC]. The present tense focuses on God's character, not the time individuals were called [Lt, NIC]. Or, the present tense indicates that God had not only called them in the beginning, he was constantly calling them to follow him [NTC].

QUESTION—What is meant by ἡ πεισμονή 'the persuasion'?

The article indicates that it refers to the persuasion just referred to in the previous verse [ICC, WBC].

1. This is to be taken in the passive sense of their being persuaded [Lt, Mor, SSA]. The Galatians were being persuaded by that new teaching to move away from simple trust in Jesus to a position of trust in Jesus plus keeping of the Jewish law [Mor].
2. This is to be taken in the active sense of the false teachers trying to persuade them [Alf, BST, Herm, Lns, NAC, NIC, WBC; TEV]. It means humanly 'contrived persuasion' in contrast to God's will and purpose [WBC]. This active sense better connects with the next clause, so that the Judaizers' attempts to persuade them is contrasted with God's calling them [NIC]. Since the verb is active, this means the persuasion to which they were yielding and cannot mean 'your persuasion', which would have the passive form [Alf]. The false teachers had persuaded the Galatians to abandon the truth of the gospel [BST]. The Judaizing missionaries must have been physically attractive, eloquent in speech, and able to put on a good show. The result of their actions was to persuade the Christians in Galatia to abandon the gospel of grace for their new theology of salvation [NAC].

QUESTION—Who is τοῦ 'the one' calling them?

God is the one who called the Galatians [Alf, BNTC, BST, Herm, ICC, Lns, Lt, Mor, NAC, NCBC, NIBC, NIGTC, NTC, SSA, TH, WBC]. It is God or Christ [NIC, TNTC].

5:9 (A) little[a] leaven[b] leavens[c] all[d] the lump-of-dough.[e]

LEXICON—a. μικρός (LN 59.15, 79.125) (BAGD 2.a. p. 521): 'little' [BNTC, Herm, LN (59.15, 79.125), Mor, SSA, WBC; all versions], 'little (bit of)' [BAGD], 'limited amount of' [LN (59.15)], 'small' [LN (79.125)].

b. ζύμη (LN 5.11) (BAGD 1. p. 340): 'leaven' [BAGD, BNTC, LN, SSA; KJV, NASB, REB], 'yeast' [BAGD, Herm, LN, Mor, WBC; all versions except KJV, NASB, REB].

c. pres. act. indic. of ζυμόω (LN 5.12) (BAGD p. 340): 'to leaven' [BAGD, BNTC, Herm, Mor, WBC; KJV, NASB, NRSV, REB], 'to ferment' [BAGD], 'to put yeast in' [LN], 'to raise' [SSA], 'to change' [CEV], 'to spread through' [GW], 'to make rise' [NCV, NET, TEV], 'to work through' [NIV], 'to spread quickly through' [NLT].

d. ὅλος (LN 59.29, 63.1): 'all' [LN (63.1), SSA; REB], 'whole' [BNTC, Herm, LN (59.29, 63.1), Mor, WBC; all versions except REB], 'entire' [LN (59.29, 63.1)].

e. φύραμα (LN 63.12, 79.92) (BAGD p. 869): 'lump of dough' [BAGD, BNTC; NASB], 'batch of dough' [BAGD, LN (63.12), Mor, WBC; all versions except KJV, NASB, REB], 'lump' [LN (79.92); KJV], 'mixture' [LN (63.12)], 'dough' [Herm, SSA; REB].

QUESTION—How is this proverb to be applied?

1. This applies to doctrine [Alf, BNTC, BST, ICC, Lns, Mor, NAC, NCBC, NIGTC, NTC, SSA, WBC]. This has to do with false theology that was perverting the Galatian churches [WBC]. The imagery of the small amount of yeast is used to describe the adverse teachings of the Judaizers. So far they hadn't had much success, but the apostle sees the potential danger of their teaching [NCBC]. The 'little leaven' is best understood in reference to the teaching of the 'agitators' [BNTC]. Here the little leaven refers to doctrine and not to persons. The whole lump refers to the Galatians and all of the doctrine they had believed [Lns]. The doctrine of circumcision that is taught by a few, is threatening to pervert the whole religious life of the Galatian churches [ICC]. A little false doctrine corrupts the whole mass (of Christians) [Alf].

2. This applies to the number of people involved [Lt, NIBC; NLT]. Paul is warning that even though there may only be a few teaching circumcision their influence could damage the nature of the Galatian churches [NIBC]. The prominent idea in this verse is that of a small and compact body disturbing the peace of the Church [Lt].

5:10 I am-convinced[a] with-respect-to[b] you in[c] (the) Lord

LEXICON—a. perf. (with pres. meaning) act. indic. of πείθω (LN 33.301) (BAGD 2.a. p. 639): 'to be convinced' [LN], 'to be persuaded' [BNTC, LN, Mor], 'to put (one's) confidence' [BAGD], 'to be certain' [SSA; CEV], 'to be confident' [Herm, WBC; NET, NIV, NRSV], 'to have confidence' [KJV, NASB], 'to be trusting' [NLT], 'to trust (in the Lord)'

[NCV], 'to feel confident' [TEV]. This verb is also translated with 'the Lord' as the subject: 'the Lord gives me confidence' [GW, REB].
  b. εἰς with accusative object (LN 90.23): 'with respect to, with reference to, concerning' [LN], 'with regard to' [BNTC, WBC], 'about' [LN, Mor; NRSV, TEV], 'in' [Herm; KJV, NASB], not explicit [SSA; CEV, GW, NCV, NET, NIV, NLT, REB].
  c. ἐν with dative object (LN 83.13, 89.119, 90.6) (BAGD I.5.d. p. 259): 'in' [BNTC, Herm, LN (83.13, 89.119), Mor, WBC; NASB, NCV, NET, NIV, NRSV], 'in union with' [LN (89.119); TEV], 'by' [LN (90.6), SSA], 'through' [KJV], 'to belong to' [CEV], not explicit [GW, NLT, REB]. It indicates a close personal relationship [BAGD].

QUESTION—What is the significance of the pronoun ἐγώ 'I'?
  It is emphatic [Alf, Lt, Mor, SSA, TH, WBC]. It emphasizes the personal, subjective character of the confidence. 'I, at least, whatever others think' [ICC], 'whatever be the case with others' [Mor], 'as for me' or 'on my part' [SSA], 'however others may evaluate matters, I at least have confidence' [WBC]. It is emphatic because of the contrast which Paul is wanting to stress by saying, 'although I have been speaking to you in a straight manner, I myself am confident over you' [NCBC].

QUESTION—What relationship is indicated by εἰς ὑμᾶς 'with respect to you'?
  The phrase εἰς ὑμᾶς 'with respect to you' identifies the persons toward whom Paul's confidence is directed [ICC, WBC].

QUESTION—What relationship is indicated by ἐν κυρίῳ 'in (the) Lord'?
  The phrase ἐν κυρίῳ 'in (the) Lord' indicates the basis for Paul's confidence [ICC, Lns, NCBC, NIBC, NIC, TH, WBC]. It indicates that Paul's assurance rests on a relationship to Jesus Christ [Mor]. Paul's confidence comes from his trust in Christ and from his knowledge that he and his Galatian friends are fellow members of Christ [NIGTC, NTC]. Paul's confidence about the Galatians was based on the love of God and the faithfulness of Jesus Christ. Paul firmly believed that the Lord had saved at least some of the Galatians [NAC]. Paul's confidence concerns the Galatians, but it is from the Lord [SSA]. Κυρίῳ 'Lord' refers to Christ [BNTC, ICC, NCBC, NIBC, NIC, NIGTC, TH, TNTC]. Paul's confidence was derived directly from his own relationship with Christ as Lord, from his commission from the Lord Christ, and from his conviction that Christ as Lord was directing his affairs and overseeing his relationships [BNTC]. It indicates the sphere in which Paul's confidence is exercised [Alf, Lt].

that nothing different[a] you-will-be-minded;[b]
LEXICON—a. ἄλλος (LN 58.36, 58.37): 'different' [LN (58.36); NCV, TEV], 'other' [Herm, LN (58.36, 58.37); NASB, NET, NIV], 'otherwise' [BNTC, Mor; KJV, NRSV], 'additional' [SSA], not explicit [NLT]. See b. [WBC; CEV, GW, REB].
  b. fut. act. indic. of φρονέω (LN **31.1**) (BAGD 1. p. 866): 'to be minded' [BAGD; KJV], 'to think' [BAGD, BNTC, Mor; NRSV], 'to believe'

198   GALATIANS 5:10

[NCV], 'to accept' [NET], 'to take' [Herm, WBC; NIV, TEV], not explicit [NLT]. This entire clause is translated 'that you will not take a different view' [**LN**; TEV], 'that you will do what I say, instead of what someone else tells you to do' [CEV], 'that you will not disagree with this' [GW], 'that you will adopt no other view' [NASB], 'that you will not adopt the wrong view' [REB], 'that you will value and comply with nothing additional' [SSA], 'that you will take no other view' [Herm].

QUESTION—What is referred to by οὐδὲν ἄλλο 'nothing different'?

It refers to the warning that Paul stated in 5:9. The Galatians will see that a little Judaistic leaven will eventually leaven the whole lump. Therefore, they should fear how they have started to go back into Judaistic legalism and stop [ICC, Lns]. Paul was confident that the Galatians wouldn't have a view different from his [BNTC]. It refers to what Paul said in 5:8–9 [WBC]. Paul believed that they had really received the gospel, therefore they must think no differently from himself [NIGTC, WBC]. Paul believed that those who have genuine faith in Jesus are not going to be persuaded to adopt a totally different way of seeking God and living for God. So Paul was confident that the Galatians would not think otherwise [Mor].

and the-(one) disturbing[a] you will-bear[b] the judgment,[c]

LEXICON—a. pres. act. participle of ταράσσω (LN 25.244) (BAGD 2. p. 805): 'to disturb' [BAGD; NASB], 'to unsettle' [BAGD; REB], 'to stir up' [BAGD, Herm], 'to throw into confusion' [BAGD, WBC; NIV], 'to distress, to distress greatly' [LN], 'to trouble' [BNTC, Mor; KJV], 'to confuse' [SSA; GW, NCV, NET, NRSV], 'to cause trouble' [CEV], 'to trouble and confuse' [NLT], 'to upset' [TEV].

b. fut. act. indic. of βαστάζω (LN **90.80**) (BAGD 2.b.β. p. 137): 'to bear' [BAGD, BNTC, Herm, Mor; KJV, NASB, REB], 'to undergo' [LN], 'to suffer' [**LN**, WBC; GW]. The phrase βαστάσει τὸ κρίμα 'will bear the judgment' is translated 'will be punished' [CEV, NCV], 'will be punished by God' [SSA; TEV], 'will pay the penalty' [NET, NIV, NRSV], 'God will judge' [NLT].

c. κρίμα (LN 30.110, 56.24, 56.30) (BAGD 4.b. p. 450): 'judgment' [BNTC, Herm, LN (30.110, 56.24), Mor, WBC; KJV, NASB], 'sentence, verdict' [LN (56.24)], 'condemnation' [BAGD, LN (56.30)], 'God's judgment' [GW, REB], 'penalty' [NET, NIV, NRSV]. This noun is also translated as an active verb with 'God' as the subject: 'to judge' [NLT]; as a passive verb: 'to be punished' [SSA; CEV, NCV, TEV].

QUESTION—Who is ὁ ταράσσων 'the one disturbing' them?

It should be understood as a generic singular [Herm, NIC, NIGTC, WBC]. If Paul thinks of an individual it is only as a representative of the whole. The real point that Paul is alluding to is to warn the Galatians of the judgment which will fall on anyone who distracts them from the truth [NCBC]. Many scholars believe that Paul has a specific person in mind, possibly the leader of the false teachers [TH]. It refers to any one who hereafter may disturb them. For rhetorical effect, their conduct is referred to not as fact but as a future possibility [ICC]. Probably there are several disturbers [NTC].

QUESTION—Whose judgment is referred to here?

It refers to God's judgment, not man's [BST, Herm, ICC, Lns, Mor, NCBC, NIBC, NIC, NTC, SSA, TH, TNTC, WBC; GW, NLT, REB, TEV].

whoever^a ever he-may-be.^b

LEXICON—a. ὅστις (LN 92.18) (BAGD 1.e.α. p. 586): 'whoever' [BAGD, BNTC, Herm, LN, Mor, WBC; all versions except GW], 'who' [LN; GW]. This entire phrase is translated 'even if he is an important person' [SSA].

b. pres. subj. of εἰμί (LN 13.1) (BAGD II.6.d. p. 224): 'to be' [BAGD, BNTC, Herm, LN, Mor, SSA, WBC; all versions].

QUESTION—What is meant by this phrase?

It implies that either Paul did not know who the agitators were or that knowing who they were he preferred to name no names [NIGTC, WBC]. It refers to someone who holds a high position [SSA, TNTC], possibly in the Jerusalem church [TNTC]. It might indicate that the person has a high position within the group. However, it could only emphasize how indefinite the reference is [TH]. It refers to any disturber [Lns].

5:11 But I, brothers,^a if still^b I-am-preaching^c circumcision,^d

LEXICON—a. ἀδελφός (LN 11.23): 'brother, Christian brother, fellow believer' [LN]. The plural form is translated 'brothers' [BNTC, Herm, Mor, SSA, WBC; NIV], 'brethren' [KJV, NASB], 'friends' [CEV, NRSV, REB, TEV], 'brothers and sisters' [GW, NCV, NET, NLT].

b. ἔτι (LN 67.128) (BAGD 1.a.α. p. 315): 'still' [BAGD, BNTC, Herm, LN, Mor, SSA, WBC; all versions except KJV, NCV, TEV], 'yet' [KJV], not explicit [NCV]. This adverb is also translated as a verb with 'I' as the subject: 'to continue' [TEV].

c. pres. act. indic. of κηρύσσω (LN 33.256) (BAGD 2.b.β. p. 431): 'to preach' [BAGD, BNTC, Herm, LN, Mor, WBC; all versions except NCV, REB], 'to proclaim' [SSA], 'to teach' [NCV], 'to advocate' [REB].

d. περιτομή (LN 53.51) (BAGD 1. p. 652): 'circumcision' [BAGD, BNTC, Herm, LN, Mor, WBC; all versions except CEV, NCV, NLT]. This noun is also translated as a passive verb: 'to be circumcised' [SSA; CEV, NCV, NLT].

QUESTION—What relationship is indicated by δέ 'but'?

Δέ 'but' with the emphatic ἐγώ 'I' puts Paul in sharp contrast with the false teachers [Mor].

QUESTION—What is the significance of the pronoun ἐγώ 'I'?

It is emphatic [Alf]. He places the pronoun forward for the sake of strong emphasis [Herm, Lns].

QUESTION—Who are the ἀδελφοί 'brothers'?
It refers to 'you, my fellow believers,' or 'you, who also believe in Christ' [TH]. By using ἐγὼ δέ ἀδελφοί 'but I, brothers', Paul aligns the Galatian believers as a whole with himself against the new teachers [SSA].

QUESTION—What relationship is indicated by εἰ 'if'?
By putting his proposition in an 'if' clause, Paul is anticipating that some are asserting that he favored circumcision in his preaching [NCBC]. Most translators favor the position that the conditional clause reflects a charge against Paul by his enemies. In that case it is implied that there was a time when Paul actually promoted circumcision. However, this conditional clause could also be interpreted as a hypothetical case: 'if I were preaching…' [TH]. This expresses an unfilled condition [ICC].

QUESTION—What relationship is indicated by ἔτι 'still'?
It contrasts Paul's present practice as an apostle with his former activity as a Jew [NIC]. Before his conversion Paul was a strenuous promoter of Judaism, but now he was changed [Alf]. The use of ἔτι 'still' with κηρύσσω 'I am preaching' implies that there was a time when he preached circumcision [ICC, WBC]. It refers to his pre-Christian life [ICC, NIGTC, WBC]. Or, the other missionaries accused Paul of being inconsistent. He preached the gospel free of circumcision to the Gentiles, but he continued to preach circumcision to the Jews [BNTC].

why still[a] am-I-being-persecuted?[b]

LEXICON—a. ἔτι (LN 67.128) (BAGD 2.c. p. 316): 'still' [BAGD, BNTC, Herm, LN, Mor, SSA, WBC; all versions except CEV, KJV, NLT], 'yet' [KJV], not explicit [CEV, NLT].

b. pres. pass. indic. of διώκω (LN 39.45) (BAGD 2. p. 201): 'to be persecuted' [BAGD, BNTC, Herm, LN, Mor, SSA, WBC; GW, NASB, NET, NIV, NRSV, REB, TEV], 'to be attacked' [NCV]. This passive verb is also translated as a noun: '(to suffer) persecution' [LN; KJV]. This passive verb is also translated actively with 'the Jews' as the subject: 'to persecute' [NLT]. This entire phrase is translated 'why am I in so much trouble?' [CEV].

QUESTION—What relationship is indicated by ἔτι 'still'?
It is not temporal as in the case of ἔτι 'still' in the preceding clause since he was not persecuted for preaching circumcision in those earlier days [ICC], so here it indicates logical opposition [Alf, ICC, Lt]. This argument is 'If I am still, as in my pre-Christian days, preaching circumcision, why do they, having learned this, continue that persecution which they began supposing that I was opposed to circumcision?' [ICC].

Then[a] the offense[b] of-the cross has-been-abolished.[c]

LEXICON—a. ἄρα (LN 89.46) (BAGD 3. p. 103): 'then' [BAGD, Herm, LN, Mor, SSA; KJV, NASB], 'as a result' [BAGD, LN], 'in that case' [BNTC, WBC; GW, NET, NIV, NRSV], 'if that were true, then' [TEV]. See c. [CEV, NCV, NLT, REB].

b. σκάνδαλον (LN **25.181**) (BAGD 3. p. 753): 'offense' [**LN**, WBC; KJV, NET, NIV, NRSV, REB], 'stumbling-block' [BAGD, BNTC, Herm, Mor; NASB]. This noun is also translated as a passive verb: 'to be offended' [SSA]; as an adjective: '(to be) offensive' [GW]. See c. [CEV, NCV, NLT, TEV].

c. perf. pass. indic. of καταργέω (LN 13.100, 13.163, 76.26) (BAGD 2. p. 417): 'to be abolished' [LN (76.26), WBC; NASB, NIV], 'to be put an end to' [LN (13.100)], 'to be put a stop to' [LN (13.163)], 'to be nullified' [Mor], 'to be removed' [BNTC, Herm; NET, NRSV], 'to be ceased' [KJV], not explicit [SSA]. This entire clause is translated 'the cross has ceased to be an obstacle' [BAGD], 'The message about the cross would no longer be a problem, if I told people to be circumcised' [CEV], 'In that case the cross wouldn't be offensive anymore' [GW], 'If I still taught circumcision, my preaching about the cross would not be a problem' [NCV], 'The fact that I am still being persecuted proves that I am still preaching salvation through the cross of Christ alone' [NLT], 'To do that would be to strip the cross of all offense' [REB], 'If that were true, then my preaching about the cross of Christ would cause no trouble' [TEV].

QUESTION—What relationship is indicated by ἄρα 'then'?

It may conclude 5:1–11 or be the reason for what is stated in 5:11a [WBC]. This statement can be taken either as the conclusion to the section 5:2–11a, or as the reason for 5:11a, or both [Herm].

QUESTION—What is meant by τὸ σκάνδαλον τοῦ σταυροῦ 'the offense of the cross'?

The message of Christ crucified is offensive to human pride. To preach Christ crucified is to tell sinners that they can't save themselves by their own good works and that only Christ can save them through the cross [BST]. The preaching of the cross provokes offense, or the cross itself is a stumbling-block because it stands for the way of salvation by grace through faith in the death of Christ. Salvation is only attained through the cross not through circumcision and the law [NIC]. Paul talks about the cross as the stumbling-block. The message about the cross means that people can't do anything to bring about their salvation. Christ had done everything that is necessary by dying in the place of sinners [Mor]. To have to receive salvation from the crucified one is an insult to all notions of proper self-pride and self-help. For many people this is a major stumbling-block in the gospel of Christ crucified [NIGTC]. The stumbling-block of the cross is that element in the death of Christ that would cause the Jews to oppose the whole event and hinder them from accepting Jesus as the Messiah. Paul implies that the stumbling-block is his interpretation of Christ's death that makes it possible for anyone to be accepted by God on simple trust, and not by doing what the Law requires [ICC, TH]. The crucifixion of the Messiah was in itself a stumbling-block to the Jews. To preach it as the means of atonement made it even more of a stumbling-block. Σταυροῦ 'cross' here stands for the atoning death of Christ [Lt]. The stumbling-block for the Jews was the fact that salvation is attained only through the death of Christ on the cross and not through other additional props such as circumcision [NTC]. The stumbling-block of the Christian message is, according to Paul, that salvation is proclaimed on the basis of Christ's crucifixion and death. This is an offense to the Jews because salvation is promised 'through faith in Christ Jesus' and by implication, renders the Jewish concept of salvation through observation of the Torah invalid. It is also a stumbling-block to the Greco-Roman culture because it implies that the Christian concept of salvation denies any validity to the way of Greek discipline [Herm]. It was unthinkable for the Jew that their Messiah could ever suffer the utter disgrace of crucifixion [NCBC]. The Jews were offended when Paul preached that Christ died on the cross and he didn't preach that a man must be circumcised [SSA].

QUESTION—What is meant by κατήργηται 'has been abolished'?

If circumcision could be maintained as the condition of salvation, the cross of Christ would cease to be a stumbling-block [Alf, ICC]. If it were true that Paul was still promoting circumcision, then his preaching about the death of Christ on the cross would no longer cause any trouble for the Jew [TH]. If Paul were preaching circumcision then the offense would cease [SSA].

5:12 Would-that[a] the-(ones) disturbing[b] you even will-cut-themselves-off/will-castrate-themselves.[c]

LEXICON—a. ὄφελον (LN 71.28) (BAGD p. 599): 'would that' [BAGD, BNTC, LN, Mor], 'O that' [BAGD, WBC], 'I would even wish that' [SSA], 'I would' [KJV], 'I wish that' [CEV, NASB, TEV], 'I wish' [GW, NCV, NET, NIV, NRSV], 'I only wish that' [NLT], not explicit [Herm; REB].

b. pres. act. participle of ἀναστατόω (LN 39.41) (BAGD p. 61): 'to disturb' [BAGD, SSA], 'to trouble' [BAGD, Mor, WBC; KJV, NASB], 'to upset' [BAGD, BNTC; CEV, TEV], 'to bother' [NCV], 'to unsettle' [NRSV], 'to incite to revolt, to cause to rebel' [LN]. This verb is also translated as a noun: 'troublemaker' [GW, NLT], 'agitator' [Herm; NET, NIV, REB].

c. fut. mid. indic. of ἀποκόπτω (LN 19.18 **fn 4**) (BAGD 2. p. 93): 'to cut off, to cut' [LN (19.18)], 'to make a eunuch of (oneself)' [BAGD, Herm; REB], 'to castrate' [Mor; GW, NCV, NET, NRSV, TEV], 'to emasculate' [SSA, WBC; NIV], 'to mutilate' [NASB, NLT]. Here it probably refers to severe mutilation of the penis or possibly to castration [LN (19.18 **fn 4**)]. This active verb is also translated passively: 'to be castrated' [BNTC], 'to be cut off' [KJV]. The phrase καὶ ἀποκόψονται 'even will cut themselves off' is translated 'would not only get circumcised, but would cut off much more' [CEV].

QUESTION—What relationship is indicated by καί 'even'?

It introduces a climax [Alf].

QUESTION—To what is referred by ἀποκόψονται 'to cut themselves off'?

1. This refers to castration [Alf, BNTC, Herm, ICC, Lns, Mor, NAC, NCBC, NIGTC, NTC, SSA, TH, WBC; GW, NCV, NET, NIV, NRSV, REB,

TEV]. This could also include those who refer to 'mutilation' [Lt; NASB, NLT], but mutilation could also refer to cutting off the penis [LN; probably CEV].
2. This refers to separation from the fellowship of the church [NIC; KJV].

DISCOURSE UNIT: 5:13–6:18 [REB]. The topic is guidance by the Spirit.

DISCOURSE UNIT: 5:13–26 [NET]. The topic is the practice love.

DISCOURSE UNIT: 5:13–18 [TNTC, WBC]. The topic is the true use of freedom [TNTC], life directed by love, service to others, and the Spirit [WBC].

DISCOURSE UNIT: 5:13–15 [BST, Mor, NAC, NIC, NIGTC]. The topic is the nature of Christian freedom [BST], love [Mor], the law of love [NAC], liberty, not license [NIC], the way of love [NIGTC].

5:13 For[a] you have-been-called[b] for[c]/to[c] freedom,[d] brothers;[e]

LEXICON—a. γάρ (LN 89.23) (BAGD 4. p. 152): 'for' [BNTC, Herm, LN, Mor; KJV, NASB, NET, NLT, NRSV], 'because' [LN], 'as for' [TEV], not explicit [SSA, WBC; CEV, GW, NCV, NIV, REB]. It expresses continuation or connection [BAGD].

b. aorist pass. indic. of καλέω (LN 33.307, 33.312) (BAGD 2. p. 399): 'to be called' [BAGD, BNTC, Herm, LN (33.307, 33.312), Mor, SSA, WBC; all versions except CEV, NCV], 'to be summoned' [LN (33.307)], 'to be called to a task' [LN (33.312)], 'to be chosen' [CEV]. This passive verb is also translated actively with 'God' as the subject: 'to call' [NCV].

c. ἐπί with dative object (LN 89.60) (BAGD II.1.b.ε. p. 287): 'for' [BAGD], 'for the purpose of' [LN], 'on the basis of' [Mor], 'to' [BNTC, Herm, WBC; all versions except KJV], 'in order that' [SSA], 'unto' [KJV].

d. ἐλευθερία (LN 37.133) (BAGD p. 250): 'freedom' [BAGD, BNTC, Herm, LN, Mor; NASB, NET, NLT, NRSV], 'liberty' [KJV]. This noun is also translated as an adjective: '(to be) free' [WBC; CEV, GW, NCV, NIV, REB, TEV]; as an adverb: '(you might live) freely' [SSA].

e. ἀδελφός (LN 11.23): 'brother, Christian brother, fellow believer' [LN]. The plural form is translated 'brothers' [BNTC, Herm, Mor, SSA, WBC; NIV], 'brethren' [KJV, NASB], 'friends' [CEV, REB, TEV], 'brothers and sisters' [GW, NCV, NET, NRSV]. Not explicit [NLT].

QUESTION—What relationship is indicated by γάρ 'for'?

It is continuative [BNTC, NIC] and reintroduces the theme of freedom that was stated in 5:1a [WBC]. It introduces an explanation [Mor]. It gives a reason for 5:12 [ICC]. It gives the reason why Paul was so passionate in his denunciation of the disturbers in 5:12 [Alf]. It may indicate another step in the argument [Herm]. 'For' at the head of a paragraph means 'in order to explain still further' [Lns].

QUESTION—What is indicated by the pronoun ὑμεῖς 'you'?
It's presence makes it emphatic [BNTC, ICC, Lns, Mor, NAC, NCBC, NIC, SSA, TH]. It accents the difference between the Galatians and those referred to in 5:12 [Lns, NCBC, NIC, TH].

QUESTION—What relationship is indicated by ἐπί 'for'?
1. It indicates the purpose for which believers have been called [NIC, NIGTC, SSA]: you were called for freedom.
2. It indicates the goal to which they have been called [Lns].

QUESTION—Who is the actor of ἐκλήθητε 'were called'?
It is God [BNTC, BST, Herm, Mor, NAC, NIC, NIGTC, NTC, SSA, TH, TNTC, WBC; NCV].

QUESTION—To what freedom is referred here?
It is freedom from Jewish nomism [WBC]. It is freedom of conscience, freedom of guilt. Christian freedom is freedom from sin not freedom to sin [BST]. It is freedom from the law [NIC, NIGTC]. It is freedom from the Torah [NIBC]. It is the freedom from complying with rules and rites [SSA].

only[a] not the freedom[b] for[c] (an) excuse[d] for-the flesh,[e]
LEXICON—a. μόνον (BAGD 2.c.α. p. 528): 'only' [BAGD, BNTC, Herm, Mor, WBC; KJV, NASB, NET, NRSV, REB], 'so' [CEV], 'but' [NCV, NIV, TEV], not explicit [GW, NLT]. This neuter is used as an adverb [BAGD]. This entire phrase is translated 'But although God has caused that you be free, do not deliberately indulge/gratify your naturally evil selves' [SSA].

b. ἐλευθερία (LN 37.133) (BAGD p. 250): 'freedom' [BAGD, BNTC, Herm, LN, Mor, WBC; all versions except KJV], 'liberty' [KJV]. This noun is also translated as a verb phrase: 'to be free' [SSA].

c. εἰς with accusative object (LN 89.48, 89.57): 'for' [BNTC, LN (89.57); KJV], 'for the purpose of' [LN (89.57)], 'to cause, with the result that' [LN (89.48)], 'as' [Mor, WBC; CEV, NCV, NET, NRSV], 'into' [GW, NASB, REB], 'to become' [Herm; TEV], not explicit [NIV, NLT]. See a. [SSA].

d. ἀφορμή (LN **22.46**, 89.22) (BAGD p. 127): 'excuse' [LN (89.22); CEV, GW, NCV, TEV], 'occasion' [LN (22.46); KJV], 'opportunity' [BAGD, BNTC, Herm, LN (22.46), Mor, WBC; NASB, NET, NRSV], 'favorable opportunity' [**LN** (22.46)], 'license' [REB], not explicit [NIV, NLT]. See a. [SSA].

e. σάρξ (LN 8.63, 26.7, 58.10) (BAGD 7. p. 744): 'flesh' [BAGD, BNTC, Herm, LN (8.63), Mor, WBC; KJV, NASB, NET], 'human nature' [LN (26.7, 58.10)], 'sinful self' [NCV], 'sinful nature' [NIV, NLT], 'physical nature of people' [LN (58.10)], 'corrupt nature' [GW], 'unspiritual nature' [REB], 'physical desire' [TEV], 'naturally evil self' [SSA]. The phrase τῇ σαρκί 'for the flesh' is translated 'to do anything you want' [CEV], 'for self-indulgence' [NRSV].

GALATIANS 5:13

QUESTION—What is indicated by μόνον 'only'?
It functions as a limitation to the action or state designated by the main verb [WBC]. It is used to call attention to an important addition to a preceding statement. Here it introduces a very significant element of Paul's teaching concerning freedom which has not been mentioned before [ICC].

QUESTION—What freedom is referred to here?
It is the Christian freedom [Mor]. It refers to the Christian freedom of the preceding clause [ICC, WBC]. It is freedom from rules and rites [SSA].

QUESTION—What is meant by σάρξ 'flesh'?
It means not merely the bodily passions and lusts, rather it means the human individual in his or her sin and depravity [Mor, NIC]. It is used in an ethical sense. It is that element of man's nature which is opposed to goodness and makes for evil [ICC, WBC]. It is our fallen human nature [BST]. It is that self-regarding element in human nature which has been corrupted at the source and which if unchecked produces the 'works of the flesh' [NIGTC]. Throughout Galatians 5–6 flesh is used as an ethical term with a negative connotation. Flesh refers to fallen human nature [NAC]. It refers to that aspect of the human self which refuses to acknowledge God and which leads to the doing of evil instead of good [TH]. The word 'flesh' sums up the impelling motive of the natural man, the moral bias of the man who is not energized by the Spirit [NCBC]. It seems to be selfish interest in contrast to God's interest [SSA].

but through[a] love serve[b] one-another.

LEXICON—a. διά with genitive object (LN 89.76, 90.8): 'through' [BNTC, Herm, LN (89.76, 90.8), Mor, WBC; GW, NASB, NET, NRSV], 'by' [LN (89.76); KJV], 'by means of' [LN (89.76, 90.8)], 'with' [LN (90.8); CEV, NCV], 'in' [NIV, NLT, REB]. The phrase διὰ τῆς ἀγάπης δουλεύετε 'through love serve' is translated 'let love make you serve' [TEV], 'constantly love each other and submit yourselves to serve' [SSA].

b. pres. act. impera. of δουλεύω (LN **35.27**) (BAGD 2.c. p. 205): 'to serve' [BAGD, BNTC, **LN**, Mor, SSA, WBC; all versions except NRSV], 'to become a slave to' [NRSV], 'to become a slave of' [Herm].

QUESTION—What relationship is indicated by ἀλλά 'but'?
It is a strong adversative and is often used to highlight a positive correlative of a preceding negative statement [ICC, WBC]. Here it contrasts freedom as 'an opportunity for the flesh' with freedom expressing itself 'through love' in service to others [WBC].

QUESTION—What relationship is indicated by διά 'through'?
It serves to identify 'love' as the conditioning cause of Christian service or that which makes possible the action of the verb δουλεύετε 'to serve' [ICC, WBC]. It indicates that love is the means by which they are to serve one another [Alf, NIC].

QUESTION—What love is meant here?
It is love between Christians [NIC].

QUESTION—What is meant by 'serve one another'?

It means 'to render service to', 'to do that which is for the advantage of'. Paul tells them to serve one another, not in the sense of subjection to the will, but of voluntary devotion to the welfare of one another [ICC]. This is not a single act of service, but a continuous attitude and activity [ICC, SSA]. To serve each other is to do our work for each other according to our Lord's will [Lns, SSA].

5:14 For[a] the whole law[b] is-fulfilled[c] in[d] one word,[e]

LEXICON—a. γάρ (LN 89.23): 'for' [BNTC, Herm, LN, Mor, WBC; KJV, NASB, NET, NLT, NRSV, REB, TEV], 'because' [LN], 'since' [SSA], not explicit [CEV, GW, NCV, NIV].

b. νόμος (LN 33.55, 33.333) (BAGD 3. p. 542 *twice*): 'law' [BAGD, BNTC, LN (33.333), Mor, WBC; KJV, NCV, NET, NIV, NLT, NRSV, REB], 'Law' [Herm, LN (33.55); CEV, NASB, TEV]. It refers to the law which Moses received from God [BAGD]. This singular form of the noun is also translated as plural: 'laws' [SSA], 'Moses' Teachings' [GW].

c. perf. pass. indic. of πληρόω (LN **33.144**) (BAGD 3., 4.b., p. 671): 'to be fulfilled' [BAGD, BNTC, Herm, Mor, WBC; KJV, NASB], 'to be brought to completion' [BAGD], 'to have (its) true meaning' [**LN**], 'to be given the true meaning to, to provide the real significance of' [LN], 'to be summarized' [SSA; GW], 'to be summed up' [CEV, NET, NIV, NLT, NRSV, REB, TEV], 'to be made complete' [NCV].

d. ἐν with dative object (LN 83.13): 'in' [BNTC, Herm, LN, Mor, SSA, WBC; all versions].

e. λόγος (LN 33.98) (BAGD 1.b.α. p. 478): 'word' [BNTC, Herm, LN, Mor; KJV, NASB], 'statement' [LN; GW], 'commandment' [WBC; NET, NRSV, REB, TEV], 'law' [SSA]. It refers to God's word [BAGD]. It refers to God's command [BAGD; CEV, NCV, NIV, NLT].

QUESTION—What relationship is indicated by γάρ 'for'?

It introduces a reason for the preceding statement [Mor]. It connects 5:14 with the final statement of 5:13 and, as a result, gives a reason why Christians should serve others through love [WBC]. It gives the reason that mutual service through love is important enough to be stated in 5:13 as the goal of the believers' freedom [NIC]. It connects this statement with 5:13c and also indicates a new matter to be introduced [Herm].

QUESTION—What is meant by ὁ πᾶς νόμος 'the whole law'?

It means the basic commandments that contain and sum up the whole law [WBC]. It is the Torah. Paul seems to be thinking of the law here in terms of a series of injunctions which is the usual English understanding of the word [TNTC]. The law is seen as a whole rather than as an aggregation of individual commandments [BNTC]. The whole law is the Jewish law not understood as a legalistic system, but as an expression of God's will [TH]. It means the whole law of Moses [Alf]. It refers to the Torah as a whole

[Herm]. It is the entire God-given moral law viewed as a unit [NTC]. All the commandments are viewed together [SSA].

QUESTION—What is meant by ἐν ἑνὶ λόγῳ πεπλήρωται 'is fulfilled in one word'?

1. It is fulfilled in (obeying) one word [Alf, BST, Lns, Lt, NIC, NIGTC; KJV, NASB]. We should probably understand λόγος in the sense of 'commandment' which it sometimes bears in the Pentateuch. The commandment in which the whole law is fulfilled is Lev. 19:18b [NIGTC].
2. It is summed up on one word [SSA; all versions except KJV, NASB, NCV].
3. It is both summed up and fulfilled in one word [NTC, TNTC].

in[a] the[b] (statement), "You-shall-love[c] your neighbor[d] as yourself."
LEXICON—a. ἐν with dative object (LN 83.13): 'in' [BNTC, LN; KJV, NASB], not explicit [Herm, SSA, WBC; all versions except KJV, NASB, NET]. The phrase ἐν τῷ 'in the (statement)' is translated 'namely' [Mor; NET].
b. ὁ (LN 92.24) (BAGD II.8.a. p. 552): 'the' [BNTC, Herm, LN; NASB], 'this' [KJV], not explicit [SSA, WBC; all versions except KJV, NASB, NET]. The neuter article stands before whole clauses [BAGD]. See a. [Mor; NET].
c. fut. act. indic. (declarative) of ἀγαπάω (LN 25.43) (BAGD 1.a.α. p. 4): 'to love' [BAGD, BNTC, Herm, LN, Mor, SSA, WBC; all versions].
d. πλησίον (LN 11.89) (BAGD 1.b. p. 672): 'neighbor' [BAGD, BNTC, Herm, LN, Mor, SSA, WBC; all versions except CEV], 'others' [CEV].

QUESTION—What is meant by πλησίον σου 'your neighbor'?
It means anyone with whom one comes in contact [Mor, NIC, NTC].

QUESTION—What relationship is indicated by ὡς 'as'?
Just as a person loves himself, he must love his neighbor [BNTC, Mor, NIBC, NIC, TH].

5:15 But if you-are-biting[a] and devouring[b] one-another,
LEXICON—a. pres. act. indic. of δάκνω (LN **20.26**) (BAGD 2. p. 170): 'to bite' [BAGD, BNTC, Herm, Mor, WBC; KJV, NASB, NET, NIV, NLT, NRSV], 'to harm' [**LN**], 'to criticize' [SSA; GW], 'to hurt' [NCV, TEV], 'to fight' [REB], not explicit [CEV].
b. pres. act. indic. of κατεσθίω (LN 20.45) (BAGD 2. p. 422): 'to devour' [LN, Mor; KJV, NASB, NET, NIV, NLT, NRSV], 'to consume completely, to destroy utterly' [LN], 'to tear to pieces' [BAGD, Herm, WBC], 'to tear at' [BNTC], 'to tear apart' [NCV], 'to discredit' [SSA], 'to attack' [CEV, GW], 'to harm' [TEV], not explicit [REB].

QUESTION—What relationship is indicated by δέ 'but'?
It marks a contrast to 5:14 [Herm, Mor].

QUESTION—What relationship is indicated by εἰ 'if'?

It introduces a construction that assumes the condition to be fulfilled and the present tense points to continuing action [Mor]. It indicates a condition and assumes the reality of the situation described [WBC]. The form of the conditional clause and the tense of the verbs imply that the apostle has in mind a condition which he knows to be, or thinks may be, even now existing [ICC]. Paul evidently is thinking of an actual case since he uses the present tense in the verbs [SSA, TH; CEV, NCV, NET, NIV, NLT, REB]. Or, no conclusion can be made from this conditional clause that actual biting and devouring occurred in Galatia. If such conditions were actual in Galatia, Paul would have undoubtedly written more than one line regarding them [Lns].

QUESTION—What is meant by ἀλλήλους δάκνετε καὶ κατεσθίετε 'you are biting and devouring one-another'?

Paul is comparing the Galatians to wild animals [NIC, NIGTC, TH; CEV, TEV]. This is a hyperbole that compares them with dogs or animals of prey biting and snapping at each other, while also tearing at and devouring their victim [BNTC]. The hyperbole describes mad beasts fighting each other so ferociously that they end up killing each other [Herm, WBC]. The verbs suggest wild animals involved in a deadly struggle [ICC, Lns, NCBC, NTC].

take-heed[a] lest[b] you-be-consumed[c] by[d] one-another.

LEXICON—a. pres. act. impera. of βλέπω (LN 27.58) (BAGD 6. p. 143): 'to take heed' [BAGD; KJV], 'to beware of' [BAGD, LN, Mor; NET, NLT], 'to watch' [BAGD], 'to watch out for' [LN, WBC; CEV, NIV, TEV], 'to pay attention to' [LN], 'to look out' [BNTC], 'to be careful' [GW, NCV], 'to take care' [NASB, NRSV]. This is translated 'I warn you that you must stop doing what you are doing' [SSA], 'see to it' [Herm]. This entire phrase is translated 'all you can expect is mutual destruction' [REB].

b. μή (LN 89.62) (BAGD B.1.b. p. 517): 'lest' [BAGD, BNTC, LN, Mor], 'that...not' [BAGD], 'so that...not' [LN], 'in order that...not' [LN, SSA], 'that' [Herm, WBC; GW, KJV, NASB, NET, NRSV], 'or' [CEV, NCV, NIV, TEV], not explicit [NLT]. See a. [REB].

c. aorist pass. subj. of ἀναλίσκω (LN 20.47) (BAGD p. 57): 'to be consumed' [BAGD, BNTC, Herm, Mor, WBC; KJV, NASB, NET, NRSV], 'to be destroyed' [LN; NIV], 'to be ruined' [SSA]. This passive verb is also translated actively with 'you' as the subject: 'to destroy' [CEV, GW, NCV, NLT, TEV]; as a noun: 'destruction' [REB].

d. ὑπό with genitive object (LN 90.1): 'by' [BNTC, Herm, LN, Mor, SSA, WBC; NASB, NET, NIV, NRSV], 'of' [KJV], not explicit [CEV, GW, NCV, NLT, TEV]. See a. [REB].

QUESTION—What is meant by ὑπ' ἀλλήλων ἀναλωθῆτε 'you be consumed by one another'?

Paul was warning the Galatians that their fighting with one another could lead to the disintegration of their fellowship and the disappearance of the churches of Galatia [NAC, NIGTC]. Either the Galatians themselves will be destroyed or the Christian fellowship will be destroyed [TH]. It means the destruction of the bond of Christian fellowship [Lns]. Your spiritual life together will be annihilated [Alf]. Here it probably means 'you might be made spiritually depleted or ineffective' [SSA].

DISCOURSE UNIT: 5:16–26 [GNT, Mor, NCBC; CEV, NCV, NIV, NLT, TEV]. The topic is the Spirit and the flesh [Mor], Christian life as life in the Spirit [NCBC], God's spirit and our own desires [CEV], the fruit of the Spirit and the works of the flesh [GNT], the Spirit and human nature [NCV, TEV], life by the Spirit [NIV], living by the Spirit's power [NLT].

DISCOURSE UNIT: 5:16–25 [BST]. The topic is the flesh and the Spirit.

DISCOURSE UNIT: 5:16–21 [NRSV]. The topic is the works of the flesh.

DISCOURSE UNIT: 5:16–18 [NAC, NIC, NIGTC]. The topic is conflict and victory [NAC], the Spirit the overcomer [NIC], walking by the Spirit [NIGTC].

5:16 **But I-say,**[a]

LEXICON—a. pres. act. indic. of λέγω (LN 33.69, 33.140): 'to say' [Herm, LN (33.69), Mor, WBC; KJV, NASB, NET, NIV, NRSV, TEV], 'to mean' [LN (33.140); REB], 'to tell' [BNTC; NCV], 'to discuss' [SSA], 'to advise' [NLT], 'to explain' [GW], not explicit [CEV].

QUESTION—What is the function of the phrase λέγω δέ 'but I say'?

The phrase λέγω δέ 'but I say' is a formula for giving additional information on a subject [Lt, NIC, SSA]. It ties together Paul's statements about love in 5:13b–14 with his present statements about the Spirit in 5:16–18. It also functions to direct the emphasis of what is being said to life in the Spirit [WBC]. In 5:2 and 5:16 it draws attention to Paul's personal appeal to his readers [NCBC, TH]. It is a common formula that Paul used to introduce a new section of material and to alert his readers to an emphatic point he was about to make [NAC]. It indicates an important statement [BNTC]. It refers to 5:13 and repeats and explains it [Alf]. It emphasizes the statement that is introduced [ICC]. It indicates that Paul is about to make an important statement [Herm].

Walk[a] **in/by-(the)-Spirit/spirit**[b]

LEXICON—a. pres. act. impera. of περιπατέω (LN 15.227, 41.11) (BAGD 2.a.β. p. 649): 'to walk' [BAGD, BNTC, Herm, LN (15.227), Mor; KJV, NASB], 'to behave' [LN (41.11)], 'to conduct (oneself)' [BAGD], 'to live' [BAGD, LN (41.11), WBC; GW, NCV, NET, NIV, NLT, NRSV]. This active verb is also translated passively: 'to be guided' [CEV, REB], 'to be directed' [TEV], 'to be empowered' [SSA].

b. πνεῦμα (LN 12.18, 26.9) (BAGD 5.d.β., 6.b., p. 677): 'Spirit' [BAGD, BNTC, Herm, LN (12.18), Mor, WBC; all versions except GW, NLT], 'Holy Spirit' [LN (12.18), SSA; NLT], 'Spirit of God' [LN (12.18)], 'spirit' [LN (26.9)], 'spiritual nature' [LN (26.9); GW]. The Spirit produces a spiritual type of conduct, unless frustrated by man's natural condition [BAGD].

QUESTION—What is meant by walking in the πνεύματι 'by the Spirit/spirit'?

1. It refers to the Holy Spirit [Alf, BST, ICC, Mor, NAC, NCBC, NIC, NIGTC, NTC, SSA, TH, TNTC, WBC; NLT]. It refers to the Spirit of God [ICC, NCBC]. It means living in close connection with the Holy Spirit [Mor]. It means 'let your conduct be directed by the Spirit' [NIGTC]. To 'walk by the Spirit' means to be under the constant moment by moment direction, control, and guidance of the Spirit [NIC]. To 'walk in the Spirit' means to go where the Spirit is going, to listen to his voice, to discern his will, to follow his guidance [NAC]. The phrase means that the Galatians should allow their whole life to be controlled or regulated by the Holy Spirit [TH]. 'Walking' is a metaphor used to indicate spiritual progress [Mor]. 'Walking' is a common Hebraism for 'conducting one's life' and thus is synonymous with 'living' [NIC]. The present tense of the imperative περιπατεῖτε 'walk' shows that Paul is not telling them to do what they have not done before. He is telling them to 'keep on walking by the Spirit' [NCBC, WBC]. The present tense indicates a present activity now in progress [ICC, NAC, NIC, TH].

2. It refers to spiritual life as opposed to 'flesh' [Lns; GW]. 'Live your life as your spiritual nature directs you' [GW]. In the following verse spirit and flesh are contrasted, referring to the new and old natures so here it means to keep walking by means of what is spirit in its nature, referring to the reborn and new man [Lns].

and no not[a] you-will-carry-out[b] (the) desire[c] of-(the)-flesh.[d]

LEXICON—a. μή (LN 69.5): 'not' [BNTC, Herm, LN, Mor, WBC; all versions except CEV, GW, NLT]. The phrase οὐ μή 'not not' is translated 'by no means' [LN], 'certainly not' [LN, SSA], 'won't' [CEV, NLT], 'never' [GW].

b. aorist act. subj. of τελέω (LN **13.126**) (BAGD 2. p. 811): 'to carry out' [BAGD, Herm, WBC; NASB, NET], 'to accomplish' [**LN**, SSA], 'to fulfill' [LN, Mor; KJV], 'to satisfy' [BNTC; TEV], 'to obey' [CEV], 'to follow through on' [GW], 'to do' [NCV, NLT], 'to gratify' [NIV, NRSV, REB].

c. ἐπιθυμία (LN 25.12, **25.20**) (BAGD 3. p. 293): 'desire' [BNTC, Herm, LN (25.12, **25.20**), SSA; NASB], 'lust' [LN (25.20), Mor; KJV]. This singular form of the noun is also translated as plural: 'cravings' [BAGD], 'desires' [WBC; CEV, NET, NIV, NRSV, REB, TEV]. This noun is also translated as a verb with 'flesh' as the subject: 'to want' [GW, NCV], 'to crave' [NLT].

d. σάρξ (LN 8.4, 8.63, 9.12, 26.7, 58.10) (BAGD 7. p. 744 *twice*): 'flesh' [BAGD, BNTC, Herm, LN (8.63), Mor, WBC; KJV, NASB, NET, NRSV], 'body, physical body' [LN (8.4)], 'physical nature' [LN (9.12)], 'physical nature of people' [LN (58.10)], 'human nature' [LN (26.7,

58.10); TEV], 'corrupt nature' [GW], 'sinful selves' [NCV], 'sinful nature' [NIV, NLT], 'unspiritual nature' [REB], not explicit [SSA; CEV].

QUESTION—What is meant by οὐ μή 'no not'?

The promise is stated emphatically by its use [BNTC, ICC, Lt, NCBC, SSA, WBC]. It expresses a strong negative statement relating to the future [NIGTC].

QUESTION—How should the clause οὐ μὴ τελέσητε 'by no means you will carry out' be interpreted?

Some have interpreted it as imperative, 'do not gratify' [TH; NRSV]. Most translations use a future indicative, 'you will not carry out' [TH; all versions except NRSV]. The words express a promise which will be realized by those who walk by the Spirit [BNTC, Herm, ICC, Mor, NAC, NCBC, NIC, NIGTC, SSA, WBC].

QUESTION—What is meant by ἐπιθυμίαν σαρκός 'the desire of the flesh'?

Our flesh is characterized by lust which stands for the strong, but sometimes evil desires that are associated with bodily living. The flesh is the physical part of our being and stands for that which is opposed to our spirit as well as the divine Spirit [Mor]. The flesh is the power that opposes God and enslaves human beings [NIGTC]. The flesh is that part of human nature which does not submit to God [TH].

5:17 For[a] the flesh[b] desires[c] against[d] the Spirit/spirit, and the Spirit/spirit against the flesh,

LEXICON—a. γάρ (LN 89.23): 'for' [BNTC, Herm, LN, Mor, WBC; KJV, NASB, NET, NIV, NRSV, TEV], 'because' [LN], 'since' [SSA], not explicit [CEV, GW, NCV, NLT, REB].

b. σάρξ (LN 8.4, 8.63, 9.12, 26.7, 58.10) (BAGD 7. p. 744 *twice*): 'flesh' [BAGD, BNTC, Herm, LN (8.63), Mor, WBC; KJV, NASB, NET, NRSV], 'body, physical body' [LN (8.4)], 'physical nature' [LN (9.12)], 'physical nature of people' [LN (58.10)], 'human nature' [LN (26.7, 58.10); TEV], 'naturally evil self' [SSA], 'corrupt nature' [GW], 'sinful selves' [NCV], 'sinful nature' [NIV, NLT], 'nature' [REB], 'your (desires)' [CEV].

c. pres. act. indic. of ἐπιθυμέω (LN 25.12) (BAGD p. 293): 'to desire' [BAGD, BNTC, WBC; NIV, NRSV], 'to desire very much' [LN], 'to rise in protest' [BAGD], 'to lust' [Mor; KJV], 'to want' [GW, NCV, TEV], 'to love' [NLT], not explicit [SSA]. This verb is also translated as a noun: 'desire' [NASB], 'desires' [Herm; CEV, NET, REB].

d. κατά with genitive object (LN 90.31) (BAGD I.2.b.γ. p. 406): 'against' [BAGD, BNTC, Herm, LN, Mor; KJV, NASB, NCV, REB], 'in opposition to' [LN], 'contrary to' [WBC; GW, NIV], 'opposite from' [NLT], 'opposed to' [NET, NRSV, TEV]. This preposition is also translated as a verb with 'self' as the subject: 'to oppose' [SSA]. This entire phrase is translated 'The Spirit and your desires are enemies of each other' [CEV].

QUESTION—What relationship is indicated by γάρ 'for'?
It confirms the opposition of flesh and Spirit stated in 5:16 and explains why that opposition exists [Alf, ICC, Mor, WBC].
QUESTION—What is meant by πνεύματος 'Spirit/spirit'?
See this question in 5:16.

for[a] these[b] are-in-opposition[c] to-one-another,

LEXICON—a. γάρ (LN 89.23): 'for' [BNTC, LN, Mor; NASB, NET, NRSV], 'because' [LN, SSA], 'and' [KJV], 'since' [Herm], not explicit [WBC; CEV, GW, NCV, NIV, NLT, REB, TEV].
  b. οὗτος (LN 92.29): 'this' [LN], 'these' [BNTC, Mor, SSA, WBC; KJV, NASB, NET, NRSV], 'they' [Herm; CEV, GW, NIV, REB], 'the two' [NCV], 'these two' [NLT, TEV].
  c. pres. mid. (deponent = act.) indic. of ἀντίκειμαι (LN 39.1) (BAGD p. 74): 'to be in opposition' [BAGD, Mor, WBC; NASB, NET], 'to oppose' [LN], 'to conflict' [SSA], 'to be contrary' [KJV], 'to be fighting' [CEV, NLT], 'to be opposed' [BNTC, Herm; GW, NRSV], 'to be against' [NCV], 'to be in conflict' [NIV, REB], 'to be enemies' [TEV].

QUESTION—What relationship is indicated by γάρ 'for'?
It gives a reason that these two are against each other which is that they are opposites [Alf].
QUESTION—What is meant by ταῦτα 'these things'?
It refers to 'the flesh' and 'the Spirit' [Herm, Mor, NAC, NCBC, NIC, NIGTC, SSA, TH, WBC].
QUESTION—What is meant by ἀντίκειται 'to be in opposition'?
The verb indicates hostility. In Paul's view the spirit and the flesh are irreconcilable adversaries [NCBC]. It indicates an ongoing opposition of the Spirit and the flesh [WBC].

so-that[a] not (the) things-which ever you-may-desire[b] these-things you-may-do.[c]

LEXICON—a. ἵνα (LN 89.49, 89.59) (BAGD II.2. p. 378): 'so that' [BAGD, Herm, LN (89.49, 89.59), Mor, WBC; KJV, NASB, NET, NIV, REB], 'so as a result' [LN (89.49)], 'that' [LN (89.49); TEV], 'for the purpose that' [LN (89.59)], 'in order that' [LN (89.59), SSA], 'as a result' [GW], 'so' [NCV], not explicit [BNTC; CEV, NLT, NRSV].
  b. pres. act. subj. of θέλω (LN 25.1) (BAGD 2. p. 355): 'to desire' [LN; KJV], 'to want' [BAGD, BNTC, LN, Mor, WBC; NET, NIV, NRSV, REB, TEV], 'to wish' [BAGD, LN], 'to choose' [SSA], 'to intend' [Herm]. The phrase ἃ ἐὰν θέλητε 'the things which ever you may desire' is translated 'what you feel you should' [CEV], 'what you intend to' [GW], 'the things that you please' [NASB], 'what you please' [NCV]. This entire clause is translated 'and your choices are never free from this conflict' [NLT].
  c. pres. act. subj. of ποιέω (LN 42.7, 90.45) (BAGD I.1.b.ε. p. 681): 'to do' [BAGD, BNTC, Herm, LN (42.7, 90.45), Mor, SSA, WBC; all versions

except NLT], 'to carry out, to accomplish' [LN (42.7)], 'to perform' [LN (42.7, 90.45)]. See b. [NLT].

QUESTION—What relationship is indicated by ἵνα ᾄσο τ'ατᾷ?
1. It indicates the result of the opposition [Alf, Herm, Lns, Lt, Mor, NIC, NTC, TNTC; all versions except CEV, NLT].
   1.1 The person is prevented from doing the good he desires [Lt, NTC, TNTC]. The phrase ἃ ἐὰν θέλητε 'what ever you may desire' is to be understood of moral strivings and yearnings, not baser impulses [TNTC].
   1.2 The person is prevented from doing the evil he desires [Lns, Mor]. Paul is saying that in our flesh we do not want to do the right things. We do not do the good things we ought to do [Mor]. The spirit in us succeeds in blocking some craving of our flesh [Lns].
   1.3 The person is prevented from doing either good or evil on his own volition [Alf, Herm, NIC]. The human 'I' wills, but it is prevented from carrying out its will because it is paralyzed through the flesh and the Spirit within. As a result, the human 'I' is no longer the subject in control of the body. The 'I' as the subject of willing is not identical with either flesh or Spirit [Herm].
2. It indicates the purpose of the opposition [ICC, WBC].
   2.1 It is the purpose of both the Spirit and the flesh [ICC, WBC]. The flesh opposes the Spirit with the desire that people not do what they want to do when guided by the Spirit and the Spirit opposes the flesh with the desire that people not do what they want to do when guided by the flesh [ICC, WBC].
   2.2 It is the purpose of God [SSA]. The Holy Spirit opposes your naturally evil self in order that you might not constantly do exactly what you naturally choose to do [SSA].

5:18 **But if you-are-being-led[a] by-(the)-Spirit/spirit,**

LEXICON—a. pres. pass. indic. of ἄγω (LN 36.1) (BAGD 3. p. 14): 'to be led' [BAGD, BNTC, Herm, LN, Mor, WBC; KJV, NASB, NET, NIV, NRSV, REB], 'to be controlled' [SSA], 'to be directed' [NLT]. This passive verb is also translated actively with 'you' as the subject: 'to obey' [CEV], with 'the Spirit' as the subject: 'to lead' [NCV, TEV]. This entire phrase is translated 'If your spiritual nature is your guide' [GW].

QUESTION—What relationship is indicated by δέ 'but'?

Δέ 'but' introduces a contrast [Mor]. Or, it functions here as a simple connective 'and'. It does not indicate contrast, but simply adds a further thought to the statements of 5:13–18 [WBC].

QUESTION—What relationship is indicated by εἰ 'if'?

It indicates a condition that assumes the reality of the statement 'since you are led by the Spirit' [WBC].

QUESTION—What is meant by this clause?

The tense of the verb suggests a continuing action 'if you continue to be led by the Spirit' [ICC, NTC, TH, TNTC]. To be 'led by the Spirit' is to 'walk by the Spirit'. To have the power to deny the desire of the flesh, to be conformed to the likeness of Christ more and more and to stop being under the law [NIGTC]. 'The Spirit leads you' should be understood as more or less equivalent to 'walk by the Spirit' in 5:16 [Lns, TH].

you-are not under^a (the) Law/law.^b
LEXICON—a. ὑπό with accusative object (LN 37.7) (BAGD 2.b. p. 843): 'under' [BAGD, BNTC, Herm, LN, Mor, WBC; KJV, NASB, NCV, NET, NIV], 'under the control of' [LN, SSA; CEV], 'to be subject to' [GW, NLT, NRSV, REB, TEV].
  b. νόμος (LN 33.55, 33.333) (BAGD 3. p. 542): 'Law' [Herm, LN (33.55); NASB, TEV], 'law' [BAGD, BNTC, LN (33.333), Mor, SSA, WBC; KJV, NCV, NET, NIV, NLT, NRSV, REB], 'the Law of Moses' [CEV], 'Moses' laws' [GW]. It refers to the law which Moses received from God [BAGD].

QUESTION—What law is referred to by the noun νόμον 'law'?

'Law' here is understood by the majority of scholars to refer to the Jewish law. However, since the noun does not have an article, some scholars understand it as referring to any law, whether Jewish or Gentile [Mor, TH]. It refers to that legalistic system from which Paul is trying to keep his readers free. See 3:23, 4:4, 5, 21 [ICC]. This refers to the Torah [Herm].

DISCOURSE UNIT: 5:19–26 [WBC]. The topic is the works of the flesh and the fruit of the Spirit.

DISCOURSE UNIT: 5:19–21 [NAC, NIC, NIGTC, TNTC]. The topic is the works of the flesh [NAC, NIC, NIGTC], the natural results of human nature [TNTC].

5:19 Now^a the works^b of-(the)-flesh^c are evident,^d
LEXICON—a. δέ (LN 89.124): 'now' [LN, SSA, WBC; GW, KJV, NASB, NET, NRSV], 'but' [LN, Mor], 'on the other hand' [LN], 'and' [BNTC], not explicit [Herm; CEV, NCV, NIV, NLT, REB, TEV].
  b. ἔργον (LN 42.11) (BAGD 1.c.β. p. 308): 'work, deed' [BAGD, LN], 'act' [LN], 'behavior' [REB]. The plural form of the noun is translated 'works' [BNTC, Herm, Mor, WBC; KJV, NET, NRSV], 'effects' [GW], 'deeds' [NASB], 'things' [NCV], 'acts' [NIV], 'desires' [NLT]. This noun is also translated as a verb: '(how people) think and act' [SSA], 'what (human nature) does' [TEV], '(people's desires) make them give in' [CEV].
  c. σάρξ (LN 8.4, 8.63, 9.12, **26.7**, 58.10) (BAGD 7. p. 744): 'flesh' [BAGD, BNTC, Herm, LN (8.63), Mor, WBC; KJV, NASB, NET, NRSV], 'body, physical body' [LN (8.4)], 'physical nature' [LN (9.12)], 'physical nature of people' [LN (58.10)], 'human nature' [LN (**26.7**, 58.10); TEV], 'naturally evil selves' [SSA], 'corrupt nature' [GW], 'sinful self' [NCV],

'sinful nature' [NIV, NLT], 'people's desires' [CEV], 'unspiritual nature' [REB].
d. φανερός (LN 28.58) (BAGD 1. p. 852): 'evident' [BAGD, Herm, LN; NASB], 'clear' [BAGD, LN; NCV], 'plain' [BAGD, BNTC, LN; TEV], 'obvious' [WBC; GW, NET, NIV, NRSV], 'manifest' [Mor; KJV], 'familiar' [SSA], not explicit [CEV, NLT]. This adjective is also translated as a verb with 'anyone' as the subject: 'to see' [REB].

QUESTION—What relationship is indicated by δέ 'now'?

It is resumptive in function, not adversative [ICC, WBC].

QUESTION—How are the nouns related in the genitive construction ἔργα τῆς σαρκός 'works of the flesh'?

These are the deeds people do when they are controlled by their sinful impulses [Mor]. Evil deeds are done and therefore called 'works.' They are done by man, but in reality they are the work of the flesh, which dominates man and dictates his activities [Herm]. 'Works' are regarded sufficiently comprehensively to include not only overt deeds but also attitudes [NCBC]. Those things which express the character of the flesh and its desires [BNTC].

QUESTION—What is meant by φανερός 'evident/clear'?

It suggests common knowledge, implying that one does not need the Mosaic law to identify the wrongness of what follows [WBC]. Paul is saying that it is well known and anyone can recognize it as 'works of the flesh' [TH]. They are the kind of things which are well known to everyone [NCBC].

which[a] (things) are sexual-immorality,[b] uncleanness,[c] licentiousness,[d]

TEXT—Some manuscripts add μοιχεία 'adultery' before πορνεία 'sexual immorality'. GNT does not mention this variant. Μοιχεία 'adultery' is read by KJV.

LEXICON—a. ὅστις (LN 92.18): 'which' [BNTC, LN, Mor, WBC; KJV, NASB], not explicit [all versions except KJV, NASB]. The phrase ἅτινά ἐστιν 'which are' is translated 'such as' [Herm], 'I will illustrate' [SSA].

b. πορνεία (LN 88.271) (BAGD 1. p. 693): 'sexual immorality' [Herm, LN, WBC; NET, NIV, NLT], 'fornication' [BAGD, LN, Mor; KJV, NRSV, REB], 'unchastity' [BAGD], 'unlawful sexual intercourse' [BNTC], 'illicit sex' [GW], 'immorality' [NASB], 'immoral ways' [CEV], 'immoral actions' [TEV]. This noun is also translated as a verb phrase or clause: 'being sexually unfaithful' [NCV], 'people unite sexually with persons who are not approved by God' [SSA].

c. ἀκαθαρσία (LN 88.261) (BAGD 2. p. 28): 'uncleanness' [BAGD, Mor; KJV], 'immorality' [BAGD, LN], 'filthiness' [LN], 'impurity' [BNTC, Herm, LN, WBC; NASB, NET, NIV, NRSV], 'perversion' [GW], 'indecency' [REB], 'filthy thoughts' [CEV], 'filthy actions' [TEV], 'impure thoughts' [NLT]. This noun is also translated as a verb phrase or clause: 'not being pure' [NCV], 'people use their sexual organs unnaturally' [SSA].

d. ἀσέλγεια (LN 88.272) (BAGD p. 114): 'licentiousness' [BAGD, Herm, Mor; NRSV], 'licentious behavior, licentious deeds, extreme immorality' [LN], 'debauchery' [BAGD, BNTC, WBC; NIV, REB], 'sensuality' [BAGD; NASB], 'lasciviousness' [KJV], 'promiscuity' [GW], 'depravity' [NET], 'eagerness for lustful pleasure' [NLT], 'shameful deeds' [CEV], 'indecent actions' [TEV]. This noun is also translated as a verb phrase or clause: 'taking part in sexual sins' [NCV], 'people are sensual' [SSA].

QUESTION—What relationship is indicated by ὅστις 'which'?

It introduces the list of works of the flesh and draws special attention to the qualitative aspect [NCBC]. It is qualitative, not merely 'which' but 'of a kind which'. It intimates that the list is not exhaustive [Lns, Lt].

QUESTION—What is meant by πορνεία 'sexual immorality'?

It means any unlawful sexual intercourse [BNTC, BST, ICC, Lns, NIGTC, NTC, SSA], including adultery and incest [NAC]. It refers to a particular instance of the more general 'impurity' ἀκαθαρσία [NCBC]. It refers to unlawful and immoral sexual relationships [WBC]. It refers to any kind of sexual sin or immoral acts [TH].

QUESTION—What is meant by ἀκαθαρσία 'uncleanness'?

It refers to the defilement of sexual sin and the result of being separated from God [NAC]. It refers to impure conduct in sexual relations [NIBC, NIC]. It refers to moral impurity [NCBC]. It refers to sexual impurity or looseness in a moral sense and the result of being separated from God [WBC]. It means sexual uncleanness [TH]. It includes uncleanness in deeds, words, thoughts, and desires of the heart [NTC]. It refers to sexual perversion [SSA].

QUESTION—What is meant by ἀσέλγεια 'licentiousness'?

It means the total loss of limits, the lack of restraint, decency, and self-respect [NAC, NIGTC]. It refers to an open and reckless contempt of propriety [BST, Lt]. It refers to looseness in sexual relationships [NCBC]. It means to disregard accepted rules and here it refers to sexual misbehavior and to conduct that knows no restraint [Mor]. It refers to sexual excesses resulting in indecent conduct [TH]. It refers to any indecent conduct, whether involving violation of the person or not [ICC]. It refers to the lack of self-control that characterizes the person who gives free play to the impulses of his sinful nature [NTC].

5:20 idolatry,[a] sorcery,[b] enmities,[c] strife,[d] jealousy,[e] angers,[f] selfishnesses,[g] dissensions, [h] divisions,[i]

LEXICON—a. εἰδωλολατρία (LN 53.63) (BAGD p. 221): 'idolatry' [BAGD, BNTC, Herm, LN, Mor, WBC; all versions except CEV, NCV, TEV], 'worship of idols' [TEV]. This noun is also translated as a verb phrase or clause: 'worshiping gods' [NCV], 'they worship idols' [CEV], 'people worship false gods and things which represent them' [SSA].

b. φαρμακεία (LN 53.100) (BAGD p. 854): 'sorcery' [BAGD, BNTC, Herm, LN, Mor; NASB, NET, NRSV, REB], 'magic, magic arts' [BAGD], 'magic spell' [LN], 'witchcraft' [WBC; KJV, NIV, TEV], 'drug

use' [GW], 'participation in demonic activities' [NLT]. This noun is also translated as a verb phrase or clause: 'doing witchcraft' [NCV], 'they practice witchcraft' [CEV], 'people perform rituals in order that evil spirits might act for them' [SSA].
c. ἔχθρα (LN 39.10) (BAGD p. 331): 'enmity' [BAGD, LN]. This plural form of the noun is translated 'hatred' [WBC; GW, KJV, NIV], 'hostility' [NLT], 'enmities' [Mor; NASB, NET, NRSV], 'quarrels' [REB], 'hostilities' [Herm], 'hostile feelings and actions' [BNTC]. This noun is also translated as a verb phrase or clause: 'hating' [NCV], 'they hate others' [CEV], 'people become enemies' [TEV], 'people are hostile to others' [SSA].
d. ἔρις (LN 33.447, 39.22) (BAGD p. 309): 'strife' [BAGD, BNTC, Herm, LN (39.22), Mor, WBC; NASB, NET, NRSV], 'discord' [BAGD, LN (39.22); NIV], 'contention' [BAGD], 'dispute, quarrel' [LN (33.447)], 'variance' [KJV], 'rivalry' [GW], 'quarreling' [NLT], 'contentious temper' [REB]. This noun is also translated as a verb phrase or clause: 'making trouble' [NCV], 'they are hard to get along with' [CEV], 'they fight' [TEV], 'people quarrel with each other' [SSA].
e. ζῆλος (LN 88.162) (BAGD 2. p. 337 *twice*): 'jealousy' [BAGD, BNTC, Herm, LN, WBC; GW, NASB, NET, NIV, NLT, NRSV], 'resentment' [LN], 'envy' [BAGD, LN, Mor; REB]. This singular form of the noun is also translated as plural: 'emulations' [KJV]. This noun is also translated as a verb phrase or clause: 'being jealous' [NCV], 'people become jealous' [CEV], 'they become jealous' [TEV], 'people fear that they lose something to another person' [SSA]. This verse denotes the various outbreaks of jealousy and the forms it takes [BAGD].
f. θυμός (LN 88.178) (BAGD 2. p. 365): 'anger, fury, rage, wrath' [LN]. This plural form of the noun is translated 'outbursts of anger' [BAGD; NASB, NET, NLT], 'outbursts of rage' [Herm], 'fits of rage' [WBC; NIV, REB], 'displays of anger' [BNTC], 'angry outbursts' [GW], 'angers' [Mor], 'anger' [NRSV], 'wrath' [KJV]. This noun is also translated as a verb phrase or clause: 'being angry' [NCV], 'people become angry' [CEV], 'they become angry' [TEV], 'people behave angrily' [SSA]. The plural form stresses numerous and repeated occurrences [TH].
g. ἐριθεία (LN 39.7, 88.167) (BAGD p. 309 *twice*): 'selfishness' [BAGD, LN (88.167)], 'selfish ambition' [BAGD, LN (88.167)], 'rivalry, resentfulness' [LN (88.167)], 'hostility' [LN (39.7)], 'dispute, outbreak of selfishness, contentiousness' [BAGD], possibly 'strife' [BAGD]. The plural form of the noun is translated 'rivalries' [Mor], 'disputes' [NASB], 'selfish ambitions' [BNTC; REB], 'selfish rivalries' [NET], 'quarrels' [Herm; NRSV], 'strife' [KJV], 'selfish ambition' [WBC; GW, NIV, NLT]. This noun is also translated as a verb phrase or clause: 'being selfish' [NCV], 'people become selfish' [CEV], 'they become ambitious' [TEV], 'people promote themselves and do not consider others/do despise

others' [SSA]. The plural form stresses numerous and repeated occurrences [TH].

h. διχοστασία (LN 39.13) (BAGD p. 200): 'dissension' [BAGD], 'discord, division' [LN]. This plural form of the noun is translated 'dissensions' [BNTC, Herm, Mor, WBC; NASB, NET, NIV, NRSV, REB], 'seditions' [KJV], 'divisions' [NLT], 'conflict' [GW]. This noun is also translated as a verb phrase or clause: 'making people angry with each other' [NCV], 'they argue' [CEV], 'they become ambitious' [TEV], 'people disassociate themselves from others' [SSA].

i. αἵρεσις (LN 33.241, 63.27) (BAGD 1.c. p. 24): 'division' [LN (63.27)], 'faction, dissension' [BAGD], 'heresy, false teaching, untrue doctrine' [LN (33.241)]. This plural form of the noun is translated 'factions' [BNTC, Herm, Mor, WBC; GW, NASB, NET, NIV, NRSV], 'heresies' [KJV], 'party intrigues' [REB], 'the feeling that everyone is wrong except those in your own little group' [NLT]. This noun is also translated as a verb phrase or clause: 'causing divisions among people' [NCV], 'they cause trouble' [CEV], 'they separate into parties and groups' [TEV], 'people associate only with those who agree with them' [SSA].

QUESTION—What is meant by εἰδωλολατρία 'idolatry'?

In a specific sense it means the worship of idols. In a general sense it means the worship of anything other than the one God [TH]. It means the worship of the image or of the god represented by it [ICC, SSA]. It means the worship of graven images and any substitute for the living and true God [NIGTC]. It means the open recognition of false gods [Lt].

QUESTION—What is meant by φαρμακεία 'sorcery'?

It means the use of any kind of drugs, potions, or spells and also magic of any kind [Mor]. It refers to the use of drugs to poison people and the use of drugs in sorcery and witchcraft [WBC]. In New Testament times this referred to the use of drugs with occult properties for a variety of purposes, especially for abortion [NAC]. 'Sorcery' translates a word which originally meant 'use of medicine or drugs,' but which has the derived meaning of the use of drugs for magical purposes [NIGTC, TH]. It refers to witchcraft, sorcery, magic art of any kind, without special reference to the use of drugs [ICC]. It is used here in the sense of sorcery, by means of which mysterious powers were erroneously ascribed to certain articles, formulas, or incantations [NTC]. It means the 'use of drugs' and was used with a purely medical sense. Greek writers used the word for magical practices in which drugs played a major role [SSA].

QUESTION—What is meant by ἔχθραι 'enmities'?

It refers to mankind's hostility against God [WBC]. The plural form stresses numerous and repeated occurrences [TH].

QUESTION—What is meant by διχοστασίαι 'dissensions'?

It refers to divisiveness in a group [NIBC]. It refers to divisions and schisms and the plural form stresses numerous and repeated occurrences [TH]. It refers to the formation of hostile splinter groups [NCBC].

QUESTION—What is meant by αἱρέσεις 'divisions'?
It refers to the development of various conflicting opinions [NCBC, WBC]. It refers to groups who hold to their opinions aggressively and divisively [NIBC]. It refers to when the divisions have developed into distinct and organized parties [Lt]. The plural form stresses numerous and repeated occurrences [TH].

5:21 envyings,[a] drunkennesses,[b] carousings,[c] and the (things) similar[d] to these,[e]

TEXT—Following φθόνοι 'envyings' some manuscripts add φόνοι 'murders'. GNT omits φόνοι 'murders' with a C decision, indicating that the Committee had difficulty making the decision. Φόνοι 'murders' is read by KJV, NET.

LEXICON—a. φθόνος (LN 88.160) (BAGD p. 857): 'envy, jealousy' [BAGD, LN]. This plural form of the noun is translated 'envyings' [BNTC; KJV, NET], 'jealousies' [Mor; REB], 'outbreaks of envy' [Herm], 'envy' [WBC; GW, NCV, NIV, NLT, NRSV], 'envying' [NASB]. This noun is also translated as a verb phrase or clause: 'feeling envy' [NCV], 'they are envious' [CEV, TEV], 'people want what others have/dislike others who have what they want' [SSA].

b. μέθη (LN 88.283) (BAGD p. 498): 'drunkenness' [BAGD, LN], possibly 'drinking-bout' [BAGD]. This plural form of the noun is translated 'drunkennesses' [Herm, Mor], 'drinking bouts' [REB], 'drunkenness' [BNTC, WBC; GW, KJV, NASB, NET, NIV, NLT, NRSV]. This noun is also translated as a verb phrase or clause: 'being drunk' [NCV], 'they get drunk' [CEV, TEV], 'people intoxicate themselves' [SSA]. The plural refers to repeated occurrences of drunkenness [NTC].

c. κῶμος (LN 88.287) (BAGD p. 461): 'carousing' [BAGD, LN], 'reveling, orgy' [LN], 'revelry' [BAGD]. This plural form of the noun is translated 'carousings' [Mor; NET], 'orgies' [WBC; NIV, REB], 'revelings' [KJV], 'wild parties' [NLT], 'carousing' [NASB, NRSV], 'excessive feasting' [BNTC], 'excessive banquets' [Herm], 'wild partying' [GW]. This noun is also translated as a verb phrase or clause: 'having wild and wasteful parties' [NCV], 'they carry on at wild parties' [CEV], 'they have orgies' [TEV], 'people revel/participate in orgies' [SSA].

d. ὅμοιος (LN 64.1) (BAGD 1. p. 566): 'similar' [LN; NET], 'like' [BAGD, Herm, LN, Mor, SSA; GW, NASB, NCV, NRSV, TEV], 'as' [BNTC]. The phrase καὶ τὰ ὅμοια τούτοις 'and the things similar to these' is translated 'and do other evil things as well' [CEV], 'and other kinds of sin' [NLT], 'and the like' [WBC; NIV, REB], 'and such like' [KJV].

e. οὗτος (LN 92.29): 'this' [LN], 'these' [BNTC, Herm, Mor, SSA; NASB, NCV, NRSV, TEV], 'that' [GW], not explicit [NET]. See d. [WBC; CEV, KJV, NIV, NLT, REB].

QUESTION—What is meant by φθόνοι 'envyings'?

It means to regard another person with ill-will because of what he has or is [NIC]. It means the displeasure aroused by seeing someone else have something [NTC]. The use of the plural means different acts or specific forms of envious desire [ICC, TH].

QUESTION—What is indicated by the phrase καὶ τὰ ὅμοια τούτοις 'and the things similar to these'?

It indicates that his list is not exhaustive [Herm, NTC], but that the Galatians will be able to recognize other 'works of the flesh' [TH]. It means that the works of the flesh are this kind of thing and from these examples it should be possible to recognize others [NCBC].

which I-say-already[a] to-you, just-as I-said-already,[b]

LEXICON—a. pres. act. indic. of προλέγω (LN 33.86, **33.423**) (BAGD 1. p. 708): 'to say already' [LN (33.86)], 'to tell beforehand' [BAGD], 'to warn' [**LN** (33.423), SSA, WBC; NCV, NET, NIV, NRSV, REB, TEV], 'to tell in advance' [BNTC, Mor], 'to tell before' [KJV], 'to tell again' [CEV, GW, NLT], 'to forewarn' [Herm; NASB].

b. aorist act. indic. of προλέγω (προεῖπον BAGD) (LN 33.86, **33.423**) (BAGD 2.a. p. 704): 'to say already' [LN (33.86)], 'to say before' [BAGD, WBC], 'to say previously' [BAGD], 'to warn' [**LN** (33.423)], 'to warn previously' [SSA], 'to warn before' [NCV, NET, NIV, NRSV, REB, TEV], 'to tell before' [BNTC, Mor; CEV, NLT], 'to tell in time past' [KJV], 'to tell in the past' [GW], 'to have forewarned' [Herm; NASB].

QUESTION—What is meant by ἃ προλέγω 'which I say already'?

It refers the reader forward to what will be said as introduced by ὅτι 'that' [WBC]. It refers to the sentence quoted in the following clause [Herm]. Paul now repeats what he told them before [Mor]. As a further warning, Paul says again what he already had said to them [NIC].

QUESTION—What is meant by καθὼς προεῖπον 'just as I said already'?

It points back to what Paul told his converts before and it seems Paul has in mind some portion of his past teaching when he was with them, since there is nothing in the immediate context that matches the content of what he states he is repeating in the last part of the sentence [WBC]. Possibly the previous occasion to which he refers was the instruction given during his missionary work among them [NCBC]. It probably refers to the same occasion which he has referred to previously. See 1:9, 4:16, 5:3 [TH]. It recalls a past event which must have been when Paul provided the Galatians with basic instruction [Herm, TNTC]. It refers to a time when Paul was with them [Alf]. This is probably during his second visit [Lt].

that the-(ones) practicing[a] such[b] (things) will- not -inherit[c] (the) kingdom of-God.

LEXICON—a. pres. act. participle of πράσσω (LN 42.8) (BAGD 1.a. p. 698): 'to practice' [BAGD, LN; NASB, NET], 'to do' [BAGD, Herm, LN, Mor, WBC; CEV, GW, KJV, NCV, NRSV, TEV], 'to carry out' [LN], 'to

commit' [BAGD], 'to behave' [BNTC; REB], 'to act and think' [SSA], 'to live' [NIV, NLT].
   b. τοιοῦτος (LN 64.2, 92.31) (BAGD 3.a.β. p. 821): 'such' [BAGD, Herm, LN (64.2)], 'such things' [Mor, WBC; KJV, NASB, NET, NRSV], 'such ways' [BNTC], 'of such a kind, of a kind such as this' [LN (92.31)], 'similar' [BAGD], 'like that' [BAGD, LN (64.2); REB], 'like this' [SSA; NIV], 'these things' [CEV, NCV, TEV], 'that sort of life' [NLT], 'things like that' [GW].
   c. fut. act. indic. of κληρονομέω (LN 57.131, 57.138) (BAGD 2. p. 434): 'to inherit' [BNTC, Herm, LN (57.138), Mor, WBC; all versions except CEV, TEV], 'to acquire, to obtain, to come into possession of' [BAGD], 'to receive' [LN (57.131), SSA], 'to gain possession of' [LN (57.131)], 'to share' [CEV], 'to possess' [TEV].

QUESTION—What is significant about the verb πράσσοντες 'practicing' in this clause?

Πράσσοντες 'practicing' is a present participle and it implies that they do these things constantly [ICC, Lns, Mor, NIBC, SSA]. Πράσσοντες 'practicing' refers to habitual practice rather than an isolated lapse [BST, NAC, NIC].

QUESTION—How are the nouns related in the genitive construction βασιλείαν θεοῦ 'kingdom of God'?

Βασιλείαν refers to the future kingdom [Mor]. Βασιλείαν 'kingdom' would actually be better translated as 'rule of God' rather than 'kingdom' [TNTC]. Βασιλείαν θεοῦ 'kingdom of God' refers to God's rule, to his activity as King [Lns, TH]. The word 'kingdom' refers to the reign of God which was to take place at the end of the age, but it may also include a present realization as it seems to have done in the teaching of our Lord [NCBC]. The kingdom of God for Paul is in the future. It is the heritage of the people of God in the age to come, the resurrection age [NIGTC]. Βασιλείαν θεοῦ 'kingdom of God' refers to the eschatological realm of heaven or paradise [Herm]. The apostle thought of the 'kingdom of God' here to be in the future and when it is inaugurated at the return of Christ from the heavens and the resurrection from the dead [ICC]. It refers to its future consummation in glory when Christ 'delivers up the kingdom to God the Father' [NIC]. The gift of the Spirit here and now is the first installment and guarantee of that coming heritage [BNTC, NIGTC]. This kingdom may be inherited by all believers in Christ. Those who consistently behave in ways that are opposed to God's nature show that they have not accepted God's rule through Christ in their lives. They will not have a part in the future kingdom [Lns, NIBC, NIC]. Those who continue to practice their former evil habits will not inherit the kingdom of God [NTC, SSA]. Κληρονομήσουσιν 'will inherit' brings out the point that people in the kingdom do not earn their place, it is a gift to them from him who died [Mor]. To inherit the 'kingdom of God' is to acknowledge God as King or to be under God's rule and authority [TH].

DISCOURSE UNIT: 5:22–26 [NAC, NIGTC, TNTC; NRSV]. The topic is the fruit of the Spirit [NAC, NIGTC; NRSV], the harvest of the Spirit [TNTC].

DISCOURSE UNIT: 5:22–23 [NIC]. The topic is the fruit of the Spirit.

5:22 But the fruit[a] of-the Spirit is love,[b] joy,[c] peace,[d] patience,[e] kindness,[f] goodness,[g] faith,[h]

LEXICON—a. καρπός (LN 3.33, 42.13) (BAGD 2.a. p. 404): 'fruit' [BNTC, Herm, LN (3.33), Mor, WBC; KJV, NASB, NET, NIV, NRSV], 'deed' [LN (42.13)], 'result, outcome, product' [BAGD], 'harvest' [REB]. The phrase Ὁ δὲ καρπὸς τοῦ πνεύματός ἐστιν 'But the fruit of the Spirit is' is translated 'But the Holy Spirit causes that people think and act very differently from that' [SSA], 'God's Spirit makes us' [CEV], 'But the spiritual nature produces' [GW], 'But the Spirit produces the fruit of' [NCV], 'But when the Holy Spirit controls our lives, he will produce this kind of fruit in us:' [NLT], 'But the Spirit produces' [TEV].

b. ἀγάπη (LN 25.43) (BAGD I.1.a. p. 5): 'love' [BAGD, BNTC, Herm, LN, Mor, WBC; all versions except CEV]. This noun is also translated as a verb phrase or clause: 'makes us loving' [CEV], 'people know that God loves them' [SSA].

c. χαρά (LN 25.123) (BAGD 1. p. 875): 'joy' [BAGD, BNTC, Herm, LN, Mor, WBC; all versions except CEV], 'gladness' [LN]. This noun is also translated as a verb phrase or clause: 'makes us happy' [CEV], 'people are joyful' [SSA].

d. εἰρήνη (LN 22.42, **25.248**) (BAGD 1.b. p. 227): 'peace' [BAGD, BNTC, Herm, LN (22.42, **25.248**), Mor, WBC; all versions except CEV]. This noun is also translated as a verb phrase or clause: 'makes us peaceful' [CEV], 'people are peaceful' [SSA].

e. μακροθυμία (LN 25.167) (BAGD 2.a. p. 488): 'patience' [BAGD, BNTC, LN, WBC; all versions except CEV, KJV], 'forbearance' [BAGD, Herm], 'longsuffering' [Mor; KJV]. This noun is also translated as a verb phrase or clause: 'makes us patient' [CEV], 'people are patient' [SSA].

f. χρηστότης (LN 88.10, 88.67) (BAGD 2.a. p. 886): 'kindness' [BAGD, BNTC, Herm, LN (88.67), Mor, WBC; all versions except CEV, KJV], 'benevolence' [LN (88.10)], 'generosity, goodness' [BAGD], 'gentleness' [KJV]. This noun is also translated as a verb phrase or clause: 'makes us kind' [CEV], 'people treat others kindly' [SSA].

g. ἀγαθωσύνη (LN **57.109, 57.109 fn28**, 88.1) (BAGD p. 3): 'goodness' [BNTC, Herm, LN (**57.109 fn 28**, 88.1), Mor, WBC; all versions except CEV, NRSV], 'generosity' [BAGD, **LN** (57.109); NRSV]. This noun is also translated as a verb phrase or clause: 'makes us good' [CEV], 'people are good' [SSA].

h. πίστις (LN 31.102) (BAGD 1.a. p. 662; 2.d.γ. p. 663): 'faith' [BAGD (2.d.γ. p. 663), BNTC, LN; KJV], 'faithfulness' [BAGD (1.a. p. 662), Herm, Mor, WBC; all versions except CEV, KJV, REB], 'reliability' [BAGD (1.a. p. 662)], 'fidelity' [REB]. This noun is also translated as a verb phrase or clause: 'makes us faithful' [CEV], 'people are reliable/ones whom others can trust' [SSA].

QUESTION—What relationship is indicated by δέ 'but'?

It is adversative and introduces a contrast [BNTC, Mor, SSA, WBC]. It is slightly adversative and introduces the fruit of the Spirit in contrast to the works of the flesh [ICC].

QUESTION—How are the nouns related in the genitive construction καρπὸς τοῦ πνεύματός 'fruit of the Spirit'?

These qualities are to be found in believers because of the change the Spirit of God has made in them. The word fruit indicates that the issue in this matter is not what man can do. A fruit is not something that is made or done [Mor]. The 'fruit of the Spirit' are not human products but the result of God's Spirit dwelling within men [NIC, WBC]. It seems certain that Paul believed there was a definite distinction between the 'fruit of the Spirit' and the spiritual gifts (charismata) mentioned in 1 Corinthians. The spiritual gifts were for special tasks and were not shared by all alike [NCBC]. The 'fruit of the Spirit' is the normal product of every believer led by the Spirit [Lt, NCBC, NIGTC, NTC, TH].

QUESTION—What is significant about καρπός 'fruit' being in the singular?

Paul is not speaking about a series of fruits that would be shared so that one believer has one fruit and another believer has a different fruit. Instead, he is speaking about a cluster in which all of these qualities are to be manifested in each believer [Mor]. The plural would suggest a variety of products. His real aim is to show the various aspects of the one harvest [NCBC]. The singular shows that the nine virtues mentioned are not different jewels, but are different facets of the same jewel [NIC]. The following qualities are various aspects of the generative power of the Spirit [NIBC]. It indicates that to Paul spiritual life is a unity and that all of these qualities are found in every believer who is led by the Spirit [TH]. The singular serves to present all the experiences and elements of character in the following list as a unity which make up the result of living by the Spirit [ICC].

QUESTION—What is meant by ἀγάπη 'love'?

1. It means expressions of love toward others [ICC, Mor, NAC, NIC, NIGTC, TH, WBC]. This love floods our lives so that we love God, Christ, and all mankind [NIGTC].
2. It means a unique inner experience or possession of believers in realizing God's love for them. Love is one of the trio of love, joy, and peace, and all are inner experiences made possible through the Holy Spirit [SSA].

QUESTION—What is meant by χαρά 'joy'?

To become a Christian means to pass from the domain of Satan into the blessing of being saved, which means love and joy [Mor]. It is joy that has a religious basis, grounded in a conscious relationship to God [ICC]. Joy results from our experience of God's grace and blessings, never dimmed by tribulation [Lns].

QUESTION—What is meant by εἰρήνη 'peace'?
1. It means tranquility of the mind [ICC, Lns, NCBC, SSA]. It probably has the same meaning as in Romans 5:1 based on a right relationship with God [ICC].
2. It means right relationships with others [BST, NIGTC, TH]. It means a Christian's peace with God [BST]. It means tranquility of mind as the result of the restoration of right relationships between people [TH].
3. It means both 1. and 2. above [Mor, NIC, NTC, WBC].

QUESTION—What is meant by μακροθυμία 'patience'?

It means being patient with other people by refusing to be irritated by the wrongs they do to us [Mor, NAC, SSA, WBC]. The main emphasis here is on a passive quality of bearing up under the stresses and strains of life [NCBC]. It means being longsuffering towards those who aggravate or persecute [BST, ICC, NIC, NTC]. It means forbearing and enduring in the midst of provocation and injury from others [TH].

QUESTION—What is meant by πίστις 'faithfulness'?
1. It means the quality of being worthy of being trusted by others [BST, ICC, Lns, Mor, NAC, NCBC, NIC, NIGTC, NTC, SSA, TH, WBC; all versions except KJV]. Since faith is a basic requirement in man's approach to God it cannot be regarded as part of the 'fruit of the Spirit' in the same way as the other virtues mentioned. Therefore, the word must mean 'trustworthiness', either in the sense of fidelity to standards of truth or in the sense of reliability in dealings with others [NCBC].
2. It means the quality of trusting others [Alf, Lt].

5:23 gentleness,[a] **self-control;** [b]

TEXT—Following ἐγκράτεια 'self control' some manuscripts add ἁγνεία 'purity', and other manuscripts add ὑπομονή 'endurance'. GNT rejects both of these additions with an A decision, indicating that the text is certain.

LEXICON—a. πραΰτης (LN 88.59) (BAGD p. 699): 'gentleness' [BAGD, BNTC, LN, WBC; all versions except CEV, KJV, TEV], 'mildness' [LN], 'meekness' [BAGD, LN, Mor; KJV], 'humility' [BAGD, Herm; TEV]. This noun is also translated as a verb phrase or clause: 'makes us gentle' [CEV], 'people treat others gently' [SSA].

b. ἐγκράτεια (LN 88.83) (BAGD p. 216): 'self-control' [BAGD, BNTC, Herm, LN, Mor, WBC; all versions except CEV, KJV], 'temperance' [KJV]. This noun is also translated as a verb phrase or clause: 'makes us self-controlled' [CEV], 'people control their naturally evil selves' [SSA].

QUESTION—What is meant by πραΰτης 'gentleness'?

It includes the quality of mildness, which is seen in a willingness to submit to the will of God [NCBC]. It implies a submissive and teachable spirit toward God that manifests itself in genuine humility and consideration toward others [NAC]. It can be understood as humble submission to God, but here it has the primary sense of gentleness and patience in dealing with others [TH]. It has the meaning of humility, courtesy, or considerateness in relating to others [NIBC].

QUESTION—What is meant by ἐγκράτεια 'self-control'?

It means mastery over one's desires and passions [Lns, NAC, NCBC, NIBC, NTC, SSA, TH]. It is the holding in of the lusts and desires [Alf].

against^a the such^b (things) there-is not (a) law.^c

LEXICON—a. κατά with genitive object (LN 90.31): 'against' [BNTC, Herm, LN, Mor, WBC; all versions except NCV, NLT], 'in opposition to' [LN]. This entire phrase is translated 'When people think and act like this, they do not violate any law' [SSA], 'There is no law that says these things are wrong' [NCV], 'Here there is no conflict with the law' [NLT].

b. τοιοῦτος (LN 64.2, 92.31): 'such' [Herm, LN (64.2), Mor, WBC; KJV, NASB, NET, NIV, NRSV, REB], 'of such a kind, of a kind such as this' [LN (92.31)], 'such as these' [BNTC; TEV], 'like that' [LN (64.2); GW], 'like this' [SSA], 'these' [CEV, NCV]. See a. [NLT].

c. νόμος (LN 33.55, 33.333) (BAGD 3. p. 542): 'law' [BAGD, BNTC, Herm, LN (33.333), Mor, SSA, WBC; all versions except GW], 'Law' [LN (33.55)]. This singular form of the noun is also translated as plural: 'laws' [GW].

QUESTION—What relationship is indicated by the phrase κατὰ τῶν τοιούτων 'against such things'?

1. This is neuter: against such qualities [Alf, BNTC, Herm, ICC, Lns, Lt, NIC, NIGTC, NTC, WBC; all versions except CEV, KJV, NLT]. Τῶν τοιούτων 'such things' refers to the items listed from 'love' through 'self-control' [WBC]. Τῶν τοιούτων 'such things' shows that the list just given is not exhaustive, but representative [Lns, NIC, SSA]. Since Paul has just completed a list of virtues, which are things, not people, it is natural to interpret his words as meaning 'against such virtues there is no law' [NTC]. It is not certain whether κατὰ τῶν τοιούτων 'against such things' is masculine or neuter, but the latter is more likely because of the analogy in 5:21 [Herm].

2. This is masculine: against such people who have these qualities [SSA, TNTC; CEV]. In view of the personal nature of the reference in 5:21 where οἱ τὰ τοιαῦτα πράσσοντες clearly means 'those who habitually behave thus', it is better to translate as 'such men' here. The phrase would then be translated 'The law was never meant for or directed against men like this' [TNTC].

QUESTION—What is meant by the phrase οὐκ ἔστιν νόμος 'there is no law'?

Νόμος 'law' without the article could be a reference to any law, but Paul is probably still thinking of the Mosaic law [NCBC, NIC, WBC]. This is a masterly understatement. It draws our attention to the fact that the kind of conduct that Paul has outlined is that which lawmakers everywhere want to bring about [Mor]. The phrase 'against such things there is no law' is probably best understood as an understatement given for rhetorical effect. It reiterates the assertion made in 5:14 that 'such things' fully satisfy the requirements of the law, since they go beyond the law's requirements [ICC, WBC]. The statement also makes it clear that the list of virtues is not given as a set of legal prescriptions, it is not to be taken as some kind of new law for Christians, as though by setting such goals and seeking to put them into practice believers can present themselves as acceptable before God [WBC]. No law forbids qualities like these. Such virtues in fact 'keep' or 'fulfill' the law [TNTC]. Paul points out that the Spirit-life is a real alternative because there is no need for any restraining law [NCBC]. Paul doesn't mean that the nine virtues which make up the fruit of the Spirit are not forbidden by law. What he means is that when these virtues are in view we are in a sphere with which law has nothing to do. These virtues cannot be legally enforced [NIGTC]. The law exists for the purpose of restraint, but there is nothing in the manifestations of the Spirit to restrain [BST, Lt, NIC, TH].

DISCOURSE UNIT: 5:24–26 [NIC]. The topic is the application and appeal.

5:24 **And the-(ones) of-Christ Jesus have-crucified^a the flesh^b with^c the passions^d and the desires.^e**

TEXT—Instead of Χριστοῦ Ἰησοῦ 'of Christ Jesus' one important manuscript reads κυρίου Ἰησοῦ Χριστοῦ 'of the Lord Jesus Christ', and other manuscripts read only Χριστοῦ 'of Christ'. GNT reads Χριστοῦ Ἰησοῦ 'of Christ Jesus' but with Ἰησοῦ 'of Jesus' in brackets in the text and with a C decision, indicating that the Committee had difficulty making the decision. 'Christ's' is read by KJV. 'Belong to Christ' is read by NET.

LEXICON—a. aorist act. indic. of σταυρόω (LN 20.76) (BAGD 2. p. 765): 'to crucify' [BAGD, BNTC, Herm, LN, Mor, WBC; all versions except CEV, TEV], 'to renounce' [SSA], 'to kill' [CEV], 'to put to death' [TEV].

b. σάρξ (LN 8.63, 9.12, 26.7, 58.10) (BAGD 7. p. 744): 'flesh' [BAGD, BNTC, Herm, LN (8.63), Mor, WBC; KJV, NASB, NET, NRSV], 'physical nature' [LN (9.12)], 'human nature' [LN (26.7, 58.10); TEV], 'corrupt nature' [GW], 'sinful nature' [NIV, NLT], 'old nature' [REB], 'naturally evil self' [SSA], 'sinful selves' [NCV], 'selfish (feelings and desires)' [CEV].

c. σύν with dative object (LN 89.105, 89.107) (BAGD 4.b. p. 782): 'with' [BNTC, LN (89.105, 89.107), WBC; KJV, NASB, NET, NIV, NRSV, REB, TEV], 'together with' [BAGD, Herm, LN (89.105, 89.107), Mor], 'along with' [GW], not explicit [CEV]. The phrase τὴν σάρκα ἐσταύρωσαν σὺν τοῖς παθήμασιν καὶ ταῖς ἐπιθυμίαις 'have crucified the flesh with the passions and the desires' is translated 'have renounced their naturally evil selves which had enjoyed and had desired evil' [SSA]. The phrase σὺν τοῖς παθήμασιν καὶ ταῖς ἐπιθυμίαις 'with the passions and the desires' is translated 'the passions and desires of' [NLT], by starting a new sentence 'They have given up their old selfish feelings and the evil things they wanted to do' [NCV].

d. πάθημα (LN **25.30**) (BAGD 2. p. 602): 'passion' [BAGD, LN]. The plural form of the noun is translated 'passions' [BNTC, Herm, Mor, WBC; all versions except CEV, KJV, NCV], 'affections' [KJV], 'selfish feelings' [CEV, NCV]. This noun is also translated as a verb with 'naturally evil selves' as the subject: 'to enjoy' [SSA].

e. ἐπιθυμία (LN 25.12, 25.20) (BAGD 3. p. 293): 'desire' [BAGD, LN (25.12)], 'lust' [LN (25.20)]. This plural form of the noun is translated 'desires' [BNTC, Herm, WBC; all versions except KJV, NCV], 'lusts' [Mor; KJV]. This noun is also translated as a verb with 'naturally evil selves' as the subject: 'to desire' [SSA]. This is translated 'the evil things they wanted to do' [NCV].

QUESTION—What relationship is indicated by δέ 'and'?

It is used in a connective, continuative fashion [ICC], not in a contrasting manner [WBC]. 'But' is used as a contrast [Alf].

QUESTION—How are the nouns related in the genitive construction οἱ τοῦ Χριστοῦ ['Ἰησοῦ] 'the ones of Christ Jesus'?

They belong to Jesus Christ [SSA; all versions except KJV]. They are Christ's [KJV]. It includes all believers and means they are members of Christ, incorporated in him [NIGTC].

QUESTION—What is meant by σάρξ 'flesh'?

See this word at 5:13 [WBC]. It has the same meaning as σάρξ in 5:16, 17, 19 [ICC].

QUESTION—What is meant by the phrase τὴν σάρκα ἐσταύρωσαν 'crucified the flesh'?

It is a strong way of saying that they no longer respond to the temptations coming from the physical nature [Mor]. We are to take the flesh, our willful and wayward self, and, metaphorically speaking, nail it to the cross. This is Paul's graphic description of repentance, of turning our back on the old life of selfishness and sin and refusing to acknowledge it [BST]. Paul indicates that all who really belong to Christ have performed this act on their flesh. It was not performed upon them, they did it themselves [Lns]. It refers to the act by which they put an end to the dominion of the flesh over their conduct [ICC].

QUESTION—What is significant about the phrase σὺν τοῖς παθήμασιν καὶ ταῖς ἐπιθυμίαις 'with the passions and the desires'?

It stresses the completeness of the crucifixion involved since not only are the outward manifestations of the flesh destroyed but also its dispositions and cravings are put to death [ICC, WBC]. The 'passions' are the outward expressions of which the 'desires' are the inner directive force [NIC]. 'Passions' and 'desires' taken together refer to 'the works of the flesh' [TH]. The article with both words is restrictive and serves to mark them as those of the σάρξ 'flesh' [ICC, NCBC].

5:25 **If we-are-livingᵃ in/by-(the)-Spirit/spirit,**
LEXICON—a. pres. act. indic. of ζάω (LN 23.88, 41.2) (BAGD 2.a. p. 336): 'to live' [BAGD, BNTC, LN (23.88, 41.2), Mor, WBC; GW, KJV, NASB, NET, NIV, NLT, NRSV], 'to conduct (oneself), to behave' [LN (41.2)]. This entire clause is translated 'if the Spirit is the source of our life' [Herm; REB], 'God's Spirit has given us life' [CEV], 'we get our life from the Spirit' [NCV], 'the Spirit has given us life' [TEV], 'Since the Holy Spirit has caused that we be spiritually alive' [SSA].

QUESTION—What relationship is indicated by εἰ 'if'?

As in 5:18, the 'if' clause refers to something that is assumed to be true [ICC, NIC, SSA, TH, WBC]. The 'if' clause is rhetorical [NCBC] and could be translated 'since we live by the Spirit' [NCBC, SSA, TH, TNTC, WBC; NIV]. It is simply stated as a fact [CEV, NCV, TEV]: we are living by the Spirit.

QUESTION—What is meant by the phrase ζῶμεν πνεύματι 'we are living by the Spirit'?

1. This refers to the entrance into spiritual life brought about by the Holy Spirit [BNTC, Herm, NIC, NTC, SSA, TH; CEV, NCV, REB, TEV]: we get our new life from the Spirit. The source of our life is the Spirit [NTC]. The phrase deals with the Spirit as the source and sustaining power of believers' spiritual life [NIC].
2. This refers to the spiritual life being lived in relation to the Holy Spirit [Alf, ICC, Lt; KJV]: we live in the Spirit. Assuming they are in such fellowship, this phrase emphasizes spiritual fellowship, mystical union [ICC]. This phrase refers to an ideal life rather than an actual life. It indicates a state which the Galatians were put in the way of attaining rather than one which they had already attained [Lt].
3. This refers to the spiritual quality of life [Lns; GW]: we live by our spiritual nature.

let-us-followᵃ also with-(the)-Spirit.
LEXICON—a. pres. act. subj. of στοιχέω (LN **41.12**) (BAGD p. 769): 'to follow' [BAGD, BNTC; CEV, NCV, NLT], 'to conduct (oneself) in accordance with' [**LN**, SSA], 'to behave in accordance with' [LN; NET], 'to live' [LN], 'to keep in step with' [Mor, WBC; NIV], 'to walk' [KJV, NASB]. This active verb is also translated passively: 'to be guided by' [NRSV]. This entire phrase is translated 'then our lives need to conform to our spiritual nature' [GW], 'let the Spirit also direct its course' [REB], 'let the Spirit also direct our course' [Herm], 'he must also control our lives' [TEV].

QUESTION—What is meant by this phrase?

'Walking' requires a constant application while 'living' requires an abiding fellowship. The practical application of this new life requires perseverance just as a child who is learning to walk needs persistence. The same Spirit who gives life gives both strength and guidance throughout life's journey

[NCBC]. This phrase deals with the Spirit as the regulative principle of believers' conduct [NIC]. The verb στοιχέω 'to follow' has the sense of walking in a straight line and so of conducting oneself appropriately [ICC, NIBC, TH]. In this sense the expression in this phrase is synonymous with the expression in 5:18 [TH].

DISCOURSE UNIT: 5:26–6:5 [BST]. The topic is reciprocal Christian relationships.

5:26 Not let-us-become^a conceited^b (ones),

LEXICON—a. pres. mid. (deponent = act.) subj. of γίνομαι (LN 13.3, 13.48): 'to become' [BNTC, Herm, LN (13.48), Mor, WBC; NASB, NET, NIV, NLT, NRSV], 'to be' [LN (13.3); CEV, NCV, REB, TEV]. This entire phrase is translated 'We (incl.) should not overestimate ourselves' [SSA], 'Let us not be desirous of vain glory' [KJV], 'We can't allow ourselves to act arrogantly' [GW].

b. κενόδοξος (LN **88.222**) (BAGD p. 427): 'conceited' [BNTC, LN, Mor, WBC; CEV, NET, NIV, NLT, NRSV, REB], 'falsely proud' [**LN**], 'boaster' [BAGD], 'boastful' [NASB], 'proud' [NCV, TEV], 'boastfully vain' [Herm]. See a. [SSA; GW, KJV].

QUESTION—How is this verse connected with its context?
1. It is the end of a preceding paragraph [Lt, Mor, NIGTC, NTC, TH; CEV, GW, NCV, NET, NIV, NLT, TEV]. The paragraph is 5:16–26 [Mor], 5:19–26 [NCV], 5:22–26 [CEV, GW, NET, NIV, TEV], 5:24–26 [NLT], or 5:25–26 [NIGTC, NTC]. It gives one consequence of following the Spirit [ICC]. The lack of any conjunction shows that it is closely connected to the preceding verse [TH].
2. It begins a paragraph continuing on in chapter 6 [Lns; REB]. The paragraph is 5:26–6:2 [REB], 5:26–6:5 [Lns]. The lack of a conjunction helps indicate that this begins a new paragraph and the vocative 'brothers' (6:1) grammatically belongs at the end of 5:26. Here Paul begins to give admonitions concerning the use of Christian liberty [Lns].
3. It is a part of the paragraph 5:25–6:6. It is linked to 5:25 by a lack of a conjunction, by continuing with another exhortation in the first person plural, and by functioning as the first of the specifics involved in following the Spirit [SSA].
4. It is a separate paragraph in itself [NIC; NASB]. It returns to the themes of 5:15, describing behavior that is opposite to mutual service through love [NIC].

QUESTION—What is meant by κενόδοξος 'conceited'?
It refers to the attitude of being puffed up with pride, arrogant, boastful [NAC, NIC, TH], putting value on things that are not really valuable [ICC, NAC, NIC, TH]. The word refers to the praise which men seek without a genuine reason [Lns]. It means not merely having an awareness of one's own superiority or importance, but having an excessive or unfounded sense of either [SSA].

provoking^a one-another,

LEXICON—a. pres. mid. (deponent = act.) participle of προκαλέω (LN **88.188**) (BAGD p. 707): 'to provoke' [BAGD, BNTC, Herm, **LN**, Mor, WBC; GW, KJV, NET, NIV], 'to challenge' [BAGD; NASB], 'to irritate' [LN; NLT, TEV], 'to make trouble' [NCV], 'to compete against' [NRSV], 'to incite to rivalry' [REB], not explicit [CEV]. This entire phrase is translated 'We (incl.) should not overestimate ourselves and claim that we (incl.) are superior to each other/compete with each other for honor' [SSA].

QUESTION—What is meant by provoking one another?

They might not realize that their actions of service might provoke someone into doing what is wrong [Mor]. It means to put themselves ahead of others [TH]. If they brag about that which they think they have, they call forth equally pretentious swagger on the part of another person [NTC]. Wanting to be glorified by men, they could cause others to want more credit and praise than they receive [Lns]. They must not provoke or challenge fellow Christians to do things they hesitate to do [ICC].

envying^a one-another.

LEXICON—a. pres. act. participle of φθονέω (LN **88.161**) (BAGD p. 857): 'to envy' [BAGD, BNTC, Herm, Mor, SSA, WBC; GW, KJV, NASB, NIV, NRSV], 'to be envious' [LN], 'to be jealous of' [BAGD, **LN**; NCV, NET, NLT, REB, TEV], 'to make others jealous' [CEV].

QUESTION—What is meant by envying one another?

In this phrase the verb is used which corresponds to the noun in 5:21, which suggests that Paul's aim is to show how the works of the flesh must be actively resisted [NCBC]. They are not to be jealous of what another believer is doing in serving the Lord [Mor]. They are not to envy another person of the praise that person receives [Lns]. They are not to grudge someone for what he has [NTC]. They must not envy fellow Christians who dare to do what they will not venture to do [ICC].

DISCOURSE UNIT: 6:1–18 [NASB]. The topic is bearing one another's burdens.

DISCOURSE UNIT: 6:1–10 [GNT, Mor, NAC, NCBC, NIC, NIGTC, WBC; CEV, NET, NIV, NLT, NRSV, TEV]. The topic is specific exhortations [NIC], mutual helpfulness [Mor], freedom in service to others [NAC], Christian life in its responsibility to others [NCBC], mutual help and service [NIGTC], doing good to all [WBC; NIV], helping each other [CEV], bearing one another's burdens [GNT; NRSV, TEV], supporting one another [NET], we reap what we sow [NLT].

DISCOURSE UNIT: 6:1–6 [TNTC; NCV]. The topic is how to deal with an offender [TNTC], helping each other [NCV].

DISCOURSE UNIT: 6:1–5 [GW]. The topic is helping carry each other's burdens.

6:1 Brothers,[a] if (a) person[b] even[c] is-overtaken[d] by/in[e] some[f] transgression,[g]

LEXICON—a. ἀδελφός (LN 11.23): '(Christian) brother, fellow believer' [LN]. This plural noun is translated 'brothers' [BNTC, Herm, Mor, SSA, WBC; KJV, NASB, NIV], 'brothers and sisters' [GW, NCV, NET, NLT], 'my friends' [CEV, NRSV, REB, TEV].
  b. ἄνθρωπος (LN 9.1, 9.24): 'person' [BNTC, Herm, LN (9.1), SSA; GW, NET], 'individual' [LN (9.1)], 'man' [LN (9.24), Mor; KJV], 'someone' [WBC; CEV, NIV, TEV], 'someone in your group' [NCV], 'anyone' [NASB, NRSV, REB], 'another Christian' [NLT].
  c. καί (LN 89.93): 'even' [LN; NASB], not explicit [BNTC, Herm, Mor, SSA, WBC; all versions except NASB].
  d. aorist pass. subj. of προλαμβάνω (LN **27.33**) (BAGD 2.b. p. 708): 'to be overtaken' [BAGD; KJV], 'to be overcome' [NLT], 'to be surprised' [BAGD, LN], 'to be caught' [**LN**, Mor; NASB, NIV, REB, TEV], 'to be detected' [BAGD, BNTC, Herm, LN; NRSV], 'to be discovered' [LN; NET], 'to be entrapped' [WBC], 'to be trapped' [CEV], 'to get trapped' [GW], not explicit [NCV]. This passive verb is also translated actively with 'brothers' as the subject: 'to discover' [SSA].
  e. ἐν with dative object (LN 13.8, 83.13, 90.10): 'in' [BNTC, Herm, LN (13.8, 83.13), Mor; CEV, KJV, NASB, NET, NIV, NRSV, TEV], 'by' [LN (90.10), WBC; GW, NLT], not explicit [SSA]. The phrase προλημφθῇ ἔν τινι παραπτώματι 'is overtaken by some transgression' is translated 'does something wrong' [NCV], 'is caught doing something wrong' [REB].
  f. τις (LN 92.12): 'some' [BNTC, LN, WBC; NET, NLT], 'something' [LN; NCV, REB], 'any' [Mor; NASB], 'a' [Herm; KJV, NIV, NRSV], 'any kind of' [TEV], not explicit [SSA; CEV, GW].
  g. παράπτωμα (LN 88.297) (BAGD 2.a.α. p. 621): 'transgression' [BNTC, Herm, LN, Mor; NRSV], 'sin' [LN, WBC; CEV, NET, NIV, NLT], 'trespass' [BAGD; NASB], 'fault' [KJV], 'wrongdoing' [GW, TEV], 'wrong' [NCV, REB]. This noun is also translated as a verb with 'person' as the subject: 'to sin' [SSA].

QUESTION—What is significant about the use of ἀδελφοί 'brothers' here?

It indicates that a new topic is going to be discussed and reiterates his affectionate regard for his readers [NAC]. The repetition of 'brothers' reflects Paul's anxiety to keep his exhortations on a personal level [NCBC]. The repetition of the address ἀδελφοί 'brothers' indicates that Paul will now present an important matter to the readers [Herm].

QUESTION—Who is referred to by ἄνθρωπος 'person'?

It is generic and is to be understood as a generic noun for any believer [ICC, Mor, NIC, TH, WBC; NCV, NLT]. In the present context the wrongdoer would certainly be a Christian [Herm]. The man is presumed to be a Christian [NCBC, SSA].

QUESTION—What relationship is indicated by ἐάν 'if'?

It indicates that it is not assumed whether anyone was in fact guilty of the offence or not [Mor]. It indicates some indefiniteness, but also suggests the probability of such a situation in the future [WBC]. It indicates that Paul is stating a hypothetical case [SSA, TH].

QUESTION—What relationship is indicated by καί 'even'?

It is intensive and puts the emphasis on the immediately following word which is the verb προλημφθῇ 'should be overtaken' [ICC, WBC] and is most likely intended to apply to the whole clause [ICC].

QUESTION—What is the meaning of the phrase προλημφθῇ ἄνθρωπος ἔν τινι παραπτώματι 'a person even is overtaken by/in some transgression'?

1. It means the sin overcomes the person so that he sins [ICC, Lns, Mor, NCBC, NIC, NTC; CEV]: if a person is overcome by some transgression. The term παράπτωμα 'sin' has the idea of falling. It is not the deliberate and planned aspect of sin that is stressed here, but the unwitting element [Mor, NIC]. Mistake rather than misdeed is the force of the word [Mor]. This person doesn't deliberately plan to do a wicked deed, but before he realizes the consequences of his actions he is overtaken in some transgression [NTC].

2. It means someone else catches the person committing a sin [Alf, BST, Herm, Lt, SSA; GW, NASB, NET, NIV, NRSV, REB, TEV]: if a person is discovered in some transgression. The preposition ἐν means that he is caught 'in' some transgression or 'while' he is sinning [SSA]. Being caught in the act of committing a sin, he is guilty of a transgression without a doubt [Lt].

you the spiritual[a] (ones) restore[b] such[c] (a person) in[d] (a) spirit[e] of-gentleness,[f]

LEXICON—a. πνευματικός (LN 12.21, 26.10, 41.40) (BAGD 2.b.β. p. 679): 'spiritual' [BNTC, LN (12.21, 26.10, 41.40), Mor, WBC; all versions except NLT, NRSV, REB], 'spirit-filled (people)' [BAGD], 'godly' [NLT]. The phrase ὑμεῖς οἱ πνευματικοί 'you the spiritual ones' is translated 'those of you whom the Holy Spirit is directing and empowering' [SSA], 'you who have received the Spirit' [NRSV], 'you, my friends, who live by the Spirit' [REB], 'you who are endowed with the Spirit' [Herm].

b. pres. act. impera. of καταρτίζω (BAGD 1.a. p. 417): 'to restore' [BAGD, BNTC, Herm, Mor, WBC; KJV, NASB, NET, NIV, NRSV], 'to lead back to the right path' [CEV], 'to help turn away from doing wrong' [GW], 'to help make right again' [NCV], 'to help back onto the right path' [NLT], 'to set right' [REB, TEV], 'to correct' [SSA].

c. τοιοῦτος (LN 64.2, 92.31) (BAGD 3.a.α. p. 821): 'such, like such, like that' [LN (64.2)], 'of such a kind, of a kind such as this' [LN (92.31)].

The phrase τὸν τοιοῦτον 'the such' is translated 'such a one' [Mor; KJV, NASB, NRSV], 'such a person' [BAGD; NET], 'a person like that' [SSA], 'this person' [Herm], 'that person' [BNTC, WBC; CEV, GW, NCV, NLT], 'him' [NIV, REB, TEV].

d. ἐν with dative object (LN 13.8, 89.84): 'in' [BNTC, Herm, LN (13.8), Mor, WBC; GW, KJV, NASB, NET, NRSV], 'with' [LN (89.84)], not explicit [SSA; CEV, NCV, NIV, NLT, REB, TEV].

e. πνεῦμα (LN **30.6**) (BAGD 3.c. p. 675): 'spirit' [BAGD, BNTC, Herm, Mor, WBC; KJV, NASB, NET, NRSV], 'attitude' [**LN** (30.6)], 'disposition' [BAGD, LN (30.6)], 'spiritual state, state of mind' [BAGD]. The phrase ἐν πνεύματι πραΰτητος 'in a spirit of gentleness' is translated 'gently' [SSA; CEV, NCV, NIV, REB], 'gently and humbly' [NLT], 'but you must do it in a gentle way' [TEV], 'Do it in a gentle way' [GW].

f. πραΰτης (LN 88.59) (BAGD p. 699): 'gentleness' [BAGD, BNTC, LN, Mor, WBC; NASB, NET, NRSV], 'mildness' [LN], 'meekness' [BAGD, LN; KJV], 'humility' [BAGD]. This noun is also translated as an adverb: 'gently' [SSA; CEV, NCV, NIV, REB], 'gently and humbly' [NLT]; as an adjective: 'gentle' [Herm; GW, TEV].

QUESTION—What is meant by ὑμεῖς οἱ πνευματικοί 'you the spiritual'?

It means those who have the Holy Spirit dwelling in them [Mor]. Paul uses this designation for all of his converts in Galatia. Since they are 'in Christ' they have become the recipients of God's Spirit [WBC]. Paul is thinking of a contrast between those who obey the Spirit and those who do not [NCBC]. All Christians have the Holy Spirit dwelling in them, but spiritual Christians are also led by the Spirit and walk by the Spirit so that the fruit of the Spirit appears in their lives [BST]. Those who are spiritual are those whose lives are guided by the Spirit [Lt, NIGTC, NTC, TH]. It refers to those who live by the Spirit and walk by the Spirit in obedience to the instructions given in 5:16–26 [ICC]. They are those who walk in the power of the Holy Spirit and according to the standard of the Holy Spirit, in contrast with natural persons outside of Christ and with fleshly Christians (5:16) [SSA]. Those who walk, are led, and keep in line with what is spirit [Lns].

QUESTION—What is meant by καταρτίζω 'to restore' in this phrase?

It is used in the ethical sense of restoring to a former good state [BST, ICC, NIC, NTC, TNTC, WBC]. It means to help the wrongdoer to stop doing wrong [TH]. It means to correct the sinner's own condition [SSA].

QUESTION—What is meant by πνεύματι πραΰτητος 'spirit of gentleness'?

1. This refers to a person's attitude and disposition [BAGD, LN (30.6), Lt, Mor, NIC, SSA]. It is the quality of gentleness, a fruit of the Spirit [NIC]. This is a characteristic of true spirituality [Lt].
2. This refers to a person's spirit [Alf, Herm, ICC, NIC, NTC, TH, WBC]. It means a human spirit characterized by gentleness [ICC].

watching[a] yourself lest[b] you also[c] should-be-tempted.[d]

LEXICON—a. pres. act. participle of σκοπέω (LN **27.58**) (BAGD p. 756): 'to watch' [**LN**, WBC; GW, NIV], 'to pay attention to' [LN], 'to pay close attention to' [NET], 'to be very cautious' [SSA], 'to consider' [Mor; KJV], 'to keep an eye on' [BNTC; TEV], 'to watch out' [CEV], 'to be careful' [NCV, NLT], 'to take care' [NRSV]. The phrase σκοπῶν σεαυτόν 'watching yourself' is translated 'to look to (oneself)' [BAGD], 'to look to (yourself)' [Herm; NASB, REB].

b. μή (LN 89.62) (BAGD B.1.b. p. 517): 'lest' [BAGD, BNTC, LN, Mor; KJV], 'that not' [BAGD, Herm, WBC; NRSV], 'so that not' [LN; GW, NASB, NET, TEV], 'in order that not' [LN], 'in order that you might not' [SSA], 'because' [NCV], 'or' [NIV]. The phrase μὴ καὶ σὺ πειρασθῇς 'lest you also should be tempted' is translated 'and don't be tempted yourself' [CEV], 'not to fall into the same temptation yourself' [NLT], 'you also may be tempted' [REB].

c. καί (LN 89.93): 'also' [BNTC, LN, Mor, WBC; GW, KJV, NIV, REB], 'too' [Herm; NASB, NCV, NET, TEV], not explicit [SSA; NRSV]. See b. [CEV, NLT].

d. aorist pass. subj. of πειράζω (LN 88.308) (BAGD 2.d. p. 640): 'to be tempted' [BAGD, BNTC, Herm, LN, Mor, SSA, WBC; all versions except NLT], 'to fall into the same temptation' [NLT].

QUESTION—What is the function of the participle σκοπῶν 'watching'?

It means more than just seeing. It involves a steady consideration, like looking at a target before shooting at it [NCBC]. This entire clause is not only a warning, but is also the motivation for meekness [Lns]. This clause also suggests that gentleness is born of a sense of our own weakness and proneness to sin [BST].

QUESTION—What is significant about the switch from the plural ὑμεῖς 'you' to the singular σεαυτοῦ 'yourself'?

It makes this personal to each believer [BNTC, Mor, NIC]. It makes the exhortation more pointed since it applies the warning to each individual [ICC, WBC]. Self-examination can only be individual [NCBC]. By switching from the plural to the singular Paul demands self-examination by each individual Christian [Herm, SSA]. Since this admonition is applicable to all the individuals involved, it is normally necessary to continue the use of a plural form [TH].

QUESTION—What is the function of the clause μὴ καὶ σὺ πειρασθῇς 'lest you also should be tempted'?

Some state that this clause is the purpose of the verb σκοπέω 'to watch'. The purpose for watching is so that one will not fall into temptation [NCBC, SSA, TH]. Others state that this is a warning. One should watch or else he will fall into temptation [TH]. This could be interpreted as being either the object or the purpose of the verb 'watch'. If it is interpreted as the object it would restrict the sphere of self-examination to areas of possible examination [NCBC]. It could be a clause of purpose after σκοπῶν σεαυτὸν 'watching yourself' or an object clause after σκοπέω 'watch' or a clause of fear, the verb of fearing to be supplied in thought. It is most likely a clause of fear since the possibility of a clause of purpose focuses on not so much to avoid falling into temptation as to cause one to be considerate of those who do fall. Also the possibility of an object clause is ruled out because in other places Paul constantly uses σκοπέω 'watch', not as a verb of effort, but in the sense 'to consider, observe' [ICC].

QUESTION—What is meant by πειράζω 'to be tempted'?

It may mean being tempted to do the same sin, but more likely it means to be tempted to see oneself as superior [Mor]. There is a temptation to develop self-righteousness and arrogance with regard to the wrongdoer. A temptation such as this presents a threat to the community by providing an opportunity for the 'works of the flesh' [Herm]. Paul warns his converts about their own vulnerability to such sins as they seek to correct in others so that they do not become self-righteous and look down on those they are trying to restore [WBC]. The verb contains the idea of being attracted to doing wrong and also the implication of yielding to this attraction [ICC, SSA, TH].

6:2 Bear[a] the burdens[b] of-one-another

LEXICON—a. pres. act. impera. of βαστάζω (LN 15.188) (BAGD 2.b.α. p. 137): 'to bear' [BAGD, BNTC, Herm, LN, WBC; KJV, NASB, NRSV], 'to carry' [BAGD, LN, Mor; NET, NIV, REB], 'to help' [NCV], 'to help carry' [GW, TEV], 'to share' [NLT]. This entire phrase is translated 'you should help each other, that is, the ones who have extreme problems' [SSA], 'when you offer each other a helping hand' [CEV]. The present imperative has the sense of 'keep carrying' [Mor].

b. βάρος (LN 22.4) (BAGD 1. p. 134): 'burden' [BAGD, BNTC, Herm, LN, WBC; all versions except CEV, NCV, NLT], 'load' [Mor], 'hardship' [LN], 'extreme problems' [SSA], 'trouble' [NCV], 'troubles and problems' [NLT]. See a. [CEV].

QUESTION—What is meant by this phrase?

Paul puts ἀλλήλων 'of one another' first in the sentence to give it emphasis [Alf, ICC, Lt, Mor, NCBC, SSA, TH, WBC]. Paul is encouraging believers to live their lives as helpful people. They should always be ready to lift the burden from other people's shoulders [Mor]. In this phrase τὰ βάρη 'the burdens', it refers mainly to the burdens of temptation that were mentioned in 6:1, but more general oppressive burdens of any kind are also in mind here [ICC, NCBC, WBC]. The burdens referred to here are all kinds of weakness, suffering, and pain, any and every burden that is hard to bear [Alf, Herm, Lt, NIC, NTC, SSA, TH].

and thus[a] you-will-fulfill[b] the law[c] of-Christ.

TEXT—Instead of the future indicative ἀναπληρώσετε 'you will fulfill', one important manuscript reads the future indicative ἀποπληρώσετε 'you will fill full', and some manuscripts read the aorist subjunctive ἀναπληρώσατε 'fulfill'. GNT reads ἀναπληρώσετε 'you will fulfill' with a C decision, indicating that the Committee had difficulty making the decision. The aorist subjunctive ἀναπληρώσατε 'fulfill' is read by KJV.

LEXICON—a. οὕτως (LN 61.9): 'thus' [BNTC, LN], 'so' [LN, Mor, WBC; KJV], 'in this way' [Herm, LN; GW, NET, NIV, NLT, NRSV, REB, TEV], 'by means of that' [SSA], 'thereby' [NASB], not explicit [CEV, NCV].
   b. fut. act. indic. of ἀναπληρόω (LN **36.17**) (BAGD 2. p. 59): 'to fulfill' [BAGD, BNTC, Herm, Mor, WBC; KJV, NASB, NET, NIV, NRSV, REB], 'to obey' [**LN**; CEV, NCV, NLT, TEV], 'to conform to' [LN], 'to complete' [SSA], 'to follow' [GW].
   c. νόμος (LN 33.55, 33.333) (BAGD 5. p. 543): 'law' [BAGD, BNTC, Herm, LN (33.333), Mor, WBC; all versions except GW], 'Law' [LN (33.55)], 'teachings' [GW]. The phrase νόμον τοῦ Χριστοῦ 'law of Christ' is translated 'what Christ requires' [SSA].

QUESTION—What is meant by καὶ οὕτως ἀναπληρώσετε 'and thus you will fulfill'?

Paul is stating that if the whole law is fulfilled in the concept of love, as he has stated in 5:14, then to share in each other's burdens is to be obedient to that law [TH]. Fulfilling the law of Christ means following the example of Christ in seeking the good of the neighbor [BNTC]. Paul believes that Christians will completely satisfy the demands of the law of Christ if they bear each others' burdens [NIC]. The thought here is not that bearing each others' burdens will by itself satisfy the law of Christ, but that the Galatians will not satisfy the law of Christ without bearing each others' burdens [SSA].

QUESTION—How are the nouns related in the genitive construction νόμον τοῦ Χριστοῦ 'law of Christ'?

Law here is not to be thought of as part of a legal code, but it points to the need for lowly service if we are truly to be followers of Jesus who has commanded that we love one another (John 13:34) [Mor]. The construction 'law of Christ' involves submission to a person rather than to a code. It is probably better to understand it in this sense than to suggest that 'law' here refers to any specific commandments or precepts of Jesus. As Christ bore the burdens of others, so the believer must do the same. This is the 'law' of true Christian relationships [NCBC]. The 'law of Christ' is to love one another as He loves us [BNTC, BST, Lns, NIC, NTC]. The 'law of Christ' doesn't require one to observe the Torah, but instead it allows one to act as Christ [NIBC]. The 'law of Christ' means either the law of God as shown by Christ in his life or the law which Christ taught [TH]. By 'the law of Christ' Paul means the law of God as Christ stated formally; just as the law of Moses is the law of God as presented by Moses. It is clear that Paul conceived of the law presented by Christ as consisting not in a body of statutes, but in the central and all-inclusive principle of love. However, whether in his present reference to that law he had in mind its content, or thought simply of the law of God presented by Christ, can't be decided with certainty [ICC].

6:3 For[a] if anyone[b] thinks[c] (himself) to-be something,[d] being[e] nothing,[f]

LEXICON—a. γάρ (LN 89.23): 'for' [BNTC, Herm, LN, Mor, WBC; KJV, NASB, NET, NRSV], 'because' [LN], 'since' [SSA], 'so' [GW], not explicit [CEV, NCV, NIV, NLT, REB, TEV].
  b. τις (LN 92.12): 'anyone' [BNTC, Herm, LN, Mor, WBC; GW, NASB, NCV, NET, NIV, REB], 'someone' [LN, SSA], 'a man' [KJV], 'you' [CEV, NLT, TEV], 'those' [NRSV].
  c. pres. act. indic. of δοκέω (LN 31.29) (BAGD 1.b. p. 201): 'to think' [BAGD, BNTC, Herm, LN, Mor, SSA, WBC; all versions except REB], 'to believe, to suppose' [BAGD, LN], 'to imagine' [REB].
  d. τις (LN 92.12) (BAGD 1.b.ε. p. 820): 'something' [BAGD, Herm, LN, Mor, WBC; KJV, NASB, NET, NIV, NRSV, TEV], 'important' [BNTC; GW, NCV], 'important/superior' [SSA], 'too important (to help someone in need)' [NLT], 'somebody' [REB]. The phrase εἶναί τι 'to be something' is translated 'to amount to something' [BAGD], 'are better than others' [CEV].
  e. pres. participle of εἰμί (LN 13.1): 'to be' [BNTC, Herm, LN, Mor, SSA, WBC; all versions except CEV, GW, NLT]. The phrase μηδὲν ὤν 'being nothing' is translated 'when you're really not' [GW], 'when you really aren't' [CEV]. This is translated by starting a new sentence 'You are really a nobody' [NLT].
  f. μηδείς (LN 92.23) (BAGD 2.b.γ. p. 518): 'nothing' [BAGD, Herm, LN, Mor, WBC; KJV, NASB, NET, NIV, NRSV, REB, TEV], 'not' [BNTC; GW, NCV], 'aren't' [CEV], 'not important/superior' [SSA], 'a nobody' [NLT].

QUESTION—What relationship is indicated by γάρ 'for'?
  1. This is connected to 6:2 [Alf, BST, ICC, Lns, NCBC, NIC, NIGTC, WBC]. This sentence gives the reason for the injunction of 6:2, 'bear one another's burdens' [ICC, NIC], and implies that conceit, thinking one's self to be something more than one really is, tends to make one unwilling to share another's burden [ICC]. Paul substantiates his admonitions by pointing to the opposite. But not to the opposite action, refusal to bear the burdens of others; he at once goes deeper, namely to the delusion from which such refusal would spring [Lns]. It seems to function not only to support what is said in 6:2, but also to set off the statement of 6:3 as being a general truth or rule of conduct [WBC]. Paul's point, it seems, is that thinking oneself to be something when actually we are nothing results in making one unwilling to bear others' burdens [BST, WBC]. The conjunction shows a close connection with the previous statement. Bearing other people's burdens involves self-sacrifice and this is totally incompatible with a sense of self-importance [NCBC]. The Galatians weren't supposed to think of themselves more highly than they ought to think. If they did, they would be inhibited from fulfilling 'the law of Christ' by bearing one another's burdens or restoring those who had been overcome by some sudden temptation [NIGTC].

2. This is connected to 6:1 [Lt]. These words are connected to 6:1, while 6:2 is an amplification of and inference from 6:1 [Lt].
3. This is connected to 5:26 [SSA]: Let us not become conceited…because the one who does so deceives himself. In this case, the positive exhortations in 6:1–2 are almost parenthetical [SSA].

QUESTION—What relationship is indicated by εἰ 'if'?
The basic framework of 6:3 is a condition introduced by εἰ 'if' followed by the consequence [SSA].

QUESTION—Who is referred to by τις 'anyone'?
Paul is probably thinking of some specific person or persons who had too high a self-esteem [NCBC].

QUESTION—What is meant by δοκεῖ εἶναί τι 'thinks to be something'?
It means to regard oneself as important [BNTC, ICC, NIC, SSA, TH; GW, NCV, NLT]. This may refer to 'anyone', referring to all human beings in comparison with God or it may refer to 'someone', referring to an individual who is evaluated by human standards [SSA].

QUESTION—What is meant by μηδὲν ὤν 'being nothing'?
1. This describes the condition of all people [BST, Lt, Mor, NCBC]. It is basic to the Christian understanding that we can do nothing at all for our salvation. Christ came to this earth and lived and died so that there would be a way of salvation. We are asked to simply believe, to trust Christ alone. Also we are totally dependent on the strength and guidance of the Holy Spirit to live out the Christian life [Mor]. No believer has any right to think of himself as any more than nothing since he owes everything to Christ [NCBC].
2. This describes the kind of people who deceive themselves [ICC, Lns, NTC]. Paul is saying that if anyone imagines that he amounts to something, while he amounts to nothing, he is deluding himself. Paul is attacking the spirit of overconfidence in oneself [NTC]. Paul doesn't claim that everyone is nothing. The fault he mentions is that person who is nothing, but thinks himself something [Lns].

he-deceives[a] himself.
LEXICON—a. pres. act. indic. of φρεναπατάω (LN **31.12**) (BAGD p. 865): 'to deceive' [BAGD, BNTC, **LN,** Mor, WBC; KJV, NASB, NET, NIV, NRSV, TEV], 'to delude' [Herm; REB], 'to deceive/delude' [SSA], 'to fool' [GW, NCV, NLT]. This entire phrase is translated 'you are wrong' [CEV].

QUESTION—What is meant by this phrase?
It means to deceive one's own mind. Paul implies that any believer who claims to be 'something' is filling his mind with fantasies [NCBC].

6:4 But each[a] (person) let-him-test[b] his-own work,[c]
LEXICON—a. ἕκαστος (LN 59.27): 'each' [BNTC, Herm, LN, Mor, SSA, WBC; GW, NASB, NCV, NET, NIV, REB, TEV], 'every' [KJV], 'all'

[NRSV]. This entire phrase is translated 'do your own work well' [CEV], 'be sure to do what you should' [NLT].
b. pres. act. impera. of δοκιμάζω (LN 27.45) (BAGD 1. p. 202): 'to test' [LN, WBC; NIV, NRSV], 'to examine' [BAGD, Herm, LN; GW, NASB, NET, REB], 'to prove' [Mor; KJV], 'to evaluate' [BNTC], 'to judge' [NCV, TEV], 'to test and approve' [SSA]. See a. [CEV, NLT].
c. ἔργον (LN 42.11, 42.12, 42.42) (BAGD 1.c.β. p. 308): 'work' [BNTC, LN (42.42), Mor; CEV, KJV, NASB, NET, NRSV], 'workmanship' [LN (42.12)], 'accomplishment' [BAGD], 'deed' [BAGD, LN (42.11)], 'act' [LN (42.11)], 'conduct' [Herm; REB, TEV], 'actions' [WBC; GW, NCV, NIV]; the collective singular is used for the plural [BAGD]. The phrase ἔργον ἑαυτοῦ 'his own work' is translated 'what you yourself are doing and thinking' [SSA]. See a. [NLT].

QUESTION—What relationship is indicated by δέ 'but'?
1. It connects 6:4 with 6:1–2 [WBC].
2. It connects with 6:2 [ICC]. This command is joined to the command in 6:2 [ICC].
3. It connects with 6:3 [Lns, Lt, NTC, TH]. The contrast is with the person who thinks he is something while being nothing [Lt]. A person's pride should be based on his own achievement, not in comparison with others [TH].
4. It connects with 5:26 [SSA]: we should not overestimate ourselves, rather, you should constantly test yourselves.

QUESTION—What is significant about ἕκαστος 'each' in this passage?
It emphasizes individual responsibility in the work of self-scrutiny [NIC].

QUESTION—What work is referred to here?
Here 'work' is a collective singular and can include both a person's conduct or his actions as well as the task which is set by God [NIC]. It means 'what one achieves, the result of one's effort' [ICC].

and then he-will-have[a] the boasting[b] in[c] himself alone[d]
LEXICON—a. fut. act. indic. of ἔχω (LN 57.1, 74.12, 90.65): 'to have' [BNTC, LN (57.1, 90.65), Mor, WBC; CEV, KJV, NASB], 'to experience' [LN (90.65)], 'to be able to' [LN (74.12)], not explicit [Herm]. This entire phrase is translated 'and then you can boast/exult only because of what you yourself are doing and thinking' [SSA], 'and then he can measure his achievement by comparing himself with himself' [REB], 'for then you will enjoy the personal satisfaction of having done your work well' [NLT], 'then that work...will become a cause for pride' [NRSV]. This entire phrase is translated by starting a new sentence 'Then you can be proud of your own accomplishments' [GW], 'Then he can be proud for what he himself has done' [NCV], 'Then he can take pride in himself' [NET, NIV], 'If it is good, then you can be proud of what you yourself have done' [TEV].

b. καύχημα (LN 25.203, 33.368, 33.371, 33.372) (BAGD 1. p. 426): 'boasting' [LN (33.368)], 'rejoicing' [KJV], 'reason for boasting' [BAGD, BNTC, Herm, WBC; NASB], 'the right to boast' [LN (33.372)], 'what (one) boasts about' [LN (33.371)], 'basis of pride' [LN (25.203); NRSV], 'matter for glorying' [Mor], 'to take pride' [NET, NIV]. This noun is also translated as a verb with 'you' as the subject: 'to boast/exult' [SSA]; as an adjective: '(to be) proud' [GW, NCV, TEV]. The phrase εἰς ἑαυτὸν μόνον τὸ καύχημα 'the boasting in himself alone' is translated 'something to be proud of' [CEV]. See a. [NLT, REB].
c. εἰς with accusative object (LN 90.23): 'in' [LN, Mor, WBC; KJV, NET, NIV], 'concerning' [LN], 'with reference to' [BNTC], 'with regard to' [Herm], 'in regard to' [NASB]. See a. [SSA; GW, NCV, NLT, NRSV, REB, TEV]. See b. [CEV].
d. μόνον (LN 58.50): 'alone' [BNTC, Herm, LN, Mor; KJV, NASB], not explicit [WBC]. See a. [SSA; all versions except CEV, KJV, NASB]. See b. [CEV].

QUESTION—What relationship is indicated by τότε 'then'?

It means that when he has tested his own actions, the following will result [ICC, NCBC, NIC, WBC].

and not in^a the other^b (person);

LEXICON—a. εἰς with accusative object (LN 90.23): 'in' [LN, Mor; KJV], 'concerning' [LN], 'with' [REB], 'by comparison with' [WBC], 'in comparison with' [Herm], 'in regard to' [NASB], 'with reference to' [BNTC]. This entire phrase is translated 'and not because of what other persons are doing or are not doing' [SSA], 'without comparing yourself to others' [GW], 'and not compare himself with others' [NCV], 'and not compare himself with someone else' [NET], 'without comparing himself to somebody else' [NIV], 'and you won't need to compare yourself to anyone else' [NLT], 'rather than their neighbor's work' [NRSV], 'without having to compare it with what someone else has done' [TEV]. This entire phrase is translated by starting a new sentence 'But don't compare yourself with others' [CEV].
b. ἕτερος (LN 58.37) (BAGD 1.b.ε. p. 315): 'other' [BNTC, LN, SSA; CEV, GW, NCV], 'another' [Mor; KJV, NASB], 'someone else' [Herm, WBC; NET, TEV], 'somebody else' [NIV], 'anyone else' [NLT, REB]. The phrase τὸν ἕτερον 'the other person' is translated '(one's) neighbor' [BAGD]. See a. [NRSV].

QUESTION—Who is referred to by ἕτερος 'other'?

This refers to either a particular wrong-doer or a general class of wrong-doers with whom someone in the church may compare himself [WBC]. If the article is restrictive, it refers to a particular imagined wrongdoer. If the article is generic, it refers to anyone [ICC]. It suggests any other person besides oneself [NCBC]. It refers to anyone else rather than to a specific individual [TH]. This refers particularly in regard to another's weakness

[NIC]. The man he was comparing himself with is general in its meaning, but particular in each case of comparison [Alf].

6:5 for[a] each (person) will-carry[b] his-own load.[c]

LEXICON—a. γάρ (LN 89.23): 'for' [BNTC, Herm, LN, Mor, WBC; all versions except CEV, GW, NCV], 'because' [LN], 'since' [SSA], not explicit [CEV, GW, NCV].

b. fut. act. indic. of βαστάζω (LN 15.188) (BAGD 2.b.α. p. 137): 'to carry' [BAGD, LN, Mor; CEV, NET, NIV, NRSV, TEV], 'to bear' [BAGD, BNTC, Herm, LN, WBC; KJV, NASB, REB], 'to perform' [SSA], 'to assume' [GW], 'to be responsible for' [NCV, NLT].

c. φορτίον (LN 15.208) (BAGD 2. p. 865): 'load' [BAGD, BNTC, Herm, LN, Mor; CEV, NASB, NET, NIV, NRSV, TEV], 'burden' [BAGD, LN, WBC; KJV, REB], 'responsibility' [GW], 'conduct' [NLT], 'task' [SSA]. This entire verse is translated 'Each person must be responsible for himself' [NCV].

QUESTION—What relationship is indicated by γάρ 'for'?

It indicates an explanation of 6:4 [WBC]. It suggests that Paul applies it to the situation that is dealt with in 6:4: one's responsibility before God [NIGTC]. The repetition of ἕκαστος 'each one' and γάρ 'for' connect 6:5 with 6:4 [SSA].

QUESTION—What is meant by φορτίον 'load' in this verse?

1. It means the person's assigned responsibility or lot [BST, Herm, Lt, Mor, NCBC, NIBC, NIC, NTC, SSA; GW]. Paul is urging believers to concentrate on their task in serving God [Mor]. It refers to the general load which everyone must carry. There are certain responsibilities that cannot be passed on to others. For instance, each must bear the burdens of his own sinful bias, the infirmity of the flesh [NCBC]. Believers are not to avoid responsibility for their own character [NIBC].
2. It means the person's weaknesses or sins [Alf, ICC]. Paul argues for the need to test oneself by the fact that every man has his own burden of weakness and sin [ICC].

DISCOURSE UNIT: 6:6–10 [BST; GW]. The topic is sowing and reaping [BST], we will harvest what we plant [GW].

6:6 And[a] the-(one) being-taught[b] the Word[c] let-him-share[d] with-the-(one) teaching[e] in[f] all good[g] (things).

LEXICON—a. δέ (LN 89.87, 89.94): 'and' [LN (89.87, 89.94)], 'but' [BNTC, SSA], 'now' [NET], 'when' [REB], 'if' [TEV], not explicit [Herm, Mor, WBC; all versions except NET, REB, TEV].

b. pres. pass. participle of κατηχέω (LN 33.225) (BAGD 2.a. p. 423): 'to be taught' [BAGD, BNTC, Herm, LN, SSA; GW, KJV, NASB, NLT, NRSV, TEV], 'to be instructed' [BAGD, LN, Mor], 'to receive instruction' [WBC; NET, NIV], 'to be under instruction' [REB], not explicit [CEV]. The passive verb is also translated actively with 'anyone' as the subject: 'to learn' [NCV].

c. λόγος (LN 33.100, 33.260) (BAGD 1.b.β. p. 478): 'Word' [BAGD, LN (33.100)], 'word' [BNTC, Herm, Mor, WBC; KJV, NASB, NET, NIV, NRSV], 'Message' [LN (33.100)], 'what is true about God' [SSA], 'what God has said' [CEV], 'God's word' [GW], 'teaching of God' [NCV], 'word of God' [NLT], 'the faith' [REB], 'gospel' [LN (33.260)], 'the Christian message' [TEV].

d. pres. act. impera. of κοινωνέω (LN **57.98**) (BAGD 2. p. 438): 'to share' [BNTC, Herm, **LN**, SSA, WBC; all versions except KJV, NLT, REB], 'to communicate' [KJV]. This verb is also translated as a noun: '(to give) a share' [BAGD; REB], '(to be) a sharer' [Mor]. The phrase κοινωνείτω τῷ κατηχοῦντι ἐν πᾶσιν ἀγαθοῖς 'let him share with the one teaching in all good things' is translated 'should help their teachers by paying them' [NLT].

e. pres. act. participle of κατηχέω (LN 33.225) (BAGD 2.a. p. 423): 'to teach' [BAGD, BNTC, Herm, LN; CEV, KJV, NASB, NET], 'to instruct' [BAGD, LN]. This verb is also translated as a noun: 'teacher' [SSA; GW, NCV, NLT, NRSV, REB, TEV], 'instructor' [Mor, WBC; NIV].

f. ἐν with dative object (LN 90.23): 'in' [BNTC, LN, Mor; KJV, NRSV], 'concerning, with respect to, with reference to' [LN], not explicit [Herm, SSA, WBC; all versions except KJV, NRSV].

g. ἀγαθός (LN 65.20) (BAGD 2.b.β. p. 3): 'good' [BNTC, Herm, LN, Mor, WBC; all versions except NLT], 'possession, treasure' [BAGD], 'various material' [SSA]. See d. [NLT].

QUESTION—What relationship is indicated by δέ 'and'?

It provides a loose connection with 6:5, simply saying that this saying follows 6:5 [Herm]. It indicates a contrast to the individuality of 6:5 [Alf].

QUESTION—What is meant by τὸν λόγον 'the word'?

It means the Christian message [WBC]. It refers to the teaching about Christ and about the divine revelation that is the source of the Christian understanding of life and salvation [Mor]. In this passage it refers to the whole Christian message [Herm, TH].

QUESTION—What is meant by the phrase κοινωνείτω τῷ κατηχοῦντι ἐν πᾶσιν ἀγαθοῖς 'let him share with the one teaching in all good things'?

1. The learner shares his material goods with the teacher [Alf, Herm, Lt, Mor, NIC, NTC, SSA, TNTC; CEV, NCV, NLT, REB, TEV]. Κοινωνέω 'share' or 'have fellowship' is a Christian euphemism for 'let him make a financial contribution' [TNTC]. The most common and the most likely interpretation of 'share' is in the sense of active giving and 'all good things' in the sense of physical goods [NIC]. Most likely the phrase 'in all good things' refers to the material needs of life, but understood in a general sense [Herm]. They are to take good care of those who taught them about the Christian way of life and should give them money or food or lodging or all of these things [Mor].

2. The teacher shares the good doctrine with the learner [Lns]. The one who instructs has the good things; the one being instructed is to proceed to participate in 'all' of them. The riches are with the teacher of the Word, the poverty is with the pupil, and the pupil is to establish 'fellowship' with the teacher so that he, the pupil, may be enriched. There are not only burdens in which we must fellowship and aid those who bear them, there are also 'good things,' spiritually and morally beneficial things, in which we should delight to have fellowship with those who possess these good things [Lns].
3. There is a mutual sharing: the teacher gives spiritual instruction and the learner gives material aid [BST, ICC, WBC]. Anyone who is taught the word should help to support his teacher. A minister sows the good seed of God's word and he reaps a livelihood [BST]. Since ἀγαθός 'good (thing)' is supposedly an inclusive term that refers to both spiritual and material good, κοινωνείτω 'let him share' should be understood as in Phil. 4:15 as referring to a mutual, reciprocal sharing in which the one taught received instruction and gave of his property. However, in view of the context, it must be assumed that here the emphasis is on the giving of material good [ICC].

DISCOURSE UNIT: 6:7–10 [TNTC; NCV]. The topic is sowing and reaping [TNTC], life is like planting a field [NCV].

6:7 **(Do) not be-deceived,**[a]
LEXICON—a. pres. pass. impera. of πλανάω (LN 31.8) (BAGD 2.c.γ. p. 665): 'to be deceived' [BNTC, LN, WBC; KJV, NASB, NET, NIV, NRSV], 'to be misled' [LN; NLT], 'to be fooled' [Herm; NCV]. This clause is translated 'make no mistake' [BAGD; GW, REB], 'don't go astray' [Mor], 'don't make a fool of yourself' [CEV], 'do not deceive yourselves' [SSA; TEV].
QUESTION—What is meant by this command?
  It is a warning against self-deception [SSA]. It is assumed to be a common introductory formula to a statement of warning in Paul's day [Mor, WBC]. It is implied that the Galatians could be holding an opinion or following a course of action which amounted to self-deception [BNTC]. It is a warning about what follows in the verse [ICC].

God not is-mocked.[a]
  a. pres. pass. indic. of μυκτηρίζω (LN **33.409**) (BAGD p. 529): 'to be mocked' [BAGD, BNTC, Mor, WBC; KJV, NASB, NIV, NRSV], 'to be ridiculed' [**LN**], 'to be sneered at' [Herm, LN], 'to be outwitted' [SSA], 'to be made a fool' [NET], 'to be fooled' [REB]. This passive verb is also translated actively with 'you' as the subject and 'God' as the object: 'to fool' [CEV], 'to make a fool out of' [GW], 'to cheat' [NCV], 'to ignore' [NLT]; with 'no one' as the subject: 'to make a fool of' [TEV].

QUESTION—What is significant about the absence of the article with θεός 'God'?

It shows that θεός 'God' is to be understood qualitatively [NCBC]. It focuses on the nature of God's being instead of on the identity of his person [NIC]. It is always qualitative and emphasizes the divine attributes of God. It designates not simply the being God, but God as divine [ICC]. The word θεός 'God' is emphatic and emphasizes that God is not a man and therefore cannot be mocked [ICC, TH]. Paul is not speaking about a ridicule of God that he will not leave unpunished, but an evasion of his laws which men try to accomplish, but can not [ICC].

For[a] what ever (a) person[b] may-sow,[c] this also[d] he-will-reap;[e]

LEXICON—a. γάρ (LN 89.23): 'for' [BNTC, Herm, LN, Mor, WBC; KJV, NASB, NET, NRSV], 'because' [LN], 'specifically' [SSA], not explicit [CEV, GW, NCV, NIV, NLT, REB, TEV].
    b. ἄνθρωπος (LN 9.1, 9.24) (BAGD 3.a.γ. p. 69): 'person' [BNTC, LN (9.1), SSA; NET], 'one' [BAGD, Herm], 'individual' [LN (9.1)], 'man' [LN (9.24), Mor, WBC; KJV, NASB, NIV], 'you' [CEV, GW, NLT, NRSV, TEV], 'people' [NCV], 'he' [REB].
    c. pres./aorist act. subj. of σπείρω (LN 43.6) (BAGD 1.b.α. p. 761): 'to sow' [BAGD, BNTC, Herm, LN, Mor, SSA, WBC; all versions except CEV, GW, NCV], 'to plant' [CEV, GW, NCV].
    d. καί (LN 89.93): 'also' [BNTC, Herm, LN, Mor, WBC; KJV, NASB], not explicit [SSA; all versions except KJV, NASB].
    e. fut. act. indic. of θερίζω (LN 43.14) (BAGD 2.a. p. 359): 'to reap' [BAGD, BNTC, Herm, LN, Mor, SSA, WBC; all versions except CEV, GW, NCV], 'to harvest' [LN; CEV, GW, NCV].

QUESTION—What is meant by this phrase?

Paul is saying that this has an important application to the way people live. It is what we sow that determines our ultimate harvest [Mor]. Paul emphasizes that there is a direct correlation between sowing and reaping. The responsibility rests on the person himself as to whether life results in blessing or judgment since God is not a deity who reverses his laws or can be tricked into believing something to be true when it is not [WBC]. 'Whatever a person may sow' could refer to anything that a man does while he is alive [TH]. 'He will reap' could refer to God's response to these actions [TH] or to his verdict on the day of judgment [Alf, Herm, TH].

QUESTION—What relationship is indicated by γάρ 'for'?

It functions as an explanation [WBC]. It explains in what respect this warning is to be heeded [Lns]. It indicates the reason for the first part of this verse [Herm].

QUESTION—What relationship is indicated by τοῦτο καί 'this also'?

Τοῦτο 'this' gives emphasis 'this and nothing else' [Alf]. Τοῦτο 'this' emphasizes the force of καί 'also'. Τοῦτο καί 'this also' emphasizes the cause-effect relationship and exact correspondence between what is sown and what is reaped [NIC].

6:8 because[a] the-(one) sowing[b] to his-own flesh[c] will-reap[d] ruin[e] from the flesh,

LEXICON—a. ὅτι (LN 89.33): 'because' [LN; NET], 'for' [BNTC, Herm, Mor; KJV, NASB], not explicit [SSA, WBC; all versions except KJV, NASB, NET].

b. pres. act. participle of σπείρω (LN 43.6) (BAGD 1.b.α. p. 761): 'to sow' [BAGD, LN]. The phrase ὁ σπείρων εἰς τὴν σάρκα ἑαυτοῦ 'the one sowing to his own flesh' is translated 'the one/person who sows to his own flesh' [WBC; NASB, NET], 'he who sows to his own flesh' [Mor], 'he that soweth to his flesh' [KJV], 'the one who sows to please his sinful nature' [NIV], 'if you sow to your own flesh' [NRSV], 'if you plant in the field of your natural desires' [TEV], 'if you plant in the soil of your corrupt nature' [GW], 'if they plant to satisfy their sinful desires' [NCV], 'if he sows in the field of his unspiritual nature' [REB], 'those who live only to satisfy their own sinful desires' [NLT], 'those who sow to their own flesh' [BNTC], 'if you follow your selfish desires' [CEV], 'the one who indulges his own naturally evil self' [SSA], 'whoever sows into one's own flesh' [Herm].

c. σάρξ (LN 8.63, **26.7**) (BAGD 7. p. 744): 'flesh' [BAGD, BNTC, Herm, LN (8.63), Mor, WBC; KJV, NASB, NET, NRSV], 'human nature' [LN (26.7)], 'human, natural desires' [**LN** (26.7)], 'natural desires' [TEV], 'sinful desires' [NLT], 'naturally evil self' [SSA], 'selfish desires' [CEV], 'corrupt nature' [GW], 'sinful selves' [NCV], 'sinful nature' [NIV], 'unspiritual nature' [REB].

d. fut. act. indic. of θερίζω (LN 43.14) (BAGD 2.a. p. 359): 'to reap' [BAGD, LN], 'to harvest' [LN]. The phrase ἐκ τῆς σαρκὸς θερίσει φθοράν 'will reap ruin from the flesh' is translated 'will reap corruption from the flesh' [NET], 'you will reap corruption from the flesh' [NRSV], 'will from/of the flesh reap corruption' [Mor; NASB], 'shall of the flesh reap corruption' [KJV], 'shall from the flesh reap corruption' [BNTC], 'he will reap from it a harvest of corruption' [REB], 'you will harvest destruction' [CEV, GW], 'from that nature will reap destruction' [NIV], 'their sinful lives will bring them ruin' [NCV], 'from it you will gather the harvest of death' [TEV], 'from the flesh shall reap destruction' [WBC], 'will harvest the consequences of decay and death' [NLT], 'will be condemned eternally by God' [SSA], 'will reap a harvest of corruption' [Herm].

e. φθορά (LN 20.38, 88.267) (BAGD 4. p. 858): 'ruin' [LN (20.38); NCV], 'destruction' [BAGD, LN (20.38), WBC; CEV, GW, NIV], 'depravity, moral corruption' [LN (88.267)], 'corruption' [BNTC, Mor; KJV, NASB, NET, NRSV], 'a harvest of corruption' [Herm; REB], 'the harvest of death' [TEV], 'the consequences of decay and death' [NLT]. This noun is also translated as a passive verb: 'to be condemned' [SSA].

QUESTION—What relationship is indicated by ὅτι 'because'?

It probably functions in a declarative manner to set off what follows as being Paul's own explanation [WBC]. The metaphor of sowing and reaping in the preceding verse is now followed by four more applications of sowing or reaping [SSA].

QUESTION—What relationship is indicated by εἰς 'to'?

It indicates the direction in which the seed fell. In a metaphorical sense, it must mean that flesh is the sphere in which a man sows [NCBC].

QUESTION—What is meant by φθορά 'ruin'?

It refers to ultimate loss; it is the opposite of life eternal [Lns, Mor, NTC]. It refers to physical death and disintegration, from which for those who sow to the flesh, there is no rising to eternal life [NIC]. It stands for that which results in death [NCBC]. Some understand the word to mean moral and spiritual decay. However, the word could also refer to physical decay and, therefore, should be understood as a term for 'death' in a general sense [TH]. It refers to the corruption and death of the body from which, for those who have not lived according to the spirit, there is no rising to eternal life [ICC].

QUESTION—What is meant by σάρξ 'flesh'?

1. It refers to the physical aspects of the person's desires [ICC, NIC; TEV]. It refers to the body, the physical element of man [ICC].
2. It refers to the person's sinful nature [BST, Lns, NIGTC, NTC, SSA; CEV, GW, NCV, NIV, NLT]. Our 'flesh' is our lower nature with its passions and desires (5:24). If our flesh is unchecked it breaks out in 'the works of the flesh' (5:19–21) [BST]. 'Flesh' is not the body but our own sin-corrupted nature [Lns].

QUESTION—How are σάρξ 'flesh' and πνεῦμα 'Spirit' compared?

1. The flesh and the Spirit are compared to the soils in which the seeds are sown [BST, Herm, Lt, NCBC, TH; GW, REB, TEV]. The sower sows either to the flesh or to the Spirit, as though casting seed into two entirely different fields and from those two different fields he reaps a harvest that corresponds to the nature of the fields themselves [WBC]. Paul presents 'flesh' and 'spirit' as two kinds of fields which yield different harvests. 'Flesh' yields a harvest of corruption and 'spirit' yields a harvest of eternal life [TH]. The sower sows 'into his flesh' or 'into the Spirit' as if they were fields. Then the sower harvests 'from the flesh' or 'from the Spirit' [Herm].
2. The flesh and the spirit do not refer to soils [Alf, ICC, Lns, NTC; KJV, NASB, NCV, NET, NIV, NRSV]. Εἰς is not 'into'; it functions as a dative. The one sows for his own flesh, to promote his flesh. The other sows for the spirit, to promote the interests of the spirit. The stress is on the two sowers and what their sowing promotes. Seed and soil are not mentioned, since no one sows without them [Lns]. What would be meant by casting seed into one's own flesh? It is evident that Paul is not

GALATIANS 6:8 247

constructing a condensed parable consistent throughout. He is using individual terms 'sow' and 'reap' in a figurative sense. Therefore, εἰς 'to' should not be taken spatially but tropically [ICC, NIC].

but[a] the-(one) sowing[b] to[c] the Spirit/spirit[d] will-reap[e] life eternal[f] from[g] the Spirit/spirit.[d]

LEXICON—a. δέ (LN 89.124): 'but' [BNTC, Herm, LN, Mor, SSA; all versions except NIV, TEV], 'if' [TEV], not explicit [WBC; NIV].
   b. pres. act. participle of σπείρω (LN 43.6) (BAGD 1.b.α. p. 761): 'to sow' [BAGD, BNTC, Herm, LN, Mor, WBC; KJV, NASB, NET, NIV, NRSV, REB], 'to plant' [GW, NCV, TEV], 'to live' [NLT]. The phrase ὁ σπείρων εἰς τὸ πνεῦμα 'the one sowing to the Spirit' is translated 'the one who pleases the Holy Spirit' [SSA], 'if you follow the Spirit' [CEV].
   c. εἰς with accusative object (LN 84.22, 89.57, 90.23): 'to' [BNTC, Mor, WBC; KJV, NASB, NET, NRSV], 'into' [Herm, LN (84.22)], 'in' [GW, REB, TEV], 'for the purpose of' [LN (89.57)], 'with respect to, with reference to' [LN (90.23)]. This preposition is also translated as a verb with 'they' as the subject: 'to please' [NCV], with 'the one' as the subject: 'to please' [NIV], with 'those' as the subject: 'to please' [NLT]. See b. [SSA; CEV].
   d. πνεῦμα (LN 12.18) (BAGD 5.g.α. p. 677): 'Spirit' [BAGD, BNTC, Herm, LN, Mor, WBC; all versions except GW], 'Holy Spirit' [LN, SSA], 'spiritual nature' [GW].
   e. fut. act. indic. of θερίζω (LN 43.14) (BAGD 2.a. p. 359): 'to reap' [BAGD, BNTC, Herm, LN, Mor, WBC; KJV, NASB, NET, NIV, NRSV, REB], 'to harvest' [LN; CEV, GW, NLT], 'to gather' [TEV], 'to receive' [NCV]. The phrase θερίσει ζωὴν αἰώνιον 'will reap life eternal' is translated 'will live forever with God' [SSA], 'you will harvest eternal life' [CEV].
   f. αἰώνιος (LN 67.96): 'eternal' [BNTC, Herm, LN, Mor, WBC; all versions except GW, KJV, NLT], 'forever' [SSA], 'everlasting' [GW, KJV, NLT].
   g. ἐκ with genitive object (LN 90.16): 'from' [BNTC, Herm, LN, WBC; all versions except CEV, GW, KJV], 'of' [Mor; KJV], not explicit [CEV, GW]. The phrase ἐκ τοῦ πνεύματος 'from the Spirit' is translated 'because he pleased the Holy Spirit' [SSA].

QUESTION—What is meant by ζωὴν αἰώνιον 'eternal life'?
   It is the resurrection life of Christ that was made available to believers by the Spirit of God who raised Jesus from the dead [NIGTC]. It is not merely life that lasts eternally. It is God's very own life, the life of the Father, the Son, and the Holy Spirit that God graciously gave to the children of God through faith in Jesus Christ [NAC]. The emphasis is on the positive qualities that go with a life which is lived in the Spirit [TH].

QUESTION—What spirit is referred to by πνεῦμα 'spirit'?
1. This refers to God's Holy Spirit [BNTC, BST, Herm, Lt, Mor, NAC, NCBC, NIC, NTC, SSA, TH; all versions except GW]. It most likely refers to a man whose intentions are directed towards the Spirit-dominated life [NCBC]. It means the Holy Spirit if 'spirit' has the same reference as in 5:16 [TH].
2. This refers to the spiritual aspect of a person [ICC, Lns; GW]. This refers to one's own πνεῦμα 'spirit', the non-material, intellectual, spiritual side of man's being, which is the seat of the religious life, and that which survives the cataclysmic experience of physical death or the day of the Lord [ICC].

6:9 But doing[a] the good[b] not let-us-lose-heart,[c]

LEXICON—a. pres. act. participle of ποιέω (LN 90.45) (BAGD I.1.b.ε. p. 681): 'to do' [BAGD, BNTC, Herm, LN, Mor, SSA, WBC; all versions except CEV, GW], 'to live' [GW], 'to help' [CEV]. This entire phrase is translated 'Don't get tired of helping others' [CEV], 'We can't allow ourselves to get tired of living the right way' [GW].
b. καλός (LN 65.22, 88.4) (BAGD 2.b. p. 400): 'good' [Herm, LN (65.22, 88.4), Mor, SSA, WBC; NASB, NCV, NET, NIV, NLT, REB, TEV], 'well' [BNTC; KJV], 'right' [NRSV], 'morally good' [BAGD], 'praiseworthy' [BAGD, LN (88.4)]. The phrase τὸ καλὸν ποιοῦντες 'doing the good' is translated 'helping others' [CEV], 'living the right way' [GW].
c. pres. act. subj. of ἐγκακέω (LN 25.288) (BAGD 1. p. 215; p. 240): 'to lose heart' [BAGD, LN; NASB], 'to be discouraged' [LN], 'to be weary' [Mor; KJV], 'to give up' [**LN**], 'to become weary' [BAGD, BNTC, WBC; NIV], 'to grow weary' [Herm; NET, NRSV], 'to become tired' [BAGD; CEV, GW, NCV, NLT, REB, TEV], 'to falter' [SSA].

QUESTION—What relationship is indicated by δέ 'but'?
Δὲ 'then' connects this verse with 6:8 [WBC]. Δὲ 'so' connects this verse with 6:8 [TH]. Its function is to introduce that which is additional and different [Lns, SSA].

QUESTION—What is meant by τὸ καλὸν ποιοῦντες 'doing the good'?
It includes everything the Christian is responsible for doing [Herm, NAC] such as restoring someone who is entrapped by sin (6:1), bearing the oppressive burdens of others (6:2), and sharing materially with those who teach the gospel message (6:6) [WBC]. The καλός 'good' refers generally to all that is morally good [NIC]. In this verse it refers generally to any action done for others or for oneself that results in well-being [TH]. In the context it is possible that Paul was thinking of helping anyone who was in need [NTC].

QUESTION—Who is referred to with ἐγκακῶμεν 'let us lose heart'?
Paul includes himself with the Galatian Christians [Mor, NCBC, SSA].

for in-its-own[a] time[b] we-will-reap,[c] not giving-up.[d]

LEXICON—a. ἴδιος (LN 57.4): '(one's) own' [LN], 'due' [BNTC, Herm, Mor; KJV, NASB, NET, REB], 'proper' [WBC; GW, NIV], 'right' [CEV, NCV], 'appropriate' [NLT], 'harvest' [NRSV]. The phrase καιρῷ ἰδίῳ 'in its own time' is translated 'when God determines/has determined' [SSA], 'the time will come' [TEV].

b. καιρός (LN 67.1) (BAGD 3. p. 395): 'time' [BAGD, BNTC, LN, Mor, WBC; all versions except KJV], 'season' [Herm; KJV]. See a. [SSA].

c. fut. act. indic. of θερίζω (LN 43.14) (BAGD 2.a. p. 359): 'to reap' [BAGD, BNTC, LN, Mor, WBC; all versions except CEV, GW, NCV], 'to harvest' [LN], 'to receive' [GW, NCV], 'to bring in' [Herm], 'to experience/witness/receive' [SSA]. The active verb is also translated passively: 'to be rewarded' [CEV].

d. pres. mid. (deponent = act.) participle of ἐκλύω (LN 23.79, **25.288**) (BAGD p. 243): 'to give up' [**LN** (25.288), WBC; CEV, GW, NCV, NET, NIV, NRSV, TEV], 'to give out' [BAGD, Herm], 'to become discouraged' [LN (25.288)], 'to lose heart' [BNTC, LN (25.288)], 'to faint' [LN (23.79); KJV], 'to faint from exhaustion, to become extremely weary' [LN (23.79)], 'to grow slack' [Mor], 'to be slack' [REB], 'to grow weary' [NASB], 'to quit' [SSA], 'to get discouraged and give up' [NLT].

QUESTION—What relationship is indicated by γάρ 'for'?

It indicates the reason for not losing heart [Lns]. It is the grounds for the preceding admonition [SSA].

QUESTION—What is meant by καιρῷ ἰδίῳ 'in its own time'?

It is probably an idiom for 'at the appropriate moment,' 'in due season,' or 'at the proper time,' without specifying what moment, season, or time is in mind [WBC]. It means 'at the moment of time that is exactly right' as determined by God [NTC, SSA]. It could be that 'the time will come' refers to the return of the Lord or to the end of the world [TH].

QUESTION—What is the function of the participle ἐκλυόμενοι 'becoming weary'?

It expresses a condition [Lns, NCBC, SSA; all versions except NLT]: if we do not become weary. The condition is implied 'if we do not relax' [Lns]. Paul states the condition here by the use of a participle to show that it is an integral part of reaping [NCBC]. The reaping is subject to their μὴ ἐκλυόμενοι 'not quitting' [SSA]. The verb puts emphasis on becoming discouraged or relaxing one's efforts [Lns, TH].

6:10 Therefore[a] then[b] as[c] we-have opportunity,[d]

LEXICON—a. οὖν (LN 89.50): 'therefore' [LN, SSA, WBC; KJV, NIV, REB], 'so' [BNTC, LN, Mor; NASB, NET, NRSV, TEV], 'consequently' [Herm, LN], 'accordingly, then, so then' [LN], not explicit [CEV, GW, NCV, NLT].

b. ἄρα (LN 89.46) (BAGD 4. p. 104): 'then' [BNTC, LN, Mor; NASB, NET, NRSV, TEV], 'so, consequently, as a result' [LN], not explicit

[Herm, SSA, WBC; CEV, GW, KJV, NCV, NIV, NLT, REB]. The phrase ἄρα οὖν 'therefore then' is translated 'so then' [BAGD].
c. ὡς (LN 67.45, 67.139) (BAGD IV.1.b. p. 898): 'as' [BNTC, Herm, LN (67.45), Mor; KJV, NIV, REB], 'when' [LN (67.45); NCV], 'while' [LN (67.139); NASB], 'whenever' [WBC; CEV, GW, NET, NLT, NRSV], 'as often as' [TEV], 'as long as' [BAGD, LN (67.139)], 'in proportion to' [SSA].
d. καιρός (LN 22.45, 67.1) (BAGD 2. p. 395): 'opportunity' [BAGD, BNTC, LN (22.45), Mor, SSA, WBC; all versions except CEV, TEV], 'time' [Herm, LN (67.1)], 'occasion' [LN (67.1)], 'good occasion' [LN (22.45)], 'chance' [TEV]. This entire phrase is translated 'whenever we can' [CEV].

QUESTION—What relationship is indicated by ἄρα οὖν 'therefore then'?

Ἄρα οὖν 'therefore then' is used to introduce the logical conclusion of the preceding statement [NIC]. It is a formula that Paul uses to draw out the logical consequence of what he has just said [NCBC]. It signals that Paul was about to conclude the ethical exhortations he had presented in this letter [NAC]. It introduces the conclusion [Herm].

QUESTION—What is meant by ὡς καιρὸν ἔχομεν 'as we have opportunity'?
1. This refers to different opportunities as they come [BNTC, ICC, NCBC, NTC; CEV, GW, NCV, NET, NLT, NRSV, TEV]: whenever we have opportunity. It implies that during the present life there are always opportunities for doing good [NCBC].
2. This refers to the present opportunity before the harvest [Herm, Lns, Mor, NAC, NIBC, NIC, NIGTC, TNTC; NASB]: while we still have the opportunity. Paul is saying that while we have life we have opportunity and we should make the most of that opportunity [Mor, NIC]. It means that in Paul's view the Christian's ethical responsibility is limited to the time in which he lives 'in the flesh' [Herm]. It is not a reference to special opportunities which come along. Instead, this is an ever-present 'season' or opportunity. It is to go on 'while, as long as, we have opportunity,' as long as life lasts and without weariness [Lns].
3. This refers to the correspondence with the opportunities [Alf, SSA]: in proportion to our individual opportunities. It means to let our state of being kind, charitable, or beneficial be in proportion to our opportunity [Alf].

let-us-be-doing[a] the good[b] to[c] all (persons),

TEXT—Instead of the present subjunctive ἐργαζώμεθα 'let us be doing' some manuscripts read the aorist subjunctive ἐργασώμεθα 'let us do' [KJV, NASB, NET, NIV], and other manuscripts read the present indicative ἐργαζόμεθα 'we are doing'. GNT reads the present subjunctive ἐργαζώμεθα 'let us be doing' with an A decision, indicating that the text is certain.

LEXICON—a. pres. mid. (deponent = act.) subj. of ἐργάζομαι (LN 90.47) (BAGD 2.a. p. 307): 'to do' [BAGD, LN, Mor, SSA, WBC; GW, KJV, NASB, NET, NIV, NLT, TEV], 'to work' [BNTC, Herm; NRSV, REB], 'to help' [CEV, NCV]. This entire phrase is translated 'we should help people' [CEV], 'to help anyone, we should do it' [NCV].
  b. ἀγαθός (LN 65.20, 88.1) (BAGD 2.a.α. p. 3): 'good' [BAGD, BNTC, Herm, LN (65.20, 88.1), Mor, WBC; all versions except CEV, GW, NCV]. This noun is also translated as an adjective: '(what is) good' [SSA; GW]. See a. [CEV, NCV].
  c. πρός with accusative object (LN 84.18, **90.58**) (BAGD III.4.b. p. 710): 'to' [BAGD, LN (84.18, **90.58**), Mor, SSA, WBC; NASB, NET, NIV, NLT, TEV], 'unto' [KJV], 'of' [BNTC, Herm; NRSV, REB], 'for' [GW]. See a. [CEV, NCV].
QUESTION—What is meant by τὸ ἀγαθόν 'the good'?
  In the singular with an article it means 'that which is advantageous' [WBC]. It refers to deeds that benefit people [NIC].

but[a] especially[b] to[c] the members-of-the-household[d] of-the faith.[e]
LEXICON—a. δέ (LN 89.94, 89.124): 'but' [Herm, LN (89.124), SSA; NCV], 'and' [LN (89.94); NASB, NET, NRSV, TEV], not explicit [BNTC, Mor, WBC; CEV, GW, KJV, NIV, NLT, REB].
  b. μάλιστα (LN 78.7) (BAGD 1. p. 489): 'especially' [BAGD, BNTC, Herm, LN, Mor, WBC; all versions except NCV], 'particularly' [SSA]. This adverb is also translated as a verb with 'we' as the subject: 'to give special attention' [NCV].
  c. πρός with accusative object (LN 84.18, 90.58) (BAGD III.4.b. p. 710): 'to' [BAGD, LN (84.18, 90.58), Mor, SSA, WBC; NASB, NCV, NET, NIV, NLT, TEV], 'unto' [KJV], 'for' [Herm; GW, NRSV], not explicit [BNTC; REB]. The phrase πρὸς τοὺς οἰκείους τῆς πίστεως 'to the members of the household of the faith' is translated 'if they are followers of the Lord' [CEV].
  d. οἰκεῖος (LN 10.11) (BAGD 2. p. 556): 'member of the household' [BNTC, LN; REB], 'member of a family' [LN], 'household' [Mor, SSA], 'family' [GW]. The phrase τοὺς οἰκείους 'the members of the household' is translated 'those who belong to the household' [BAGD, Herm, WBC], 'those who belong to the family' [NET, NIV], 'them who are of the household' [KJV], 'those who are of the household' [NASB], 'those who are in the family' [NCV], 'those of the family' [NRSV], 'those who belong to our family' [TEV], 'our Christian brothers and sisters' [NLT], 'followers of the Lord' [CEV].
  e. πίστις (LN 31.102) (BAGD 2.d.α. p. 663): 'faith' [BAGD, BNTC, Herm, LN, Mor, SSA, WBC; KJV, NASB, NET, NRSV, REB, TEV], 'believer' [GW, NCV, NIV], not explicit [CEV, NLT].

QUESTION—What is the meaning of μάλιστα 'especially'?

Giving charity especially to our brethren is required no more than doing other spiritual good especially to our brethren. They and we are of one divine family or household, we are joined together with them as we are with no others. This is the reason for Paul's 'especially', it applies to 'the good' in every respect [Lns]. We as Christians are to have a special concern for the welfare of fellow believers [NAC, WBC]. Fellow Christians have first call upon us [Lns].

QUESTION—How are the nouns related in the genitive construction τοὺς οἰκείους τῆς πίστεως 'the members of the household of the faith'?

Believers 'in Christ' make up 'the household of faith.' This is metaphorical for the corporate unity of Christians [WBC]. The phrase refers to fellow Christians [Herm]. The phrase suggests that Christians are like members of one family. Their faith in Jesus Christ is what distinguishes them [TH]. Τῆς πίστεως 'of the faith' means the active Christian faith, faith in Jesus Christ. The phrase τοὺς οἰκείους τῆς πίστεως 'the members of the household of the faith' means those who are members of that household [ICC]. The distinguishing characteristic of the Christian household is 'the faith in Jesus Christ' [ICC, Mor, NCBC, WBC]. The phrase τοὺς οἰκείους τῆς πίστεως 'the members of the household of the faith' appears to be little more than a colorful description of all true Christian believers [NCBC]. The phrase τοὺς οἰκείους τῆς πίστεως 'the members of the household of the faith' means those who share the gospel [NTC].

DISCOURSE UNIT: 6:11–18 [BST, GNT, Mor, NCBC, NIC, NIGTC, TNTC, WBC; CEV, GW, NCV, NET, NIV, NLT, NRSV, TEV]. The topic is the essence of the Christian religion [BST], conclusion [Mor, NCBC], summary and conclusion [NIC], concluding comments and final greeting [NIGTC], the autographed conclusion [TNTC], subscription [WBC], final warnings [CEV], final warning and benediction [GNT], Paul summarizes his teachings about circumcision [GW], Paul ends his letter [NCV], final instructions and benediction [NET], not circumcision but a new creation [NIV], Paul's final advice [NLT], final admonitions and benediction [NRSV], final warning and greeting [TEV].

DISCOURSE UNIT: 6:11–16 [NAC]. The topic is the apostolic seal.

6:11 See[a] in-how-large[b] letters[c] I-have-written[d] to-you with-my hand.[e]

LEXICON—a. aorist act. impera. of ὁράω (LN 24.1, 30.45) (BAGD 1.c. p. 220 εἶδον): 'to see' [BNTC, Herm, LN (24.1), Mor, WBC; all versions except GW, NLT, REB], 'to take notice of, to pay attention to' [LN (30.45)], 'to notice' [BAGD, SSA; NLT], 'to look' [GW, REB].

b. πηλίκος (LN **79.126**) (BAGD 1. p. 656): 'how large' [LN; GW, KJV], 'what large' [BAGD, BNTC, Herm, **LN**, Mor, WBC; NASB, NCV, NIV, NLT, NRSV], 'what big' [CEV, NET, TEV], 'how big' [REB], '(the) large' [SSA].

c. γράμμα (LN **33.35**) (BAGD 1. p. 165): 'letter' [BAGD, BNTC, Herm, **LN**, Mor, WBC; all versions], 'character' [SSA].

d. aorist act. indic. of γράφω (LN 33.61) (BAGD 1. p. 166): 'to write' [BAGD, BNTC, Herm, LN, Mor, SSA, WBC; all versions].

e. χείρ (LN 8.30) (BAGD 1. p. 880): 'hand' [BNTC, Herm, LN, Mor, WBC; all versions except GW, NCV, NLT], 'handwriting' [BAGD; NLT]. The phrase ἔγραψα τῇ ἐμῇ χειρί 'I have written to you with my hand' is translated 'I'm writing this myself' [GW], 'I use to write this myself' [NCV], 'I myself am writing to you' [SSA].

QUESTION—What is the mood of the verb ἴδετε 'see'?

1. It is imperative [Alf, BNTC, BST, Herm, ICC, Lns, Lt, NCBC, NIC, NTC, TH, TNTC, WBC; all versions except CEV, KJV]: see. Its purpose is to arouse attention and to highlight the importance of what follows [WBC].

2. It is indicative [CEV, KJV]: you see.

QUESTION—What is significant about Paul writing in large letters?

Writing in his own hand is a token of the genuineness of the letter [Mor, NTC]. He wanted to emphasize the importance of what he was writing in these final verses [BNTC, BST, Herm, ICC, Mor, NIGTC, NTC, SSA, TH, WBC]. This emphasizes the following words about circumcision, which was the key issue among the Galatians [SSA]. This special emphasis is given to the following summary of the argument of the letter and to a final warning [NTC]. The size of the letters would have about the same effect as that of bold-face type in a modern book or double underlining in a manuscript [ICC].

QUESTION—What is referred to by ἔγραψα τῇ ἐμῇ χειρί 'I have written to you with my hand'?

1. He is referring to this paragraph [BNTC, BST, Herm, ICC, Lt, Mor, NAC, NCBC, NIBC, NIC, NIGTC, NTC, SSA, TH, TNTC, WBC]. This interpretation would indicate that the letter had been dictated up to this point and then Paul wrote this concluding portion with his own hand, and therefore the aorist would mean that Paul placed himself at the time this letter is read in Galatia [Lns].

2. He is referring to the whole letter which he has written himself [Alf, Lns]. Paul is referring to the entire epistle and says that all of it came from his own hand. None of it was dictated and all of it was written in large script [Lns].

6:12 As-many-as[a] desire[b] to-make-a-good-showing[c] in[d] (the) flesh,[e]

LEXICON—a. ὅσος (LN 59.7) (BAGD 2. p. 586): 'as many as' [BAGD, LN, Mor; KJV], 'some' [SSA; NCV]. The phrase ὅσοι...οὗτοι 'as many as...these' is translated 'all who' [BAGD], 'those who' [BNTC, WBC; NASB, NET, NIV, NLT, NRSV, REB], 'those people who' [Herm; CEV], 'these people who' [GW], 'the people who' [TEV].

b. pres. act. indic. of θέλω (LN 25.1): 'to desire' [LN, SSA; KJV, NASB], 'to wish' [Herm, LN, Mor], 'to want' [BNTC, LN, WBC; GW, NET, NIV, NRSV, REB, TEV], 'to try' [CEV, NCV, NLT].
c. aorist act. infin. of εὐπροσωπέω (LN **88.236**) (BAGD p. 324): 'to make a good showing' [BAGD, **LN**, WBC; NASB, NET, NRSV], 'to make a good impression' [Mor; NIV], 'to make a fair showing' [BNTC], 'to make a nice appearance' [Herm], 'to make a fair show' [KJV], not explicit [NCV, NLT]. The phrase εὐπροσωπῆσαι ἐν σαρκί 'to make a good showing in the flesh' is translated 'that what they do outwardly might please the Jews' [SSA], 'to make a big deal out of a physical thing' [GW], 'to be outwardly in good standing' [REB], 'to show off and boast about external matters' [TEV], 'to show how important they are' [CEV].
d. ἐν with dative object (LN 83.13, 89.5): 'in' [BNTC, Herm, LN (83.13, 89.5), Mor; KJV, NASB, NET, NRSV], 'with regard to' [LN (89.5)], not explicit [WBC; NCV, NIV, NLT]. See c. [SSA; CEV, GW, REB, TEV].
e. σάρξ (LN 8.63, 26.7, 58.10) (BAGD 6. p. 744): 'flesh' [BNTC, Herm, LN (8.63), Mor; KJV, NASB, NRSV], 'human nature' [LN (26.7, 58.10)], 'earthly things' [BAGD], 'physical thing' [GW], 'external matters' [NET, TEV], not explicit [NCV, NLT]. This noun is also translated as an adverb: 'outwardly' [SSA, WBC; NIV]. See c. [CEV, REB].

QUESTION—What is meant by εὐπροσωπέω 'to make a good showing'?
To the Jewish mind the finest outward display of a man's serious intentions towards piety was his willingness to submit to circumcision. This is what Paul meant by 'to make a good showing' [NCBC].

QUESTION—What is meant by ἐν σαρκί 'in the flesh'?
Literally it refers to circumcision 'in the flesh', but more generally it signifies whatever is external as opposed to that which is spiritual [WBC]. It refers to outward things with special reference to the external rite of circumcision [TH].

these are-compelling[a] you to-be-circumcised,[b]
LEXICON—a. pres. act. indic. of ἀναγκάζω (LN 37.33) (BAGD 1. p. 52): 'to compel' [BAGD, BNTC, Herm, LN, Mor, WBC; NASB, NIV, NRSV], 'to force' [BAGD, LN; GW, NCV, NET, NLT, REB, TEV], 'to insist' [SSA], 'to constrain' [KJV], 'to tell' [CEV].
b. pres. pass. infin. of περιτέμνω (LN **53.51**) (BAGD 1. p. 652): 'to be circumcised' [BAGD, BNTC, Herm, **LN**, Mor, SSA; all versions except CEV, REB], 'to get circumcised' [CEV]. This verb is also translated as a noun: '(to receive) circumcision' [WBC], '(to force) circumcision' [REB].

only[a] in-order-that not they-may-be-persecuted[b] for-the cross of Christ.
LEXICON—a. μόνον (LN 58.50): 'only' [BNTC, Herm, LN, Mor, WBC; KJV, NET, NRSV, TEV], 'solely' [SSA], 'simply' [NASB], 'only aim' [GW], 'only reason' [NIV], 'sole object' [REB], 'for just one reason' [NLT]. This entire phrase is translated by starting a new sentence 'And they don't want to get into trouble for preaching about the cross of Christ' [CEV],

'They are afraid they will be attacked if they follow only the cross of Christ' [NCV].
b. pres. pass. subj. of διώκω (LN 39.45) (BAGD 2. p. 201): 'to be persecuted' [BAGD, BNTC, Herm, LN, Mor, SSA, WBC; NASB, NET, NIV, NLT, NRSV, TEV], 'to get into trouble' [CEV], 'to be attacked' [NCV]. This verb is also translated as a noun: '(to suffer) persecution' [KJV], '(to avoid) persecution' [GW], '(to escape) persecution' [REB].

QUESTION—What relationship is indicated by μόνον 'only'?
It indicates that this was the driving force as Paul saw it [Mor]. This was the only purpose the new teachers had in promoting circumcision [SSA].

QUESTION—How are the nouns related in the genitive construction σταυρῷ τοῦ Χριστοῦ 'cross of Christ'?
The cross here stands for the death of Christ together with its significance, particularly that of bringing about a relationship with God based on faith alone [TH]. Σταυρός 'cross' is used by metonymy for the crucifixion of Christ or more generally for the whole doctrine of salvation through the crucified Jesus as against that of justification by works of the law [ICC]. Σταυρός 'cross' stands for Christ's death on the cross [SSA]. The cross stands for the whole doctrine of salvation through the crucified Jesus as against that of justification by works of law [NIC].

6:13 For[a] not-even the-(ones) being-circumcised[b] keep[c] (the) Law[d] themselves[e]

LEXICON—a. γάρ (LN 89.23): 'for' [BNTC, Herm, LN, Mor, WBC; KJV, NASB, NET], 'because' [LN], 'since' [SSA], 'and' [NLT], not explicit [CEV, NCV, NIV, NRSV, REB, TEV]. This is translated 'It's clear that' [GW].
b. pres. pass. participle of περιτέμνω (LN 53.51) (BAGD 1. p. 652): 'to be circumcised' [Herm, LN, Mor, SSA, WBC; CEV, KJV, NASB, NCV, NET, NIV, NRSV], 'to have (oneself) circumcised' [BAGD, BNTC; GW]. This verb is also translated as a noun: '(to advocate) circumcision' [NLT], '(to accept) circumcision' [REB], '(to practice) circumcision' [TEV].
c. pres. act. indic. of φυλάσσω (LN 36.19) (BAGD 1.f. p. 868): 'to keep' [BAGD, BNTC, Herm, Mor, WBC; KJV, NASB, NLT], 'to observe' [BAGD], 'to follow' [BAGD; GW], 'to obey' [LN; CEV, NCV, NET, NIV, NRSV, TEV], 'to comply with' [SSA]. This verb is also translated 'are (not) thoroughgoing observers of' [REB].
d. νόμος (LN 33.55, 33.333) (BAGD 3. p. 542): 'Law' [Herm, LN (33.55); NASB, TEV], 'law' [BNTC, LN (33.333), Mor, WBC; KJV, NCV, NET, NIV, NLT, NRSV, REB], 'Mosaic law' [SSA], 'Law of Moses' [CEV], 'Jewish laws' [GW]. It refers to the law which Moses received from God [BAGD].

e. αὐτός (LN 92.37): as a plural: 'themselves' [BNTC, Herm, LN, SSA, WBC; GW, KJV, NASB, NCV, NET, NRSV], not explicit [Mor; CEV, NIV, NLT, REB, TEV].

QUESTION—What relationship is indicated by γάρ 'for'?

It confirms what was stated in the previous phrase begun by μόνον 'only'. The only reason that the Judaizers were compelling the Galatian Christians to become circumcised was a desire to avoid persecution [ICC, WBC].

QUESTION—Who is referred to by οἱ περιτεμνόμενοι 'the ones being circumcised'?

1. It refers to Gentiles who have accepted circumcision [ICC]. The Judaizers probably claimed that their motive for getting Gentiles circumcised was a sincere zeal for the law. But Paul shows that their only motive was to escape persecution since once the Gentiles were circumcised, the Judaizers did not require them to conform to the whole law [ICC].
2. It refers to the Judaistic teachers [Alf, BST, Lns, Lt, Mor, NCBC, NIC, NIGTC, NTC, SSA, TH, WBC]. What is emphasized in Paul's statement that these people 'do not obey the Law' is not their inability to follow the Law, but their indifference toward obeying it. In a sense Paul is saying 'they want you to follow the Law, but they themselves don't obey it' [TH]. The perfect 'those who have been circumcised' may have seemed more correct to a copyist than the present which could be interpreted to mean 'those who have themselves circumcised.' But the present can also be interpreted as indicating 'those who favor and advocate circumcision.' The context points to the latter interpretation for it is clear that Paul is referring to the Judaizers [NTC].
3. It refers to Jews in general [NCBC, TNTC]. This phrase is best understood to refer to Jews whose habitual practice is circumcision, rather than the Gentiles who are now tempted to take that step [TNTC]. Paul points out that not even the circumcised keep the law. The most natural meaning would seem to be that they cannot keep the law because its demands are impossible. Paul isn't criticizing them for failure to keep the law, but for failure to recognize their inability to do so. If they would have recognized this failure they would certainly not have insisted on the Gentiles attempting to do what they themselves had failed to do [NCBC].

but they-want[a] you to-be-circumcised[b]

LEXICON—a. pres. act. indic. of θέλω (LN 25.1) (BAGD 1. p. 355): 'to want' [BNTC, Herm, LN, WBC; all versions except KJV, NASB], 'to desire' [LN, SSA; KJV, NASB], 'to wish' [BAGD, LN, Mor].

b. pres. pass. infin. of περιτέμνω (LN 53.51) (BAGD 1. p. 652): 'to be circumcised' [BAGD, BNTC, Herm, LN, Mor, SSA; all versions except CEV, KJV, NASB], 'to have (oneself) circumcised' [BAGD], 'to have (someone) circumcised' [CEV, KJV, NASB]. This verb is also translated as a noun: '(to receive) circumcision' [WBC].

in-order-that they-may-boast[a] in[b] your flesh.[c]

LEXICON—a. aorist mid. (deponent = act.) subj. of καυχάομαι (LN 33.368) (BAGD 1. p. 425): 'to boast' [BAGD, BNTC, Herm, LN, Mor, SSA, WBC; NASB, NET, NIV, NRSV, REB, TEV], 'to glory' [BAGD; KJV], 'to brag' [CEV, GW, NCV, NLT].

b. ἐν with dative object (LN 83.13, 89.5): 'in' [BNTC, Herm, LN (83.13, 89.5); KJV, NASB], 'with regard to' [LN (89.5)], 'about' [Mor, SSA, WBC; CEV, GW, NCV, NET, NIV, NLT, NRSV], 'of' [REB], not explicit [TEV].

c. σάρξ (LN 8.63) (BAGD 1. p. 743): 'flesh' [BAGD, BNTC, Herm, LN, Mor, WBC; KJV, NASB, NET, NIV, NRSV], 'body' [GW], 'it' [NLT]. It refers to the flesh that is circumcised [BAGD]. This entire phrase is translated 'in order that they might boast about you to those Jews who would persecute them that you underwent that physical rite because they insisted' [SSA], 'All they want is to brag about having you circumcised' [CEV], 'so they can brag about what they forced you to do' [NCV]. ῾Υμετέρᾳ σαρκὶ 'your flesh' is translated 'your submission to that outward rite' [REB], 'that you submitted to this physical ceremony' [TEV].

QUESTION—What is meant by this phrase?

Paul implies that the legalizers' concern was not for the law as a matter of principle but for the sake of boasting about those who followed their teaching. The more Gentiles they could notch up as having been circumcised, the weightier the evidence which they could claim of their zeal for the law [NIGTC]. The fact of the Gentiles' circumcised organs gave the Judaizers a reason to boast of their accomplishments [Lns, NTC].

QUESTION—What is meant by ἐν τῇ ὑμετέρᾳ σαρκὶ 'in your flesh'?

It means 'in the fact that you have been circumcised,' which would be the sign of your conversion to legalistic Judaism [ICC].

QUESTION—What is meant by σάρξ 'flesh'?

It stands for the rite of circumcision performed on the flesh [SSA, TH].

6:14 But for-me may-it- not -happen[a] to-boast[b]

LEXICON—a. aorist mid. (deponent = act.) optative of γίνομαι (LN 13.3, 13.107) (BAGD I.3.a. p. 158): 'to happen, to occur, to come to be' [LN (13.107)], 'to be' [LN (13.3)]. The phrase μὴ γένοιτο 'may it not happen' is translated 'by no means' [BAGD], 'far from it' [BAGD], 'God forbid' [BAGD, BNTC; KJV, NLT, REB], 'never' [SSA, WBC; CEV, NCV], 'far be it' [Herm], 'may it never be' [NASB], 'may it not be' [Mor], 'may I never' [NET, NIV, NRSV]. This entire phrase is translated 'but it's unthinkable that I could ever brag about anything' [GW], 'as for me, however, I will boast' [TEV].

b. pres. mid. (deponent = act.) infin. of καυχάομαι (LN 33.368) (BAGD 1. p. 425): 'to boast' [BAGD, BNTC, Herm, LN, SSA, WBC; NASB, NET,

NIV, NLT, NRSV, REB, TEV], 'to glory' [BAGD, Mor; KJV], 'to brag' [CEV, GW, NCV].

QUESTION—What relationship is indicated by δέ 'but'?

The phrase ἐμοὶ δέ 'but for me' indicates a decisive taking up of a different position [Mor]. In contrast to the false teachers and others who brag about circumcision, Paul now begins to declare that he boasts only in the cross of Christ [TH]. In contrast with the boasting of the Judaizers, which has its sphere and basis in the mere material flesh of men, Paul presents as his ground of boasting the cross of Christ [ICC].

except[a] in[b] the cross of-our Lord Jesus Christ,

LEXICON—a. εἰ (LN 89.131): 'except' [BNTC, Herm, LN, Mor, SSA, WBC; CEV, GW, NASB, NET, NIV, NLT, NRSV], 'save' [KJV], 'but' [REB], 'only' [TEV]. The phrase ἐμοὶ δὲ μὴ γένοιτο καυχᾶσθαι εἰ 'for me may it not happen to boast except' is translated 'is my only reason for bragging' [NCV].

b. ἐν with dative object (LN 83.13, 89.5): 'in' [BNTC, Herm, LN (83.13, 89.5), Mor, WBC; KJV, NASB, NET, NIV], 'about' [LN (89.5); TEV], 'with regard to' [LN (89.5)], 'that' [SSA], not explicit [CEV, GW, NCV, NLT, NRSV, REB].

QUESTION—How are the nouns related in the genitive construction τῷ σταυρῷ τοῦ κυρίου ἡμῶν Ἰησοῦ Χριστοῦ 'the cross of our Lord Jesus Christ'?

It stands for the historical fact that Jesus was crucified. It also stands for the whole significance of the event, not only for mankind in general but for Paul in particular [NCBC]. The cross in this verse represents the atoning death of Christ which opens the way of justification by faith apart from the works of the law [NIC]. The plural 'our' includes all the Galatians and so says much more than 'my' would imply. He is 'our Lord' by the fact that he purchased and won us as his own through his death on the cross. His name is 'Jesus' or Savior. His title is 'Christ' which means 'the Messiah anointed of God' [Lns].

through[a] which/whom (the) world[b] is-crucified[c] to-me and-I to-(the) world.[b]

LEXICON—a. διά with genitive object (LN 90.4, 90.8): 'through' [BNTC, Herm, LN (90.4, 90.8), Mor, WBC; NASB, NCV, NET, NIV, REB], 'by' [LN (90.4); GW, KJV, NRSV], 'by means of' [LN (90.8), SSA; TEV], 'because of' [CEV, NLT].

b. κόσμος (LN **41.38**) (BAGD 7. p. 447): 'world' [BAGD, BNTC, Herm, LN, Mor, WBC; all versions], 'world system' [LN]. The phrase ἐμοὶ κόσμος ἐσταύρωται κἀγὼ κόσμῳ 'the world is crucified to me and I to the world' is translated 'I no longer value what those who do not trust Christ value and they do not value what I value' [SSA].

c. perf. pass. indic. of σταυρόω (LN 20.76) (BAGD 2. p. 765): 'to be crucified' [BAGD, BNTC, Herm, LN, Mor, WBC; all versions except CEV, NLT, TEV], 'to be dead' [CEV, NLT, TEV]. See b. [SSA].

QUESTION—What relationship is indicated by διά 'through'?

It indicates instrument, means, or agent [WBC].

QUESTION—What is referred to by δι' οὗ 'through which/whom'?

1. It refers to the cross [Herm, ICC, Lns, Lt, NCBC, NIC, NIGTC, NTC, TH; all versions except KJV]: through the cross. Since the cross is the instrument of crucifixion, δι' οὗ 'through which' should be understood as of the cross and not of the Lord [NIC]. 6:14b explains the meaning of the preposition ἐν 'in' in the phrase 'in the cross of our Lord Jesus Christ' [Herm]. It characterizes the cross as the instrument through which he had wholly severed connection with his old world of Pharisaic dignity and legalism. It does not describe the process by which the cross achieved this result [ICC]. Paul glories in the cross because by means of it a crucifixion has taken place for him and in him [Lns].

2. It refers to Christ [Alf; KJV]: through our Lord Jesus Christ.

QUESTION—What is meant by ἐμοὶ κόσμος ἐσταύρωται 'the world is crucified to me'?

The 'world' here indicates the mode of life which is characterized by earthly advantages, viewed as obstacles to righteousness [WBC]. The 'world' refers to all unbelievers [BNTC, BST, NCBC]. For Paul the 'world' means mainly his former way of life as a Pharisee [NIC]. The 'world' means not so much the physical world of space and time, but instead the world system that in its basic values and orientation is alienated from God [NAC]. The 'world' is most likely used to describe a way of life in which human worth is measured by external circumstances [TH]. The world for Paul was that of Israelite descent, circumcision, the rank and dignity of a Pharisee and the righteousness that is in law [ICC]. The 'world' refers to all those earthly pleasures and treasures, honors and values that tend to draw the soul away from Christ [NTC]. 'Crucified to me' means that the natural world has stopped having any claims upon him [NCBC].

QUESTION—What is meant by κἀγὼ κόσμῳ 'and I to the world'?

To be crucified to the world means to walk in the light, to bear the fruit of the Spirit, and to live in the freedom with which Christ has set us free [NAC]. To be dead to the world in which human worth is measured by external circumstances is to regard all those external factors as without value as far as being rightly related to God is concerned [TH]. Paul had become dead to all those who place their confidence in earthly pleasures and treasures, honors and values that tend to draw the soul away from Christ [NTC].

6:15 For[a] neither circumcision[b] nor uncircumcision[c] is anything,[d] but (a) new[e] creation.[f]

TEXT—Instead of οὔτε γάρ 'for neither' some manuscripts read ἐν γὰρ Χριστῷ Ἰησοῦ οὔτε 'for in Christ Jesus neither'. GNT reads οὔτε γάρ 'for neither' with an A decision, indicating that the text is certain. Ἐν γὰρ Χριστῷ Ἰησοῦ οὔτε 'for in Christ Jesus neither' is read by KJV.

LEXICON—a. γάρ (LN 89.23): 'for' [BNTC, Herm, LN, Mor, WBC; KJV, NASB, NET, NRSV], 'because' [LN, SSA], not explicit [CEV, GW, NCV, NIV, NLT, REB, TEV].

b. περιτομή (LN 53.51) (BAGD 2. p. 652): 'circumcision' [BNTC, Herm, LN, Mor, WBC; KJV, NASB, NET, NIV, NRSV, REB], 'the state of having been circumcised' [BAGD]. This noun is also translated as a verb phrase: 'to be circumcised' [SSA; CEV, GW, NCV, NLT, TEV].

c. ἀκροβυστία (LN 11.52) (BAGD 2. p. 33): 'uncircumcision' [BAGD, BNTC, Herm, Mor, WBC; KJV, NASB, NET, NIV, NRSV, REB], 'being uncircumcised' [LN]. This noun is also translated as a verb phrase: 'to be uncircumcised' [NCV], 'to not be circumcised' [SSA; CEV, GW, NLT, TEV].

d. τις (LN 92.12): 'anything' [BNTC, Herm, LN, Mor, WBC; KJV, NASB, NET, NIV, NRSV], 'nothing' [REB]. The phrase οὔτε περιτομή τί ἐστιν οὔτε ἀκροβυστία 'neither circumcision nor uncircumcision is anything' is translated 'God values neither that a person is circumcised nor that a person is not circumcised' [SSA], 'It doesn't matter if you are circumcised or not' [CEV], 'Certainly it doesn't matter whether a person is circumcised or not' [GW], 'It is not important if a man is circumcised or uncircumcised' [NCV], 'It doesn't make any difference now whether we have been circumcised or not' [NLT], 'It does not matter at all whether or not one is circumcised' [TEV].

e. καινός (LN 58.71) (BAGD 3.b. p. 394): 'new' [BAGD, BNTC, Herm, LN, Mor, WBC; all versions except NLT], 'new and different' [NLT]. The phrase ἀλλὰ καινὴ κτίσις 'but a new creation' is translated 'but God values that a person live completely differently by means of the Holy Spirit/because Christ died on the cross' [SSA].

f. κτίσις (LN 42.35, 42.38) (BAGD 1.b.α. p. 456): 'creation' [BAGD, BNTC, Herm, LN (42.35, 42.38), Mor, WBC; GW, NASB, NET, NIV, NRSV, REB], 'creature' [LN (42.38); KJV, TEV], 'person' [CEV], 'people' [NCV, NLT]. See e. [SSA].

QUESTION—What relationship is indicated by γάρ 'for'?

It indicates that this verse is the reason for something preceding, possibly 6:14c, 14a or 14a-c [SSA]. This gives the reason for glorying only in the cross [ICC]. It explains why the cross of Christ is everything to Paul [NTC]. This explains how the Judaizers are involved [Lns].

QUESTION—What is meant by καινὴ κτίσις 'a new creation'?

It involves the whole process of conversion made possible through the work of the Holy Spirit. It implies a new nature with a new system of desires, affections and habits all brought about through the supernatural ministry of the Holy Spirit in the life of the believer [NAC]. Those who are now 'in Christ' have been given the 'Spirit of Christ' and have, in baptism, 'put on' Christ. They 'belong to Christ', enjoy the 'new life' and as such are 'new creation' [Herm]. It is the new life, the life of regeneration which the Holy Spirit brings about in a person's heart [NTC]. It seems to be the total renewal caused by Christ [NCBC].

6:16 And as-many-as[a] live[b] by-this rule,[c]

LEXICON—a. ὅσος (LN 59.7) (BAGD 2. p. 586): 'as many as' [BAGD, BNTC, LN, Mor; KJV], 'all those who' [WBC; GW, NLT], 'those who' [Herm; NASB, NCV, NRSV, TEV], 'all who' [SSA; NET, NIV, REB], 'you' [CEV].

b. pres. act. indic. of στοιχέω (LN 41.12) (BAGD p. 769): 'to live' [LN, SSA; NLT], 'to walk' [Mor; KJV, NASB], 'to behave in accordance with' [LN; NET], 'to conduct (oneself) in accordance with' [LN], 'to follow' [BAGD, BNTC, Herm, WBC; CEV, NCV, NIV, NRSV, TEV], 'to conform to' [GW]. The phrase κανόνι τούτῳ στοιχήσουσιν 'live by this rule' is translated 'take this principle for their guide' [REB].

c. κανών (LN **33.335**) (BAGD 1. p. 403): 'rule' [BAGD, BNTC, Herm, **LN**, Mor, WBC; all versions except GW, NLT, REB], 'principle' [LN, SSA; GW, NLT, REB], 'standard' [BAGD].

QUESTION—What is the function of this verse?

It is a benediction of peace and mercy upon those who will follow this rule as well as upon the Israel of God [ICC, NAC, NIC, TH].

QUESTION—What relationship is indicated by καί 'and'?

Verse 6:15 states the objective principle; καί 'and' in 6:16 adds the subjective use of this principle [Lns].

QUESTION—Who is referred to by ὅσος 'as many as'?

The reference is to members of the new humanity who are guided by this principle, in contrast to those who maintain the continuing validity of circumcision and similar legal requirements [NIGTC]. It includes all of such people whether they live in Galatia or elsewhere [Lns].

QUESTION—What is referred to with κανόνι τούτῳ 'by this rule'?

It refers to the statement that Paul just made in 6:15, 'Neither circumcision nor uncircumcision means anything; all that matters is a new creation' [WBC]. Paul must mean the principle he stated in 6:14–15 concerning the central importance of the cross [NCBC]. The κανών 'rule' is apparently the principle just presented about the 'new creation' [NIGTC]. Most scholars believe that Paul was referring to the principle of justification by faith that he had summarized in 6:15 under the 'new creation' [NAC]. This rule is the one by which a person places his complete trust in Christ crucified, and that, therefore, he regulates his life by this principle [NTC]. It refers to the principle that Paul stated in 6:15 [Herm, ICC, Lns, SSA].

peace upon[a] them and mercy[b]
LEXICON—a. ἐπί with accusative object (LN 90.57): 'upon' [Herm, LN, Mor; NASB, NLT, NRSV, REB], 'on' [BNTC, LN, WBC; GW, KJV, NET], 'to' [NCV, NIV], 'with' [TEV]. This entire phrase is translated 'God will treat you with undeserved kindness and will bless you with peace' [CEV], 'are the ones whom God will cause that they be peaceful and will pity' [SSA].
  b. ἔλεος (LN 88.76) (BAGD 2.a. p. 250): 'mercy' [BAGD, BNTC, Herm, LN, Mor, WBC; all versions except CEV], 'kindness' [CEV]. This noun is also translated as a verb with 'they' as the subject: 'to pity' [SSA].
QUESTION—What is meant by εἰρήνη 'peace'?
 See this word at 1:3.
QUESTION—What is meant by ἔλεος 'mercy'?
 Mercy is basically the grace of God, although mercy has particular regard to the needy condition of the recipient, whereas the emphasis in grace is on the undeserved character of God's goodness [NIC]. Mercy could be interpreted as God's kindness or goodwill [TH].

and upon[a] the Israel[b] of-God.
LEXICON—a. ἐπί with accusative object (LN 90.57): 'upon' [Herm, LN, Mor; KJV, NASB, NRSV], 'on' [BNTC, LN, WBC; NET], 'to' [NCV, NIV], 'with' [TEV], not explicit [SSA; GW, NLT, REB]. This entire phrase is translated '(if you follow this rule) you will belong to God's true people' [CEV].
  b. Ἰσραήλ (LN 93.182) (BAGD 3. p. 381): 'Israel' [BNTC, Herm, LN, Mor, WBC; GW, KJV, NASB, NET, NIV, NRSV, REB]. The phrase τὸν Ἰσραὴλ τοῦ θεοῦ 'the Israel of God' is translated 'the (*true*) divine Israel' [BAGD], 'God's true people' [CEV], 'God's people' [NCV, TEV], 'the new people of God' [NLT], 'Israel, that is, God's true children' [SSA].
QUESTION—What relationship is indicated by καί 'and'?
 It is explicative and introduces the same thing under a new aspect [Lt, Mor].
QUESTION—How is the genitive construction Ἰσραὴλ τοῦ θεοῦ 'Israel of God' related to the phrase ὅσοι τῷ κανόνι τούτῳ στοιχήσουσιν 'as many as live by this rule'?
  1. Only one group is involved [Alf, BST, Lns, Lt, Mor, NAC, NCBC, NIBC, NTC, TH, TNTC, WBC; CEV, GW, NIV, NLT, REB]: peace and mercy be upon all who do so. The construction 'Israel of God' stands for the whole body of believers whether Jew or Gentile [Mor]. It is best to understand the 'Israel of God' as an eschatological reference to the whole people of God including converted Gentiles and completed Jews [NAC]. The 'Israel of God' is in implied contrast to the 'Israel after the flesh'. It represents not the faithful converts from the circumcision alone, but the spiritual Israel generally, the whole body of believers whether Jew or Gentile [Lt].

2. There are two groups of Christians [BNTC, Herm, NIC, NIGTC; KJV, NASB, NET, NRSV]: peace and mercy be upon all who do so and also upon the Israel of God. Paul extends the blessing beyond the Galatian Paulinists to those Jewish Christians who approve of his rule in 6:15 [Herm].
3. There are two groups and two wishes [ICC]: peace be upon all who do so and mercy be upon the Israel of God. The expression 'Israel of God' should be understood as applying to Jews and not to the Christian community. However, in view of the qualifying phrase τοῦ θεοῦ 'of God', not the whole Jewish nation is included in 'Israel of God', just the pious Israel, the remnant according to the election of grace. The benediction falls into two distinct parts. In the first part Paul invokes peace upon those who recognize and act in accordance with the principle of 6:15. In the second part Paul invokes the mercy of God through which they may obtain enlightenment and enter into peace upon those within Israel who even though as yet unenlightened are the true Israel of God [ICC].

DISCOURSE UNIT: 6:17 [NAC]. The topic is brand marks of Jesus.

6:17 Of-the rest,[a] (let) no-one cause[b] troubles[c] to-me;
LEXICON—a. λοιπός (LN 63.21, 67.134) (BAGD 3.a.β. p. 480): 'rest, remaining' [LN (63.21)]. The phrase τοῦ λοιποῦ 'of the rest' is translated 'from now on' [BAGD, BNTC, LN (67.134); GW, NASB, NET, NLT, NRSV], 'from henceforth' [KJV], 'henceforth' [Herm, LN (67.134), Mor], 'in the future' [BAGD; REB], 'anymore' [CEV]. Not explicit [SSA, WBC; NCV, NIV, TEV].
  b. pres. act. impera. of παρέχω (LN 13.127, **90.91**) (BAGD 1.c. p. 626): 'to cause' [BAGD, BNTC, Herm, LN (13.127, 90.91), WBC; NASB, NET, NIV], 'to cause to, to cause to experience' [LN (90.91)], 'to give' [**LN** (90.91); NCV, TEV], 'to make' [GW, NRSV, REB], not explicit [Mor, SSA; CEV, KJV, NLT].
  c. κόπος (LN 22.7) (BAGD 1. p. 443): 'trouble' [BAGD, BNTC, Herm, LN, WBC; all versions except CEV, KJV, NLT], 'difficulty' [BAGD], 'distress' [LN]. The phrase κόπους μοι μηδεὶς παρεχέτω 'let no one cause trouble to me' is translated 'let no one/man trouble me' [Mor; KJV], 'do not trouble me' [SSA], 'I don't want anyone to bother me' [CEV], 'don't let anyone trouble me with these things' [NLT].

for[a] I carry[b] the marks[c] of-Jesus in[d] my body.
LEXICON—a. γάρ (LN 89.23): 'for' [BNTC, Herm, LN, Mor, WBC; KJV, NASB, NET, NIV, NLT, NRSV, REB], 'because' [LN; TEV], 'since' [SSA], 'after all' [GW], not explicit [CEV, NCV].
  b. pres. act. indic. of βαστάζω (LN 15.188) (BAGD 2.c. p. 137): 'to carry' [BAGD, LN; GW, NRSV], 'to bear' [BAGD, BNTC, Herm, LN, Mor,

WBC; KJV, NASB, NET, NIV, NLT, REB], 'to have' [SSA; NCV, TEV], 'my own (body scars)' [CEV].
  c. στίγμα (LN **8.55, 33.481**, 90.84) (BAGD p. 768): 'mark' [BAGD, BNTC, Herm, **LN** (8.55, 33.481), Mor, WBC; KJV, NET, NIV, NRSV, REB], 'scar' [LN (8.55, 33.481), SSA; CEV, GW, NCV, NLT, TEV], 'brand' [LN (8.55)], 'brand-mark' [NASB]. The phrase τὰ στίγματα τοῦ Ἰησοῦ 'the marks of Jesus' is translated 'marks which indicate I belong to Jesus, marks which indicate that I am the slave of Jesus' [**LN** (90.84)], 'scars that prove I belong to Christ Jesus' [CEV], 'scars on my body that show I belong to Christ Jesus' [NCV], 'scars that show I belong to Jesus' [NLT], 'scars I have on my body show that I am the slave of Jesus' [TEV], 'scars like a slave's brand; these show that Jesus is my master' [SSA].
  d. ἐν with dative object (LN 83.13): 'in' [LN, Mor; KJV], 'on' [BNTC, Herm, SSA, WBC; all versions except KJV].
QUESTION—What relationship is indicated by γάρ 'for'?
  It introduces the physical reason why they should stop causing him trouble [Lns, Mor, NCBC, NIC].
QUESTION—How are the nouns related in the genitive construction στίγματα τοῦ Ἰησοῦ 'marks of Jesus'?
  The expression seems to indicate that Paul had been physically abused during his work for Jesus and that his body still showed the scars [Mor]. They were wounds that Paul received while being persecuted for the cause of Jesus [Alf, BNTC, BST, Herm, ICC, Lns, Lt, NAC, NCBC, NIC, NTC, SSA, TNTC]. To Paul the 'marks of Jesus' are distinguishing marks which show that he is a slave of Jesus Christ. The most probable interpretation of the entire phrase is that Paul has in mind the scars, the marks of suffering and affliction which he carries on his body as a result of his obedience to his Lord [TH].
QUESTION—What is referred to by ἐν τῷ σώματί μου 'in my body'?
  It should be understood literally as a reference to Paul's physical body [SSA].

DISCOURSE UNIT: 6:18 [NAC]. The topic is the benediction.

6:18 The grace[a] of-our Lord Jesus Christ (be) with[b] your spirit,[c] brothers.[d] Amen.[e]

TEXT—Following ἀμήν 'amen', some manuscripts add πρὸς Γαλάτας 'to Galatians', and other manuscripts read πρὸς Γαλάτας ἐγράφη ἀπὸ Ῥώμης 'to Galatians it was written from Rome'. GNT does not mention these variants.

LEXICON—a. χάρις (LN 25.89, 88.66) (BAGD 2.c. p. 877): 'grace' [BAGD, BNTC, Herm, LN (88.66), Mor, WBC; all versions except CEV, GW], 'kindness' [LN (88.66)], 'favor' [BAGD, LN (25.89)], 'goodwill' [LN (25.89); GW]. This noun is also translated as an adverb: 'graciously' [SSA]; as an adjective: '(to be) kind' [CEV]. This entire verse is translated 'I pray that our (incl.) Lord Jesus Christ will graciously guide

and sustain you/will graciously accomplish what he desires within you my brothers. Amen' [SSA], 'My friends, I pray that the Lord Jesus Christ will be kind to you! Amen' [CEV].
  b. μετά with genitive object (LN 90.60) (BAGD A.II.1.c.γ. p. 509): 'with' [BAGD, BNTC, Herm, LN, Mor, WBC; all versions except CEV]. See a. [SSA; CEV].
  c. πνεῦμα (LN 26.9) (BAGD 3.b. p. 675): 'spirit' [BAGD, BNTC, Herm, LN, Mor, WBC; GW, KJV, NASB, NCV, NET, NIV, NRSV], 'inner being' [LN], 'you' [NLT, REB, TEV]. See a. [SSA; CEV].
  d. ἀδελφός (LN 11.23): 'brother' [BNTC, Herm, LN, Mor, SSA, WBC; KJV, NASB, NIV], 'Christian brother, fellow believer' [LN], 'friend' [CEV, REB, TEV], 'brother and sister' [GW, NCV, NET, NLT, NRSV].
  e. ἀμήν (LN 72.6) (BAGD 1. p. 45): 'amen' [BAGD, BNTC, Herm, Mor, SSA, WBC; all versions], 'so let it be' [BAGD], 'truly' [BAGD, LN], 'indeed' [LN].
QUESTION—What is the function of this verse?
  It is his second benediction and he prayed that the grace of the Lord Jesus Christ would be with the Galatians [NAC, TH]. Paul closes each of his letters with a grace benediction [Mor, NIC, WBC].
QUESTION—What is meant by χάρις τοῦ κυρίου 'grace of the Lord'?
  See χάρις 'grace' at 1:3. This term is used here as part of a benediction formula so not too much theological meaning should be read into it [TH].
QUESTION—What is meant by πνεύματος ὑμῶν 'your spirit'?
  It refers to the inner personality which is the contact point between God and his children [NTC]. Paul is mindful of their spiritual needs [Mor]. The spirit is what is to triumph over the flesh [Lns]. Probably here 'spirit' and 'you' are synonymous [NIC].
QUESTION—What is meant by ἀδελφοί 'brothers'?
  It highlights Paul's continued affection for his converts [Alf, ICC, Lt, Mor, WBC]. By using this term Paul expresses the confidence that they will overcome [TH].
QUESTION—What is the significance of the ἀμήν 'amen'?
  It confirms his sincerity [Lns, NIC, NTC]. This was the usual ending to a prayer and means 'May it be so' [TH]. It emphasizes Paul's strength and depth of feeling [ICC]. In using this term Paul means to add weight to his conclusion. It was intended as a prayer 'so let it be' [NCBC]. It is a formula of confirmation [NIGTC]. It is a means of reinforcing Paul's own preceding words concerning his erring converts [SSA].